# Ideology and social order

**International Library of Sociology**

Founded by Karl Mannheim

Editor: John Rex, University of Warwick

Arbor Scientiae
Arbor Vitae

A catalogue of the books available in the **International Library of Sociology** and other series of Social Science books published by Routledge & Kegan Paul will be found at the end of this volume.

# Ideology and social order

**Eric Carlton**
Department of Social Studies
Teesside Polytechnic, Cleveland

**Routledge & Kegan Paul**
London, Henley and Boston

*First published in 1977*
*by Routledge & Kegan Paul Ltd*
*39 Store Street,*
*London WC1E 7DD,*
*Broadway House,*
*Newtown Road,*
*Henley-on-Thames,*
*Oxon RG9 1EN and*
*9 Park Street,*
*Boston, Mass. 02108, USA*
*Set in 10/11 Times Roman by*
*Kelly, Selwyn & Co., Melksham, Wiltshire*
*and printed in Great Britain by*
*Unwin Brothers Limited*
*The Gresham Press, Old Woking, Surrey*

*ISBN 0 7100 8474 9*

# Contents

# 1   Models of analysis

In the social sciences, unlike the natural sciences, experimentation is infamously difficult. Social scientists would like to have an armoury of validatory techniques which were comparable with those of the natural sciences, but the very nature of their discipline makes this impossible. Some measure of comfort may be drawn from the view that sociology, for example, is still only a young science,[1] and therefore still lacks the technical sophistication of the natural sciences. But the conclusion is inescapable that the apologists are clutching at consolatory straws.

However, the view that the social sciences are merely quasi-sciences should be qualified in a number of ways. The argument begs the question, what *is* a science? Should a science be defined in terms of its aims, its 'content', or its method?

The aims of a science are presumably:
  (i) Objectivity
  (ii) The establishment of order
  (iii) The framing of testable hypotheses
  (iv) Prediction
If we again take sociology as our example, its claim to be a science rests almost entirely on (ii) i.e. on its capacity to order and classify its material. It can frame hypotheses, as (iii), but they are not always convincingly testable – even to sociologists' satisfaction. Where the hypotheses are plausible, they are also frequently unexceptional. Sociology can be little more than the documentation of the obvious, but then sometimes the obvious needs precise documentation. Perhaps if sociology does no more than confirm what is 'known' impressionistically it will have rendered a valuable service. It can, in fact, do rather more than this, at both the theoretical and empirical levels.

The limits imposed upon the social sciences derive directly from the nature of their 'content' which in turn determines their capacity

1

for verification and prediction. The subject matter of the social sciences is human affairs and, unlike the behaviour of, say, the molecular structure of hydrogen, little can usually be said which is not subject to some degree of qualification. As T. Bottomore puts it, 'In the natural sciences, it is possible to conceive an ultimate, closed theoretical system, while in the social sciences this is inconceivable because in human affairs genuine novelty can result from human volition.'[2]

In the social sciences, only very limited experimentation is possible. The controlled experiment, so common in the natural sciences, is extremely difficult, mainly because social scientists cannot isolate their materials like chemicals in a test-tube. They cannot create artificial experimental situations of The Island of Dr Moreau variety in which the requisite variables can be manipulated at will and the experimental conditions maintained as desirable constants. Perhaps the preoccupation of social anthropologists with simple societies stems, in part, from the desire to see human society 'as it was', untouched by the withering hands of colonialists and missionaries. There is an underlying assumption that in these static societies, institutions can perhaps be seen in a 'purer', more original form,[3] and that from their examination certain conclusions can be extrapolated about institutions in particular, and about human society in general.[4]

With limited experimentation, measurement itself must remain uncertain. Indeed, in some instances the situation is made even more unsatisfactory simply because social scientists are unable to define adequately exactly what it is they are trying to measure. In psychology, for example, the debate is still wide open on such issues as intelligence and personality testing. No one, as yet, has unambiguously defined precisely what intelligence and personality *are*. Tests may be valuable indicators, but they are hardly explanatory mechanisms.[5] Perhaps Professor Eysenck is right, it may not be possible to say any more than that 'Intelligence is what Intelligence tests measure' – whatever that happens to be.[6] Here again, the difficulty is the subject matter itself. Precision may be impossible in human affairs.

The whole problem of experimentation and, by extension, precision in the social sciences is also vitiated by time and cost factors. In a number of areas of enquiry, social experiments have to be reasonably large-scale if they are going to be worthwhile. The samples must be large enough to give significant results, and the cost can be virtually prohibitive where the agencies concerned are already working on a financial shoestring. Money may well be forthcoming for, say, surveys of voting behaviour at election time, but, by contrast, the outlay involved in any really adequate study of the social and educational implications of abolishing the 11 plus could be another matter. Where studies have to be both large-scale and long-term, the necessary support must usually either come from government agencies or industrial concerns who may contend – perhaps rightly – that in cost-benefit terms the anticipated results will not merit the expense of the exercise. Investment in social research compares unfavourably with that of scientific research, possibly because it is felt that sociological conclusions are often rather marginal to the needs of both the policy-makers and the requirements of an insistent industrial machine.

It may be argued, therefore, that the social sciences are sciences by dispensation rather than by right. They have certain well-established capacities, but these are necessarily circumscribed by both the nature of the phenomena to be examined and the relatively narrow range of investigatory techniques which are available. For instance, statistical techniques are highly developed, and it is possible to make certain predictions about group behaviour within calculable margins of error. As R. Lipsey has pointed out, if this were not so concerns such as insurance companies would hardly be in business.[7] On the other hand, what any *one* individual within the group would *actually* do, is a much more difficult proposition. The problem becomes even more tortuous when the investigator has to rely upon public responses as opposed to hard statistics such as birth and death rates. The snags are obvious; the investigator is largely at the mercy of the respondent. In surveys concerning sexual behaviour, for example, there may still be a tendency towards polarities of performance; respondents – understandably – tend either to be hopelessly innocent or impossibly virile. This can stem from either an eagerness to impress or simply an impatience with the whole survey operation. There is some evidence to suggest that in some areas the public is becoming a little irritated by enthusiastic young researchers armed with a questionnaire in one hand and a few concepts in the other who probe superficially at the psyche and its secrets merely to satisfy the demands of some minor dissertation.

Social science, then, is limited in its operations and in its more general acceptance by many factors over which it has little or no control. Its techniques will undoubtedly be refined, and its predictive capacities increased, but it is never likely to reach the levels of precision of the natural sciences. This is acknowledged by some sociologists with something approaching resignation. 'There is not, at the present time, any general body of sociological theory which has been validated or widely accepted.'[8]

Sociology is really a set of perspectives. It is a form of description, a type of analysis and a method of interpretation. It is only a science in anything like the accepted sense, if a science is to be defined

3

primarily in terms of its *method*. Sociologists are often able to establish statistical correlations between different sets of variables, for instance, between housing conditions and the juvenile crime rate.[9] But only the most intrepid theorist would argue for a direct *causal connection* between housing and delinquency. Such connections may have a certain psycho-social plausibility, but beyond that no sociologist may venture with certainty. There are so many variables which could qualify the association. As Alan Ryan puts it, 'successful causal laws are those which apply under the most *im*probable conditions'.[10] Most modern sociologists would take a more modest line and remain content with the establishment of correlations, and the identification of *trends* rather than laws.[11]

If the method of science is taken as the key eligibility factor, sociology may be seen as an embryonic science. It employs a range of sophisticated statistical techniques and, in general terms, is capable of defining and classifying its material. It is able to advance falsifiable hypotheses which it is then prepared to test and modify where necessary on the basis of observation and limited experimentation.

But the method of sociology need not be confined to this set of empirical determinants. It has been maintained that 'A science is properly independent only when it can successfully defend its claim to frame and use its own categories'.[12] On this criterion, sociology can be said to have virtually arrived – but then so could scientology, or the age-old 'science' of astrology for that matter. Categories are important, but even where they are distinctive in relation to other disciplines, they are still disputed. Unlike hypotheses, categories are not susceptible to verification by induction and experiment. Only within the confines of its own sphere of competence, can it be argued that the categories of sociology have their own peculiar validity. And it has been something of a mixed blessing that sociology has borrowed a number of those categories such as structure, function, organism, etc. from the biological sciences. In fact, one could go further and insist that in their adapted forms they are not, strictly speaking, categories at all, but merely *analogies*.

It is partly because of this unsatisfactory state of affairs in social investigation, that the emphasis has shifted to *theoretical* analysis. The move has been away from the purely quantitative approach – mere 'grubbing for facts' as C. Wright Mills called it[13] – and towards a more qualitative interpretation of social action. Obviously, the two approaches are not mutually exclusive, but complementary in their contributions to social knowledge. However, in many academic circles, sociology has now come to be virtually equated with sociological theory.

This increasing stress upon theory may be a salutary departure. It can certainly be refreshing – if often confounding.[14] Whatever, it has further reduced the claims – or pretensions – of sociology to be a science. Its practitioners seem to be increasingly removed from the scientific ideals of precision, verification and prediction. But then these may not really be their objectives. They are much more concerned with what Max Weber called an 'interpretive under-standing' of human action. Does it help to know the facts and figures relating to, say, particular revolutions, or is it more instructive to know something of the characteristics of revolution as a recurring social phenomenon?[15] The shift here is to cognition rather than codification.

Theory must share a reciprocal relationship with empirical research. Admittedly, the method of investigation must, as Auguste Comte insisted, be largely determined by the nature of the pheno-mena to be investigated. After all, handing round questionnaires to prostitutes in the Bayswater Road would almost certainly prove rather fruitless – something a little more subtle is obviously re-quired.[16] But social investigation without the necessary conceptual framework might prove equally abortive. There must be some way of ordering the data, a method of making interpretive sense of the facts. This is where theory can come into its own; this is where *models of analysis* are required.

Models are one of the ways in which the general principles for-mulated by sociologists are related to the 'real world'. In a sense, they 'reproduce' what happens in the real world even though the model will incorporate chosen variables.[17] To this extent, the model represents a simplified convenience-construct which enables us to make limited deductions about the 'more complex and elusive real system'.[18]

Some theorists would go further and insist that 'we know a structure completely only if we can construct it, materially or intellectually'.[19] That is to say, our knowledge of a structure – and this is particularly pertinent to the structure of social institutions – is mediated by models.

### Ideal-type analysis

A particularly interesting use of the model is that found in the writings of Max Weber especially in his studies of religion and bureaucracy. His theories of 'rational action'[20] are associated with 'ideal-type' analysis,[21] that is analysis in terms of constructs which must be both objectively possible and subjectively meaningful.

This all sounds rather abstract put in this way. Perhaps some elaboration of the 'ideal-type' is necessary as this kind of analysis has acted as a paradigm in the comparative study of social institutions.

It is important, first of all, to make very clear what the 'ideal-type' is *not*; this is a source of some confusion to those who are

5

being introduced to the vocabulary of sociology.

(i) It is not an Average-Type: it is not possible to construct such a model in 'scattergram' terms, by determining the mean of a situation or type of system. Similarly, it is not simply a composite of known and documented systems.

(ii) It is not a Lowest-Common-Denominator-Type: it is not a model which represents some hypothesised original or basic type. In the study of religion, for example, it has been a common reductionist error to see one kind of religious experience as the social antecedent of all other kinds and varieties of religious expression.[22]

(iii) It is not an Extreme-Instance-of-the-Case: for instance, in a study of totalitarianism, it would be wrong to think of German Nazism as an ideal-type simply because it represents an extreme or seemingly 'pure' example of a totalitarian system.

(iv) It is not a Typical or Representative Example: it is not what might be termed a 'good example' of any particular phenomenon. For example, Aztec-ruled Mexico at the time of the Spanish conquest in the early sixteenth century might be said to provide an excellent example of a human sacrificial system based upon familiar notions of 'sympathetic magic'. But a good example – even the best example – is not what is meant by an ideal-type. In fact, the ideal-type may not *correspond to any known existing instance of the type.*

(v) It is not a Hypothesis: a hypothesis, by definition, can theoretically be proved or disproved. This is not the case with ideal-types. Models are simplifications, they are constructs. To this extent, they cannot be either true or false; they can only be seen as valid or invalid, useful or useless, depending upon the nature of the 'reality' which they mirror in obliquely qualified ways. Paradoxically, they are conscious distortions of reality which may enable us to understand real-world systems.

An ideal-type corresponds to an *idea* – not to reality. It is constructed by abstracting certain aspects of empirical reality and excluding others – depending upon the bias of our interests – and forming these aspects into an internally coherent system. As such, it provides a limiting case with which concrete phenomena can be contrasted; 'an unambiguous concept by which classification and comparison is facilitated'.[23]

Ideal-types, then, are simply analytical tools, and it follows that many different such models can be constructed in relation to the *same* phenomenon, say, autocracy. Everything depends upon which features we need to highlight; which elements we wish to bring into focus. Any model can, therefore, be more or less useful in so far as it helps us to arrive at an understanding of social events which is both causally adequate and cognitively illuminating.

Ideal-types are 'used' by simply comparing the actual courses of events with the model. In this way, we can order reality, as it were, by both isolating certain factors and identifying the differentiae. For example, in economics it is possible to construct rational models (taking rational to mean a logical correspondence between means and ends) of, say, systems of perfect competition, and, by comparison, assess the non-rational deviations from the model in *actual* free-market situations.

Valuable as this kind of ideal-type analysis can be, it hardly takes a sociologist to see that it is fraught with all kinds of difficulties. Models, being man-made constructs, are obviously manipulable; and that being the case, it is possible to include or exclude the desired variables and derive the equally desired conclusions. In addition, problems of fallibility arise in cases where the applicability of rational models is in doubt. Are there situations where comparisons between ideal-type models and actuality are patently unmeaningful? It could be argued, for instance, that any examination of primitive hunting magic as a means of ensuring hunting success does not fit any kind of rational model situation which ideally calls for better weaponry. Although this might be countered by simply maintaining that as hunting magic may have *in*direct confidence-inspiring functions, its role as a *non*-rational means can be 'measured' in model terms.

To be fair, Weber was well aware of the shortcomings of his own system. He insisted that no ideal-type is likely to be permanently useful. For Weber, no set of concepts could be applied indefinitely, and no system of classification had absolute validity. In fact, he maintained that in his own sociology he had given us but one of many possible sociologies. In effect, Weber, like many others, recognised the narrow range of methodological possibilities open to sociologists. The model, though lacking the elegance of those used in the physical sciences,[24] is still a convenient analytical aid when applied with refinement and discretion.

## The classification of societies

According to Emile Durkheim,[25] the broad aims of sociology are the:
  (i) Definition of subject matter in terms of some observable characteristic(s).
  (ii) Description of the normal types after the study of many cases.
  (iii) Classification into species, etc.

7

(iv) Comparative and causal investigation of the reasons for variation.

(v) Attempts to discover any general laws which might emerge.

With some reservations and qualifications, this would still be very generally endorsed by sociologists.[26] Its a reasonably modest classificatory programme with the hope that its taxonomic procedures will eventually yield something approaching scientifically satisfactory conclusions. In a sense, taxonomic knowledge implies prediction. 'The classification of objects involves a prediction of how they will behave in given circumstances, and hence the classification of objects is associated with the classification of situations.'[27]

Classificatory schemes are not only useful adjuncts to scientific and scholarly enquiry,[28] they are necessary to the process of reducing data to manageable proportions. Taxonomies must not be mere inventions, but classifications of material in accordance with relevant principles.

A perennial problem in sociology has been just *how* to classify societies. What typologies are really universally applicable – or even generally useful?[29]

For convenience, we can categorise the views most commonly advanced as being either Evolutionist or Episodic in type.

## (a) Evolutionist

The pre-supposition in these schemes is that all societies pass through the same general phases with varying degrees of developmental inevitability. In one form or another, the movement is usually from simplicity to complexity, and this is reflected in a society's organisational arrangements. Development is related to such features as political procedures, division of labour, kinship patterns, military organisation, cultic practices, and so on. Sometimes, as with L. T. Hobhouse, an attempt is made to establish some correlation between social and economic development and moral and intellectual progress.[30] Such schemes, usually associated particularly with Auguste Comte, Herbert Spencer, L. T. Hobhouse and – to some extent – Karl Marx and Emile Durkheim, are *heuristic* in so far as they explicitly assume that certain variables are the keys to correct classification.

## (b) Episodic

These schemes are also developmental to the extent that they classify societies in terms of a transition from one stage to another. They too are concerned with forms of social and economic organisation,[31] but they are related mainly to the differences between pre-industrial and industrial systems. The theorists concerned have, therefore, often resorted to simple but significant dichotomies which really, in one way or another, express the differences between these fundamentally distinct types of society.[32]

There is nothing essentially *wrong* with these typologies; in fact, as models of social development and organisation, they should only be judged on the basis of their utility or otherwise. Models are really forms of conceptual short-hand, and in their own ways these have already proved their usefulness to social analysts. But how meaningful are they for specific studies of pre-industrial societies? We have already noted how many of them presuppose, or at least anticipate, the transition to the industrialised state – something which will not concern us in the ensuing discussion. One of the difficulties with developmental schemata is the insinuation of progress. There is the implicit assumption that all stages give way, more or less inexorably, to the final and most desirable stage which is equated with a variety of – possibly incompatible – end-states ranging from the rule of science to the classless society. Implicit values of this kind are not particularly helpful in any analysis of pre-industrial systems.

A common and more apposite classificatory scheme would be the simple division of societies into Slave, Caste, Estate and Class based systems. This also has developmental overtones, but is more appropriate especially to the study of *complex* pre-industrial societies. Although it too is concerned with economic and political arrangements, etc., it is essentially a stratification-based typology. As such, it is firmly rooted in a sociology which claims stratification studies as its own – and perhaps only – distinctive area of investigation.[33] In fact, there is a reductionist tendency within the discipline to equate stratiological interpretation with sociological explanation. To 'see' social issues primarily in terms of class, is first to misunderstand the full connotations of stratification,[34] and second to minimise the capacities of the discipline itself.[35]

The term stratification is generally used to cover all forms of social ranking which, in most societies, is not based on any *single* criterion, for example, economic advantage, but on a multiplicity of criteria including age, sex, race and religion. The entire business of differentiation in society is enormously complex, and is inextricably bound up with the notion of social evaluation. The basis upon which prestige is conferred on any member of a particular society may be fairly easily identified, but status-criteria in general defy any precise theoretical formulation.[36]

The point at issue here is whether or not stratification-based typologies are the only really useful forms of classification for complex pre-industrial societies. The fact is that except for analyses

9

in terms of hydro-agriculture (see Chapter 4) they are the classifications most currently employed; and this, despite the fact that stratification typologies are subject to so many qualifications. If, on the other hand, stratification *models* of the ideal-type variety were used, the entire operation might be more worthwhile, but – as yet – theorists are not inclined to conceptualise about 'pure' Slave, Caste, Estate and Class based societies for comparative purposes.

In the study of complex pre-industrial systems, methodologies are necessarily limited. Documentation is often sparse; there is a paucity of information, especially of a statistical kind, in certain important areas. For example, in Classical Athens – which is said by some to be a slave-based society[37] – there are no reliable figures as to the actual numbers of slaves or the population. It is invidious to make judgments of *value* where they are based upon disputable facts.

Given that normal survey and case-study methods are, therefore, impossible, ideal-type models can be valuable despite their deficiencies. But should they be based on stratificatory typologies? Or would some other kinds of classification be more fruitful? This is really the crucial point of this whole discussion. The weakness of stratificatory typologies is that they are primarily concerned with one dimension of the social complex. Admittedly, there are other – particularly economic – implications in the Slave-Caste-Estate-Class classifications, but essentially the stress is upon the structural layering of these kinds of society, and the inequalities of wealth, prestige and power which characterised them.

Can the emphasis be shifted? Is it possible to realign the same variables and produce a comparably credible analysis? Take, for instance, Estate societies. The term Estate is often used interchangeably with the term Feudal, although they are not strictly synonymous. All Estate societies are not Feudal, but arguably all Feudal societies are Estate in type. Estate, as a classification, connotes social ranking and disparities in the distributive process, but Feudalism, as a *system*, is essentially a method of social control. Thus, the same kind of society can obviously be viewed from another perspective.

A stratificatory typology is structural; it stresses how a society *was*. In this sense, it tends to be inflexible and descriptive. Alternatively, an analysis in terms of control mechanisms emphasises social organisation;[38] it is more dynamically concerned with the *processes* which sustain the system and keep the structural components in being. Of course, the structural components of a society must be closely related to the control mechanisms which operate within it. But which conditions which? To what extent is it a question of reciprocal influence? These are matters which can probably only be elucidated in actual cases.

10

However, it must be stated clearly at the outset of this entire general discussion, that although the concern here is with *processes*, it is not going to be preoccupied with problems of change. Whilst it is conceded that the development of sociology as an academic discipline grew out of the need to interpret a rapidly changing world,[39] it is a contention of this thesis that sociology has for too long been enmeshed in arguments about social change. Theories of social change proliferate, as does the literature to appraise them.[40] In fact, it might be argued that sociology has become a mere documentation of change and its concomitant, the emergence of industrialised society. But the fact that is particularly evidenced by a study of complex pre-industrial societies is that *stasis*[41] – a virtually unchanging social order – is not only interesting in its own right, but is probably far more important to any understanding of society. Stasis – which we associate with traditional systems – has been the condition of societies for most of history. How, for instance, can a society such as Ancient Egypt retain an essential homogeneity for three thousand years? This kind of problem has been largely overlooked by the theorists. Stasis *needs* to be explained much more than change, and it inevitably involves a close examination of such key issues as social control and ideology. It is therefore central to this thesis that an analysis in terms of institutionalised control is important, and that within the context of pre-industrial societies, this cannot be divorced from considerations of ideology.

# 2 Functions of social control

In a discipline such as sociology, where deviancy commands so much attention, it is probably worth noting that there is no such thing as an *anarchic* society known to history. Indeed, the very expression is something of a contradiction in terms. The idea of a society itself presupposes some kind of order.

In all societies, there are rules governing behaviour between and within groups. These rules may or may not be codified – as is the case in simple societies, but they are of such a nature that they ensure some measure of uniformity, regularity and predictability of conduct between members. Arbitrary behaviour would obviously lead to social chaos, and is therefore never institutionally condoned, except in highly qualified ways. For example, the Roman Bacchanalia festivals were marked by uncharacteristically *overt* licentiousness, but these were merely periodic institutionalised 'lapses' of a deviant nature which contrasted with normal behaviour patterns[1] and acted as forms of social catharsis.

Social control is the term normally used to denote the processes which ensure that individuals conform to the norms of the group. Interests vary both between and within groups, and control mechanisms operate to resolve conflicts of interest and promote an acceptable degree of social harmony. But they may be – and certainly *can* be – more than this. Control implies regulation; social adjustment may be by persuasion or coercion. The suppressive nature of control, especially in particular societies must also be considered.

If complex pre-industrial societies are to be analysed in terms of social control we must first examine the nature and functions of control mechanisms. These can then be related to the legitimating role of ideology to determine whether or not a viable typology is possible.

Social control is variously defined. It can be seen as 'the regulation of behaviour by values and norms . . . (in contrast to) regulation by force'[2] or the process by which 'people are led to conform to one another's institutionalised expectations'.[3] Because any definition must include both the notion of internalisation as well as that of inculcation[4] – in effect, the passive and active sides of social control – we must be careful to distinguish between the *types* of control, their functions, and the *means* or agencies whereby these are transmitted.

In very general terms, the types of control in literate societies are fairly obvious. But they and the means whereby they are expressed can take a great variety of forms. They are usually mediated through socialisation agencies such as familial and educational institutions, which in turn are reinforced by politico-legal and religious sanctions.

For simplicity of analysis, they may be categorised as those embodied in:

(i) Laws: legal codes of conduct.

(ii) Customs: Conventions which constitute uncodified but highly institutionalised norms of behaviour which may be peculiar to specific groups. These could cover almost anything from kinship obligations to the seemingly social trivia of etiquette and fashion.

(iii) Moral precepts: which may be prescribed to promote social harmony or because of some believed intrinsic good.

(iv) Religious precepts: interpretations of the will of the gods in terms of ritual and ethical obligations which are normally given by priests or other professional cultic functionaries.

These categories are not, of course, mutually exclusive. In practice, they overlap in various ways together with their associated and supportive sanctions.

How then is social control effected? And what theories can we advance to explain its operations?

## 1 Social control is facilitated by particular mechanisms

Having said this, a cautionary word is necessary. The texts are replete with allusions to the conspiratorial nature of control mechanisms. 'Social control is police forces and the armies. It is propaganda. . . . It is also tapped telephone lines, censored letters and banned books. Social control is keeping the masses ignorant . . . (it) is teaching people that resistance is futile . . . man has invented an infinite variety of such devices, so great has been his fear of deviation and instability.'[5]

Mechanisms of control need not be invented for authoritarian purposes. They may simply function as control instruments in particular societies. The secret police in Rome, for example, was undoubtedly formed as a counter-subversive arm of the state, but it is highly arguable whether any of the state cults – which were also

13

very effective as control mechanisms – were similarly organised. A mechanism of control may not be deliberately designed for that purpose. In fact, quite innocuous institutions such as the family, which are usually regarded in a rather neutral way, can unwittingly function as agencies of control.

Of course, to speak of the *function* of a mechanism may tell us nothing at all about its ideal or 'original' purpose, if indeed these can be discussed in any meaningful way. For instance, some writers regard education as an instrument of oppression.[6] Be that as it may, it would be extraordinarily rash to argue that this was *all* it is, or that it always functioned as such, or that it was consciously contrived in any society for this specific purpose. Education, in certain identifiable situations, may well encourage conformity and complaisance, but in other equally identifiable situations it can be closely associated with revolutionary fervour and unrepentant individualism.[7] In this respect, education as a favourite example of a repressive mechanism is something of a two-edged sword; it can obviously be both an aid to conformity and a source of liberation.

Such qualifications about mechanisms and their functions might be taken a stage further. Not only can the seemingly neutral be used for control purposes, the apparently 'natural' can be similarly exploited. It could be argued, for example, that the notions of loyalty and disloyalty are complex psychosocial responses which are natural or inimical to human beings in a variety of situations. But these responses can crystallise into such values as patriotism, or even into quasi-legal concepts such as treason. In this case, the 'natural' has metamorphosised to become an extremely potent institutionalised control mechanism.

The mechanisms of social control function in a number of ways:

(*a*) *They tend to forestall strains in society by the resolution of incompatibilities and inconsistencies in social arrangements.*

In this way they may prevent potential conflict from becoming *actual*. Parsons refers to this as 'nipping deviant tendencies in the bud'.[8]

This could be well illustrated by a brief analysis of the different procedures which various societies have adopted to solve the problem of succession. There are several ways in which societies can make priority-statements which will give precedence to one claimant rather than another and thus eliminate – or at least reduce – socially divisive disputation.

*Royal incest*

Incest has been practised by members of the royal houses in several pre-industrial societies, notably Ancient Egypt, Inca Peru and .

14

pre-Western Hawaii. The normal arrangement was brother-sister marriage so that their progeny would inherit and thus ostensibly maintain the purity of the royal line.

In Ancient Egypt, for example,[9] the sister's main function was to produce an heir for the god-Pharaoh; she was a wife in this reproductive sense only.[10] The Pharaoh would have innumerable concubines who also bore royal offspring – the self-styled Ramesses the Great (d. c. 1230 BC) had over 100 children dependent upon his favours – but their claims were effectively thwarted by the royal brother-sister system.

Royal incest, therefore, had a number of useful functions. It ensured the continuation of an 'uncontaminated' divine succession; it outlawed any counter-claims by other royal children; and it established yet further differentiae – if this were needed – between the ruling house and its subjects.

*Affinal exclusion*

In effect, affinal exclusion has basically the same function as incest, but it is achieved by the opposite means. As a 'device', it is particularly associated with a much more recent ruling house in Egypt, namely the 'slave' or Mameluke dynasty[11] which began in the thirteenth century AD. This Egyptian slave-dynasty is unique in Occidental history. It derived from the early days of Islam when the Caliphs of Baghdad recruited body-guards from the ranks of their slaves to quell the rising tide of discontentment among their less subservient Emirs. The slaves became increasingly highly placed in the Islamic hierarchy as successive Caliphs came to rely upon their growing administrative expertise and military efficiency. After a coup in AD 1260, and their defeat of the Mongols under Gengis Khan,[12] the Mamelukes came to power and ruled Egypt for some 250 years.

The Mamelukes perpetuated the slave 'myth'. By contracting marriages with other slaves who had no inherent rights, they effectively outlawed the claims of ambitious in-laws who, as slaves themselves, were automatically disqualified from office except as a gift of the Sultan.

*Cosmic birth*

As a type of 'explanation' the cosmic myth often succeeds in eliminating overt disputation concerning succession. Although it takes many forms, all insist that the claimants in question are divine progeny. In more or less successful ways they allay suspicions about the sometimes spurious claims of would-be rulers.

15

Such legitimations can be found in a wide variety of systems. These range from the lofty metaphysical procedures surrounding the selection – or perhaps more accurately, *identification* – of the Tibetan Dalai Lama as 'he who must be born at the right time'[13] to the highly pragmatic and perhaps cynical rationalisation of the dynastic coup in Imperial China which was seen not as treason but as a transfer of the 'divine Mandate'.[14]

## Rival elimination

The elimination of any dangerous opposition is not necessarily the last desperate recourse of a threatened heir-apparent. It has been a well-established procedure in several simple and advanced pre-industrial societies.

The Buganda in pre-colonial days held that a chief's vitality might be unwittingly transferred to his sons, particularly the eldest. So, as a rather drastic precaution, the firstborn was strangled by the midwife who attended the birth. Similar acts were performed with other sons on special occasions and this became institutionalised as a form of sacrifice.[15] Ostensibly, it was done to maintain the chief's physical strength upon which the prosperity of the tribe was said to depend, although it is difficult to avoid the conclusion that it was really a type of ritualised political expediency.

Consolidation of power was also ensured by the elimination of siblings. Mutesa, the first Bugandan chief to meet white explorers, had arranged for the disposal of some ninety relatives who might have had tenuous designs upon his royal preserves.[16]

Among more advanced societies, sibling elimination was a notable feature of the Ottoman Sultanate in Turkey. Several rulers were infamous for their treatment of wives and concubines who for relatively minor misdemeanours – not least of all the inexcusable failing of growing old and undesirable – were ceremoniously drowned off Seraglio Point near the Topkapi Palace at Istanbul.[17] Possible counter-claims to the throne were dealt with in an equally peremptory manner. For example, a seventeenth-century Sultan, Muhammad III, whose position and accession were shadowed by rival brothers and half-brothers, had nineteen of them strangled with the traditional bowstring, and seven of his father's concubines – already pregnant with further claimants – drowned in the prescribed manner.

All these mechanisms presuppose the institutions of monarchy and chieftainship which are themselves most commonly justified in terms of succession issues. Societies thus devise procedures or exploit known practices in order to solve a singularly awkward problem and obviate unnecessary hierarchical discord and possible civil strife.

They may not always succeed in these aims, but their continued acceptance in so many societies attests their general effectiveness.

(*b*) *Control mechanisms may act to prevent specific conflict-occurrence by a variety of insulation expedients.*

Insulation mechanisms may be purely ideological, protecting the individual or society by erecting barriers of conviction and belief. But the most common and possibly the most effective way in which these operate is by a combination of insulation and isolation. The monastic seclusion sought by some medieval clergy fulfilled several functions. It enabled them to escape from a disenchanting world and gave them conditions in which they could pursue their own special interests in a secure ecclesiastical environment. Perhaps, more than anything else, it provided both a spatial and spiritual protection which neutralised the world's capacity to hurt them further.

This need to be insulated from the world has been the recourse of innumerable movements, and can still be seen in some modern Bruderhof and commune systems. It is at least plausible that the ability to cut oneself off from the source of anxiety, helps adherents to sublimate their tensions and frustrations, besides giving them a conducive setting in which to discover a new sense of community.

Such quasi-utopian expedients usually require some measure of isolation. It is arguable that the most famous blueprint for society written in ancient times, *The Republic*,[18] could only have been realised in a geographical context which afforded the necessary degree of isolation. Presumably, this would also have guaranteed it an initial freedom from violation as well. This kind of separatist neutrality is still reflected in the increasingly vulnerable 'curtains' and uneasy relations which exist between modern Communist and Mixed Economy systems.

(*c*) *Control mechanisms tend to canalise responses to strain and tension in socially approved ways.*

To this extent such mechanisms provide a means of social catharsis. Witchcraft accusations primarily – but not exclusively – in simple pre-industrial societies, function to redirect, or at least deflect, a sense of hostility between members. There are many explanations of witchcraft, none of them exhaustive or wholly satisfactory, but in many societies it does seem to 'contain' aggression in certain ways by reducing the possibilities for *overt* hostility.[19]

In a very different way, and in a very different context, the 'bread and circuses' policy in Ancient Rome performed a very similar role.[20] The gladiatorial displays[21] and the periodic distribution of grain are plausibly thought to have reduced the ever present possibility of insurrection. They appear to have been particularly effective expedients where, as in Rome, there was a sizeable plebeian population, which was largely unenfranchised and cosmopolitan, living at near-subsistence level.

17

(*d*) *Control mechanisms may make socially disapproved responses difficult or costly.*

In other words, control mechanisms often have a deterrence function. The sanctions most obviously connoted here are those of social approbation and disapprobation. Social responses which involve stricture, disrespect and possible ridicule can be particularly potent in relatively close-knit societies where there are intricate nexi of strong local ties.

Athenian women, for example, although not kept in any form of domestic purdah,[22] sometimes envied the relative freedom of their Spartan counterparts.[23] But it is difficult to imagine any serious violation of the accepted female role in Athenian society where they had no vote and were regarded as jural minors.[24]

At more formal levels of organisation, the legal sanctions which operated in complex pre-industrial systems were sufficient deterrents in themselves. Again in Athens, in the very early part of the fifth century BC, citizens were empowered to nominate for banishment those whom they felt had done any grave disservice to the state.[25] The constraints on a man in public life were considerable, as they were also in the Roman Republican system where once a man's period as consul had ended, he could be arraigned for crimes alleged to have been committed whilst he was in office. Socially disapproved actions could not only be made difficult and costly, under some circumstances in systems which were more repressive, they could be virtually impossible – except perhaps as token gestures of defiance. And these were usually rather temporary.

(*e*) *Control mechanisms can operate to resocialise the deviant.*

Again, this can be effected in a number of ways. The procedures naturally vary from society to society, and very markedly within societies, depending upon the level of operation and the gravity of the offence.

The techniques associated with the resocialisation process are much more characteristic of modern, technological societies than pre-industrial systems. Attempts to reform the deviant were not notable features of simpler societies; there were usually more expeditious ways of solving this kind of problem. In our kind of society, the deviant may be resocialised by means of some accepted reformative treatment. In extreme cases, this can mean imprisonment, but in many instances simply involves hospitalisation of some kind or another, particularly where specialised treatment is required, as in the case of alcoholics and addicts. Psychotherapy is also employed as a technique of social regeneration – but it is not without its critics.[26]

Resocialisation, in some societies, can be an unconvincing euphemism for ideological conversion. The political deviant may be subjected to the kinds of well-proven behavioural techniques loosely but popularly dubbed 'brainwashing'. These have been dispassionately developed to a high level of sophistication,[27] and have come a long way from the instrumental torture associated with pre-technological systems.

If all else fails –

(*f*) *Control mechanisms can operate to remove the causes of tension and anxiety.*

There are usually legal and quasi-legal means which can be employed as ultimate solutions. Where mechanisms of reform and insulation prove inadequate, there is always the possibility of segregation by imprisonment or exile, and – finally – of elimination itself. No society is without its sanctions, systems simply vary in the types they devise, the circumstances in which they operate, and the stages at which they are invoked.

## 2 Social control requires legitimation

As Max Weber has argued,[28] 'imperative coordination' in societies is based, in practice, upon a complex of interests which are not purely economic. Observance of society's norms, whether legalised or not, may be simply matters of habituation and custom. The strivings for pecuniary and general economic advantage will be tempered by the constraints imposed by given allegiances and sensed loyalties. But as an 'induction from experience', no system voluntarily limits itself to an appeal to material, affectional or even ideal motives as a basis for guaranteeing its continuance. A belief in *legitimacy* is also essential. And this can be both inculcated or cultivated in a variety of ways.

The type of legitimacy will determine a range of responses and effects in different societies. It will affect the type and degree of obedience which is both given and required. It will determine the kind of administration which must of necessity guarantee that obedience. It will also influence the mode in which this authority is exercised – whether it is in fact persuasive or coercive. In general, the effect of all these operations will be a function of the type of legitimacy employed.

Fundamentally, then, legitimation can be seen as a function of the interrelation between the structural and the cultural systems of society. It underpins the organisational status quo with justificatory supports. That is to say, it 'explains' control whilst, in itself, not being a direct mechanism of control.

Talcott Parsons[29] makes this point in his analysis of the functions of legitimation in differentiated and undifferentiated societies. In differentiated or advanced societies which are characterised by a relatively clear demarcation of functions within the institutional complex, there is usually a marked independence between the culturally-grounded bases of legitimacy, for example, religion, and the lower order operative mechanisms such as the functioning of, say, the economic markets. On the other hand, in undifferentiated societies there is a relative *dependence* of the operative mechanisms on cultural values. This is very obvious in simple societies where, for instance, economic matters are largely conditioned by kinship relations, and not by profit maximisation as in more advanced systems.

Legitimation can also be seen as a 'grounding' for the normative order of society. The normative order is hardly *self*-legitimating; social arrangements are liable to be questioned even in traditional societies. Authority may therefore base its appeal on a subtle amalgam of custom and national pride. Legitimations, whether resting on time-honoured traditions or emotional chauvinism, justify how a society *ought* to operate. This need not imply the presence of *moral* imperatives in the narrow sense of the term, but – as Parsons emphasises – it does imply an essential 'rightness' in the institutionalised order.

It follows from this that legitimation can therefore be seen as a means of supplying the requisite *self-evidence* for the system. It defines the reasons for members' rights and, by definition, the imposition of all necessary prohibitions. It justifies both the system's expectations of members and the constraints laid upon them. All can be interpreted as that which is self-evidently 'proper', and consequently needful for the harmonisation of societal interests.

In Ancient Israel, for example, the connection between ritual practice and certain cultic centres such as Dan, Bethel and particularly Jerusalem was supported by venerated traditions regarding the special sanctity of those centres.[30] Or again, similar 'irrefutable' validations can be seen in the association between socio-ritual practices such as the keeping of the Sabbath Day and the foundation myth of a six-day Creation. As far as we know, these things may never have been seriously questioned. They were accepted for both religious and socio-political reasons. And the same is true in countless ways for other societies. By perpetual practice, tradition becomes sanctified as social 'truth'.

### 3 Social control can be reinforced by ideology

Ideology can be regarded as both a reinforcing and legitimating mechanism of control. But to say this implies that ideology is, in some way, the servant of the social process, a convenient aid to the realisation of normative expectations. Ideology can be shown to be much more than this. Indeed, it is a principal contention of this whole discussion that ideology has been – and perhaps in qualified ways still is[31] – a major influence in that process. The extent and nature of its reciprocally interactive role in society is an important yet relatively neglected issue in the social sciences.[32]

Legitimation is inextricably linked with the problem of *meaning* in society. Every society which has persisted for any length of time, particularly if it has developed even a modest degree of complexity, has also evolved some interpretation of its own way of life. If members of a society are to fulfil their social obligations, it follows that 'there must be available a morally acceptable explanation of the society's particular system of institutional arrangements, including its social disparities'.[33] Societies tend to invest with value the most important goals of social activity. And although there are ubiquitous disparities between aspiration and achievement, the ideal standards are retained and, in turn, buttressed by the operation of reinforcing ideologies which are supported by this and other-worldly sanctions.

Ideological frameworks provide symbolic meaning-systems for those involved. An examination and interpretation of such meaning-systems was one of Emile Durkheim's main contributions to the social sciences.[34] He insisted that ritual behaviour which was ostensibly 'vertical' and supplicatory, actually signified an expression of human values and therefore had a latent horizontal adequacy. In worship – and this could also apply to secular rituals – men merely represented themselves to themselves. In these 'collective representations', they interpreted society and their own place in the social order.

This view is subject to all manner of qualifications and criticisms,[35] but at least it has the merit of highlighting the social implications of belief-systems. After all, when a priest of the temple of Marduk at Babylon, washed and clothed and even 'fed' the image of the god, it can hardly be supposed that he regarded the acts as any more than symbolical. In his recognition of Marduk as the tutelary deity of Babylon, his rituals were also a symbolic way of ensuring the preservation and well-being of the state. To this extent, his acts were social and ostensibly practical. In serving the god, he was also indirectly reaffirming the socio-political status quo and the – at various times – hegemonic supremacy of the Babylonian state in relation to other minor city-states in Babylonia.[36]

Ideology also provides justifications for a range of social activities. This can be particularly well illustrated in the case of war. In Assyria, for example, as with so many societies, the real motives for starting a war were never frankly admitted.[37] Presumably, these were primarily economic but this was not stated explicitly, instead the king claimed that he was embarking on a new expansionist or

21

punitive campaign in obedience to Ashur, a principal Assyrian deity. The customary reasons for war were all recognised, violation of treaties, provocation, etc., but the command of the god was given as the sufficient cause of the campaign in the official accounts. Socio-political factors and ideological factors, 'the will of Ashur', became synonymous.[38]

Ideology, then, adds a special – perhaps convenient – rationality to social arrangements. Indeed, in some systems, as Hannah Arendt has pointed out, ideology may constitute a form of *total* explanation by the application of a single idea to the various realms of reality.[39] Where it does not, or cannot, supply the necessary legitimations, ideology can play a reinforcing role. In this capacity, it will simply constitute a further validation of policies and values which have been primarily determined by non-ideological factors. In some circumstances, it may be coercive, in others it will merely act as a motivational inducement. Whatever, in its reinforcing role, ideology bridges the gap between incredulity and expediency.

# 3   The problem of ideology

Having glanced briefly at the place of ideology as a reinforcing and legitimising mechanism in social control, we must now look at some theories of ideology in much more detail. We will be particularly concerned with the nature and functions of ideology and their interactional complexity in institutional contexts.

These issues have been overlaid with numerous associations and connotations which have not always contributed to the business of clarification.[1] What is ideology? John Plamenatz – rephrasing Talcott Parsons[2] – speaks of ideology as 'a set of closely related beliefs or ideas, or even attitudes characteristic of a group or community'.[3] Similarly, ideology can be seen as that which provides 'a common universe of ultimate values ... (involving) a common cognitive orientation toward goals and (the) means for their attainment. . . .'[4] This kind of definition leaves us wondering just what is – or even can be – meant by 'ultimate values', and exactly how these are to be ascertained within any given community. Can we even meaningfully speak of ideas which are 'characteristic' of a group? That is to say, can we distinguish ideas which are so peculiar in *essence* (as opposed to the form in which they are expressed) that they can be clearly seen to constitute the differentiae of that group? Are discernible values to be equated with distinguishing characteristics? This approach to social analysis suggests that different societies, particularly historical societies, have identifiable ethoi of their own, which is a highly debatable issue.[5]

Perhaps a more satisfactory definition of ideology is 'a pattern of beliefs and concepts (both factual and normative) which purport to explain complex social phenomena with a view to directing and simplifying socio-political choices facing individuals and groups'.[6] Such a general definition does not explicate the many nuances of the term or specify the variety of intellectual systems which have been

23

styled ideologies. Neither does it define the different modes in which they may have been legitimised or the internal balance between the factual and ethical components.

There are two predominating types of theories of ideology which relate to the general area of social control.

## Interest theories

These see ideology variously as a mask, a guise or a weapon. History is regarded as an unending struggle for advantage between those who have power and those who seek it.[7] The structure of society reflects these interminable agona. Ideology is therefore an expedient devised by authority systems to secure and justify their aims and policies.

Ideology is a contrivance which perpetuates a distorted view of the social process and therefore, constitutes a system of related illusions about the state in particular and society in general.[8] This view of ideology necessarily sets it against a 'scientific' appreciation of the situation. To this extent, ideology may be seen as a substitute for exact knowledge.

Using the term to denote not the illusion, as such, but the belief or value-system, it is then argued that the ideology of the dominant classes is used to enhance their class interests by justifying the established order to the detriment of the oppressed classes. In one sense, ideology is seen as an exploitative value-system which is imposed upon the masses.[9] In another sense, it is regarded as a contrivance which both mystifies and misleads the masses by encouraging a false awareness of the historical process and of their place in the whole scheme of things.[10] In yet a further sense it is seen as a pervasive yet vulnerable illusion which is ultimately subject to the practical realities of production relations within society.

Interest theories of ideology can be criticised on a number of grounds. In their cruder forms, they imply an inadequate psychology; they do not – perhaps cannot – explain *how* or *why* the ideology in question is accepted and believed. They seem unable to bridge the causal gulf between a specific belief and a particular form of social response. In general terms, it is not known why some people sense a natural affinity with certain value-systems and others do not; why some react positively and others negatively to the same ideological stimuli. Interest theories do little to clarify this particular problem. How did it come about, for instance, that in Ancient Greece the various warring city-states were prepared temporarily to forego internecine strife for an armistice celebrated by a festival of games? The periodic cessation of warfare makes sense in any system, but why in *this* form? And why do we not find this a common practice in other societies? To insist, as interest theories must, that this was really a device to further the covert interests of a privileged minority is not to explain either the fascination which the games had for ordinary Hellenes or the binding solemnity of their ritual performance.

It can also be argued that interest theories are inclined to be rather simplistic in that they tend to ignore alternative explanations.[11] It may well be that ideologies do obscure social categories, but in some circumstances, they very clearly define them. This apparent contradiction is very evident in racist ideologies. Paradoxically, although ideologies may stabilise social expectations and strengthen social consensus, as interest theories maintain, they may also upset social expectations and weaken consensus. Ideologies both maintain and undermine social norms; both relieve and exacerbate social tensions. This is very apparent in religious ideologies which do not necessarily function as opiates of the people. Religion certainly does often support the hierarchical status quo, and sanction injustices, and neutralise the possibilities of social agitation. But it also constitutes a source of intellectual enquiry, as in the medieval Church where it ultimately led to social protest and political change.[12] Religion has also functioned as a revolutionary force in some societies, and institutionalised religion has frequently been the generative agent of social reform.[13] Religion, therefore, can be both cohesive and divisive. To insist that it is any *one* kind of a thing is to ignore its ambiguous role in actual historical circumstances.

It must be said then of interest theories that they are historically questionable. It can hardly be doubted that ideologies can be what the interest theorists say they are. They can be contrivances; they often act as exploitative mechanisms – but they are not always or necessarily either of these things. There is ample evidence in traditional societies to show that ideologies did condition social relations and that those same ideologies really were believed by exploiters and exploited alike.

To summarise: the argument that 'interest' is a particular form of rational action which derives from a class position does not explain how (i) as a historical phenomenon an ideology has been formulated, or (ii) as a psychological phenomenon, it has been acquired and believed. In short, interest theories even when carefully defined are inadequate; where they are not, they can be made to cover every contingency and thus lose their meanings.[14]

## Strain theories

These see ideology as a symptom of – or even as a remedy for – dislocation in the social structure. In general, strain theories maintain

25

that all societies are riddled with insolvable antinomies, that is to say, the co-existing presence of equally persuasive opposites. Societies are characterised by the desire to maintain stability whilst recognising the need for change. But the apparent inevitability of change[15] – particularly in modern societies – can bring dislocations[16] which ultimately prove to be unmanageable.[17] Societies are also vexed with the problems of how to maintain or increase a measure of efficiency whilst at the same time preserving a vestigial humanity. This, in turn, involves further problems of precision and flexibility, of how to reconcile the cry for liberty with the stifling necessity of political order.

These issues, however, were not so marked in complex pre-industrial societies where change was slow and hesitant. Questions of humanity and flexibility were usually subordinated to the require-ments of stability and political order.[18] And the question of liberty was perhaps something of a non-issue in a 'pre-Greek world' where freedom, as we have come to understand it, just did not exist.[19] But traditional societies had their own particular versions of these problems – pre-eminently those related to the issues of stability and social control.

These problems were largely resolved in terms of ideology, and the innumerable frictions arising from them were often contained by ideological imperatives. In one way or another, all men 'live lives of patterned desperation'.[20] Thus ideology can be seen as a patterned response to patterned strains. On this interpretation, the presence of, say, religion in society could be construed as a symptom of social malintegration and, at the same time, a functional remedy. In its remedial capacity, religion may be seen to have several related functions. It may purport to explain these social discrepancies, or it may try to obscure their 'real' nature;[21] failing this – or even in addition to this – it may endeavour to ameliorate their effects.[22]

As with interest theories, there is the assumption that ideological and scientific modes of thought are at variance with one another. This incompatibility is often expressed in terms which suggest the irreconcilability of social myth with that which is thought of as empirically true.[23] Most human action is seen as unreflective. Society tends to encourage non-reflection by presenting inadequate sets of choices, and simply indicating approved ways of behaviour. In traditional societies particularly, there may be no clear empirical references or 'solutions', although sometimes alternative referents such as religion and myth can be effective in given situations. The consequence is that eventually the imperfections within the system become too great and mechanisms are reflectively evolved to deal with them. The strains, therefore, are held to call forth various kinds of response, both rational and non-rational. Ideology is regarded as a non-rational response in terms of ideas and symbols.[24] But again, no satisfactory explanation is given as to why people respond to certain symbols rather than others, or why it is that some symbols gain and others lose their force in particular situations.[25]

Science may actually be contrasted with ideology with the clear implication that scientific reasoning produces solutions which are unquestionably superior.[26] Ideology is regarded as being selective in its use of empirical evidence. Subjects and areas of discussion may be treated eclectically or simply arbitrarily dismissed altogether. Science, which may also be selective, is seen to differ in its objectives in that it aims at understanding rather than persuasion. Alternatively, whereas science engages problems rationally, ideology often merely employs expressive symbols and slogans to excite public feeling. Science informs where ideology simply moralises and arouses emotional reactions.

This allegation that ideology has low cognitive functions but a high affective impact must be seriously qualified. It is undoubtedly true that people sometimes like to hear certain sentiments expressed which they do not entirely understand. But ideology as an effective form of supra-social explanatory system is well-attested regardless of the fact that in any given instance it does not appear to accord with a scientific evaluation of the situation. Anything more than a cursory glance at this kind of analysis will show that these distinctions between ideological and scientific modes of thought are largely relative and academic.[27] In actual instances, they usually overlap. Ideology may impede science, as the late Gilbert Murray has insisted in connection with Greek religion and culture.[28] He argues for a 'failure of nerve' on the part of the Greeks, and their consequent inability to espouse a truly rationalistic philosophy and realise their own humanistic and scientific potential. On the other hand, ideology may act as a spur to science, as Robert Merton has argued in relation to Protestantism and post-Reformation scientific development.[29] And it is undeniable that science can serve ideology, a point very persuasively made by Carl Friedrich in delineating a distinction between the character of pre-industrial autocratic societies and modern technology-aided totalitarian systems.[30]

In general, ideologies do command attention where other systems of explanation – political, scientific and so forth – tend to be either cognitively inadequate or emotionally unsatisfactory. But the influence of ideologies on the wider social process defies simple calculation. It is impossible to quantify an influence and it is even difficult to correlate the holding of any belief with a given life-style or a particular pattern of behaviour. The cause and effect issue cannot be resolved because the additional variables involved in the inter-active process cannot be held as constants. And because it is not

27

THE PROBLEM OF IDEOLOGY

therefore possible to isolate the determinative potential of the belief variable, its importance can only be assessed with qualifications. But this should not detract from its study or undermine its importance. A knowledge of men's fundamental beliefs will not explain everything about their actions in the real world. 'But insofar as these actions reflect a mutual adjustment between ideology and social realities, an understanding of ideology becomes a necessary condition for the understanding of the action.'[31] So although we may not be able to specify the precise contribution of ideology to the social order, we can identify it in terms of its functions. Even though its 'nature' is hard to define, its effects – especially in traditional societies – are both subtle and pervasive.

## The functions of ideology

Probably all ideologies are characterised by contradictions, inconsistencies and exaggerations of one kind or another. The language of ideology can itself be the vehicle of distortion. Religious ideologies in particular thrive on metaphor which involves a 'semantic tension'[32] between associated images. Language, of course, evokes a multiplicity of referential connections and symbolic associations, and ideology provides a potent kind of organising principle for the 'correct' ordering of this experience. Ideologies dispel conceptual uncertainty by supplying a blueprint, a panacea, a heuristic answer where other institutional aids have proved inadequate.

In very broad terms, the main functions of ideologies can be classified under four headings:

### (i) Cathartic functions

The argument here is that in various ways ideologies can act as emotional release mechanisms. In religious movements, for example, the catharsis involved can be seen in the cultic exercises where the actual content of the rituals may be secondary to the euphoria-generating conditions in which they are performed. More specifically, social catharsis may be concerned, in some systems, with the 'identification' of suitable social scapegoats. This is not an unusual phenomenon. It can be found in pre-industrial societies,[33] but it is perhaps more commonly a feature of modern totalitarian systems. This is starkly evidenced by the Nazi policies of institutionalised anti-Semitism and systematic genocide.[34]

Ideologies comprise the 'creative syntheses of idea elements'[35] into coherent packages. This makes acceptance easier, partly because they carry the necessary imprimatur and are therefore not to be questioned, and partly because they tend to anaesthetise the

28

intellectual – and doubting – processes. A fact of incalculable worth to authoritarian regimes. Some individuals within the system demur at the margins, but – by and large – they will conform and comply according to the socially provided cues.

### (ii) Morale-maintenance functions

Ideologies can have sustaining functions which usually operate in either of two main ways. These have a kind of complementarity in that they represent primary and secondary level defences against morale-threatening incursions.

At the primary level, ideology may deny authenticity to certain levels of reality. Racist ideologies, for example, hold that the criteria for the classification of ethnic groups can be clearly identified. To specific groups they may even deny an essential humanity, and these are consequently proscribed or generally treated as inferiors. The simple form of the theory is that some people look different and therefore, ipso facto, *are* different. (Although the reverse might be argued in the case of Jewish people.) Others display no markedly different characteristics, but are categorised as inferior on arbitrary bases which are possibly expediency-motivated.[36]

The intellectualisation of racial differences as theories of race is a relatively recent phenomenon,[37] but ethnic differentiation with inferior-superior connotations has been with us for a very long time.[38] The Ancient Egyptians – particularly of the northern Delta areas – saw the inhabitants of Upper Egypt as inferior slave material.[39] The Sumerians both despised and feared the nomadic mountain people on their borders.[40] For the Greeks, all non-Greeks – including the highly sophisticated Persians – were barbaroi, that is, foreigners or strangers, a category which carried pejorative overtones.[41] Very similar sentiments were entertained in Imperial China vis-à-vis the outside world which, in theory, was supposed to acknowledge the centrality and authority of the Imperial Court. The Emperor was believed to hold special mandates in relation to the non-Chinese world of which, needless to say, the non-Chinese world was contentedly unaware.[42] These attitudes were by no means uncommon, and are reflected in the records of many traditional societies. Essentially, they constitute a refusal to recognise – possibly for self-interested reasons – the common humanity of other hypothetically 'lesser' peoples.

Where it becomes impossible or merely imprudent to deny certain orders of reality, ideologies may function to maintain morale by a transvaluation of common experience. This can, of course, involve a re-evaluation or rationalisation of that which can no longer be denied but which is nevertheless considered to be an affront to that experience. Thus, to take the race example once again, it may not be a sense of innate superiority but a nagging suspicion of common ordinariness which compels one group to denigrate others. Where differences do not obviously exist, they must be contrived. Distinctions are made which reflect favourably on the denigrating group, and may then be validated by 'successful' social arrangements. Spartan society, for instance, consisted basically of three strata: the helots or serfs perhaps numbering about 150,000, other subjugated Lacadaemonian peoples – Messenians and the like – numbering possibly about 40,000, all controlled and exploited by an élite body of citizen Spartiates of whom there were probably only about 4,000–5,000. The Spartans, the descendants of the original invading Dorians who had either dispersed or suppressed the indigenous peoples, were well established in southern Greece from the latter part of the eighth century BC. Their military supremacy,[43] reflected in their hegemonic authority over a large part of southern Greece, became crystallised in a peculiar social ideology and distinctive social organisation.[44]

By denying or transvaluating that which is objectionable or simply humiliating, ideologies function to sustain a sense of importance and social well-being. However, having said this, there is the complementary proposition that ideologies can serve to *reaffirm* a particular reality. Peter Berger advances this kind of argument in connection with the functions of religion: 'Religion legitimates social institutions by bestowing upon them an ultimately valid ontological status, that is, by locating them within a sacred and cosmic frame of reference. . . .' This, he continues, 'is typical of primitive and archaic societies. . . .'[45] It follows from this that ideologies can have:

### (iii) Solidarity-reinforcement functions

Ideologies customarily operate to promote unity – at least, among adherents. This can involve the rehearsal of venerated traditions, or the reiteration and perpetuation of popular myths. This point is made by Emile Durkheim in relation to religion.[46]

It is asserted, for example, that the Quetzalcoatl myth is 'the most diffusive of all presences of Middle America'.[47] Said variously to have been a 'white-bearded stranger' who, in the remote past, refined the Mayan calendar; a god of the air who descended to the later Toltecs to teach them art, wisdom and kindness; the patron of learning and magic for the still later Aztecs, Quetzalcoatl emerged as the apotheosis of the Middle American culture-hero. The myth represents the qualified unity of many pre-Columbian cultures and the continuity of their traditions. Ironically, it now recalls their ultimate downfall in the hands of the conquistadores. Cortes reached the coast of Mexico in 1519, the year of the predicted return of Quetzalcoatl. The Aztec emperor, Montezuma II, who had been trained as a priest, seems to have really believed – at least initially – that Cortes must be the messianic hero fulfilling his promise to re-visit his people, an identification which the Spanish adventurer was only too ready to exploit.[48] The emperor's paralysis of will and consequent indecision – ostensibly for ideological reasons – contributed significantly to his own subsequent destruction and that of pre-Columbian Mexican civilisation.[49]

Myths therefore sometimes constitute the basis of a unifying ideology. Unlike fables where the matter of historicity can be confidently dismissed, myths may contain some vestigial historical truth. A myth may be a grossly distorted or representational account of some half-remembered incident which has a special significance for the collectivity in question. Alternatively, a myth may simply be a pre-theoretical way of transmitting social truth and justifying current social practices – particularly in traditional societies.[50] Whatever, myths often have some form of didactic function[51] and are therefore the symbolic vehicles whereby ideological truth is conveyed.

In traditional societies, there is commonly an inextricable connection between myth and ritual. 'Myth says what ritual does'[52] succinctly summarises this view. But the relationship is not invariable, and where it occurs, it is often difficult to accord primacy to one or the other.[53] In religious systems, truth is communicated in terms of insights and perceptions, 'symbolic rituals reinforce [the worshippers'] sense of otherness and, in their own ways, convey the message for those initiated into their meanings'.[54] These inspirational enactments increase the potency of belief-systems as agents of social control.

### (iv) Advocatory functions

It can be argued that ideologies articulate the strains which impel them. This has two principal effects. First, it forces the masses to recognise the nature of the issues involved and, second, it polarises their response to those issues.

Such a theory would have limited applications in traditional societies where relevant issues are not necessarily brought before the people. However, in archaic societies such as the Greek poleis where political procedures were arguably democratic, it does have a qualified applicability. Even in Sparta, a state which claimed to be a democracy but whose constitution marks it as an unusual form of oligarchy, key issues passed through a three-tier hierarchical process before action could be taken. Quite apart from the rather nominal views of the two kings who ruled jointly, matters passed

31

from the elected body of five ephors to the gerousia, or body of elders, and thence to the ecclesia, the citizens themselves. Really critical matters such as declarations of war were dealt with in this manner. The way was therefore open for persuasive orators to influence the people by reference to both practical necessity and the ideological mores of Spartan tradition.[55] The appeal to tradition and particularly the susceptibility to demagogic influence was even more significant in ostensibly open societies such as Athens. In some modern states, the masses have often been relatively free of any marked ideological commitment – except possibly for practical and personal advantage.[56] Usually there have been notable disparities between the impelling ideological 'range' of the élite and that of the lower strata. This was not so in many of the Greek poleis where lay participation in political and social affairs was encouraged.[57]

The general weakness of this kind of functional analysis is that it suggests patterns of behaviour which are only tenuously related to realised ends. For example, how can one demonstrate a functional relationship between, say, the entrail readings of Roman augurs and increased social solidarity? In fact, according to the theories, the ends in question are often so vaguely expressed that one is left unsure as to whether they have been realised or not. After all, social solidarity is extraordinarily amorphous, and morale-maintainance quite impossible to assess with any degree of confidence. To what extent any action or ideology has contributed to the attainment of these goals cannot be known with certainty. To suggest, as Merton does,[58] that we should look not only at the manifest functions but also the *latent* functions of an institution may tell us very little in these circumstances. The concept of latent function merely names or indicates such means-ends relationships, it does not explain them. How symbols 'work' is still not clear – it seems simply adventitious that they appear to do so.

Theories of ideology tend to be diagnostically convincing but functionally suspect. Both interest and strain theories pass from the hypothesised sources of the ideology to the consequences of its operation without demonstrating how and why. They tend to be presented as self-evident propositions although they can only be tentative – if plausible – hypotheses.

## Types of ideologies

The well-established distinction between conservative ideologies and liberal or revolutionary ideologies[59] seems unexceptional but generally valid. The term conservative ideology is virtually self-explanatory. It signifies that which supports the interests and values of existing social arrangements. Such an ideology may be imposed or perpetuated by a dominant ruling group, but as we have already noted, this is by no means necessarily the case. A conservative ideology may well be associated with, or actually identified with, the religious belief-system of a society. As such, it would uphold the structural and institutional norms of that society whilst at the same time legitimating its traditions. The fabric of every complex pre-industrial society was so permeated by ideological considerations of this kind, that it is often virtually impossible to divorce, say, various substantive legal and political issues from the religious sanctions usually connected with them. So that when, for example, Ramesses II, king of Egypt, wished to make a peace treaty with Hattusilis, king of the Hittites, after the inconclusive battle of Kadesh (c. 1295 BC), the gods were necessarily invoked. The text of the treaty was written in the neutral cuneiform Akkadian – at that time the language of international communication – on two silver tablets. One was taken back to Hatti, i.e. Hittite Anatolia, and presented to the Hittite storm-god, and the other copy was laid 'at the feet of' Re, the Egyptian sun deity. In each case, the king took an oath before his god and – more indelibly – before other human witnesses, so that the treaty was both invested and deposited with divine sanction and authority.[60]

Whereas conservative ideologies are concerned with the preservation of the social status quo, revolutionary ideologies – by definition – are more interested in the possible disruption of the current social order. Conservative ideologies seek to maintain social stasis, revolutionary ideologies are directed towards social change.

Revolutionary ideologies are not really a feature of traditional societies. It is possible to find examples of revolutionary *philosophies* which, if taken to their logical conclusions, could have meant some modifications to the current system. But these usually had a limited and rather cerebral appeal. The work of Plato – and presumably that of his mentor, Socrates – would fall into this category.[61] Despite the establishment of his Academy in the early part of the fourth century BC, Plato's teachings did not really claim widespread attention. His appeal was essentially to the intellectual and the aesthetic, and although he impressed many of his students who later occupied positions of authority in Greece and elsewhere, it can probably be argued that his influence has been largely posthumous.[62] His contemporaries were probably less impressed than scholars have been since.[63] This may, of course, suggest that he was ahead of his time and could therefore only be truly appreciated by later generations; on the other hand, it could indicate that his teaching was not *significantly* different from that of some others among the Athenian intelligentsia.[64] Whatever, there is surely a germinal truth in A. N. Whitehead's comment that the history of

33

Western philosophy ever since has consisted of 'mere footnotes to Plato'.[65]

In traditional societies also there have been attempted *reforms* which contemporaries certainly viewed as revolutionary in intent although it is doubtful if the thinking behind them can be graced with the term ideology. The monetary and political reforms instituted by Solon in Athens in the sixth century BC, and by Pericles a century later represented sweeping changes. But these were very much changes *within* the system; the essential character of Athenian political and social life was already established.[66] Similarly, the agricultural and social reforms of Tiberius and Gaius Gracchus (normally referred to simply as the Gracchi) in second-century BC Rome were regarded by their conservative patrician opponents as disruptive and dangerous.[67] But except for an incipient egalitarianism, it would be extravagant and perhaps misleading to attribute the limited changes which did take place to the presence of a revolutionary ideology.

In the ancient world perhaps one of the nearest things to what we might regard as an ideological revolution – as opposed to mere palace coups d'état which were not entirely unknown – were the religio-political innovations introduced by Amenophis IV, a Pharaoh of the Eighteenth Dynasty. Coming to the throne of Egypt c. 1376 BC, he changed his name to Akhenaten, 'the glorious sun-disc', and moved his capital from the traditional Thebes to a new site near the present village of Tell-el-Amarna. He tried to alter the entire religious emphasis to a near-monotheism,[68] the worship of the Aten, the sun's disc. In doing so, he violated the sacred traditions already vested in a powerful priesthood. These astonishing changes, by contemporary standards, were accompanied by a new and possibly less autocratic style of monarchy. This relaxation was reflected in unusual and refreshingly naturalistic conventions in art – until this time, for instance, it had been unknown to portray the god-king, posing as a mortal, leisurely playing with his wife and children. Needless to say, the reforms did not outlive his death. There is evidence to suggest that his memory was vilified and his monuments, the remaining physical evidence of his revolutionary activities, in a number of instances either destroyed or defaced. The now famous Tell-el-Amarna letters, correspondence between the palace and the governors of outlying Egyptian territories, confirm the weakness of the monarchy during this period.[69] They consist mainly of desperate pleas for assistance in the attempt to repel invasions by hostile tribes. The restoration of the earlier religious forms and the reconstitution of the traditional norms of monarchy, were probably necessary to carry the nation through this turbulent period which lasted until the accession of Ramesses II about 1300 BC.

The uncertainty of rule came to be identified with the unprecedented and sacrilegious changes which had taken place, and this made failure inevitable.

In general, then, a conservative ideology explains and defends existing institutions, especially those concerned with government, the economy and the social structure, whereas revolutionary ideology attacks the existing social order. But there are also two variants, the reactionary ideology and the counter-ideology.

Reactionary ideologies, which can derive from either conservative or revolutionary forms[70] usually support the restoration of certain revitalised or resuscitated versions of a traditional or conservative system. Viewed in this way, the reactionary ideology is particularly characteristic of complex pre-industrial societies whose orientations were, by definition, archaic. Almost invariably, any attempted reforms were, in effect, endeavours to recapture something of the known or assumed glories of the past. Utopian aspirations, as we tend to define them, were virtually unknown to archaic man. His thinking tended to be retrospective rather than prospective; indeed, his ideal world bore an unremarkable resemblance to his own.[71]

In this respect, we are necessarily dependent upon the literati whose interests were sometimes inseparably linked with the authority structure. But these are really the only records we have. These represent the most articulate voices of the ancient world; the sentiments of the anonymous masses usually only reach us indirectly through the remnants of ritual practice or hastily scribbled graffiti. Anything we 'know' about the feelings and opinions of the lower orders of society have normally been communicated by professional scribes and priest-historians whose task has been to preserve and enhance the systems' traditions. A possible general exception to this might be found in the broader terms of intellectual enquiry of the Greeks, but even this is subject to some qualification.

Counter-ideologies can be seen as those belief-systems which justify the norms of deviant groups or movements which have no ostensible desire to change the existing social order. To this extent, the ideology of such a group will only be seen as deviant or 'counter' in the wider social context. Within the group it will constitute its own form of conservatism, and on analysis may even be seen as a reactionary ideology which is being consciously contained. This situation could arise for esoteric reasons, to maintain some prized exclusivity, or simply because it is believed that any attempt to propagate the ideology would either be unsuccessful or would inevitably lead to an adulteration of standards and a consequent weakening of the movement.

In traditional societies, the term counter-ideology might most usefully be applied to certain forms of circumscribed religious

35

movements. For example, Mithraism, a popular cult especially among Roman legionaries from the second century AD onwards, could be regarded as a type of counter-ideology when compared with the persecution-inviting revolutionary ideology of Christianity during the same period. Indeed, it can be argued that in times of social instability, there will be a tendency for ideologies to proliferate.[72] Conflict situations produce more intensively institutionalised counter-movements with competing ideologies.[73] These need not represent a spectrum of protest, merely half-articulated expressions of disenchantment – but this would depend on the society in question.

This raises the perplexing – and more intriguing – dependent/independent variables problem. Why, under certain conditions, does the ideology dominate the situation? And why, under *other* conditions, does the whole ideological edifice appear to crumble before the practical impact of non-ideological considerations? Under some circumstances, ideological factors seem to be determinate, in others they appear to be subordinate to the prevailing socio-economic pressures. The task for the sociologist is to try to identify these situations and analyse the differences.

Useful as these customary sociological categories are in relation to ideology, their relevance is somewhat oblique, and therefore not entirely appropriate for the present discussion. What is suggested instead is the application of a conceptual model which is more directly related to the basic constructs of Archaic and Seminal types of society. A distinction is, therefore, proposed between cosmic and civic ideologies; between systems which are supernaturalistically orientated and those which are humanistically-orientated.

This polarity involves the concomitant question of how far we can distinguish ideology from religion. For functionalist theorists who take an inclusivist view of religion, ideology and religion are virtually the same thing simply because they *function* in similar ways.[74] Ideology is held to refer to secular explanations whilst religion advances theological explanations for similar and even the same phenomena.[75] But this lack of any really clear distinction raises all kinds of definitional problems. Religion can be seen as part of an overall ideological spectrum, and as such can be classed as a *form* of ideology, and may function as ideology in given conditions.[76] But ideology is not the predication of religion. The two terms cannot be equated as though they were synonymous. A function of religion does not 'explain' religion, nor can the sum of those functions exhaust the meaning of religion.

Ideology and religion obviously have a great deal in common, but exclusivist theorists[77] would argue that they should be regarded as analytically distinct. Religion refers to a supernatural order

36

which has a believed relevance for human action, whereas ideology is concerned with social systems. It follows, on this analysis, that cognitive ideological statements are in principle usually capable of being confirmed or disconfirmed by reference to empirical facts, but even the most cautious statements about the non-empirical or superempirical order are not. 'What distinguishes religious belief from other kinds of social beliefs is that in some way . . . it refers to, and looks for validation in, a dimension beyond the empirical-technical realm of action.'[78] If, therefore, the term religion per se is to have any academic credibility, it must be differentiated from more inclusive ideological systems, and be definitionally linked with the supernatural. In short, all religions are ideologies, but not all ideologies are religion.

As ideal constructs, cosmic and civic ideologies are to be distinguished by their general orientations. Cosmic ideologies have unambiguous supernaturalistic orientations. Belief in the gods predominates, and service to the gods is the central focus of human activity. The social order will be seen in some ways to be contingent on the cosmic order. Perhaps both orders are thought to enjoy a form of mystical congruence. The imperatives of the ideology are, therefore, unquestioned, and the demands of the ideology are totalising in their ultimacy. Cosmic ideologies may be universalising in their attitudes to the world, and try to absorb or if necessary destroy other competing belief systems. Alternatively, they may be extremely introverted, regarding themselves as provinces of special revelation and divine favour. This is to be guarded against all incursions, and is not to be shared with the non-elect. Early Islam would approximate to the former, and Judaism at particular periods, to the latter. Christianity, in its many forms, could approximate to both. In general, the ideologies of ancient societies were cosmic in type, and tended to be introverted and specific. In a qualified sense both Egypt and Athens are alike in this respect.

Broadly speaking, cosmically-oriented systems have diffuse other-worldly goals which may range from the care of the soul to the destiny of a particular group or society. There will be a consonance between their beliefs and values; no obvious or marked disparities will be evident between their theological-normative structures and their substantive value-orientations. Cosmic ideologies and religions can, therefore, be thought of in synonymous terms.

In contrast, civic ideologies have clear humanistic orientations. There may be some nominal adherence to the gods, but the concerns of the group or state will be the main focus of activity. The demands of a civic ideology will be totalising not in their ultimacy but in their applications. As with cosmic systems, they may take either conversionist or introversionist forms, or even both in conducive

37

situations. For example, Marxist ideology which is civic in type and has a universal appeal, crystallises in adapted forms in particular contexts. (The parenthetical problem here is if an ostensibly universalising ideology such as Marxism is both adopted and adapted for specific rationalistic purposes, does it then remain the same ideology?) The Athenians encouraged the adoption of democratic civic forms in other poleis, although this was hardly done with any conscious sense of mission.

Generally, civically-oriented systems will have specific this-worldly goals which are concentrated on the welfare of a particular community. The emphasis is secular and rationalistic. Where either a diffuse or vestigial religious ethic exists, the operative values of the society may not be consonant with its weak theological structures. Civic ideologies, therefore, are forms of belief-system which, by definition, can hardly be categorised as religions.

Neither Egypt nor Athens fits either one of these constructs neatly. But if cosmic and civic are viewed as the extremes of a continuum, it can be hypothesised that Egypt, especially in its Old Kingdom form, will approximate to the cosmic model whilst Athens will be seen to share many of the characteristics of the civic model.

Ideology, then, is a belief-system, and as such is a particular configuration of ideas and attitudes in which the elements are bound together by some dominant form of constraint. Viewed in this way, it constitutes a kind of special knowledge. It is here that we must avoid any etymological confusion between the knowledge of experience (Greek gnosis) – the 'prudence' of Hobbes and Burke – and intuitive knowledge (Greek eidos) which forms the basis of ideology. We may, therefore, regard ideology as being governed by a reductionist principle[79] in so far as an attempt is being made in ideological statements to reduce certain complexities to rule.[80] Reductionism in this form seems effectively to control or exclude error by reference to an impersonal – possibly supernatural – source which is beyond question. It is a return from Probabilistic models to Deterministic models of social causation.[81]

Probabilistic models stress relationships – which may be expressed numerically – rather than causes. They are interventionist in emphasis; they contain the tacit assumption that men and society can actually change things and shape their own destinies. Except for an implicit humanistic agnosticism, they are strictly non-philosophical. Deterministic models, on the other hand, are – by definition – necessitarian. They are mechanistic and often teleological, emphasising a purpose or goal. Not infrequently they are supernaturalistic, having specific value-orientations such as ultimate justice, truth, etc.

The operation of actual ideological systems may involve a subtle amalgam of both. The overall philosophy may be one of transpersonal causation; what happens may be seen as the outcome of almost any transpersonal agency from the will of the gods to some immutable 'law of history'.[82] But, at the same time, it may be held that such transpersonal principles can only be actualised by men. For instrumental reasons, the transpersonal must become personal.

It is, therefore, a principal contention of this thesis that social order is functionally related to the prevailing ideology in a society, and that this, in turn, conditions the mode of acceptance of the control mechanisms employed.[83] Not only does ideology relate to the respective poles of acceptance and rejection of existing institutions, it may itself determine the forms and even the nature of those institutions. This argument envisages a continuum ranging from ideal eunomia to ideal anomia, literally, from social good order to social disorder. Of course, no society has perfect order, and no known society has ever been completely anarchic and without any order at all. These are simply model polarities with which to compare actual situations. The argument then hypothesises that these can be plausibly linked with the relevant ideological imperatives. Where there is a totalising ideology, there will be a eunomic society, but where there is a non-totalising ideology – or the lack of any identifiable or coherent ideology – there will be an anomic society. Revolutionary ideology, on the other hand, need not produce a state of anomia, partly because it has a unifying effect on at least part of the society, and partly because successful revolutionary ideologies have a habit of becoming transmuted into conservative ideologies. It follows from this, therefore, that eunomia which is maintained by conservative ideology is consonant with social stability, and that anomia which can be associated with an absence of ideology is consonant with certain forms of social instability.

But there is one important qualifying codicil to these propositions which relates specifically to the issue of control. Whether the ideology in question is cosmic or civic in type, the theory or theology of the ideology may not be enough. As a belief-system it may be eminently persuasive and coherent but this may not be sufficient to effect social good order. What counts finally is the *implementation* of the ideology, the specificity of control, and the necessary evocation of obedient response.

# 4 Theories of cultural development

The intention in this section of the discussion is not to try to trace the origins and document the histories of development of particular ancient civilisations. Rather it is to outline certain general patterns of development and in doing so to examine some of the theoretical issues associated with them. The emphasis here then is nomothetic. This study will concentrate on the recurrent and, where possible, the universal: it is not *primarily* concerned with the particular or the unique. Specific instances can, of course, be interesting in themselves, but where they are cited it will be as examples of general socio-historical problems. But this too must be qualified. Social verities are difficult to determine. All perceived truth is relative,[1] but social truths are positively elusive. The student can, therefore, only recourse to a more defensible prehensive approach, treating the unique and the individual with extrapolatory caution, and grouping events into classes in the hope that a possible trend or even 'law' may emerge.[2]

The human habitation of our planet represents a mere fraction of the age of the planet itself. Excavations from 1959 onwards in the Olduvai Gorge in Kenya have somewhat surprisingly increased the size of that fraction. 'Man' in the very broadest sense of the term, has apparently existed for something like two million years,[3] although the date of the emergence of 'true' men is uncertain as are their precise links with sub-men. Eoliths or 'dawn stones' which appear to have been roughly chipped and shaped as hand tools have been found in many parts of the world. These date back more than a million years. But of the hominids of this Palaeolithic or Old Stone Age period, very little is known. In fact, anything which pre-dates the last glacial period, that is about 50,000 years ago, must be highly conjectural. Even the connections between Cromagnon or 'true' man who 'appeared' about 30,000 years ago,[4] and the intermediate Neanderthal species is uncertain, if indeed it even existed.[5] Whatever, when the last ice age began to recede, and tundra with its plentiful and accessible game gave way to forest, the hunter also very slowly gave way to the agriculturalist.

All the Palaeolithic groups lived by hunting, fishing and gathering. This required little in the way of economic sophistication although there is archaeological evidence of communal hunts which at least suggests the beginnings of social organisation. From even this Lower Palaeolithic period, there are traces of primitive religion and possibly belief in life after death; the dead were buried in uniform postures together with food and weapons, and protected by stones. Later, burial rites became more elaborate, and these together with other possible fertility rituals[6] indicate the rudiments of religious ideology. The famous cave-paintings of Lascaux and Carnac date from this Upper Palaeolithic period, that is c. 40000–c. 10000 BC. These paintings which have been executed with considerable artistic skill represent stags, reindeer and bison being pierced by arrows.[7] No one is sure why they are there. They may, of course, be there for no particular reason – a form of early interior decoration or mere Palaeolithic doodlings. But it is at least reasonable to suppose that they may have comprised part of some primitive hunting ritual which was designed to influence the mysterious forces of nature to give the hunters success in their expeditions. At the same time, the ritual may have acted as a psychological spur which increased both their courage and their confidence for the chase.

The Neolithic or New Stone Age cultures which followed were very widespread both in space and time. They also differed considerably in type. Perhaps the most significant advances were made in the areas of simple technology and the development of a food-producing economy. 'Plant and animal domestication, which initiated the so-called Neolithic level of culture, quite possibly ranks as the most significant discovery in the history of mankind.'[8] Men were now freed from complete dependence upon wild food resources and therefore less affected by the natural fluctuations in the availability of those resources. Though still subject to seasonal variations, they had a more direct control over food production which eventually resulted in the accumulation of surpluses. This consequently had important implications for future economic patterns and social organisation. By c. 7000 BC or a little later, fully-fledged agricultural settlements had been established[9] in south-west Asia and these provided a solid foundation for the urban civilisations which were to follow.[10]

This is the tidy, conventional and – to some extent – speculative account of the emergence of proto-urban societies[11] which immediately preceded the Chalcolithic[12] and Metal Age civilisations with

41

which we are most concerned. On investigation, certain awkward questions are raised, and some qualifications are needed. The main problem is of the frustrating chicken-and-egg variety, namely, what – if any – was the key variable in the 'urban revolution'? This, in turn, raises a host of supplementary issues about the effects of diffusion, the nature of social organisation and the role of ideology.

The great early civilisations of Mesopotamia, Egypt, the Indus valley and the Hwang-Ho valley were preceded by prehistoric Neolithic cultures the natures of which are, to a limited extent, identifiable. There is little doubt that these earlier cultures were essential proving grounds for the civilisations which followed. They constituted the foundations and anticipated some of the social arrangements, but could they have supplied the necessary impetus which the transformation seems to have required? Milton Covensky writing of what he regards as the primary civilisations, namely Mesopotamia and Egypt, insists that 'while that prehistory was a necessary prerequisite for [their] emergence, it is not of itself a sufficient explanation. For [their] rise . . . constituted a leap, a breakthrough an emergence of genuinely new ideas, institutions, and values.'[13]

Before we investigate this problem and its related issues, we must glance briefly at the diffusionist implications of the term 'primary civilisations'. There is a long-standing debate between extreme diffusionists such as Heine-Geldern,[14] who it may be thought tend to belittle man's ingenuity, and others – the majority – who appear to have a higher regard for man's inventive ability. The matter is extremely technical and involved and is now aggravated by intense nationalistic feelings, but specific points should be made. A rigid diffusion-invention dichotomy is probably untenable. Although there is some evidence[15] that some civilisations have had more than one life-span and have, in effect, been 'invented' at least twice, it is generally conceded that the early civilisations were not contemporaneous in their *origins* even though they co-existed at a particular period in the ancient world. Archaeological findings confirm that Mesopotamian urban cultures pre-date those of Egypt, and that these were followed by the Indus civilisations centred on Harappa and Mohenjo-daro, with the Hwang-Ho (Yellow River) civilisation considerably later still. Very much depends upon just how the term 'urban civilisation' is defined,[16] but in general terms, Mesopotamian civilisation dates from *c.* 3750 BC, Egyptian from *c.* 3250 BC, the Indus valley *c.* 2500 BC and the Hwang-Ho *c.* 1500 BC. Chronologically, therefore, a diffusionist hypothesis has some plausibility, and this is supported by the general similarities of certain structural and ideological features. But there are also certain marked dissimilarities, as the ensuing discussion will show, between the two primary civilisations, and especially between these and the Indus valley cultures about which we are admittedly still somewhat in the dark.[17]

The diffusion-independent development issue is further complicated by the presence of the later Meso-American cultures. The Inca civilisation of Peru dates from only the thirteenth century AD, and the Aztecs of Mexico even later, from the fifteenth century, although modern scholarship is pushing back the date of the earlier Mayan cultures,[18] certainly to before the Christian era. And this leaves out of account the yet more ancient and rather mysterious Olmecs and Toltecs.[19] Gideon Sjoberg insists that; 'As to the cities of the Americas, only the most fertile imagination (at the present state of knowledge) can conceive of these as products of diffusion from the Old World.'[20] But how conclusive is this? A case has been building up for some time in favour of some form of cultural transmission to the New World. The architectural parallels, for example, between the ziggurats and pyramids of the Middle East and Meso-America may not be entirely coincidental. The extreme antiquity of some of the ceremonial centre complexes, at Monte Alban in Oaxaca, for instance, have so far defied precise archaeological classification, and have naturally excited all kinds of speculation.[21] Not least of all, the ancient and widespread Quetzalcoatl myth, which holds that the area was once visited by wise white-bearded strangers who would one day return, lends some credence to the diffusionist argument.

How then was it possible for the primary civilisations, however these are identified, to even begin? There appear to have been sudden flowerings of new and advanced cultures. Were they solely the outcome of indigenous factors and was their maturation slower than scholarship seems to indicate, or was there some common impulse which generated such remarkable developments? Covensky argues that 'historians have not yet worked out an answer'.[22] In fact, one of the most eminent of all orientalists, the late Henri Frankfort expressed serious doubts as to whether the origins of civilisation in the Near East could even be ascertained.[23] However, a number of hypotheses have been put forward ranging from the reasonably persuasive to the intriguingly bizarre. Many of them, whilst conceding the importance of a variety of factors, are frankly reductionist in type. They attempt to reduce the complexities of the problem by relating development to a principal or key variable. Nevertheless, they merit our attention.

**Environmental theories**

These state, in their most popular form, that the great primary civilisations evolved in river valleys where the rich alluvial soil

43

permitted extensive cultivation. This supported growing concentrations of population and thus we have the beginnings of urban cultures. In this, its crudest form, and despite its obvious merits,[24] environmental theory is open to some objections. Robert Braidwood *et al.*[25] have shown that the theory of a significant climatic change between *c.* 12000 BC and 8000 BC which brought about the crucial change from food collection to food production can probably be discounted. They also insist that the first *village* settlements were located in hill country and not in river valleys. But they still are unable to explain the transition from village settlements to what they term 'incipient urbanisation', that is developed urban communities. With additional refinements, the plausibility of environmental theories is greatly enhanced. When the emphasis is shifted from the specificity of a simple riverine valley approach, to include broader ecological and economic implications, the result is more persuasive though still not conclusive.

Perhaps the most notable proponent of the economic determinist position was the late Gordon Childe.[26] He stressed the dominant role of material factors, arguing that the 'urban revolution' was a direct result of the 'food-producing' revolution which brought with it the necessary surplus of wealth. This in turn facilitated a surplus of population and financed a hierarchy of specialists and artisans which generated its own ruling class. Villages eventually gave way to larger urban communities which employed the bureaucratic and cultic techniques which characterised the primary civilisations. Robert Braidwood has largely followed Childe's general approach and has repudiated the conventional method of classifying pre-history in terms of materials and artifacts. He has abandoned the Old Stone Age–New Stone Age–Chalcolithic Age–Bronze and Iron Age schema, and instead has opted, like Childe, for a classification in terms of economies. Braidwood's simple alternative is a developmental stage theory with food-gathering and hunting, food-gathering with restricted hunting, food-collecting, food-producing and finally food-producing/incipient urbanisation divisions.[27] Implicit within this schema is the view that where food-production can be most easily established, that is in fertile river valleys, there is a greater likelihood of incipient urbanisation.

Few would dispute that for the development of a primary civilisation there must be a favourable ecological base. This is, of course, also true of later technological revolutions. No one is really surprised that the Esquimaux have not industrialised. There have to be certain pre-conditions for development; ecological minima in terms of resources are essential. The problem turns on the question of exactly just what these minima are. Some societies have developed in the most unlikely environments.

Viewed retrospectively, the flat salt marshes of the Persian Gulf hardly suggest a cradle of civilisation. The bare featureless landscape does not seem to be appropriate as the birthplace of Mesopotamian culture. Granted there was the richness of the soil in the Tigris–Euphrates valleys, but the inundations could be unpredictable and disastrous – a situation which may have given rise to the very ambivalent view of the gods in Mesopotamian theology.[28] In material resources also, Mesopotamia was relatively poor. Unlike Egypt, it had very little stone for building, hence the resourcefulness in the manufacture and extensive use of baked brick which was employed on a truly monumental scale in the ziggurats and palace-temple complexes. On the other hand, like Egypt, it had few natural sources of either wood or metals, and was dependent on an effective amalgam of both trade and conquest to make good these deficiencies.

Similar limitations apply to a number of Meso-American societies. The rain forests of Central America were hardly conducive to the purely physical establishment of the Mayan culture. To hack and prise a civilisation out of near impenetrable jungle was no mean feat for a people with only a rudimentary technology. Or again, how many would have anticipated the emergence of a civilisation with the architectural grandeur and organisational sophistication of the Incas on the arid uplands of Peru? The evidence is reasonably conclusive: an adaptable ecological base may be a necessary condition for the development of a primary civilisation, but it is hardly a sufficient one.

### Technological factors

Equally valid reservations can be adduced where attempts are made to make technology – important though it is – the *key* variable in development. Gideon Sjoberg insists that there is 'no one-to-one correspondence between technology and urban development [but] the association is exceedingly high on a long-term basis'.[29] Possession of even the elements of technology conferred some very real comparative advantages in ancient societies. It sometimes required relatively little technology, by contemporary standards, to achieve quite spectacular results.

Looking back to the early civilisations, one is tempted to think of these advantages in purely architectural terms. The mute and shattered masonry at, say, Karnak, is eloquent testimony to the advanced techniques of the Egyptian builders. Rudimentary technology raised the hundred-foot granite obelisk of Queen Hatshepsut, and erected the monumental temple-complex which could house ten European cathedrals, to the honour of the sun-god, Amon-Re.[30]

45

This material evidence of ancient man's constructional ingenuity – impressive as it is – reminds us that technology was used very largely for ideological purposes. It had limited 'practical' applications. Cultic centres have few overt utilitarian functions.

Transportation was facilitated by technological advances, the use of wheeled vehicles and the utilisation of wind-power for ships were revolutionary innovations in the pre-industrial world. Among the by-products of these were the advantages to commerce and overseas trade. As large urban centres evolved, trade became increasingly important. Both Egypt and Mesopotamia had to import wood and metals. In some cases, notably Athens and Rome, there was a growing dependence on overseas colonies for the necessary supplies of grain.[31] It can be argued, in fact, that with conquest and the expansion of the trade in luxury goods from the East, there were changes in the life-style of these cities and a 'softening' of attitudes among the traditionally austere and economically frugal nobilities. Perhaps the development of technological skills and the increase in commerce can be positively correlated with the changing ethoi of these societies.[32]

Simple technology was also involved in advances in symbolic communication as is evidenced by the processing of papyrus in Egypt, for example. There may be sequential patterns, but it would be erroneous to try to establish any *causal* relationships between the development of these techniques and the emergence of literacy and numeracy in ancient cultures.

Important as technology has proved to be, the reservations concerning the cruciality of its role remain. So much depends upon the definition of the term. Are the chippings of a Stone Age hunter technology? Obviously, the simplest artifacts require some skills which may be generously dignified by the term technology, but is such an interpretation meaningful? Handicrafts, the extractive activities of hunting, collecting and fishing are certainly skills which can be developed to a high degree of efficiency, but is this proto-science? By technology, we surely think of architectural and agricultural techniques and particularly man's gradual liberation from animate sources of energy. But accepting, for convenience, this general understanding of the term, it must still be said that some complex pre-industrial systems arose without any appreciable degree of technological sophistication. Again, the Maya provide an interesting example. The plough, the wheel – except for non-productive applications in children's toys[33] – and rudimentary metallurgical techniques, were all missing from early Meso-American cultures. Perhaps even stranger is the absence of literacy, in anything like the commonly accepted sense of the term. The Maya had certain notational systems which they employed with great accuracy especially in astronomical calculations.[34] The Peruvian civilisation of the Incas lacked any conventionalised symbols for representing sounds or concepts other than numbers. They did have a mnemonic device, the quipu, which was really little more than a series of coloured knotted strings which provided a crude but effective code mainly for accounting purposes.[35] The achievements of such cultures as those in Sri Lanka (Ceylon) dating from *c.* third century BC, and particularly the relatively little documented Khmer culture in the ninth century AD in Cambodia whose ruins include some of the most spectacular temple complexes ever built in the pre-industrial world,[36] also testify to the fact that comparatively little technology was required in the development of some early civilisations.

## The oriental despotism thesis

Some consideration must be given – within the general sweep of this discussion – to the influential oriental despotism thesis. This is something of a digression which interrupts the flow of the argument because it is not exclusively a theory about development. It really combines a theory about patterns of development with ecological implications, together with a theory of social control containing unmistakable anti-Marxist overtones. It's a fairly heady concoction, and its explicit bias should not detract from its persuasive scholarship.

Karl Wittfogel's main thesis[37] is that social systems can be shaped by hydraulic systems. He argues that although water is no more essential to agriculture than, say, the lie of the land, the nature of the plants, the temperature and the fertility of the soil, it is – in a qualified sense – a factor which can be *controlled*. Where rivers and large streams are found in arid and semi-arid areas, and where large-scale irrigation schemes are therefore required to bring fertility to these water-deficient lands: (a) the supply of water becomes a variable which can be manipulated, and (b) this control is almost invariably in the hands of governments or centralised agencies who alone can finance and operate such schemes – usually to their own advantage.

In elaboration and in support of his general thesis, Wittfogel presents his own typology of systems. He first of all distinguishes different types of society in terms of their agriculture. In effect, he correlates the agricultures and the irrigation systems associated with them, with the kinds of societies which emerged in these particular conditions. 'Rainfall based systems', i.e. where there was no large-scale irrigation but where, nevertheless, the areas were highly fertile such as in feudal Europe, are distinguished from 'hydrocultures', i.e. where there was small-scale irrigation – often where the areas are broken by hills and small valleys as in Greece or feudal Japan. These kinds of conditions, he maintains, encouraged

47

the evolution of multi-centred societies. 'Rainfall based systems' and 'hydrocultures' are then differentiated from 'agrohydraulic' systems where large-scale agriculture required substantial and *centralised* works of water control. Wittfogel argues that it was these systems which facilitated the monopolisation of political power. As examples of these systems, Wittfogel particularly cites Classical China, Ancient Mesopotamia and Egypt, and pre-conquest Mexico and Peru.

The thesis maintains that the necessity for hydraulic works gave rise to a new class of administrators, and that their exercise of control degenerated into forms of despotism. Wittfogel distinguishes between 'simple', 'semi-complex' and 'complex' hydraulic societies depending upon the *extent* of control over land, private trade and mobile property. And he also differentiates between 'core', 'sub-marginal' and 'marginal' hydraulic societies depending upon the *degree* of control which was often a function of the degree of centralisation. This distinction between the extent and degree of control is valid especially in societies where levels of power have spatial relations.

This control of a single, essential commodity, we are told, was directly related to the imposition of absolute control. Rival institutions were checked. Competitive forces such as, say, the feudal knights or the self-governing guild cities which arose in medieval Europe, were either inhibited or proscribed. After all, the growth of such bodies as the medieval banking houses and trading companies can be seen both as manifestations of incipient capitalism[38] and embryonic democracy,[39] in so far as they were movements towards the fragmentation of autocratic power. No independent institutions were therefore allowed to develop to challenge autocratic rule.[40] Adequate traditions were also lacking in such societies, at least in the forms which might modify or even neutralise the abuses of the state. The masses were exploited. Ownership of property was allowed but strictly controlled. Stratification patterns were not primarily determined by property-holding or other economic factors but by a person's position in the bureaucratic hierarchy. It was a proximity relationship to the foci of political power. Although, there was a certain amount of social conflict, there could not therefore, by definition, be any class struggle, as such. Wittfogel writes of 'total submission and total terror'; an atmosphere of suspicion and mutual distrust. Among rulers and people alike there was a condition of 'total loneliness'. There were occasional uprisings, and palace coups, but there was no basic change in the pattern of despotism. The only limitation – which was self-imposed – is what he terms 'the law of diminishing administrative returns', that is the situation in which it pays progressively *less* to administer further territories and social groups.[41]

There is a certain diffusion of aims in the oriental despotism thesis. At one level it is a polemic against Marxism. [42] It is a refutation of the Marxist unilinear theory of social evolution; 'Oriental' societies do not conform neatly to the five-stage scheme. Although, as Donald Macrae points out, this may be something of a 'straw-man' argument which Wittfogel is inclined to labour. After all, a typology of societies need not indicate *inevitable* stages. It is also a refutation of the Marxist class-struggle theory; in 'Oriental'-type societies an independent capitalist structure *could not* emerge. Control was exercised in such a way that no real class-struggle was possible. It is also a refutation of the view that freedom stems from centralised systems. For Wittfogel, centralisation must, by definition, contain something of despotism; real political freedom can only come through *independent* class relations. What he does not stress is that despotisms tend to be worse for those closest to the holders of political power. The serf and the peasant, whose lot was certainly unenviable, were usually relatively untouched by the arbitrariness of the despot.

There are a number of criticisms that can be – and have been – made of the thesis. Perhaps the most pungent overall criticism is simply that it tends to supplant one general theory, namely Marxist social development theory, by another which may not be significantly better. What particularly concerns us here, however, is that all general theories must be subject to particular criticisms. Are oriental despotisms historical or ideal-types? The thesis can only carry complete conviction if it is seen in model terms, but it is doubtful whether Wittfogel intends this. He develops his argument from actual examples, and whilst this is both interesting and plausible, his case is partly invalidated by the presence of too many historical exceptions.

Not all despotisms are to be found in hydraulic societies. Resource-control is an important factor, but there are other factors, particularly of a military nature, which are equally essential for the task of sustaining despotic systems. [43] Complementarily, not all hydraulic societies breed despotisms. Water-control in hydraulic societies was in fact, often fragmented. In Mesopotamia, it was often shared between the government and the temple authorities, and it is probably worth asking whether sectional interests could always be reconciled. Similarly, in China, water control was often in the hands of local gentry, [44] again suggesting the absence of a completely centralised hydraulic system. It can be further argued that not all areas where conditions for a hydraulic society existed in fact produced such a system. There is no evidence for the early exploitation of, for example, the peoples of California and New Mexico although it has now been shown to be technically possible as vast irrigation schemes have since been undertaken there.

Even despotisms must have secondary supports. Despots must, to a qualified extent, be subject to the system and this necessarily involves the co-operation of others. Rulers may even seek alliances with opposing groups to secure particular ends. The continuance of noble families in such societies despite dynastic changes shows that they were an integral part of the power structure and is indirect evidence of the fact that rulers were, to some degree, dependent upon them. S. N. Eisenstadt contends that, 'Holders of political power have to justify their goals according to the basic values of society'.[45] But do they? Given that despots must mobilise support and delegate authority, do they also *have* to justify their actions and their policies? This begs questions such as: how do we determine exactly what *are* the basic values of society? Can these values be changed, and how is opinion formed and manipulated? And are we thinking in terms of long- or short-run situations? After all, the Roman people, and particularly the nobility, bore the capriciousness of Caligula for two years before deciding that enough was enough. Obviously, the limits to despotic control differ with societies. In broad terms, the public awareness of the abuses of despotism could be more easily contained in complex pre-industrial systems. In modern societies, the spread of education, the ease of communications and the presence of the mass media operate in strangely ambiguous ways in the area of control. They both add to the public knowledge whilst, at the same time, rendering that knowledge more vulnerable and the manipulation of opinion more feasible.

Wittfogel seems to imply that despotisms are dominated by *one* overriding consideration, namely, the maximisation of power. But despotic rule cannot be shown to be invariably egocentric. Motives and aims tend to be mixed – even confused. For instance, Dionysius I, the tyrant of Syracuse (d. 367 BC) no doubt built the fortifications of the city, especially the fortress of Euryalus, partly to repel the Carthaginians, and partly to erect monumental reminders of his own fame and power. Nevertheless, he did have cultural aspirations,[46] and his beautifying of the city has provided posterity with magnificent Greek remains which rival those of the mainland.

Obviously, there is no one kind of despotism. Some historical despotisms have been ideologically-based, this is particularly the case in Ancient Egypt. Others have been rooted in a revolutionary idea which was then converted into military power based on success. If or when the promise was betrayed, or success ran dry, or the ideology was questioned, there were a number of possible consequences. The system collapsed or was overthrown, as in the case of the Mongolian Khanates of the Golden Horde. Or it has – and still frequently does – become 'respectable', as in the case of Augustus and the rise of Imperial Rome towards the close of the first century

BC. On the other hand, it may simply fall apart into manageable sub-empires under ambitious subordinates – the rather ignominious fate of the hurriedly conquered world of Alexander the Great in the fourth century BC.[47]

Complete or 'pure' despotism of an entirely arbitrary and capricious kind may never have persisted for very long *anywhere*. But a qualified despotism based upon resource-control, aristocratic support, ideological sanctions and a concomitant plebeian passivity has certainly been a feature of some of history's most stable systems. Indeed, it might almost be taken a stage further and argued that it was a *condition* of that stability.

### Social factors

Gideon Sjoberg takes a balanced multi-variable approach to the problem.[48] He writes of the necessary preconditions for the emergence of urban society and, in general terms this overlaps with the related issue of primary civilisations. He identifies three principal factors, an ecological base and an 'advanced' technology, which we have already considered, together with a well-developed social organisation with an established power structure. The presence of this third variable has not been overlooked by other commentators, but its importance has probably been minimised. 'It is hardly fortuitous that the great cities of the pre-industrial world have been those within powerful kingdoms or in the heartland of an empire.'[49] It is the powerful state that can successfully ward off incursions by ambitious neighbours, and aggressively extend its own rule and cultural influence over a wide area.[50] It is within a relatively stable system that political continuity and economic viability make development possible. Institutional controls guarantee the necessary social order which, in turn, provide the foundations for cultural achievement. This is not to argue that stability is *absolutely essential* for cultural advance, after all the Golden Age of Greece – and certainly of Athens – between *c.* 500 and 400 BC was during the Persian and Peloponnesian Wars. But then it could be argued that the threat of external aggression can be a unifying factor which brings its own particular kinds of stability.

To concentrate on the matter of the surplus which facilitates concentrations of population and wealth is really to put the cart before the horse. The surplus, which of course was necessary for the development of ancient civilisations, could surely only be accumulated where the right kind of social and political arrangements permitted. Economic organisation requires social organisation. The logistics of realising the surplus – the mobilisation of labour, the irrigation works, the collection and distribution systems –

51

all these need sophisticated administrative procedures and controls. Bread was usually a direct by-product of bureaucracy.

By implication, Talcott Parsons appears very generally to endorse this position[51] with certain variables added. He stresses, first of all, the matter of literacy. He argues that what he terms 'archaic societies' are characterised by 'craft' or priest literacy. This would, as we have seen, be difficult to sustain in relation to Meso-American cultures[52] but perhaps these should not be regarded as archaic societies – though it is difficult to see how else they can be categorised.[53] If Parsons's 'archaic societies' category is equated with what we have previously termed primary civilisations, the main difficulties disappear. This emphasis upon literacy as a distinguishing feature of the city in relation to other early settlements, is also supported by Childe.[54] But this calls into question just how these terms are to be usefully defined. Sir Mortimer Wheeler tends to use the terms urbanisation and civilisation synonymously, although he has also suggested that the former precedes the latter.[55] He agrees that the hallmarks of a civilisation are a settled community which can support non-agricultural specialists, and a durable administration capable of producing public works. He does not appear to consider writing as a necessary component of civilisation. But here we may be in danger of confusing the *pre-conditions* of civilisation, and the characteristics of early urban communities, which are not quite the same thing.

The existence of writing implies a literati, a bureaucracy – no matter how informal – which is capable of recording and allocating a society's resources.[56] This, too, entails some form of institutionalised educational programme which may well be closely linked with a cultic centre. Parsons also argues for the presence of a cosmological religious system – but whether this is an actual pre-condition or simply a characteristic is a very interesting question.

Archaic societies, by definition, must have developed settlement patterns and therefore property arrangements. This must necessarily, by extension, involve such concepts as ownership and legality. This, in turn, implies the existence of elementary rules, codified or otherwise, to condition and validate these arrangements. Codes of conduct together with the elaboration of the language whereby they are articulated tend to generate a sense of group identity. There may even be the crystallisation of an embryonic ethnicism. The normative structures and their symbolic expression increasingly define *the* people and *the* state and endow them with a separateness which marks them off from their neighbours.

**Moral factors**

In *A Study of History*,[57] Arnold Toynbee advances what can probably best be termed a quasi-moral explanation of development and, indeed, decline. He rejected race and environment as critical factors in the genesis of civilisations, and instead appears to plump for a combination of physical, social and psychological forces.[58] But Toynbee's interpretation also contains a more elusive variable; there is the implicit notion of 'character' and the imputation of moral worth in the life-cycles of his twenty-one civilisations,[59] although as Toynbee explicitly states, 'there is no known law of historical determinism'.[60]

The process of civilisation growth, according to Toynbee, is dominated by a pattern of 'challenge-and-response'. Growth continues when a civilisation successfully meets every challenge which may range from a severe climate to a threat of aggression. It expands primarily in qualitative terms; size is not an important criterion. It achieves a measure of 'progressive integration' and becomes differentiated by its unique 'style'. Growth is interrupted when its 'creative minority' are unable to respond adequately to a serious challenge. Breakdown is followed by decline and dissolution, although Toynbee concedes that in some cases, for example, Roman civilisation, this may take some hundreds of years. The later stages may, in fact, be marked by an imperialist and expansionist phase with an accompanying reliance on force as an instrument of authority. Disintegration is inevitable: in no historical case has a civilisation proved equal to every challenge.

As a philosophy of history, Toynbee's thesis has a kind of sweeping incontrovertibility. But on closer inspection, it is marred by a number of theoretical flaws and definitional uncertainties. What *is* a civilisation? Are there adequate criteria to determine what can and what cannot be included in this category? For example, in the context of Hellenic culture, can Sparta really qualify as a *separate* civilisation, as Toynbee suggests? The thesis also seems to contain too many pre-suppositions as to the course civilisations must take in order to merit the term. Toynbee implies that civilisations have only one life-cycle, although – on a different interpretation – it can be seen that some have several creative blossomings in the course of their histories; Egypt and Mesopotamia would be particular cases in point. It is also questionable to what extent any civilisation is marked by 'dominant' characteristics. For instance, was Hellenic civilisation always predominantly 'aesthetic', as Toynbee also suggests? In view of the highly political nature of Athenian development and the militaristic orientations of Spartan, Theban and later Macedonian society, it is evident that alternative readings of the same situation are possible.

Pieter Geyl makes the point that it is virtually impossible on Toynbee's analysis, to pinpoint the 'moment' of breakdown of any

53

civilisation. At any particular level, similar manifestations may attend both the growth and decline of a specific civilisation.[61] And Pitirin Sorokin[62] has argued that if the smallest 'culture-area' – the individual – is not completely integrated, then neither is any civilisation. If all civilisations are, therefore, cultural composites, is it possible for that which is not integrated to disintegrate?[63] And when is a civilisation 'dead'? Does this mean that all cultural values – the arts and sciences – no longer exist? Or does it mean that they are no longer *practised* and actually forgotten? If a more generous estimate is accepted, it can be seen that the modern world is not devoid of the pervasive influences of ancient cultures, and that – in some cases – their practices have actually been incorporated into present institutions.[64] So it is debatable whether any civilisation can be dead in toto.

These criticisms of Toynbee must extend, in some measure, to any attempt to formulate a general and inclusive theory of development. The immensity – and perhaps the presumptuousness – of such a task is enough to deter most scholars. It is perhaps to Toynbee's credit that in his own encyclopedic study, he has seriously endeavoured to plot patterns of change, and to indicate his own possible solution to what he regards as man's dilemma.

A somewhat different moral approach is taken up by Robert Redfield. He follows Childe in stressing the importance of the 'urban revolution' and the development of the food-producing society. There are also hints of Arcadian nostalgia, the suggestion that ancient society glowed with organic mutuality. 'Within those early communities the relationships among people were primarily those of personal status. In a small and intimate community all people are known for their individual qualities of personality . . . men and women are seen as persons, not as parts of mechanical operations. . . .'[65] Redfield parts company with Childe on the issue of economic interests. He insists that in these early communities men did not work primarily for material wealth; incentives to work were various and largely non-economic. Instead, they arose 'from tradition . . . from religious considerations and moral motivations of many kinds . . . the nexus which held people together, was moral. Humanity attained its characteristic, long-enduring nature as a multitude of different but equivalent systems of relationships and institutions each expressive of a view of the good. Each precivilized society was held together by largely undeclared but continually realised ethical conceptions. . . .'[66]

Redfield's moral emphasis provokes certain questions. If this is the condition of *pre*-civilised society, what are the ethical criteria for defining civilised society? And although he tends to lapse into a kind of empathetic idyllicism, his interpretations are worth noting. Whilst accepting Childe's ten primary characteristics of 'civilised life',[67] Redfield nevertheless adds his own qualifications regarding the technical order. Apparatus and artifacts are viewed as vitally important, but he is insistent that in folk societies, the moral and institutional order predominated over the technical order. In civilised communities, however, this situation is not exactly reversed, but the balance is altered, and the technical order assumes a greater importance. Implicit in his treatment of these themes, one detects a certain optimism that eventually the balance will be redressed.

## Religious factors

Religious and ideological factors are not always clearly distinguishable from moral factors, and they are associated in the evaluating literature (i.e. of Toynbee, Redfield et al.) with social factors.

The presence of religion is inescapable in ancient societies; it is a ubiquitous historical phenomenon. Similarly in the literature: the consideration of religion is unavoidable in any treatment of traditional systems. But to what extent was it a factor in the emergence of those systems?

H. Frankfort, although coming to no final conclusion on this issue, has been among the principal advocates of religion as a crucial variable in the civilising process. He contends that the ancients did not make the same distinctions in their modes of cognition as modern man. Nature and man did not stand in opposition, but were part of the same animate, cosmic order. '[They] saw man always as part of society, and society as imbedded in nature and dependent upon cosmic forces . . . natural phenomena were regularly conceived in terms of human experience and that human experience was conceived in terms of cosmic events.'[68] A very similar approach is taken by Mircea Eliade especially in the study of the structure and significance of mythopoeic thought,[69] and also by E. O. James in his analysis of early religious ideas.[70] In general, the abiding impression left by these and similar writers is that the establishment and organisation of human communities were not only intellectual and technical achievements, but moral and spiritual achievements as well.

Religious factors as a characteristic – if not a determinant – of primary civilisations are stressed also by Braidwood.[71] He maintains that the distinguishing feature of the advanced food-producing phase (in Mesopotamia from c. 4250 to c. 3750 BC) was an 'incipient urbanisation' involving towns *with temples*. Sjoberg makes a similar point.[72] He observes that many students of pre-industrial societies overlook the uniformities these displayed in the realm of religion. Whilst not wishing to minimise their divergencies, he argues that we cannot deny the perennial and recurrent religious themes which persisted in these systems.[73] Parsons, too, generally endorses this emphasis upon the role of religious ideology in complex pre-industrial societies. He shows that in such highly sophisticated civilisations as Ancient Egypt and Mesopotamia, no clear differentiation exists between the social and religious orders. Religion functions as an independent variable within the institutional complex, and its normative patterns of thinking and practice permeate all social activities. In Parsons's words, 'Continuing social evolution further involved creating systems of human order able to persist and develop within this basic contingent relation between the divine and human conditions.'[74]

That religion is a *main* factor in the creation of primary civilisations is an argument advanced by Rushton Coulborn.[75] He maintains that religion provided society with a basic unity and purpose. This raises the issue of exactly how religious ideology 'works'. Did it constitute the initial stimulus of civilisation, was it actually the organising principle of early societies, or did it merely supply the sanctions necessary to support an existing social order? This will be the theme of our ongoing discussion.

### Extra-terrestrial 'factors'

The need to account for the apparent sudden flowering of the primary civilisations – however they are to be defined – has given rise to some rather bizarre explanations of an extra-terrestrial kind. There is now a surfeit of popular literature purporting to be either the result of scientific enquiry[76] or revealed truth[77] which argues a theory of special origins.

This attempt to link the origins of civilisation with a specific source has grown from mere pan-Egyptian and pan-Mesopotamian theories to hypotheses which locate these origins in the submerged Pacific continent of Mu or the similarly undiscovered submerged Atlantic continent of Atlantis. The presumably final and equally unanswerable extension of these[78] is the claim that the real source of civilisation is, in fact, extra-terrestrial.[79] This is really not quite so strange as it sounds considering that some eminent scientists are toying with variants of the same idea.[80] A detailed critique of these theories is not really germane to the present discussion.[81] It hardly needs stating that they are historically unproven and perhaps unprovable, although to the mystics this is an unimaginatively conservative and rather blinkered theoretical position. Perhaps it should be added in their defence, however, that, despite the fact that such theories contain innumerable inconsistencies and unresolved loose ends, they do constitute one kind of possible explanation.

56

The conventional theories which we have been considering still remain historically ambiguous and unsatisfactory. Where there remain cognitive vacua, the most improbable explanations may be considered as likely candidates to fill the void.

# 5 Comparative typologies: Egypt and Athens

The hypothesis which is gradually emerging from an analysis of the relationships between development, stability and social control, is broadly Durkheimian in type.[1] It is apparent that there is some correspondence between the cohesiveness of a society and its prevailing ideology. (A similar correspondence might also be very tentatively posited between ideology and societal longevity, but the measurement criteria[2] for this must remain extremely uncertain and could never be established with any finality.) The same idea is implied in Talcott Parsons, although it is not explicitly stated or developed in any great detail.[3]

It is impossible finally to demonstrate a direct correlation between a belief-system and any social form or pattern of behaviour. Tests of validity are not only inappropriate in such areas, they are actually impossible; a hypothesis of this kind can, at best, never be any more than persuasive. But, despite the paucity of information at our disposal – especially in the case of some ancient societies – a further and more specific examination of these relationships will at least indicate the plausibility of such a hypothesis.

It is obviously not possible to attempt to synthesise the institutional arrangements of the principal traditional systems in relation to their ideologies. It is proposed, therefore, to study two ancient societies in particular, namely, Ancient Egypt and Classical Athens, although relevant allusions of a comparative nature will be made to other traditional systems. In the case of Egypt, references will often be made to the contemporaneous societies of Mesopotamia, and in the case of Athens, there will be frequent references to other Greek states, especially Sparta, with occasional additional comparisons with Ancient Rome.

An outline of the histories of these two societies is therefore obviously necessary (see Chapter 6), to give some substance to the ensuing analysis. But the primary intention is not to present an accumulative chronicle of events but a comparative examination of their institutional and structural complexity. In particular, to assess the development, persistence and functional importance of their institutions with special reference to the common features and differentiae which characterised them. And to relate the entire analysis to the motto themes of ideology and social control.

In order to evaluate these relationships, a model polarity can be hypothesised between Archaic and Seminal types of society. Egypt and Athens have not been chosen at random. They represent what is probably in the ancient world the closest approximation to this paradigm.

The section which follows is greatly indebted to the germinal analysis of Talcott Parsons.[4] He defines the Archaic type of society as that which is characterised by 'craft literacy and cosmological religion'.[5] The cultural elaboration of the cosmological system is linked with the literacy of the priesthood, and this ensures the perpetuation of a written tradition. This predominantly esoteric literacy is limited to specialised groups which constitute the administrative élite of the society. The cultic centres, the temples, from which the priests mediate the religio-cultural traditions may also be the focal points of social organisation. Kinship and community interests may well be subordinated to their service; their maintenance will pattern the economic arrangements of the society.

The relatively elaborate administrative functions are generally controlled by lineages rather than appointed officials. Political and religious offices overlap, especially at the very apex of the administrative hierarchy, possibly in the person of a priest-king who predominates in a three-tier system of ruler, nobility and people. In some societies, such as Classical China, a discernible mercantile 'wedge' is also apparent at the intermediate levels.[6]

The structure of society might be notably hierarchical, as in Egypt, or more segmental, as in Mesopotamia, a pattern of development which was reflected in urban rather than kin-based communities. In both cases, the control of these societies – given the level of religio-cultural symbolisation – required tightly controlled ritual and political administrations. The relative decentralisation of Mesopotamian society gave the constituent units more autonomy but less stability than in Egypt.

The 'seed-bed' society is much less clearly defined by Parsons.[7] Fundamentally, it constitutes a culturally innovative society whose impact may have been relatively small at the time of its developmental period, but whose influence has since been quite incalculable. Its cultural products have become dissociated from their society, but have had special consequences for many subsequent societies.

'Seed-bed' societies are typically small-scale with unusual bases of independence which involve a 'differentiation of *the society as a whole* from the others to which it is closely related. It had to become a new *type of society* [Parsons's italics] not merely a new sub-system within an already existent type.' In this respect, Parsons distinguishes both Ancient Israel and Greece as 'seed-bed' societies.

In very general terms, this study accepts Parsons's typologies. It is particularly influenced by Parsons's delineation of the Archaic society, and accepts, with some minor qualifications, the singularity of the type of society designated 'seed-bed'.[8] The principal reservations about 'seed-bed' societies concern the extent to which any society can really be a 'new type'. The key differentiate of both Israel and Greece had their anticipations and reflections in other systems.[9] But this is not to deny that the cultural chemistry was unique in each case. Viewed retrospectively, they were both very special kinds of society.

However, for our present purposes, Parsons's delineations of these two types of society, though important, are both insufficient and – to a degree – inappropriate. Instead, a somewhat more precise dichotomy is hypothesised to highlight certain fundamental differences in orientation which may be related to ideological considerations.

The Archaic type of society may be seen as displaying the following principal characteristics:

(i) A pervasive theocratic ethic which is integrally harnessed to the interests of the state.

(ii) Bureaucratic control in the hands of a hierarchy of specialists who may be sacred or secular officials; precise differentiation may be difficult at particular operational levels. These may hold their rank either by birth or by appointment[10] – although again the distinction is not always clear in actual cases.[11]

(iii) Circumscribed intellectual enquiry with scholar-literacy only.

(iv) Minimal institutional and role differentiation.

(v) Particularistic ascriptive status valuation.

(vi) A qualified socio-cultural exclusivity and self-conscious ethnicity.

(vii) Political inflexibility.

(viii) Social equilibrium: a homogeneous and relatively static social order.

(ix) Relative permanence.

(x) Retrospective orientations. This Arcadian preoccupation with the glories and traditions of the past is perhaps the key variable in the Archaic society model.

No actual traditional system exactly conforms to this ideal construct, but ancient Egypt probably comes closer to it than any known historical society. All the characteristics apply to a greater or lesser extent. The deviations from the model are relative to the Egyptian period in question. Ancient Egypt was by no means a completely unchanging society, it was subject to some disruption and instability during its long history.[12] Perhaps the period which most closely resembles a 'pure' Archaic society is that of the Old Kingdom, c. 2700–c.2200 BC, before internal strife and external incursions had brought about a temporary breakdown in the traditional order. But the system's orientations were perennially and obstinately retrospective. Disruption called forth uncomprehending dismay from the intellectuals. 'The land is despoiled . . . the storehouse of the king is a come-and-get-it for everybody, and the entire palace is without its taxes.'[13] The class and value system might be severely shaken, and violence might rule in the streets, but the solution was invariably seen in terms of a return to the past – to the stability and security of centralised control.

One of the most important distinguishing factors which emerges in this model-actuality comparison is an ideological one. Not only was Egypt a theocratic (god-ruled) system, it was also a theobasilic (god-king) system. This is possibly the most significant difference between Egypt and its Archaic-type contemporary, Mesopotamia, and is almost certainly connected with the autonomy-centralisation issue which also separated them. In Mesopotamia, the lugal, the 'great one', though supreme, was a mere servant of the gods, especially his tutelary deity. In Egypt, on the other hand, the king was god.

By comparison, the Seminal type of society may be characterised as possessing:

   (i) A humanistic ethic. Religious ideologies exist and – in qualified ways – may be influential but they are not effectively harnessed to the needs of the state.

  (ii) No ongoing bureaucracy of specialist officials. Administration may be loosely aristocratic or widely diffused through a proletarian assembly system. There may be no clear differentiation between sacred and secular spheres. Rituals can, in fact, be the province of many-roled leaders, but there may be no highly institutionalised system of professional religious functionaries, as such.[14]

 (iii) Intellectual freedom and high literacy.

 (iv) Comparatively high institutional and role differentiation.

  (v) Achievement status valuation.

 (vi) Socio-cultural and ethnic inclusivity.

(vii) Political flexibility and experimentation.

61

   (viii) Social disequilibrium – a heterogeneous and relatively unstable social order.
   (ix) Relative impermanence.
   (x) Prospective orientations. A social optimism prevails which in turn gives rise to new dimensions of qualified Utopianism – the conviction that the future could be better than the past.

Again, no actual ancient society is represented by such a scheme, although Classical Athens resembles it in many important respects. A comparison with Ancient Israel – Parsons's other 'seed-bed' society – is not particularly fruitful. Certainly for the purposes of this discussion, Seminal societies cannot be simply equated with 'seed-bed' societies. In this analysis, Seminal should be taken to connote the experimentally creative system which is both influential but unstable. It may be embryonically humanistic and ethoically precocious[15] in its anticipation of 'advanced' social forms and structures.

Classical Athens 'fits' the Seminal typology in most important respects. Some qualifications, however, must be made concerning the issue of socio-cultural and ethnic inclusivity. The Greeks of the Classical period – partly as a result of the ever-present Persian threat – had become increasingly conscious of their common bonds. They were united specifically by language and religious traditions, although the strength of these religious ideas had already begun to wane.[16] The Greeks recognised their internal differences, their separate traditions and their political heterogeneity. But they were also conscious of a body of shared tradition and of a cultural homogeneity which they believed marked them off from the barbaroi of the non-Greek world.

Despite this attitudinal stance, there were qualified exceptions in *practice*. The more cosmopolitan city-states, especially Athens, encouraged aliens to settle in the city and participate in the life of the community.[17] These resident aliens, or metics, who may – with the slaves – have constituted a majority of the population, were not allowed full citizenship. They had no vote, and were mainly engaged in petty trade and manufacturing, although some were prominent members of the commercial classes. 'Many traders were certainly metics, and some prominent bankers, but we hear only of those who became in some way conspicuous. We have no statistics for the smaller fry, so that it is not easy to guess at the full proportions.'[18]

The typification of the Seminal society as one characterised by prospective orientations also requires some explanation when related to Classical Athens. The Athenians cannot really be regarded as proponents of progress and initiators of social reform in anything like the modern sense. They were a pre-scientific people who, like other traditional peoples, did not – and perhaps could not – envisage a world significantly different from their own. The idea of progress is predominantly a feature of technological societies, or at least societies which have come to appreciate the possibilities inherent in an emergent science. But the Greeks did display a public-spiritedness and sense of social responsibility which were not unconnected with their unquenchable political optimism. How much this can be reconciled with the social scepticism or the guarded Utopianism which paradoxically were both later reflected in *The Republic*, is open to dispute. The Greeks were certainly resourceful and original, 'they inherited little but their native vitality, a barren soil, the sunshine and the sea'.[19] With this limited endowment, they fashioned a remarkable civilisation. The Athenians, in particular, possessed a humanistic confidence in the enduring qualities of their own culture not least of all their 'natural' democratic processes. Alvin Gouldner sees this rationality as an identifiable trait in the Athenian 'social character' which is related to 'low object attachment'. Such people 'select goals and means rather than having these imposed by un-examinable tradition and rather than being bound to them by deeply affective sentiments or by a fear-laden belief in their sacred character'.[20] For a while, they seemed on the threshold of embracing a consistently rationalistic ethic. It was incipient within the system, but – for good or ill – was never fully realised. It has been suggested that the Greek failure to achieve a truly humanistic society was a contributory factor in its ultimate decline.[21] Certainly the gropings toward a liberal society foundered as the structural deficiences and ideological inconsistencies gradually became apparent. Academic diagnoses are both numerous and inconclusive.[22] It may be that humanistic hubris is at least one cognitive key to the problem of societal impermanence.

# 6  Patterns of historical development

Any analysis of the respective structures and value-orientations of Egyptian and Athenian societies necessarily requires some appreciation of their historical biographies. It is therefore important to trace periods of development and consolidation, of dormancy, resurgence and eventual decline in both societies.

## Egypt

The life of Egypt was dominated and sustained by what Herodotus termed 'the gift of the Nile'. In a land with negligible rainfall, the annual inundations commencing in July and reaching their peak early in September, became the focus of both practical activity and reverential concern.[1]

The earliest villages date from about 5000 BC. A cemetery of this period has been found at Deir Tasa in Middle Egypt containing food, ornaments and Neolithic tools. By this time, therefore, the people were leading a settled, agricultural existence. They had developed relatively sophisticated techniques for the making and firing of pottery, the fashioning of simple jewellery, and even the manufacture of eye make-up which may have had a prophylactic as well as a cosmetic function. The archaeological evidence[2] suggests that from late pre-historic times, perhaps c. 3500 BC, a steady inflow of immigrants was taking place in Lower, i.e. northern, Egypt, possibly from Mesopotamia. Cultural traits such as decorated brickwork, balanced groups of animals as an artistic motif, and particularly the appearance of cylinder seals, points to some acculturation process at work under influences probably emanating from the Tigris–Euphrates area. Although the appropriation of these diffused cultural elements seems in no way to have determined the developmental patterns of the Nile civilisation, Egyptian development shows a clear diversity and is always identifiably unique.

By *c.* 3400 BC, two kingdoms, those of Upper (southern) and Lower (northern) Egypt had evolved. These co-existed for about 300 years, but were united – probably by conquest – by Menes (who may also be identified with a monarch called Narmer) the king of Upper Egypt, who traditionally became the founder of the First Dynasty.[3]

The first two dynasties, sometimes referred to as the Archaic period, date from *c.* 3200 to *c.* 2700 BC.[4] A great deal of detail is, of course, lacking, but the achievements of the period can be reasonably summarised. The unification of the 'Two Lands' was completed, although the duality of rule continued to be reflected in the respective and often duplicated practices of both 'kingdoms' and was symbolised by the double crown of the monarch. Both military and civil administration were organised, and the autocratic nature of control firmly established. Bureaucratic authority was facilitated by the emergence of literary skills. Possibly there had been forms of pictorial writing in pre-dynastic times, but certainly by the First Dynasty, a type of syllabic alphabet had been evolved.[5]

The irrigation system and the cultivation of disposable land were well advanced in this period. Trade too was highly developed. The caravan routes of the Fertile Crescent had long been in operation, and the waterway of the Nile provided a ready means of transportation. This is evidenced by the wide range and distribution of both imported and exported products. Architecturally and artistically, the first impressive steps were being made. Stone was being used in small quantities, and free-standing sculptures were a feature of the latter part of the period. The chief building material, however, for such structures as the royal tombs still remained sun-dried or mud brick. These were located at Sakkarah (just south of modern Cairo) near the capital of Memphis, and were often so large that they may have been constructed as burial equivalents or barely scaled-down sepulchral facsimiles of contemporary palaces.[6]

During the pre-dynastic period, it may be that independent tribal groupings had animal totems which were regarded as sacred and which were eventually elevated to the rank of gods. It follows that internecine struggles may have resulted in a series of hegemonic political structures which were, in turn, reflected in the prevailing religious order. The conqueror's deity would probably be regarded as supreme, whilst the deities of the conquered, though still worshipped, would occupy a subordinate place. By the time the tribal groups had coalesced into two kingdoms, the southern falcon-god Horus and Buto, the serpent-goddess of the north, were among the most important deities,[7] and this oligotheistic principle was later represented in the symbolisation of the united kingdom.[8] There is evidence

65

too that, by the Archaic period, the authority of the king had full ritual sanctions. Food, weapons, chairs and other utensils were part of the furnishings of the royal tombs, as was the boat in which the spirit of the monarch was to travel with the sun-god. As in Sumeria,[9] attendants were killed or immolated within the tombs so that they could serve their masters in the next life.

The Old Kingdom period covering the Third to the Sixth Dynasties (i.e. *c*. 2700–*c*.2200 BC) probably epitomises the full flowering of Egyptian culture. The unquestioned power of the god-king possibly reached its zenith during the Fourth Dynasty. The absolute monarch was regarded as the owner of all land and property and the source of all law. The king's chief minister, the vizier, administered justice from the capital at Memphis. He controlled the grain supply, the treasury, the army, public works and the priest-hoods through a body of trained officials. The most important offices of state were in the hands of the nobility who were almost invariably members of the king's own family.[10] Even the governors of the forty-odd nomes, or administrative districts, had become appointees of the king, although formerly these had been inde-pendent. This may have happened during the Fourth and Fifth Dynasties by granting lands to the nobles as a guarantee of the provision of services and food for the royal tombs. Until this time, the governorships of the nomes seem to have been held by the nobles on some form of rotational system which required the king's formal sanction. The concession of permanent tenure increased their power and their independence towards the end of the Old Kingdom period.

Trade increased during the Old Kingdom, especially with the Lebanon. At the same time, the turquoise and copper mines of Sinai were being exploited to advantage. All formal trade, however, was in the hands of the king and the nobles, and the enormous revenues which accrued were used extensively for state-cult purposes. The Egyptian pantheon by now consisted of a bewildering array of deities. Those who represented the cosmic forces, especially Re the sun-god, had been venerated from early times; other local gods such as Osiris gradually came to national prominence.[11] But the Pyramid Texts[12] make it clear that the operational religion of Egypt was the state-cult of the god-king who – apparently inconsistently – was both personally divine and at the same time the servant of the gods.

The unapproachable and inviolable nature of kingship lent an authority to the monarch that was believed to persist after death. This was the Pyramid Age when the increasing capital resources of the state were largely devoted to providing funerary complexes and what were ostensibly[13] gigantic monument-tombs for the kings.

The colossal expenditure involved in these ventures may have contributed to the eventual decline in what has become known as the First Intermediate period.

The time usually designated the First Intermediate period, which lasted for some 150 years, witnessed a breakdown of the established social order. It is not quite certain what exactly precipitated the social chaos which apparently ensued. It was a phase of Egyptian history analogous, in some respects, to our own Dark Ages, not only in the sense that little is known about it, but also because of the extent of social dislocation which attended it. The paucity of the records hardly helps, but it is reasonably clear[14] that a measure of central control was relinquished whilst autonomous groups struggled for power. The traditional social verities were challenged and behavioural norms called into question. It was an ideologically traumatic time for Egyptian culture which never quite recovered from this chastising – and perhaps salutary – experience.

The Middle Kingdom period which followed lasted from c. 2050 to c. 1800 BC, and mainly concerns the relatively long-lasting Twelfth Dynasty. During the Eleventh Dynasty, attempts were begun to restore some semblance of normality to the socio-political order. This task was consolidated during the Twelfth Dynasty. The power of the nomarchs, the district governors, and that of the monarch was re-constituted with a new capital at Thebes in Upper Egypt. The cult of the god-king was re-affirmed, and in order to lend divine support to his enterprises, Amun, the local god of Thebes was admitted to the Egyptian pantheon where he joined the sun-god Re of Heliopolis ('the city of the Sun' just north of Cairo), Ptah of Memphis and Osiris of Abydos. Order was re-established; the nobles enjoying increased prestige with the 'democratisation of the cults', a development which appears to be reflected in the burial customs of the period.[15] Towards the end of the Old Kingdom, when nobles seemed to be gaining in power, their tombs became larger and those of the kings less ambitious. In the Middle Kingdom, although the tombs of the nobles are clearly less ostentatious than those of the kings, it can be seen from their contents and the Coffin Texts that they were empowered to use similar prayers and rituals to those used by the king to achieve beatitude in the next world.

This was also a period of political and economic expansion. A campaign in Canaan (modern Israel) strengthened a weak frontier, a canal was built around the First Cataract and the boundaries of Egypt extended south into Nubia as far as the Second Cataract. A canal was also built linking the Delta with the Red Sea, and trade was encouraged as far afield as Crete, then developing its own very significant civilisation, Asia Minor and Arabia.

By this time, the Egyptians had made appreciable strides in the sciences. Mathematics was well developed, although they were probably not as advanced in it as their Mesopotamian contemporaries. They were very competent at practical geometrical applications, as their monumental architecture shows. They had devised an accurate calendar, but although they made careful astronomical observations, it is still not certain to what extent they had developed any coherent body of theory about the physical nature of the cosmos.[16]

Towards the close of the Twelfth Dynasty, there were renewed internal struggles. This era of division and general social debility is now termed the Second Intermediate period and spanned the five subsequent dynasties, i.e. the Thirteenth to the Seventeenth c. 1800–c. 1550 BC. The widespread unrest made it possible for Egypt to be infiltrated by miscellaneous groups of foreign invaders usually collectively designated the Hyksos or Shepherd Kings. They were almost certainly tribes of Semitic peoples who eventually arrived in such numbers that by c. 1730 they controlled the Delta.[17] Within 100 years they dominated Lower Egypt and had compelled Upper Egypt to accept their authority. They brought with them the horse-drawn chariot, body armour and the compound bow, all of which must have contributed considerably to their military successes.

There was a very limited degree of assimilation of the Hyksos who were the effective rulers of a series of shadow Theban kings. The Egyptians appear to have had ambivalent attitudes towards them. There seems to have been a grudging admiration for their hardiness and rough efficiency, but at the same time they were despised as uncouth barbarian intruders. With the decline of their power and the concomitant rise of another Theban house, the Eighteenth Dynasty was established c. 1570 BC under Ahmose I who eventually drove the Hyksos from Egypt. Thus was initiated the New Kingdom or Empire period[18] which lasted – despite further political upheavals – for some 500 years.

The Empire is usually regarded as the Golden Age of Ancient Egypt. Until this time, no serious expansionist policies had been pursued by the state. The relatively isolated situation of Egypt in earlier times had presumably made such policies unnecessary. But with the growing need to repel the incursion of would-be invaders and check the depredations of border tribes, it became a short step from defence to offence. The task of reconstruction became one of expansion. Having mobilised the necessary forces to oust the Hyksos and reconquer Nubia and secure the traditional territories, the implementation of imperialist policies was a natural progression. Firm control was exerted over the regional governors and the centrifugal tendencies of earlier periods were minimised by authoritarian government.

By c. 1400 BC, Egypt had extended her power to the south beyond the Sudan as far as the Fourth Cataract in Ethiopia which is about 1,000 miles from the Delta. The river trade even brought gold, ostrich plumes and slaves from Central Africa. Cyprus came within the Egyptian sphere of influence, and this gave her much-needed copper. Canaan and Syria were also under the suzerainty of Egypt, although several neighbouring powers, namely the Mitanni in Syria and the old Kassite Kingdom of Babylonia exerted counter-influences in their respective areas.[19] The later formidable force of the Assyrians to the north-east was still largely dormant, although there were soon to be some uneasy stirrings of the terror to come. The most immediate threat to the Egyptians was the growing power of the Hittites in Anatolia (Turkey). It may not be entirely coincidental that the period of greatest Hittite power c. 1360, was also a time of political weakness and indecision in Egypt. Akhenaten was pre-occupied with domestic and religious reforms but cared seemingly little for foreign policy. The Hittites had mastered the use of iron which gave them superior weapons, and their strength was eventually tested at Kadesh c. 1295 by the Nineteenth Dynasty Pharaoh[20] Ramesses II (the Great). Both protagonists claimed that they had gained the day, but from the later settlement made between the two powers it can be reasonably inferred that it was actually something of a stalemate.

The Empire is particularly noteworthy for its art and literature. The treasures of Tutankhamun (c. 1352–1344 BC) date from this period, as does also the monotheistic interlude of the mystical Akhenaten who reigned from c. 1369–c.1353 BC. The restoration of Egyptian power after the Hittite threat can be mainly attributed to the rulers of the Nineteenth Dynasty, who established a new capital at Tanis in the Delta. In particular, Ramesses the Great who commemorated his achievements – often in rather overweening and exaggerated terms[21] – in monumental stone structures. The most notable of these buildings include the incredible temple complex at Karnak near Thebes, the hall alone of which could contain the cathedral of Notre Dame; and the gigantic rock temple and figures at Abu Simbel in Nubia.

Hittite power began to decline c. 1200, at a time which coincided with the incursions of the rather mysterious 'Sea-peoples' who were probably heterogeneous groups of proto-Greeks and others from the western Mediterranean.[22]

The 'Sea-peoples' and other Libyan invaders were ultimately repulsed by Ramesses III of the Twentieth Dynasty (c. 1200–c. 1090 BC) the last ruling house of the Empire period. Throughout its 100 years or so, it remained powerful enough to discourage attacks from outside although Egypt's Asiatic possessions were being gradually whittled away by alien successes on her eastern borders. The domestic agricultural wealth of the nation remained unimpaired, as did the supply of gold from the south. The chief difficulties seem once again to have been internal. The authority of the central government weakened and its control of local officials became consequently uncertain. This applied particularly to the powerful priesthoods, especially that of Amun. Perhaps it was a failure of management which, in turn, was aggravated by the presence of large contingents of foreign mercenaries who proved to be increasingly unresponsive to discipline. Once again the north became administratively separate from the south, a division in which the priests played an important and calculating role.

The great days were now over. For the next 500 years of the Post-Empire period, Egypt was controlled variously by dynasties of Nubians and Ethiopians. 'What was lacking was not a government or a way of life, but the intensity and efficiency of extra achievement, the artistic and literary successes that in the past had raised Egypt above the level of the commonplace and routine organisation.'[23]

The ultimate humiliation came with successive conquests by ascendant world powers, the Persians in 525 BC, the Greeks commanded by Alexander in 332 BC, and finally the Romans under Pompey in 63 BC. The last three dynasties, the Thirty-first to the Thirty-third, were those of the Ptolemies, acculturated Macedonians who built up the academic reputation of Alexandria and observed the traditional mores and practices like fervent new converts to an ancient faith. But their enthusiasm could hardly support the crumbling hollow shell of Egyptian culture, or counter the erosiveness of their own internecine struggles. Fittingly it was the opportunistic Romans who not only presided over the death throes of a civilisation but also gave it the decisive coup de grâce.

### Greece

It is hardly meaningful to consider – even briefly – the history of Athens without setting it in its overall Hellenic context. But this too has its limits because, unlike Egypt, Greek civilisation was no *one* kind of a thing. The Greek culture was homogeneous only in its unilateral love of heterogeneity. There were, admittedly, the unifying forces of the common language and common cults symbolised by joint participation in the games at Olympia traditionally founded in 776 BC. But within this loose general framework there was an immense diversity which was eventually to be reflected in the fratricidal Peloponnesian War.

The evidence is now conclusive that there had been flourishing proto-Greek civilisations in Crete from *c.* 2000 to *c.* 1400 BC (probably under Egyptian influence) and on the southern mainland centred on Mycenae from *c*. 1400 to *c*. 1200 BC.[24] Various invaders, notably the Dorians, settled in Greece from the north *c*. 1100 BC and gradually evolved a civilisation which, although having a character of its own, owed much to the cultural traditions which had been assimilated. This period which lasted for about 300 years down to *c*. 800 BC, is still sometimes referred to as the 'Dark Ages' although, in the light of more recent archaeological evidence, this may be regarded as at least inappropriate, if not actually something of a misnomer. Life at this time certainly seems to have been simpler and generally less ostentatious than during previous cultural phases. All the evidence[25] points to lower levels of architectural achievement and artistic excellence during this formative 'interim' period of Greek civilisation.

By the eighth century BC, an emergent Greek civilisation existed. It was eventually centred on the mainland and the adjacent islands and also in the coastal regions of Asia Minor known as Ionia. The Ionian Greeks who had migrated to Asia Minor as early as the tenth century had, by the sixth century, become noted for their intellectual precocity[26] and maritime enterprise. It was during the eighth century also that, among the singular Greek institutions,[27] the embryonic polis or city-state began to form.[28] Before long, many of these states were founding their own colonies throughout the eastern Mediterranean world. For example, Megara and Chalcis founded Chalcedon and Byzantium respectively, and Corinth, which led in western colonisation[29] established her most famous colony at Syracuse in Sicily in 735 BC. Other colonies were established in the Black Sea area, in North Africa and in Italy[30] where Athens – which played a relatively small part in this expansionist and migratory activity – founded Tarentum (modern Taranto). Established mainly in the eighth and seventh centuries, these new states, though independent, maintained generally good relations with their mother cities. As part of Magna Graecia, they recognised a common identity, although the practice of colonisation probably promoted changes in the social realignments of some individual Greeks who in times of stress between founding poleis, were inclined to espouse the cause of their protective parent cities. The migratory impulse was primarily economic, and the mother cities were often quick to encourage emigration in order to relieve political and economic pressure in their own areas.

Exploration and colonisation had far-reaching results.[31] They created in the colonies a demand for the products of the mother country. This, in turn, led to an increase in trade and the need to exploit the new sources of raw materials. As time passed, this new found wealth from the development of overseas markets, the

71

importation of luxury goods from the east, and the emergence of a money economy[32] all had their effects upon Greek society, particularly that traditionally austere body, the land-owning aristocracy. The position of the aristocracy was also undermined by the concomitant growth of merchant groups, manufacturers, artisans and especially resident aliens. The unforeseen consequence of this was political as well as economic instability.[33] The colonisation which the city fathers had encouraged as a safety-valve, resulted eventually in the creation of classes which finally brought about the upheavals which they had feared. Various steps were taken in different poleis to stem the tide of revolutionary unrest. Sparta restricted the use of coinage. Thebes pronounced as ineligible for political office anyone who had engaged in trade within the last ten years. But Athens, on the other hand, welcomed immigrants and encouraged all kinds of economic development, although the ruling classes long resisted the demands of this insistent commercial pressure. There is little doubt that this conflict of ideologies was a contributory cause of the ultimate clash between Athens and Sparta in the fifth century.[34]

The rise of the poleis was coincidental with the decline in the institution of monarchy throughout the Greek world. Kings were relegated to the ranks of the dominant aristocracies and assumed the roles of ritual and genos (clan) leaders. Even in Sparta where a form of dual monarchy was retained, the kings themselves had diminished responsibilities; real authority lay with the ephors or city elders. Poleis, especially those developed by the Dorians, were often centred on a citadel of some kind – although again this was not so in the case of the Spartans where the state focused on a very modest group of villages.[35] The object originally was probably purely functional; citadels provided a strong base from which the surrounding subject peoples could be efficiently administered. Gradually participatory procedures evolved within the poleis, although control still remained largely in the hands of the aristocracies.

Between *c.* 800 and *c.* 500 BC, the aristocracies gained in wealth and prestige, perhaps at the cost of both kings and people. Their power was little affected by the growing prosperity of the merchant classes whose ranks some of them joined. The increasing numbers of absentee landlords found that they often had a great deal in common with those with commercial interests. It was the aristocracy which was usually best able to mobilise colonial contingents and organise the necessary investment for trading purposes. Entrepreneurial ventures were risky, and overseas trade was particularly precarious, but for the successful – or the lucky – profits could outweigh the uncertainties. Political office was monopolised either by members of the noble families in general or by one dominant noble family or clan in particular[36] as for example, the Bacchiadae who from the middle of the eighth century ruled Corinth for nearly 100 years, or the Alcmaeonidae who were the most important clan in Athens.[37]

It was the aristocrats who had the required legal expertise to preside over the rudimentary courts and take care of the administration of justice. But where there was no clearly codified law, we find bitter complaints about the rapacity and venality of those who presumed to arbitrate the claims of others.[38] The aristocracy was also able to legitimate its power in religious terms. As clan heads, they were the repositories of ritual knowledge. The gods were not, as yet, seriously questioned: the born leaders were those who alone could offer them the customary addresses and the most efficacious gifts.

The period from *c.* 650 to *c.* 550 BC, is sometimes known as the 'Age of the Tyrants'. The term 'tyranny' is correctly used when it refers to the illegal or unconstitutional way in which a person seizes power rather than the ways in which that power is exercised. The Greek tyrants[39] were usually aristocrats. Not one of them established an enduring monarchy, although in a few cases the family stayed in power for some time.[40] Most frequently, the sons of the tyrants who often possessed neither the efficiency nor charisma of their fathers lost power after a period of oppressive and unpopular rule.[41]

Tyrants sometimes increased their power by the reorganisation of tribal units and even by the introduction of new régime-supporting cults, but it must not be thought that their period of rule was one of unmitigated oppression. In fact, some of them were benefactors to their respective states and made significant contributions to the artistic and architectural enrichment of the cities.[42] Tyrants obviously differed in their reasons for aspiring to power, but the conditions which tended to produce them have a certain similarity. The states in question were usually of a commercial cast, where – it may be argued – it was easier for factions to exist. It is perhaps noteworthy that states outside the mainstream of commercial life, and with firmly established aristocracies such as Sparta, rarely if ever produced tyrants.

From the seventh century onwards, a number of law codes were formulated and published. The earliest of these was traditionally that of Zaleucus of Locris, a colony in southern Italy, although this was predated by the reforms in Sparta attributed to the legendary Lycurgus *c.* 800 BC. Presumably such codes were largely based upon customary bodies of rules which were already in existence, and were therefore attempts to rationalise and modify what was already current practice. There was a pressing need to transfer authority from the clan to the polis particularly in relation to the dispensation of justice. The establishment of rudimentary courts became necessary in a growing and increasingly differentiated society. The legislators too wanted to protect the noble families and their estates, and naturally to safeguard the rules of inheritance. The codes themselves were relatively simple, and might even be memorised.[43] They were nothing like as complex as those of the Mesopotamian states 1,000 years before, or as subject to government interpretation as those of Egypt.

About 620 BC, a famous but largely unknown code was published by an Athenian commissioner named Dracon whose name – perhaps a little unjustly – has become synonymous with severity. In 594 BC, the governing body of the Athenian polis chose Solon as its archon for the year. This gave him considerable latitude to institute various political and economic reforms, mainly in an attempt to redress the balance between the richer and poorer families – a problem which had virtually brought Athens to the point of revolution. His agricultural reforms involved a switch from cereal- to olive-growing, and a greater concentration upon rudimentary industry in the city itself. As with so many who try to make sweeping changes and yet at the same time try to steer a middle road, Solon eventually disappointed many of his supporters. His failure to redistribute the land in the ways which would have pleased the poor alienated some support, and his cancelling of debts hardly endeared him to the middle classes. But the impetus of his reforms helped to usher Athens into a new age of prosperity, and precipitated her rise to fame as the commercial and intellectual centre of the Greek world. His reform of the constitution also edged Athens considerably nearer to what the Greeks understood by democracy.[44]

Solon was possibly the 'morning star' of the Greek achievement but his 'new deal' was only observed for about ten years. Reaction, particularly by the landowners, hardened and the recently democratized state gave way to the tyranny of Peisistratus. He was a strategos, or general, who had just distinguished himself in inter-state warfare – a fraticidal pastime of the Greeks – and who seized power in 561 BC. His period of power, although characterised by the customary banishments of political opponents and the confiscations of land, was also accompanied by a policy of commercial and cultural enlightenment which did nothing to hamper Athens in her bid to become the leading state in Greece.

The ascendant power in the Mediterranean world at this time was that of Persia.[45] The Persians who had established satrapies, or administrative areas, in Asia Minor, inevitably came into conflict with the Ionian Greeks, and this precipitated the long-drawn conflict between the Greeks and the Persians[46] which was not finally resolved until the accession and subsequent victories of Alexander in the fourth century. Contemporary with the imminence of the Persian threat, early in the fifth century, political reorganisation was taking place in Athens under the capable leadership of Cleisthenes. This helped to create in its citizens a greater sense of participation in the life and policies of the city; Athens became more important than the sectional interests of its clans. Its developing ethos possibly prepared the way for this emergent state to withstand the onslaught to come.

The first rather abortive Persian expedition foundered in 492 BC, when the fleet was defeated by the weather. The second attack two years later was repulsed on the plains of Marathon by a relatively small army of Athenians and Plataeans. The Spartans, who were probably the most invincible military force in Greece, could not march to help them, ostensibly for religious reasons – they insisted that the moon was not yet full and that the time was not therefore propitious. The most ambitious Persian invasion came in 480 BC. This too was beaten by the developed sea power of the Athenians at Salamis, and by a contingent of Spartans and their allies at Plataea, but not before Athens itself was partly destroyed.

The defeat of the Persians who retired to Asia still a formidable but humiliated power, heralded the golden age of Athenian achievement. Athens strengthened her position by forming the confederation of Delos[47] purportedly as a common front against further anticipated Persian incursions. From about 472 BC, this confederacy developed empire-like characteristics under the hegemony of Athens. The transition was virtually complete by 454 BC when the confederacy funds, which were now contributed by the allies virtually as tribute, were transferred from Delos to Athens. The growing power and ambition of the Athenian confederacy now brought it into direct confrontation with the Peloponnesian league in southern Greece led by Sparta, Corinth and Aegina. Despite the Thirty Years' Peace treaty which was made in 445 BC, war broke out in 431 BC and lasted with uneasy periods of truce until 404 BC.

The era between the defeat of the Persians and the outbreak of hostilities with Sparta, saw the full flowering of Athenian culture. The Periclean period of Athenian history was the time of its greatest splendour,[48] but it was extraordinarily brief, only fourteen years between 445 and 431 BC. Pericles, an Athenian aristocrat and general, was probably the chief architect of Athenian expansionism. Under his chequered leadership, new colonies were founded and the revenues of state increased largely by heavier subsidies from the allies[49] within the Delian league. The literary, artistic and architectural accomplishments of the period can only be described as spectacular. The cultural ethos and intellectual curiosity of Athens attracted gifted men, and probably at no other period in history has such a concentration of talent been seen operating in one community.[50]

75

The influential and highly militaristic state of Sparta became increasingly suspicious of Athenian intentions, and disturbed by her growing eminence in the Greek world. A precarious détente had been reached in the middle of the century, but eventual open conflict was really inevitable. Sparta was supported principally by her allies in the Peloponnesian league, a loose confederacy of states led by Aegina and Corinth, who were probably envious of Athens' commercial success. The immediate cause of the war – the secession of Megara from the Peloponnesian league and her alliance with Athens – is of only precipitatory importance. The underlying problems were political and ideological. Sparta, a non-democratic state, posed as the champion of democracy in her confrontation with Athenian expansionism. And Athens, reputedly the personification of liberal democracy, exhibited the true nature of her repressive imperialistic policies.[51] There was an oscillation of fortune in the war until the catastrophic destruction of a huge Athenian force at Syracuse in 413 BC in a vain attempt to secure the Sicilian corn trade. The Athenian allies were in revolt, and the Persians gave support to Sparta, but the Athenians struggled on gaining some intermittent successes. The end for Athens came in 404 BC with the capture of the bulk of her fleet at Aegospotami and a three months' siege of the city which brought her to unconditional surrender. The terms were humiliating but not disastrous. After a turbulent period of social and political unrest, a form of democracy was restored and Athens again settled down to a time of relative peace as a second-class power.

There were brief moments of resurgence during the earlier part of the fourth century. Alliances and allegiances changed with baffling rapidity. Athens reformed her confederacy on more modest lines. The almost mesmeric quality of the Spartan arms began to fade, and she was beaten by her erstwhile friends, the Persians, after having defeated her former allies, the Corinthians who were on this occasion also joined by the Athenians. Persia was still a power to be reckoned with, and she imposed a 'King's Peace' upon the Greeks in 386 BC. This confirmed her authority in Asia Minor, checked the power of Sparta, and allowed Athens to reform her confederacy – although without quite the imperial arrogance which had marked the earlier Delian league. But there was little respite from war. Athens defeated the Spartans at sea, and the Thebans defeated them on land, the overweening ambition of Thebes then drew the traditional enemies, Sparta and Athens, into a coalition against her. This unsuccessful bid to curb Theban power left all the participants economically and unilaterally exhausted, and made way for the emergence of Macedonia. The collapse of the Athenian confederacy in 354 BC and the weakness of both Sparta and Thebes

76

indirectly facilitated the rise of Macedonian power first in Greece under Philip and later in the entire Middle East under his son, Alexander.

This spelled the final eclipse of Athens as a power, although her cultural influence lived on; her reputation as a centre of learning continued even in Roman times. Despite the brevity of her 'golden age', her accomplishments have become enshrined in living traditions and the memorials of her creativity can still excite the wonder of new generations. What we know about Ancient Greece is very largely what we know about Athens. Justly or not, Athenian culture has become almost synonymous with the Greek achievement.

# 7 Agencies of socialisation

As far as we can ascertain, man's biology is not sufficient for social life; in fact, in and of itself it could constitute a decided hindrance.[1] A learning or socialisation process of considerable complexity is required if social adaptation and integration are to take place. 'Correct' socialisation may even be seen as a means towards 'social maturity', that is an extension of one's roles and an expansion of one's ability to appreciate the role-definitions of others.[2]

Socialisation therefore is the process whereby people are initiated into the evaluations of any particular culture, and must be functionally similar in all societies. It is the process by which the 'barbarian invaders of each generation'[3] are conditioned to the norms of their native system. In short, it is the means whereby individuals – infants or adults – come to 'define their situations in accordance with institutional prescriptions'.[4] Put more simply, 'socialization is learning that enables the learner to perform social roles'.[5]

Socialisation processes are held to inhibit tendencies towards deviant behaviour[6] by the inculcation and internalisation of norms which reflect the essential 'rightness' of the system. They therefore help to promote a certain consistency of behaviour which is maintained in varying situations. The individual should not be regarded as a mere object of the contemporary environment; he is capable of selective and self-initiated action. According to one view, this conception is necessary to explain the individual's resistance to fundamental change and 'the persistence of ideological trends in the face of contradictory facts and radically altered social conditions . . . and why people in the same sociological situation have different or even conflicting views on social issues. . . .'[7] It follows, therefore, that immoderate views of either biological or environmental

78

determinism are both simplistic and reductionist and tend to discount the complexities of actual personality structures. The interaction between the individual and his environment and the resolution of their respective contributions is the subject of interminable debate.[8] For the purposes of this discussion, it must simply be accepted that the reciprocal nature of that interaction is, in part at least, a function of the socialisation process which we can intrepidly attempt to describe but only tentatively try to explain.

Socialisation is indissolubly linked with social order. In all societies, the processes of social control operate to inhibit deviations from the established rules. The normative order is maintained by traditions inculcated in the socialisation process. Nowhere is this more evident than in complex pre-industrial societies where the levels of stability and cohesion resulted in continuities which are largely foreign to modern systems.

The principal agencies of socialisation in traditional societies were the family and the kin-group. These constituted the informal guardians of orthodoxy and conformity. Kinship determined legal, ritual and – in a very broad sense – politico-economic status. The transmission of the culture was thus mainly undertaken by what might be termed 'internal' agencies. Formal or 'external' education as we understand it, was only institutionalised for a minority in these societies, and even this was often closely associated with ritual centres. Other external influences such as the communications media which in our society can act as purveyors of insistent heterodox opinion were, of course, unknown to traditional systems. It is, therefore, necessary to examine these agencies and try to gauge their contribution to the phenomenon of social order in the societies in question.

## The family and kinship

The French sociologist Le Play, who is usually credited with the development and popularisation of the social research technique of participant observation, suggested a typology for families in agrarian societies.[9] He regarded the *patriarchal family* as typical of agricultural communities where stable occupations and long-standing traditions enabled it to resist change and disruption. The anthropologist Ralph Linton also identified a similar type based upon consanguinal relations.[10] This type too, which may take a joint or extended family form, was also seen as typical of societies with stable relations and firm foundations. It may therefore be very numerous,[11] comprising consanguine and affinal relations together with household and other servants on the larger and more prosperous estates.[12] Linton emphasised not only the defining characteristic

79

of blood relationships, but also the complementary importance of parent-child relationships. Descent was usually traced through the male line, a practice intrinsic to the patriarchal tradition which reflected the general authority structure of society. We know that this model has only a general applicability. Descent is usually traced unilineally, although in historical cases this may be of a matrilineal type as in Egyptian society. Whatever, authority within these systems was firmly vested in the males.[13]

The kin groups of a society compose a structural sub-system of that society. They have a unity of their own, but in being closely interwoven with the overall institutional complex, they are part of a superordinate pattern.[14] In this way, the family and kinship systems comprised integral strands in the patterns of control which operated in traditional societies. Not only had they social functions in so far as they were ultimately responsible in most societies[15] for the socialisation of the child, they had legal functions also. They legitimised procreation by delineating the bounds within which sexual relations were permitted. By extension, they therefore regulated modes of inheritance, most commonly in terms of patrilineal transmission and succession. This, in turn, conferred status and often confirmed a member's place in the political order. In addition, family and kinship systems had important economic functions. Families might hold and transmit property as a group, and in some societies, notably China, an extended family group might operate as a joint economic unit. This was common in societies where patterns of mutual obligation and reciprocity were customary, and norms dictated that members co-operated for economic purposes. In the absence of highly institutionalised state-aid systems, this provided a substantial measure of security.

Family and kin groups were frequently also religious units. Ceremonial, which might take simple or elaborate forms, was carried out at all levels and was inseparable from the notion of kinship responsibility.[16] Family and kinship systems were essentially *authority* systems, and it is here that we must consider in what ways they were subject to determinative ideological influences.

*Egypt*

There was a relatively low degree of formalisation of the Egyptian legal system compared with the developed codes in Mesopotamia.[17] One result of this is that we know comparatively little about the formalities and litigation relating to marriage, divorce and property settlements, the position of women (see Chapter 8) and related issues in Egyptian society. What we do know almost exclusively concerns the nobility and the privileged classes. It is therefore particularly difficult to know to what extent extrapolations can be made to the other classes whose memory was not so honoured by mortuary-cult artists.

We know that the Egyptian nobility adhered to matrilineal kinship patterns. Although inheritance was therefore through the female line, there is evidence that like so many agrarian societies, male children were preferred.[18] Certainly among the nobility, transmission rights were vested in the women, but *control* lay with the men.

'Marriage is very seldom mentioned in surviving literary and pictorial records.'[19] We know the formalities were completed before an appointed official, and a property settlement was made whereby the husband contributed two-thirds and his wife one-third. If either party died, the survivor was entitled to the entire estate, but could only dispose of the proportion that he or she had contributed.

By comparison, the Assyrian (Mesopotamian) system seems to have been rather more flexible. Marriage could be either matrilocal or patrilocal. Sometimes it might take the form of a barely disguised purchase by the husband, but there were other forms which involved the bringing of a dowry by the bride. It is perhaps significant that this always remained her property and that of her children; neither her husband nor his brothers were allowed to make claims upon it. Similar inalienable rights also attached to other gifts which the bride received even if she were eventually divorced by her husband.[20]

In both Egypt and Mesopotamia, arranged marriages seem to have been the norm – certainly among the aristocracy. We are assured, however, that in Egypt, at least, there was some degree of freedom of choice of marriage partners.[21] As evidence, love poems are cited, 'Her hair is black, blacker than the night, blacker than sloes. Red are her lips, redder than beads of red jasper, redder than ripe dates. Lovely are her twin breasts.' But here a salutary word is necessary. Extant papyri recount stories of love and valour, of heroism and tragedy, similar in general content to those found in the corpus of mythology of many other peoples. Some appear to recount actual incidents from the remote past. Others – and this is particularly the case with Mesopotamian and Greek myths, with their fabulous creatures and unlikely adventures – are either entirely fictitious or imaginative and distorted reconstructions based upon some vestigial folk memories.[22] It may, therefore, be unwise to make categorical inferences about the nature of the societies in question from such source material, although the accounts may indicate something of the values and practices of particular milieux at particular times. As J. A. Wilson acutely observes in his very important contribution to Egyptian studies,[23] 'objective evidence does not exist. It certainly does not exist in the art of ancient Egypt, which was as timeless and propagandistic as the literature. It does not exist in the physical remains resulting from excavation, but this is an extremely limited witness, which only occasionally can deny or corroborate the written record.'

Our inferences and extrapolations then must be guarded, they must be weighed against other internal and external evidence. On these bases, reasonable assumptions can still be made. This applies particularly to the problems of interpretation of certain institutional Egyptian practices. Take, for example, the phenomenon of brother-sister marriage. The evidence is not clear on this issue. There were marriages between couples who referred to one another as brother and sister who clearly did not live in the same house, and were certainly not children of the same parents. In New Kingdom times, the term 'sister' was usually employed by the husband instead of the term 'wife', although this practice was not followed in the courts. The Greeks believed that brother-sister or half-brother-half-sister marriage took place in ancient Egypt, and that this was confirmed by observed practices among the nobility. Some of the Pharaohs appear to have married their sisters and even their daughters, ostensibly to maintain the purity of the royal line because it was believed that divine legitimacy was derived matrilineally (see Chapter 8). However, the *institutionalisation* of brother-sister marriage among the Pharaohs may have been a Ptolemaic innovation. Herodotus, the fifth-century Greek historian, reminds us that when the Persian king, Cambyses, asked the Egyptian judges if this was, in fact, permitted, they replied that there was no specific law which permitted it, but that there was a law which allowed the king to do as he pleased.[24] Whatever, no single instance has been found of an Egyptian, at any level of society, marrying his *full* sister,[25] although marriage to a sister's daughter does seem to have been allowed. This compares with Mesopotamian society where the emphasis was upon affinal rather than consanguineous relations. Here a form of levirate-sororate marriage obtained. After only betrothal, over which her father had complete authority, a girl became a full member of her future husband's family. If he died, she would then marry one of his brothers or another near relative. Conversely, if the girl died, her husband-to-be would either avail himself of one of her sisters or insist upon the return of the betrothal gifts.[26]

There appears to have been no marked segregation of the sexes in Egypt during the maturation period as is found in some societies.[27] Segregation had the ostensible function of protecting a girl's virtue during puberty, thus enhancing her marriageability. The value of chastity varies from society to society, but – as a very general rule – virginity has some economic worth, and parents may take elaborate steps to secure a girl's marriage prospects by ensuring her inviolability. It may be, as Sjoberg points out, that these norms are attainable only where women lack 'freedom' and where parents retain control of the marriage process. Perhaps these ideal patterns could 'be fulfilled only by the urban upper class'.[28]

In both Egyptian and Mesopotamian societies, concubinage was not uncommon among the social élite. But it would be difficult to sustain the charge that this derived directly from the hypothesised greater sex drive of the male or that it was a necessary concomitant of the arranged marriage system.[29] No doubt for the males, the prospect of greater sexual versatility had its attractions, and may well have been a welcome by-product of the system. (Such freedom hardly applied to women who could be punished by death for adultery.) In individual cases, it may have been the actual reason for that particular union, but as a *practice*, it is a near certainty that concubinage was bound up with status and economic factors. The Egyptian text entitled *The Book of the Dead* actually differentiates between 'wives' and 'concubines', suggesting a distinction between polygamy and concubinage in Egyptian society. And this says nothing of the slave-girls (who were surely not all musicians, as so many of the wall-paintings seem to depict) who were a feature of many of the more prosperous households. In Mesopotamian society, there appear to have been different norms operating at different periods. In the Old Babylonian period, the evidence suggests that women had a higher status than in Neo-Babylonian times. Among the Assyrians, we are told,[30] a man was not strictly allowed a plurality of wives; the term 'wife' belonged to one legal spouse only. The concubine, although in many ways functioning as a second wife, was frequently a promoted slave. She did not wear the veil, given by the husband to his legal wife at the marriage ceremony, and was always regarded as of inferior status.

The extended and more particularly the joint family was a characteristic of the social élite. Besides its function as an agency for procreation and socialisation, it also provided an effective measure of security in a society which, compared with modern western systems, always lived near the margins of subsistence. 'The large extended family fills many of the functions that in industrial cities are assumed primarily by governmental welfare agencies.'[31] The Egyptians appear to have favoured large families, so much so that the Greek historian Strabo[32] reports with some astonishment that, in contrast to the Greek experience, the Egyptians made a point of rearing all the children which might be born to them. The Heka-nakht letters of the Eleventh Dynasty,[33] give us some idea of the family life of a small landowner about 2050 BC. It is clear that the writer who is away looking after his northern estates at Memphis is trying hard to maintain complete authority over his sons who are associated with him – though hardly as partners – in the task of estate management. He obviously does not treat them equally, and exercises his control at a distance through his concubine who seems to be finding the increasing frictions rather too much for her.

In a different context, the Mesopotamian legal codes indicate something of their attitudes to children and child-rearing. Apparently, there were scarcely any limits to a father's rights over his children. In some legal documents he is described as a 'master' and 'owner' of his children, and could if necessary deposit them with a creditor as security for the repayment of a debt.[34] This was very marked in the case of adopted children. By the act of adoption the father secured extensive rights which were upheld by law. Under the law code of Hammurabi 182, for instance, drawn up c. 1740 BC, we find that under certain circumstances a child who repudiated his foster parents had his tongue cut out. Adopted children were expected to give presents to their father equal in value to those they would eventually inherit.[35]

In a relatively undifferentiated system such as Ancient Egypt, it is quite impossible to divorce both the formal and informal institutional arrangements from religion. Ideological influences informed social procedures; the pleasure of the gods was the cultivated desideratum of society. Thus the deities were invoked in connection with marriage, 'I adore Hathor [the sky goddess], I adore the Lady of Heaven, I address myself to her. . . .'[36] In Montet's view, although there is no direct documentary evidence for it, newly wed husbands and wives, and possibly all their relatives, would congregate at the temple of the city-god to offer sacrifices and receive a blessing.[37] Egyptians were certainly known to try to fix the horoscopes of their children in relation to specific divinities and their calendar of auspicious and inauspicious days. Herodotus records[38] that 'Among other discoveries, the Egyptians have ascertained the god to whom each month and day is sacred, and they can therefore tell, according to the date of the child's birth, what fate is in store for him, how he will end his days and what sort of a person he will become.' Apparently, this practice was regarded with fatalistic veneration. The most trivial factors might be determinative of the gravest consequences, it was up to the practitioners to discern the fatal or favourable omens.[39]

Similar kinds of divination and belief in the efficacy of signs are to be found in Mesopotamian society. These too were often related to horoscopic interpretations. Babylonian astrology, for instance, was intimately associated with meteorology; the observation of the winds, the colour of the stars, the occultation of planets and eclipses. There were other subsidiary forms based upon different types of augury; the flights of birds, the spreading of oil on water, indeed – as in Egyptian divination – almost anything could be held to have a cryptic significance. Hemerology, the 'science' of good and bad days, was also employed, not simply for high-level decision-making, but also to direct the uncertain steps of ordinary people in their day-to-day affairs. The family was particularly involved because unusual or abnormal births were considered – depending upon the circumstances – to be especially ominous or propitious. The belief was entrenched that every new member of society was subject to certain features of the physical world which dictated his conduct.[40]

In addition, therefore, to its customary roles, the family also performed strategic economic and ritual functions. In a reciprocal way, these helped to maintain its existence and reinforce its status. This was achieved, not least of all, by sustaining its ideological ties with the past. Social order was sanctified by tradition.

## Greece

Very much more is known about family and kinship patterns in Greece than in Egypt. Athens and Sparta are comparatively well documented, particularly during the Classical and Hellenistic periods, although there are still significant gaps in our knowledge.[41] The fact that this relative wealth of material is available must derive in part from the fact that literacy in Greece was not confined to a class of specialist scholar-amanuenses. Not only did more people write, but the range of material concerns in Greece was much wider. Social and political comment, particularly in dramatic form, was encouraged, and in the 'grand century'[42] we can see in Herodotus and Thucydides the beginnings of institutional analysis and historical interpretation.[43]

Aristotle maintained[44] that the oikos was not only the smallest unit of the state, it was also an essentially 'natural' unit which comprised the male, the female, the children and the servant.[45] The Greek oikos was more than a mere household in anything like the contemporary sense. It was a corporate and integral unit which existed to support its members, and define their status vis-à-vis the state. 'An oikos was therefore a living organism which required to be renewed every generation to remain alive; it supported its living members' needs for food and its deceased members' needs for the performance of cult rituals.'[46] The members of the oikos, the extended family together with dependants and servants, were part of the wider kinship system based on the genos, or clan, which was organised on patriarchal principles.[47] The organisation of the poleis or city-states, required that kinship should be legally defined, and in Athens, by the fourth century BC, the state recognised for practical purposes, the anchisteia, the kinship-group extending to the first cousin as defining certain limits of kinship obligation. It was the

85

anchisteia which was entitled to succeed to vacant estates, and which had legal duties and responsibilities in the event of death within the group. Members were responsible for burying their own dead, and for seeking revenge or some alternative form of satisfaction – perhaps ritual purification – should a kinsman be murdered.[48] The oikos-centricity of Greek society was closely linked with the relative impregnability of the aristocracy (literally, the rule of the best families) where the leaders of the state were almost invariably drawn from the nobility.[49] Both Solon (sixth century) in practice, and Plato (fourth century) in theory sought to divest the oikos of some of its authority by the transference of that authority to the magistrates or guardians. But this was really a perpetuation of aristocratic rule in another – though somewhat more meritocratic – form.[50]

The senior male or kurios had final authority within the oikos. Indeed, he had the same absolute rights over his children as he had over his slaves. As head of the family, he even had the right to sell his children into slavery if he wished, although this was prohibited in Attica after the social reforms of Solon early in the sixth century BC. Even so, a father could still dispose of his child by the recognised practice of exposure.[51] Similarly, a man retained the right to repudiate his wife even though he might not be able to adduce a valid reason for doing so. In fact, a wife's adultery, if established in the courts, made repudiation obligatory; a failure to 'put her away' could theoretically render him liable to atimia (literally, without honour) that is, a loss of civil rights.[52] A man was at liberty to consort with prostitutes (hetairai) if he wished,[53] but he was not allowed actually to live with a mistress or concubine, that is to establish formally an alternative oikos.[54] Technically, neither citizen men nor women were permitted to set up houses with foreign, or non-citizen, spouses on pain of enslavement or a heavy fine.[55] It is also worth noting that in a society which so obviously espoused the principle of male superiority, an adultress although punished, was not – as was an adulterer – liable to punishment by death. The lover of the adultress could be killed by the husband with impunity if caught in flagrante delicto. Indeed, the kurios enjoyed legal immunity if he killed an adulterer caught with any of the women of his household, including not only his wife, but his mother, sisters or daughters also. This can be interpreted as an inverted assertion of the patriarchal principle; an offence against a woman was indirectly an offence against her kurios, whether husband, father, or guardian. Barrenness too, in all probability, was a common ground for repudiation, as it was a man's duty to ensure the survival of his oikos. Divorce was a simple informal process for the male, but rather more difficult for the female, although women could initiate divorce proceedings possibly through the good offices of a sympathetic city elder.[56] In any case, the woman's marriage dowry would have to be returned to her original kurios, presumably her father. A girl could marry without a dowry in Athens, but it was the exception rather than the rule. It may be that the existence of the dowry distinguished legal marriage from mere concubinage. The law appears to have been enacted so as to protect not only marriage but the very institution of the oikos. Family law was, in effect, public law. Ostensibly private matters could be occasions for public concern and – where necessary – legislation.

The male principle can be seen also in the relative seclusion of upper-class women in Athenian society.[57] Apparently women were rarely allowed out unaccompanied except possibly to certain religious festivals. The everyday shopping was usually done either by the males – even the kurioi themselves – or by slaves.[58] Most of their time was occupied with the affairs of the household within which they had their own quarters – the gynaikeia. The Athenians seem to have had an almost obsessive concern with virginity and its vulnerability. But, as we have already seen in the case of other traditional societies, this is very much bound up with the status and economic considerations surrounding the question of marriageability. In Greek society, this was reflected in the age-at-marriage issue. The customary practice has to be inferred from the texts, but there seems to be little doubt that generally girls were married quite early, that is between about fifteen and eighteen years of age, although it appears that men, on the other hand, married much later, being possibly ten or more years older than the girl. There were no formal rules in Athens governing the minimum age at marriage. Possibly some girls were wed as soon as they reached puberty at twelve or thirteen. Certainly they could be *betrothed* before puberty, the marriage becoming 'effective' at the post-pubertal stage, but there is no evidence that they married before puberty, as was sometimes the case in Rome.

Love as a necessary pre-condition *for* marriage seems to have been exceptional enough to excite comment.[59] This must not be confused with love *within* marriage. There is ample evidence that Athenian families enjoyed the 'normal' affectionate relations which we associate with family life.[60] Freedom of choice in marriage was certainly not the rule; the match was made primarily by the kurioi concerned. Upper-class women, however, may have had more freedom of choice in this respect. This contrasts interestingly with the situation in Rome, say during the Augustan period, where the lower classes appear to have been relatively untouched by the normative strictures of patrician morality.[61] There is some indirect evidence, particularly from the dramatists[62] that the Peloponnesian War brought about some relaxations in Athenian attitudes to women.

Homosexuality was common in Greece, and even actively encouraged among the youths of the military sets in Sparta.[63] But homosexuality as an *exclusive* alternative to heterosexuality was treated with considerable scorn.[64] In fact, the practice of sodomy was severely circumscribed by law in Athens, and boys still at school were legally protected against sexual assaults and procurement. There appears to have been some inconsistency in such arrangements,[65] but then in all societies there are strange gaps between formal social prescriptions and actual practices. The ideal in Greece seems to have been a kind of qualified or disciplined bisexuality, or more correctly paraphilia (literally, that which accompanies love). Versatility was obviously the thing. At some time or another, every Athenian male was expected to marry, although there were no formal sanctions against bachelorhood, as there were in Sparta.

Incest was not legally forbidden in Athens, but unions between parent and child were considered an abomination,[66] and similar religious taboos operated in the case of children of the same mother. Half-brothers and sisters of different mothers were allowed to marry. Indeed, endogamy, that is unions between members of a social group limited to close relatives was often encouraged, particularly where these would preserve and reinforce family ties.

Considering the paucity of conception control techniques then available, Athenians reared relatively small numbers of children.[67] There were perennial economic reasons for this, especially the anxiety that the family estates might have to be divided among too many heirs.[68] There were ways in which families could be limited. Abortion was not illegal, but the husband's consent was necessary. If a third party procured an abortion for a free woman or a slave, it was deemed an offence against their kurios. The law only intervened to protect the rights of the unborn child's master-to-be, that is its father or slave-owner.[69] Religion had more scruples than the law on this issue; and Aristotle advised that the foetus should not have 'life or feeling' if abortion is to take place (*Politics*, VII. 14). Failing abortion, there was always exposure or the selling of the child into slavery. It is impossible to know the extent of any of these practices, although the evidence for the institutionalisation and even ritualisation of exposure in Sparta is reasonably well attested.[70] In Thebes, infanticide is said to have been unknown,[71] although a law outlawing a practice surely indicates that there were at least some sporadic instances of it.

An Athenian could gratify his sexual appetites in a number of extra-marital ways, but he *married* to produce legitimate children – and these for three main reasons. To continue the oikos, to afford him some measure of security in his failing years, and finally to bury him and maintain the family shrine. The Athenian young were socialised to treat the aged with considerable respect. The obligation to assist parents was upheld by law, and those who neglected their duties were liable to both a fine and partial deprivation of civil rights. The obligation to bury parents was even more stringently upheld; this was regarded as a primary filial responsibility.

It is interesting that in a society which lived near the margins of subsistence, where presumably some premium was put upon youthful virility and warrior potential, such a regard for old age should exist. Theoretically, the old are expendable, they no longer make any direct contribution to the economy or the security of the state, yet – as in so many traditional societies – they were often treated with something approaching veneration. Was it because, in a qualified way, they represented the 'living memories' of the society? This is, of course, much more the case in non-literate societies where the old represent the only 'records' of the clan or tribe.[72] Or was it felt that because they had reached relatively advanced years in a society with a low average life expectancy that the gods must have favoured them? Was longevity ipso facto a sign of blessing?[73] Or was it simply an acknowledgment – an institutionalised anticipation – of the fact that one day the young too would be old and would therefore require similar attention from their own children? In societies where kinship obligation has not been supplanted by welfare services, the very presence of the elderly and the infirm can be a salutary reminder of the vulnerability of old age.

Religion permeated the entire fabric of kinship and family organisation in Greece.[74] 'All Greek social groups were also religious unions.'[75] Each phratry had its own altar at which sacrifices were performed. Each genos had its ancestor-hero, and each family had its own domestic cult which was corporately related to others in their common recognition of deities in the Olympian pantheon. On the other hand, how much religion influenced the actual operation of the kinship and family systems is difficult to calculate. Certainly marriages were celebrated with religious observances,[76] and the birth and reception of children into the oikos were accompanied by the appropriate rituals. Some cultic affiliation appears to have been a nominal requirement for eligibility for higher office, but this is largely inferred from the formal responses which were necessary at the dokimasia or preliminary scrutiny of magistrates. These may have been no more significant than certain kinds of formal oath-taking in our own society. What, however, does seem to be inescapable is the importance of the rituals in honour of the dead, presumably to ensure their well-being in the nether world. The ancestor cults were, of course, an extension of the patriarchal principle, and served to reinforce the traditional structure of the

89

existing society[77] and therefore functioned as ideological mechanisms of control.

## Education

The socialisation of the young, even in pre-industrial societies, was hardly confined to the family. The family itself was subject to external normative pressures and influences. Durkheim has pointed out how parents themselves are bound to conform to customs which if ignored will have serious repercussions for the children.[78] He maintained that children were educated for particular social milieux, and were therefore socialised to conform to the requisite normative structures. This implies a measure of *ascription* in the stratification system; the achievement principle was not a pronounced feature of traditional societies (see Chapter 8). Durkheim distinguished between education and pedagogy, that is between the general operation of the socialisation process and the theories of how that process is to be consciously pursued.[79] Education, in this broad sense, is to be found in all societies. Pedagogy, on the other hand, is very much more a characteristic of affluent societies, or at least an indulgence of a leisured class.[80]

One of the most important differences between early societies and modern industrial societies is that, whereas in the latter education is directed towards the communication of empirical knowledge, and the application of that knowledge to the industrial process, in the former it was concerned also with transmitting a way of life[81] which, in turn, involved the regulation of behaviour. Knowledge, as distinct from the learning of particular skills, was imparted mainly to minorities who were destined to rule and administer according to traditional codes. Education was not a principal agent in the rationalisation of the world but a cognitive aid which enabled men to adjust to the exigencies of life. As such, it was an essentially conservative force, and thus a potent mechanism of social control.

In viewing education as the communication or transmission of knowledge, we should first of all differentiate between the transmission and that which is transmitted, between the mode of communication and the content of that which is communicated. Then we can recapitulate our opening themes by examining the ostensible purpose of this communication.

Oral transmission in pre-literate societies had its obvious limitations. Information was disseminated by public proclamations, by religious functionaries, and by the dramatisations of itinerant storytellers and entertainers. This precluded the possibility of keeping accurate records and accounts, so necessary to expanding bureaucratic systems; although this would have to be qualified in the case of those Middle American societies which flourished with only rudimentary mnemonic aids. Orally transmitted knowledge is certainly subject to unwitting or conscious distortion, which again make accurate communications doubtful. But again, some credit must be given to those systems which inculcated the virtue of precise recall, and trained some in the development of this facility. [82]

With the advent of literacy, the position changed radically for the privileged, but the oral diffusion of knowledge to the illiterate masses necessarily continued. The importance of the written word should not be underestimated. [83] 'To this day, many sociologists fail to appreciate the impact of writing upon society. At once a conservative and revolutionary force ... its existence has made civilization and city life possible. Writing ... permitted the accumulation of a vast store of learning. ... On the other hand writing fixes – even stultifies – ideas, beliefs and behaviour patterns over time and space.' [84] Literacy had a special status in pre-industrial societies. It was the guarded prerogative of the few who were also, therefore, the custodians of the esoteric or sacred lore. Even the sheer ability to write was sometimes endowed with mystical properties and believed to confer special powers. In China, for example, amulets containing small written slips were often believed to ward off illness and evil spirits. It is said that the masses regarded the intelligentsia competing for places in the bureaucratic hierarchy with special respect. They apparently viewed 'a successfully examined candidate and official [as] by no means a mere applicant for office qualified by knowledge [but also as] ... a proved holder of magical qualities'. [85]

In general terms, it might be argued that the writing system in traditional societies was so complex that it actually hindered the transmission of knowledge. This was aggravated by a paucity of writing materials and implements, but it was the scripts themselves which presented such formidable difficulties for the initiates. This applied where simple ideograms were used, as in early Egypt, and more particularly in Classical China where the ideographic script contained some 6,000 characters which had to be individually memorised. [86] The situation was made even more complicated when scripts which were originally ideographic became syllabic, that is when signs such as the cuneiform symbols of the Sumerians were invested with phonetic qualities besides retaining something of the ideographic properties. [87] It hardly needs stressing that the learning of such languages required assiduous effort on the part of the student who would almost certainly be a member of a leisured class which had the time to devote to such exercises. The Greeks, of course, were an exception in this respect. The rationalised 22-letter alphabet, probably derived originally from the Phoenicians [88] presented none

91

of these difficulties, although literacy still remained the privilege of the minority. Complex writing systems inhibited the diffusion of knowledge. Craft-literacy and the measure of control it afforded functioned to reinforce the existing social order by increasing the authority of the ruling hierarchy. Mass literacy, even in relatively advanced societies such as Athens, was possibly regarded as both impracticable and undesirable.

Education in complex pre-industrial societies was largely an urban phenomenon. Not unusually, it was closely associated with ritual centres, and even among the upper classes where education was frequently in the hands of private tutors,[89] religious considerations often predominated. Because educational institutions were commonly related to the state religious system, it followed that instruction of the young was usually the prerogative of religious practitioners who defined formal learning as the inculcation of the sacred lore. Again, Greece is something of an exception in this respect, but even Athenian rationality did not preclude metaphysical considerations. Curricula may have been narrow, as some commentators reiterate, and memorisation of texts was a tedious feature of traditional educational procedures,[90] but if these were not centres of intellectual innovation, they were at least centres of intellectual discipline.

The purpose of education in traditional societies cannot simply have been to perpetuate the inequalities of the system, as some scholars adduce.[91] Undoubtedly, it often functioned in this way. It did facilitate various forms of control, and screened the public from unwelcome or – as some saw it – contaminating influences; one has only to note the attitudes of successful Chinese emperors to the prospect of European incursions.[92] But, imperfect as education was by modern standards, it helped to form the creative minorities of traditional systems. And these still cause posterity to wonder[93] at their architectural and artistic achievements. (For comparative purposes see Appendix: The Sumerian achievement, pp. 97–.8)

## Egypt

Royal children – who were produced in appreciable numbers – were taught by private tutors. The children of some nobles appear to have joined them in what was, in effect, a royal school. There is evidence of this as early as the Fourth Dynasty.[94] The highest form of education was a priestly training which was also undertaken by the Pharaoh.

In fact, our knowledge of the educational process in Ancient Egypt is confined very largely to the temple schools where the children of the more privileged classes were taught. Certainly by the time of the New Kingdom, education began in a class of perhaps twenty pupils[95] at the age of four or five and continued into the teens. We know, for example, of a person who later became a high priest of the god Amun, who had to study at the 'writing school' at the temple of the Lady of Heaven for twelve years.[96] Intending priests were not uncommonly sons of incumbent priests who cherished similar ambitions for their children. The boys who were designated as prospective officials were given over to the religious authorities for training although the temples usually operated as day schools and not boarding schools.

Each department of the government service had its own school to which members of that department had the right to send their sons. In the upper 'forms', a boy was given some of the work of that department, so that he was partially trained by the time he entered the service. There was apparently no compulsion for a boy to follow his father in this way, although paternal influence could be to his advantage where they shared the same spheres of activity.[97]

Education was very basic, and consisted mainly of reading, writing and number. Fortunately for archaeologists, papyrus was considered too valuable for school exercises, and small, durable limestone blocks were often used instead, some of which are still extant. More senior scholars graduated to the use of reed pens and black and red inks on papyrus rolls. Red was normally used for the title of a work, and black for the text, but the scribe – who was also something of a draughtsman – might also use other colours to illuminate the text. More senior children were taught the rudiments of history, and geography, and had a thorough grounding in certain classic texts which were inculcated through repetition and memorisation.

Officials might be required to undertake quite a variety of jobs in the course of their duties. A familiar task was the writing of petitions for illiterate people to their overlords. This required some eloquence and felicity of expression. A document of the Twelfth Dynasty entitled 'The Eloquent Peasant' gives models of different kinds of petitions, and shows that 'free-lance' scribes could make a handsome living pleading the causes of their customers.[98] In fact, student officials had to familiarise themselves with a number of subjects which might range from humanistic disciplines such as law to an acquaintance with simple technical processes. Mathematics was not an abstract pursuit, as it could be among the Greeks. For the Egyptian scribe it had strictly practical applications. Much of the work of government, for example, dealt with the intricacies of taxation. Where assessments were made – as they often were – in terms of corn-yields, the scribe had to be capable of calculating the production levels of the respective cultivable areas of land, and computing the state's tax requirements accordingly.

93

Discipline was strict for the social aspirant, and teachers' complaints about the indolence of their pupils has a familiar ring. The scribe Amenmose[99] tells his charges that 'the way to get strong is by practising every day . . . if you slack for a single day you will be beaten. A youngster's ear is on his back; he only listens to the man who beats him.' Similar injunctions were given to pupils in ancient Sumeria.[100] The view here is simply that if animals must be broken before training, corporal punishment will also produce results in the lazy or obstinate child, although it is better if he responds to the appeals of ambition and good sense.

The texts are silent on the matter of the education of women. Presumably for the upper orders, this would consist mainly of a quasi-domestic initiation into the social graces and etiquette which befitted their class. Of others we know little except that even slave-girls cultivated musical talents as flute-players.

Boys destined for the religious life had the same basic education as those intent on following a secular career – if that term has any real meaning in the context of ancient Egyptian culture. As their education progressed, they were expected to master the esoterica of their profession, the gods – their titles and epithets and their divine mythologies. They had also to be acquainted with the complexities of the prescribed rituals with which the gods should be honoured. Candidates were only fully admitted to the priesthood after formal examinations which sealed their consecration and confirmed their position in the social hierarchy.

The practicalities of Egyptian education were of only complementary importance. Its purpose was the inculcation of traditional verities and the continued preservation of ma'at, the principle of harmonious eternality without which, it was said, universal chaos would inevitably ensue. In more mundane terms, this meant the training of a literate élite, and through them the perpetuation of a stable social order. Social arrangements confirmed divine requirements; ideology sustained the social system.

*Athens*

Even in the culturally buoyant Athenian society of the fifth century BC, education was a traditional rather than a political obligation. Custom was strong, but it is uncertain whether education was legally enforceable.[101] Education was not state-controlled, but left to individual initiative and even where the state supported special pupils, who were usually children of veterans or those who had died in the service of the polis, their tuition was contracted out to private teachers. Inferences have been made from plays of the period that there was something approaching universal literacy in the Athenian community,[102] but these are 'arguments from silence' which must be treated with reserve. The argumentum ad hominem extrapolation from the situations of some humble literary citizens – Aristophanes' Strepsiades in *The Clouds*, for instance – to the mass must remain an uncertain business.

In general, children were taught in the houses of their teachers, particularly at the elementary level. These must be distinguished from the palaistrai which were forms of gymnasia equipped with baths, changing rooms and sports area where the youths exercised. Physical training had a high priority in Greece.

Normally, parents were responsible for their children's school fees, and it can therefore be reasonably assumed that the amount of education received by any child was largely conditioned by its parents ability to pay. In Plato's words, 'The sons of the wealthy are sent to school later than the others and are able to stay there longer.'[103] This probably meant in practice that more prosperous parents were able to see their sons through the epheboi stage; the boys could continue their education to eighteen and over.

The evidence suggests that teachers' pay – certainly at the elementary level – was rather meagre. The question of a teacher's status is not just a matter of retrospective assessment, it was of some concern in antiquity, as Demosthenes makes quite clear.[104] '... his was a ... badly paid profession, and therefore rated very low in the Greek scale of social values. ... Throughout the whole history of the antique world the schoolmaster's was a humble trade, plied by those who had seen better days or had no other skill to offer the community.'[105] In effect, the schoolteacher had no special qualifications for the job, but then it is difficult to apply such a yardstick to a society where no formal credentials were available anyway.

The educational system in Athens was rooted in the desire for a basic literacy combined with some musical and athletic skills. Between the ages of seven and fourteen, Greek boys attended the palaistra (wrestling school) for physical education and the music school for simple literacy and musical instruction. The gymnasium (literally, the stripping place) was used by older boys, and its activities were a much more serious affair. Considerable care was taken in the selection of the specialist gymnasts who trained the athletes.[106] The music schools may, in some cases, have actually occupied the same site as the palaistra. Here boys were taught to read and write, and given exercises in simple number. Papyrus and ink were used, as were also ostraka, clay tiles and wax-covered blocks which were marked with a stylus. But great emphasis was put upon committing facts to memory. Recitation of the classics, particularly Homer, was an essential ingredient of any educational

95

programme. There is some evidence to suggest that this was not a simple didactic technique, but a method of inculcating moral precepts and drawing object-lessons on a range of related Homeric themes: war and peace, courtesy, courage, diplomacy and political wisdom, and especially duties towards parents and the gods.[107]

Discipline could be severe in the Athenian palaistra. The school day began at daybreak and holidays were irregular. Children did not attend school during the numerous civic and religious festivals. More prosperous families were able to exercise more control of their young by entrusting them to a paidogogos, that is a slave who accompanied them to and from school. For most boys, education finished when they were fourteen. Beyond that age, 'higher education' – for those who could afford specialist teachers – centred on the gymnasium which was a public institution. Young men might also avail themselves of instruction by the Sophists, itinerant teachers of rhetoric who sometimes enjoyed considerable reputations and even more considerable incomes. Not that all Sophist teachers were expensive, as was, say, Plato's contemporary, Isocrates. But Plato, perhaps a little unfairly, reserved some of his sharpest barbs for these men – particularly Protagoras and Gorgias – who attracted 'great numbers of students by the smallness of their charges and the magnitude of their professions'.[108]

Music was also an integral part of Athenian education. The lyre, the aulos – a type of flute – and singing were all taught, and possibly dancing as well. The apparent necessity for even a rudimentary musical education possibly echoes the Pythagorean philosophy of the fundamental relationship between music and number. This was thought to reflect the 'harmonia' of the universe – the essential balance of the cosmic and societal orders.[109] Choral and instrumental displays were often part of the many celebrations and festivities which both mirrored and endorsed the state ideology.

Until the fourth century, there were no schools for girls,[110] but education was not exclusively a male-orientated business. There is evidence[111] to show that many were given a basic literacy, but very few received any kind of higher education. This compares interestingly with the freer and ostensibly less discriminatory practices which were adopted in Sparta which is generally regarded as a more regimented and less egalitarian society.[112]

Greek education, particularly in its physical aspects, betrayed many of the signs of its early military character and its strong aristocratic orientations. It remained, throughout the fifth century certainly, an education for the élite with adaptations for a society in which there was increasing citizen participation. The ideal persisted: the inculcation of arete – the conception of cultivated excellence – was an integral part of the educational process. In its earlier form, that of the man who is 'both beautiful and good', it may have been merely a 'resplendent fiction'.[113] Certainly it was 'aesthetic rather than literary, athletic rather than intellectual'.[114] By the latter part of the fifth century, arete had metamorphosised from a kind of moral virtue to the capacity for conspicuous and practical efficiency.[115] Such changes were encouraged, though not necessarily initiated by the Sophists.

According to some authorities,[116] there was a time when religion was the bond of Greek political life. Indeed, it can be seen as the 'only restraining pressure exerted against the future separatist tendencies of independent city-states and against the dangerous individualistic quality of the Greek temperament'.[117] Despite the unifying qualities of Greek religion, this is probably an overstatement. It may be more accurate to regard the real religion of the fifth century as 'a devotion to the city itself'.[118] In fact, by this time both philosophers and dramatists were seriously questioning the ancient myths. The Olympian gods had long failed to edify, a point forcibly made by Euripides (especially in the *Medea*) and were worthy of little more than ridicule, a view that is quite explicit in the work of Aristophanes.[119] Certainly the old ideology was breaking down. With the Sophists, there was a growing intellectualism and with it an incipient humanism. Social behaviour became marked by overt and acknowledged utilitarian attitudes, so that towards the end of the fifth century, Adeimantus can ask 'But suppose there are no gods?'[120] In this, he appears to be speaking for many others beside himself. After a century of qualified achievement, Athens' self-confidence was shattered and its scepticism increased by the defeat which ended its political hegemony.

Athenian education was different in emphasis from that of Egypt. It was not primarily oriented towards the maintenance of the social status quo or simply the perpetuation of a particular form of bureaucratic hierarchy. It was – in broad terms – directed towards the realisation of the 'good life'. This it was assumed depended on the 'development of the whole personality in a balanced relationship of its physical, intellectual, aesthetic and moral aspects. It was an ideal seldom attained and eventually corrupted in the course of Greek history, but it has left a deep impress on western civilization.'[121]

## Appendix   The Sumerian achievement

The Sumerians were the major power in Lower Mesopotamia for over 1,000 years; between *c.* 3000 and *c.* 1800 BC their achievements were, in relative terms, quite exceptional. They established an urban civilisation based upon agriculture with an involved economic system based upon a complex division of labour and a merchant

97

class using a form of money economy – a very advanced innovation for the period. They created the political unit which we know as the city-state which, in this case, was organised and administered on theocratic principles which involved a highly elaborated set of religious ideas and beliefs. These states developed a class of literate administrators – bureaucracies – which, unlike their contemporaries, the Egyptians, formulated and utilised legal codes. They also developed an extensive literature and are usually credited with the invention of the cuneiform script, and perhaps even the art of writing itself. Their artistic skills too were considerable: the cemetery finds at Ur including the jewellery of Queen Shub'ad and the famous 'ram in the thicket' statuette all show exquisite workmanship predating the first dynasty of Ur, i.e. pre-*c.* 2650 BC.[122] The Sumerians evolved considerable technological expertise. Their technical mastery of their irrigation systems – so vital to their economy – involved the construction of canals, dykes, dams and reservoirs. They were skilled in the uses of copper and bronze, and to compensate for their limited access to wood and stone, they cultivated the art of building in brick. This was used particularly in the incredible ziggurats – the flat-topped pyramids which were used for ritual purposes.

Not least of all, there are certain 'legacies' in areas which are perhaps more commonly associated with education. Mesopotamian culture generally was highly sophisticated.[123] It developed the sexagesimal system which we still use in the calculation of time and in navigation. In chemistry, there were experiments with filtration, and in very early times, some hundreds of drugs had been successfully identified. And in astronomy, a major pre-occupation of the priests, the length of the year had been computed, and eclipses were predicted – an achievement which was again vital for their religious purposes.

Unlike Egypt, Sumeria was a 'true' theocratic system. The king was at the same time both monarch and priest – but never a god. As ruler, he was merely the steward of the tutelary deity. Indeed, legend had it that the people were created as serfs on the estates of the gods 'to be burdened with the toil of the gods that they might freely breathe'.[124] Ideologically, it was essentially a contingent system exhibiting an operative interrelationship between the societal and cosmic orders, and necessitating attitudes of complete dependency and resignation.

# 8   Systems of social differentiation

This study is not the place for an elaborate digression on the respective merits and demerits of the main theories of stratification.[1] But it should be made clear that it repudiates as misguided and misconceived the notion that sociology is somehow to be equated with the study of stratification (see Chapter 1). And it regards as axiomatic that the term stratification should not be confused with that of class. In this examination of the social structure of complex pre-industrial societies, it will be taken that stratification is the more inclusive term[2] which 'denotes the differential ranking of the human individuals who compose a given social system and their treatment as superior and inferior relative to one another in certain socially important respects'.[3]

The term class, on the other hand, should not be used in a loose, amorphous sense as a catch-all category for social analysis, for example, 'social class is a large body of persons who occupy a position in a social hierarchy by reason of their manifesting similarly valued objective criteria. These latter include kinship affiliation, power and authority, achievements, possessions, and moral and personal attributes. Achievements involve a person's occupational and educational attainments; possessions refer to material evidences of wealth; moral attributes include one's religious and ethical beliefs and actions; and personal attributes involve speech, dress, and personal mannerisms.'[4] The concept of class should be taken to mean the more specific ranking of individuals according to economic criteria: 'class has denoted those holding a common position along some continuum of the economy. While this has sometimes been a continuum of wealth or income, and, at other times, occupations, in the strictest Marxist usage it has denoted basic forms of relationship to the modes of material production.'[5] The term class, then, expresses those social relations – and by definition, specifically power relations – which are determined by the individual's proximity to the ownership of the means of production.

Stratification, therefore, is synonymous with ranking, the idea that there is a hierarchy of social positions which are graded according to a *variety* of criteria, which involves inequality of privilege. But this too must be qualified. Is it possible on this general definition to equate social stratification with social differentiation? It is arguable whether, like stratification, all differentiation implies 'significant discontinuities in the distribution of goods and services, or of property, rights and obligations',[6] although it may well imply gradations of prestige. Differential access to wealth and power is not necessarily congruent with differential status,[7] although in practice they are often closely interconnected. 'In contrast to the economically determined "class situations" we wish to designate as "status situation" every typical component of the life fate of men that is determined by a specific, positive or negative, social estimation of *honour*.'[8] Wealth and power are not always consistent with social esteem, a fact which is particularly highlighted in the study of traditional societies. In fact, poverty itself seen as an ethical or religious task as with, say, certain Hindu gurus, may be held to confer high prestige on the individuals concerned.[9] 'In the past the significance of stratification by status was far more decisive [than classes] . . . above all, for the economic structure of the societies.'[10]

Social differentiation, then, is a term with even broader connotations than social stratification. It does encompass the notion of social levels or layers with their superior–inferior implications; the idea of ascription and achievement modes of strata allocation, and the examination of the life-chances and life-styles of the respective strata in question. It is similarly concerned with ideology and the extent to which it justifies the system or scale of ranking. But social differentiation also includes primary distinctions made upon such criteria as age, sex and race. To regard these too as forms of ranking requires considerable qualification in specific social contexts. The matter of race, in particular societies, will not admit of any overt or explicit treatment in terms of simple stratification. For example, in Ancient Greece during the fourth century, many Greeks became increasingly unwilling to hold fellow Greeks as slaves. A complex of elements was involved: cultural, nationalistic and almost certainly ethnic. Distinctions were being made but the reasons were not clearly analysed or explicated. When the policy – if such it can be called – was in its developmental phase, if any ranking was taking place at all, it was largely in the form of intellectual categorisations not as an institutionalised practice. Similarly, the Egyptians, although tolerant of divergent ideas, were not necessarily tolerant of other peoples. They made a distinction between 'men' and Libyans,

Asiatics and Africans.[11] Fellow Egyptians were 'humans'; they were 'people' – or perhaps more precisely *the* people – but about foreigners there was some vestigial doubt. The actual basis of the distinction is difficult to determine. In one sense, it does not seem to have been narrowly religious, perhaps because the religious ideas of other peoples often contained recognisable – and therefore acceptable – common features. But it was broadly ideological in as much as it involved the notion of politico-ethnic separateness.

Any attempted analysis of the structure and organisation of human society is vitiated by the ubiquitous and rather intangible concept of status. It appears as something of a universal value which is expressed in a great variety of ways in different societies,[12] and – as Weber has emphasised – can have particular relevance for traditional systems especially where long periods of economic stability characterise the normal state of affairs.[13] The status factor links the ranking system with the norms and values of a society.[14] In industrialised contexts it is usually related to consumption – patterns and styles of life rather than amounts or sources of income. And in both traditional and modern societies, it is possible to identify hierarchies of status which are distinguishable from those of class.[15]

In pre-industrial systems[16] social differentiation was inextricably linked with ideology. Some authorities maintain that traditional social structures were suffused with a kind of cosmic awareness.[17] Extreme as this may seem, the evidence does suggest that there was certainly a pervasive sensitivity to the religious factor, even though this may not have been clearly articulated at all levels of society. Unsurprisingly, it was expressed differently by different strata. For example, in Classical China, although Confucianism continued as the state religion it did not develop specialised religious roles or organisations.[18] Confucianism can be seen more as a humanistic philosophy than a personal belief system,[19] but it did permeate the state organisation, 'turning the Chinese state into a special type of church-state'.[20] Confucian ideology increased in importance as a criterion for social ranking, and merged with political-literary criteria in definitions of status. Although the salvationist Taoist faith too attracted adherents from all classes especially during the Han period (206 BC–AD 220) and later Buddhism in the T'ang dynasty (AD 618–907) also achieved wide recognition, the religion of the *people* remained persistently atavistic being mainly concerned with sundry nature deities and the traditional ancestor cults.

The ranking systems of pre-industrial societies had a certain rigidity; this tends to be a characteristic of ascriptive valuation situations. But it is arguable whether these systems were quite as inflexible as has sometimes been supposed. 'One of the most striking

101

of the features that set the pre-industrial city apart from its industrial counterpart is the all-pervasiveness of its stratification system, above all the rigid class structure.'[21] Undoubtedly, this situation obtained in the lower echelons of most societies, but it can be shown that there was considerable flexibility in the hierarchies of status especially among influential entrepreneurial and merchant groups in urban situations. As Eisenstadt points out in relation to the legal definition of status groups, 'the range encompassing legally free groups varied greatly from one society to another . . . most . . . societies exhibited a tendency toward weakening such definitions. . . . It was also mostly – if not entirely – in the cities that the cultural, religious and professional elites often cut across any fixed status groups.'[22]

These groups were normally dissociated from territorial and kinship associations, and were usually found less among the lower peasant and unskilled urban strata *and* the hereditary aristocracy than among the rural and – especially – urban middle classes. This dissociation of the upper classes was more common in some societies than others. The Chinese literati, for example, affected to despise trade though profiting indirectly from its operations, whilst the Athenian aristocracy – many of whom were actively engaged in commercial ventures – entertained far more ambivalent attitudes to economic enterprise. For the societies in question, these and other organisational activities provided some cultural diversity. In relatively rigidified traditional structures, they also gave a measure of mobility to both the opportunistic and the privileged. Such groups reflected the growing recognition of the achievement principle in what were predominantly ascriptive status systems.[23]

Achievement status was also possible among the military where warrior prowess and tactical expertise were important criteria for social and political advancement. Not least of all, ideological requirements generated categories of religious functionaries who often came to constitute exemplary élites. These categories were sometimes based on ascriptive valuations, as, say, in Renaissance Italy where it was possible to appoint pre-pubertal cardinals. Politico-pecuniary considerations were important, and the Vatican was not above a little indulgent nepotism where necessary.[24] But the medieval Church could also be a channel of mobility for any who had the necessary devotion and learning.

In some traditional societies, religious categories might be kin-based as in Ancient Israel[25] or otherwise rooted in hereditary castes.[26] But those engaged in the tasks of religious leadership and communication were not always drawn exclusively from particular strata. Indeed, it was the religious sphere which was probably most open to questionings of an ethico-oracular kind. But even the prophetic challenge was usually protological[27] and was therefore

102

made within the existing ideological frameworks.[28] Revelation-based systems have a habit of spawning further and higher revelations which can be both debilitating and self-renewing depending on circumstances.[29] These are generally only acceptable if they are compatible with the socio-cultural norms of the society in question.[30]

As a very general rule, the more undifferentiated the institutional system, the more undifferentiated and less mobile were the groups – economic, military, religious, etc. – to be found within it. And the fewer and more crystallised these groups were, the more static the society remained. Alternatively, the more highly differentiated the institutional system, the more differentiated and more numerous were the groups which constituted mobile elements within it. These contributed to the openness and relative flexibility of such societies and rendered them more susceptible to influences for change. It is instructive to see how this analysis now applies to Egypt and Athens.

## Egypt

We have already noted (Chapter 6) that Egypt had a long and chequered history marked by expansion and contraction, incursions and invasions – particularly during the later phases – and the ascendancy of foreign dynasties. But during this entire period not only did she retain an essential cultural homogeneity, she also managed to avoid essential structural discontinuities. 'The structure of society in Egypt changed very little during the three thousand years of history, the general pattern being disturbed only by the two intermediate revolutionary periods, and for not more than a couple of decades during the Amarna interlude which, because of its total aberration from the Egyptian norm, is sometimes given an isolated prominence for this very reason.'[31]

The pyramid shape which is so evocative of Ancient Egypt and its achievements is often said to symbolise the structure of the society itself.[32] Theoretically, there were no classes or castes in Egypt. Except those of royal blood, all were legally commoners 'before the throne'.[33] In practice, however, authority was delegated downwards from the king at the apex through a widening hierarchy of officials to the peasants or fellahin at the base.

The state was controlled by the king and his chief ministers with the vizier as his principal administrator. These were aided by the high priest of the current state deity who was responsible with the priests for maintaining the many cultic centres (periodic changes in theological emphasis[34] were sometimes functions of the relative strengths of the respective priesthoods); and the commander of the army, whose tasks included not only national security, but also the organisation of resource-seeking expeditions. For example, he might

103

be required to obtain slaves; on other occasions, it might be for important raw materials. In the reign of Amenophis II, a king of the Eighteenth Dynasty, the army is said to have brought back 90,000 captive workers from one campaign alone.[35] Sometimes the king would intervene in these expeditions personally, particularly where they affected his own person. Ramesses II, for instance, was especially interested in obtaining the stone for his own monuments.[36]

The country was governed in the name of the king by means of a developed bureaucracy of scribes, archivists and other administrators through descending grades of artisans, masons and agricultural overseers to the masses who laboured mainly in the fields, on dykes and canals, in workshops and on building sites. Whether they worked on an official's estate or on the lands and in the craft centres associated with the temples, they were all theoretically responsible to the king from whom they derived their livelihood as a kind of bounty. As subjects, they were obliged to pay part of their crops to their superiors as taxes, and they were also liable for both military duties, if required, and for service in the corvée, a form of forced labour exacted by the government for the construction of various public works. Their rights were therefore minimal; they were entirely dependent upon the munificence of the monarch and his administrative subordinates.

Among the lower orders, there is little evidence of social mobility, but at the upper levels there appears to have been considerable mobility. Once a member of the bureaucracy, promotion was always possible for the favoured and the gifted. 'The king was always on the lookout for able men and once he spotted a potential talent, movement to a higher echelon could quickly follow.'[37] Parsons makes a similar point: 'status was diffuse. . . . Yet it could break through the very strict forms of kinship ascription, making it possible for more able people to be advanced more routinely from lower to higher positions of service.'[38]

In the very early years, during the First and Second Dynasties, the rather meagre evidence suggests that the main division in Egyptian society was between a large serf population of the indigenes and a nobility which was racially different and culturally superior.[39] But with the gradual fusion of the races, the situation was slightly ameliorated. The development of an artisan class and the enlargement and diversification of the bureaucracy brought a measure of social mobility for both the fortunate and the politically energetic.

For the peasant, the horizon was always limited, but for the scribe advancement was an ever-present possibility. We are told that scribes tended to despise manual work. A late Egyptian school exercise says, 'Be a scribe who is freed from forced labour and protected from all (manual) work.'[40] Temple scribes and highly-skilled artisans may have held regular positions on an hereditary basis in particular community and hierocratic organisations which had some measure of operational independence.

In traditional societies, élites tended to be urban in character.[41] In urban centres they were usually safer in times of social disturbance than in the less well protected rural areas. Certainly intellectuals gravitated towards the larger cities. This was particularly the case in the later Mediterranean world – especially in Greece and Asia Minor. Urban living provided the necessary contacts with the few academic communities. But for the ruling élites, the cities were the centres of control. Here they could best ensure a grip on the key administrative organisations, and in maintaining their positions, enhance their own self-image as a privileged group. This general picture, however, must be qualified to some extent in relation to Ancient Egypt. The centres of control were not always urban in the commonly accepted sense, but were often concentrated on temple complexes which operated as semi-autonomous economic communities.

The temple organisations comprising cultic centres and their adjacent estates were often endowed with enormous wealth, mainly for the upkeep of the attendant priesthoods and the maintenance and extension of the complexes themselves. Because of its variations, it is probably unwise to generalise unilaterally about the role of the priestly class, but it was possibly 'the most variable feature of importance in agrarian societies'.[42] In Egyptian society, however, it can probably be seen as a relatively *in*variable feature of importance.

Ideology appears to have been one of the primary stimuli behind the Egyptian economy. For example, we learn that Ramesses III, the founder of the Twentieth Dynasty, who probably ranked among the more generous benefactors of the priestly class, gave vast riches to the temples.[43] The record shows that his gifts to the gods and their servants included 169 towns, 113,433 slaves, 493,386 cattle, 1,071,780 plots of land; and – among other things – 2,756 images of the gods containing 1,400 pounds of gold and 2,200 pounds of silver.

The customary bases of mobility must therefore be modified in respect of Egyptian society. Age – a common criterion in many simple societies – though venerated, did not ensure upward mobility within the system. Wealth too was also open to qualifications. In what was, in effect, a state economy with minimal entrepreneurial activity, wealth – in relative terms – was held mainly by state and temple officials. The emergence of a merchant or capitalist class was, therefore, severely inhibited if not actually impossible. Even the work of the professional class of artisans was harnessed primarily to the needs of the state. Merit, on the other hand, whether military or administrative, certainly had its rewards. And what in general terms might be called charismatic merit – the prerogative of the ritual functionaries – could also pay high dividends.

The lowest order in traditional systems was, of course, the slaves. M. I. Finley is probably right when he asserts that, 'The pre-Greek world – the world of the Sumerians, Babylonians, Egyptians, and Assyrians . . . was, in a very profound sense, a world without free men.'[44] Possibly in all traditional systems, therefore, there was no such thing as freedom as we have come to understand it, merely varying degrees of unfreedom. But in many pre-industrial societies, as in Ancient Greece, the legal and – less commonly – the occupational distinctions between the slave and the peasant were reasonably clear whereas, in Egyptian society, the line was sometimes blurred. The work of the peasant was often indistinguishable from that of the slave; the landed estates owned slaves and employed serfs for similar kinds of work. But by the time of the New Kingdom, quite separate terms had come to be used to differentiate between the slave and the servant (literally, listeners or followers).

The slave was usually a foreign captive, often from Nubia or Libya, or sometimes Syria and Canaan. In fact, it has been argued that during the Old Kingdom period, there were no slaves other than prisoners-of-war; this is partly inferred from the fact that in the building of the pyramids, the annual corvée of the peasantry was probably sufficient for the task on hand.[45] The actual occupations of slaves could vary enormously. They could be employed as they were in the fifteenth century BC for example, mining copper and turquoise in the Sinai in reasonably harsh conditions.[46] Yet in reviewing again the exploits of the king Amenophis II, we find that in the seventh year of his reign, his campaign captives included 270 women 'the favourites (or musicians?) of every foreign country . . . in addition to their paraphernalia for entertaining the heart . . .'[47] These ladies, who might technically be regarded as slaves, were presumably destined for the royal harem as both concubines and entertainers. We also find that the general growth in the slave population and the demands of the developing expansionist policy of the Empire put such strains upon the system that the army considered the possibility of using slave troops.[48]

Slaves could be owned by the state, by temple priesthoods or by private individuals. They could be sold, bequeathed or hired, and the state required that all slaves had to be duly registered after purchase. A papyrus published in the 1930s sheds some light on the process.[49] It shows that when a young female slave was purchased by barter from Syria, oaths were exchanged in the presence of witnesses and the contract was registered with a tribunal. This compares with the careful legal transactions which were recorded in relation to the rights of slaves and owners in Mesopotamia where the private ownership of slaves was on a comparatively small scale.[50]

Rights of slaves do not appear to have followed a particularly consistent pattern. They could be severely treated, especially if they were runaways,[51] but this may have been relatively rare. For the same offence, in Mesopotamia, branding and mutilation were not uncommon penalties. This punished the recalcitrant slave without actually impairing his economic efficiency, and was a favourite practice of the Assyrians.[52] On the other hand, Egyptian slaves had certain legal rights. They could own property and land and this is evidenced by an extant tax-assessor's scroll which includes slaves with priests, soldiers, etc., who were all under the general oversight of a high civil or religious administrator.[53] Slaves were even allowed to marry free-born women, and could be emancipated by an official act.[54] This again compares with Mesopotamian practices whereby slaves could be articled as craft apprentices,[55] and could also be manumitted or adopted by their masters, although there are no known laws to protect the slave from maltreatment by their masters.[56]

Traditional societies did not seriously question the morality of slavery, it was very much an accepted institution. In as much as people needed to rationalise such practices, justifications were made either in terms of economic necessity or in terms of the natural inferiority of the slave himself. In Egypt, the scribes referred to slaves as being 'without heart', that is to say, 'without understanding' and therefore insisted that they had to be driven with a stick like cattle.[57] There was really no reason for Egyptian society to reflect on the ethical implications of slavery or even on the aesthetic niceties of the slave's condition. It was a taken-for-granted institution common to their contemporaries in the ancient world. Slavery was feared as the potential plight of any citizen. It was certainly the accepted fate of the captive,[58] either by war or piracy, and often the debtor as well.[59] The morality of the situation was not even an academic question. Slavery was merely the last rung on the social ladder; for the individual concerned, chattel slavery was the ultimate in non-status.

Turning from specific ranking systems to the more general forms of differentiation, it is necessary to look at the social position of women in Ancient Egypt.

In Egyptian society, women appear to have enjoyed a similar status to men, although writers are not entirely agreed on this point.[60] Few definitive statements are possible because so much has to be inferred from inadequate and perhaps ambiguous sources. It needs to be reiterated that cosy homilies about married life[61] and idyllic feasting scenes in the wall-paintings which seem to show women enjoying equal status with men,[62] may not really depict the social situation 'as it was' for women of all strata. They may, in fact, be well-meaning but distorted reflections of social actuality. This raises – at least as a passing parenthetical thought – the extent to which the art of any society, ancient or contemporary, represents the normative or substantive patterns of behaviour and belief.

What can be said with some certainty is that Egypt was a matrilineal society. 'The ancestors are always traced farther back in the female line than the male line. The father was only the holder of the office, the mother was the family link . . . [also] in respect of property; that goes through . . . the mistress of the house; we never find a . . . master of the house.'[63] All landed property apparently descended in the female line from mother to daughter. If a man married an heiress, he enjoyed her property only as long as his wife lived. On his death, it passed to her daughter or her daughter's husband. This had very important implications for the matter of royal succession, and may be related to the question of why Pharaohs sometimes married their sisters and even their daughters.

> The marriage laws of Ancient Egypt were never formulated and knowledge of them can be obtained only by working out the marriages and genealogies. It becomes evident that a Pharaoh safeguarded himself from abdication by marrying every heiress without any regard to consanguinity, so that if the chief heiress died, he was already married to the next in succession and thus retained the sovereignty . . . the throne went strictly in the female line. The great wife of the king was the heiress; by right of her the king came to the throne . . . [his] birth was not important. He might be of any rank, but if he married the queen, he became king. The queen was queen by right of birth, the king by right of marriage.[64]

It seems that a prince could never become Pharaoh simply by being his father's son; he had to be his wife's husband. The woman conferred kingship. When the Eighteenth Dynasty Pharaoh Tutankhamun died, his young widow Ankhesenamun wrote to the Hittite king saying, 'My husband is dead and I have no son. Send me one of your sons and he will be my husband and lord of the land of Egypt.' Tutankhamun had also become king by marrying the 'daughter of the god.'[65] A man of little rank and obscure birth could become king. This is illustrated by the career of Heri-Hor who rose from a modest military rank to become Viceroy of Nubia and Commander of the Army to military dictator and Pharaoh in the Post-Empire period c. 1090 BC.

But there are qualifications of unambiguous matriliny. John A. Wilson, one of the foremost modern authorities,[66] agrees that the legitimacy of rule was conditioned by the royal descent of the mother and of the father, and that according to the rather tortuous theology of succession, the first wife was both the daughter and the consort of the god. He feels that this contributes to the 'strong matriarchal trend in the theory of royal succession in Egypt' and adds that this 'was the reason for brother-sister marriages by some of the Pharaohs'.[67] But he also stresses that the position of women is 'not very clear'. Women appear to be chattels *and* channels of transmission: queens certainly enjoy considerable esteem, but '[slave women] and concubines had no legal status and could be dismissed at will'.[68]

Marriage contracts which have survived seem to show that women's rights were respected. A late contract dating from *c.* 580 BC – which in substance may be based on earlier contracts – records a prospective husband taking an oath that if he leaves his wife 'either from dislike, or preferring another', he will return the dowry and a share of all paternal and maternal property for the children which she may bear.[69] There is no evidence that marriage was indissoluble, and divorce may have been relatively simple for both parties.[70]

Among the very few professions which were open to women, mourning, dancing, midwifery and the priesthood appear to have been the most common. But inevitably, the account is very incomplete since 'it is only the wives and daughters of the well-to-do [who] have left us their portraits'.[71] There is some evidence for prostitution as a practice, although the sources are meagre. The Doulaq Papyrus (*c.* 1400 BC) translated by Flinders Petrie tells of the infatuation of Setna, a prince about whom there are a number of legends, for Tbutui who appears to have been a prostitute in the service of the temple of Bastit which was dedicated to the Egyptian cat-goddess.[72] But temple prostitution does not appear to have been as highly institutionalised as it was in, say, Mesopotamia.

The overall picture which emerges is neither clear not consistent. What can be discerned are impressions of the ubiquitous residues of ancient social life. The position of women, at the lower levels, was presumably not very dissimilar from that of women in other traditional societies. Life was hard, insecure and not over-long. Where the matrilineal principle obtained, women had the power to transmit, but only rarely the power to control. At the upper levels, the situation – certainly in Egyptian society – is much more clearly defined. It is one of privilege and esteem, and – in the case of queens – was bound up with a form of bio-theological rationale.

Any analysis of the ranking systems of ancient Egypt must be vitiated by the problem of change within a 'changeless' tradition.[73] Theoretically, there was no rigid caste system in which all were contained despite the changing generations. There was a status

109

continuum which extended from the gods to men and even to animals and inorganic objects. The society demanded talented artisans and administrators, therefore there had to be a qualified mobility within the system.

There is a paucity of information concerning the class divisions in the Old Kingdom, although the main divisions became crystallised at a very early period. We may generally hypothesise, however, that this was closely linked with religious ideology. 'The future life of each class of society was treated as an advance over this life.' This extended through all grades within the system. 'Thus the hope of eternal life would be an advance within one's own rank.'[74] By the time of the New Kingdom, these divisions had, paradoxically, both widened and become less well defined. Increased wealth brought a realignment of the divisions and the introduction of new professional groups. These constituted an intermediate status category which enhanced the old distinctions between master and peasant. At the same time, the occupational distinctions between peasants and slaves possibly narrowed to the extent that many slaves were better placed than their legally 'free' counterparts.

The growing numbers of interest groups and increasing socio-economic differentiation meant inevitably that a greater degree of flexibility evolved within Egyptian society. This process was accentuated by the increasingly relaxed attitude to foreigners and resident aliens. The once monolithic system began to feel the strain of containing competing autonomoi – a pluralism of independent and semi-independent social groups which challenged the total nature of the traditional autocracy. External pressures began to mount, and the adaptive internal structures were ultimately unable to withstand them. Social differentiation and fragmentation are sometimes welcomed as the precursors of change and liberalisation; they may also be tell-tale tumours of societal mortality.

### Athens

In the structure of Homeric society,[75] the key distinction was between the aristoi or land-owning aristocracy and their dependants in a type of proto-feudal organisation where status was largely based on wealth and military prestige. These were the salient dimensions which determined the gradations of dependency. All were more or less bound directly or indirectly to local lords. Some served as retainers in the households (oikoi) of the aristocracy whilst other worked in a serf-like capacity in their fields. These early communities also included slaves and property-less workers (thetes) who were sometimes hired by the households, and freemen who were mainly herders and craftsmen.[76]

110

The expression 'household' is really inadequate as a translation of oikos because the Greek term can connote a grouping which is both larger and more complex than the simple household of modern Western society. It would consist of all the members of the lord's family, including his sons (until his death), general retainers, hired servants and slaves. 'It is likely that, at least during certain periods, the ties of common membership in an oikos transcended even communal commitments. It was the basic social and economic unit in early Greek society',[77] which ultimately gave way to the more inclusive demands of polis organisation.

By the early seventh century BC, there was a growing shortage of agricultural land in Attica, the area controlled by Athens. This, it is argued,[78] intensified the conflict between the classes and increased the power of the eupatridai – the 'well-born' landed aristocracy. They were able to squeeze many of the small farmers out of business by the imposition of high-interest loans which the independent growers could only repay by forfeiting their personal security, and sometimes that of their families, and 'share-cropping' for the big landowners. This assimilation of the formerly independent holdings and the social injustices which attended virtually untrammelled aristocratic control,[79] eventually precipitated the reforms of Solon at the beginning of the sixth century BC. These were designed to 'advance the community idea . . . by protecting the weaker majority from the excessive . . . extra-legal power of the nobility'.[80]

Solon established a system of four classes of citizens based on income from property. These were categories of 500, 300, 200 and under 200 bushels, depending on crop returns. Only members of the first two classes were admitted to high public office,[81] and members of the lowest class were excluded from any public office though admitted to the Assembly and the courts. In effect, Solon abolished the birth qualification and introduced a property qualification; this increased the numbers of citizens eligible for public office. The first three classes constituted about 40 per cent of the citizen body, but during the fifth century BC when the total number of citizens grew from about 40,000 to about 50,000 this proportion increased to an estimated 50 per cent.[82]

Although the Solonic reforms laid the groundwork for a new conception of community, they also had – perhaps unwitting – divisive effects. Alvin Gouldner argues that the reforms helped to bridge the status incongruences that had developed by providing a system that enabled men whose income and class positions were improving to have a correspondingly large share in political powers and honours and that this, in turn, strengthened their loyalties to the community and made their energies and resources more willingly available.[83] But they also gave, as never before, institutional

111

articulation to the true class divisions in Athenian society. The old ascription-based status distinctions of the nobility began to give way to the achievement-orientations of the wealthy. They favoured the intermediate categories, the upwardly mobile and the politically ambitious. The extremes of the stratificatory spectrum, the nobility and the poor, remained permanently discontented. Social cleavage crystallised around property considerations; class-consciousness, in the strict economic sense, became a reality.

It is extremely difficult to analyse the structure of Athenian society during the Classical period without anticipating yet further analyses of the political and economic spheres. The simple division of the society into citizens and non-citizens involves political considerations in as much as 'citizen' for the Greeks was essentially a political term. On the other hand, if emphasis is – perhaps rightly – given to the saliency of wealth and property, the economic dimension has been invoked. In short, differentiation in Athenian society involves a number of possible dichotomies. The aristoi and the demos (i.e. the mass of ordinary citizens whether urban or rural); the citizens and the non-citizens (metoikoi) who were without political affiliation; and – what is by no means the same thing – the free and the unfree. In a further rather special category comes also a valid distinction between male and female, because, in one sense, the free Athenian woman was a non-citizen. She was without direct political representation, yet her status was quite different from that of the metic and very different from that of the slave, both of whom were types of non-citizen.

Perhaps the least confusing categorisation of strata in fifth-century BC Athens would be:

|  |  |  |
|---|---|---|
| free | citizens | (a) four classes of males encompassing the aristocracy to the free proletariat |
| unfree | non-citizens | (b) women and children<br>(c) resident foreigners (metics)<br>(d) slaves |

This categorisation really needs a number of qualifications. For instance, it should be stressed that aristocratic women and children– despite their relative wealth – were just as politically *un*represented as those of the 'people'. It also begs the question of exactly what is meant by 'free' and 'unfree'. Some of these issues, at least, should be elucidated in the ensuing discussion.

Gouldner too points out that any analysis of stratification in Classical Greece must take account of a number of dimensions, and he particularly identifies four main issues:[84]

112

(i) Whether or not persons derived their income from owner-ship, operation, or investment in landed properties or from mercantile or manufacturing properties.

(ii) The differences between citizens and foreigners.

(iii) The distinction between residence and landholding in urban and rural areas.

(iv) The distinction between the free and the slaves.

All these issues should be noted, but with some reservations. Points (i) and (iii) have marked economic orientations, and it is arguable that these have a limited applicability in the context of Athenian society.[85] It can be disputed whether considerations of professional and educational status weighed very heavily in a society where it was possible for slaves to hold responsible positions. 'Most bank managers were slaves, as were clerks in public audit departments. Many were shopkeepers, craftsmen and business agents.'[86] It can also be contested whether even the desirability of wealth was a social sine qua non in a community where resident non-citizens (metics) were in the forefront of entrepreneurial activity.[87] The Athenian value-system was undoubtedly conscious of wealth and its growing importance. In the city there were some hundreds of families of outstanding wealth.[88] But its humanistic emphasis on honour and the quality of life cannot be fully appreciated in materialistic terms.

The aristocracy were largely rentiers whose income derived either from their estates of which they were often absentee landlords, or from manufacturing or slave-hire,[89] or perhaps from some combination of these. They were therefore able to devote their time to learning or to political or military activity,[90] or – not infrequently – to nothing in particular. It was probably in the military sphere that the aristocracy operated with a measure of ease and confidence. It was here that 'the well-born, like the nobility of much later nations, felt at home and claimed the right to command'.[91]

The vast majority of citizens were either small farmers, craftsmen or tradesmen. Greece being primarily an agrarian society, the main attachment was to the soil, and possibly about three-quarters of the citizen families of Athens owned some landed property, although often barely enough for a livelihood. The extremes of wealth and poverty were probably to be found in the urban rather than the rural population.

The proportions of the population to be found in the main social categories is a matter of some dispute. Attica, the area – about the size of Bedfordshire – controlled by Athens (although all called themselves Athenians) is estimated by R. Flaceliere to have had a total population of about half a million of whom roughly two-fifths were 'free'. Included in this figure, he calculates that there were

113

about 40,000 citizens, 20,000 metics, and perhaps as many as 300,000 slaves.[92] H. D. Kitto, on the other hand, gives a much lower estimate: a total population of 350,000 of whom about 210,000 were 'free', including 20,000 citizens and 35,000 metics, leaving a slave population of about 140,000.[93] H. Bengtson[94] gives quite different figures. His view is that the population of Athens was between 105,000 and 120,000 whilst the total population including rural Attica was approximately 210,000–235,000; of these perhaps as many as 35,000 were citizens.[95] To add to the complexities, M. I. Finley advances yet further figures. He gives 250,000–275,000 as the total population, of whom perhaps 60,000–80,000 were slaves. Using army figures based on Thucydides, he calculates that in 431 BC, there might have been as many as 40,000–45,000 citizens.[96] Perhaps a third of these had hoplite status, that is, they enjoyed the – perhaps to us – doubtful privilege of being able to supply their own heavy armour and general accoutrements of war. This suggests that they belonged to that intermediate stratum of citizens which it is tempting, though possibly inaccurate, to dub middle class. However, it does give us, in the light of very inadequate and disputed statistics, some idea of the class distribution of Athenian society.

On any estimate, therefore, the citizens, i.e. the male voters, comprised only a fraction – perhaps as low as a tenth – of the total population. And from the uncertain inferences which can be made from the available sources, this was not out of keeping with the balance found in other Greek states. Within this enfranchised category, a certain flexibility obtained. Some mobility did exist for the lower orders of citizen; the mercantile means of advancement were beginning to operate in Classical times, but commerce was still hardly a prestigious pursuit. Wealth could buy a grudging recognition, but breeding was important; it was barely possible for the demos to aspire to the ranks of the aristocracy. Political and military merit were acceptable, but neither age nor cultic pretensions – which only involved a very narrow range of professional practitioners – really conferred any particular advantages. Even service with the military reflected the prevailing ranking system. In very general terms, the higher and intermediate orders served with the army, whilst the navy – though commanded by the nobility – recruited, especially as rowers, large numbers of metics and slaves.

However, it should be added in fairness to the Athenian system that, in practice, there was a great deal of necessary co-operation and fraternisation between the lower strata. On public works, slaves, metics and poor citizens might be employed under similar conditions. There is the well-known example of the building of the Erechtheion in 408–404 BC. Of the 71 men engaged in the work, 16 were slaves, 35 were metics, and 20 were citizens.[97] Downward mobility, on the other hand, was also a feature not so much of the occupational structure as the status hierarchy of Athenian society. Under certain circumstances, for example a successful prosecution under the anti-pederasty laws,[98] it was possible for a citizen to lose his citizenship rights (atimia) for a specified period.

Any consideration of the Athenian non-citizen must first of all take account of that rather anomalous category, the metics. These resident foreigners were probably mostly Greek by birth and had migrated to Athens for a variety of reasons; the relative security of a large and powerful state, and the opportunities of an expanding economy.

As we have seen, they constituted an appreciable proportion of the total Athenian population during the Classical period. They were liable to most of the ordinary citizens' financial obligations, particularly the leitourgiai, i.e. the public service and festival expenses, besides a small special tax which was peculiar to their class. The metics had educational disadvantages: although permitted to exercise in the gymnasia (which were barred to slaves) they were excluded from ephebic training, the stage of education for the more privileged Athenian males between sixteen and eighteen years. Marriages between metics and citizens were probably sanctioned by law[99] although after 451 BC the children of such marriages did not qualify for citizenship. Metics could acquire household chattels and own slaves, but were only exceptionally allowed to buy houses, for which they needed special permission. Their rights to their possessions, however, were upheld by law.

Pericles, in comparing Athens with some other cities, eulogised on the liberal nature of Athenian society and institutions. 'Our city is open to all men: we have no law that requires the expulsion of the stranger in our midst, or debars him from such endeavour or entertainment as he may find among us.'[100] But legally, the metic had to be represented in court by a citizen who acted as his patron, and could even be put to the torture – although this may have been seldom enforced. The differential social value of the metic is also evidenced by the fact that the murderer of a metic could not be executed – only exiled – although this was the statutory punishment for the murder of a citizen.

Metics had relative freedom as far as religion was concerned, and could even import and celebrate their own native cults, some of which found adherents among citizens themselves.[101] This liberty extended to special places at specifically Athenian festivals, such as the Panathenaic games.

Although the metic population was distributed throughout the administrative districts (demes), they possessed no political rights, and were allocated purely subordinate tasks. The spheres in which

115

they flourished were those of manufacture and trade. They had considerable liberty to develop their commercial interests, particularly banking and importing, and many of them became prosperous additions to the community. They had virtual monopoly of the metal-working trades, were prominent in weaving, tanning and pottery-making; and one of them, Chaerephilus, owned the largest salt-curing business in Athens.

It is highly probable, therefore, that metics were treated as well if not better in Athens than in any other states. They had the liberty to advance their own economic interests, but this must be balanced against the fact that political ambition was denied them. They had no power to change their own political situation. In commerce and trading they were retained because they were useful. In religion, there were virtually no restrictions, perhaps because the cults were only of marginal practical concern in the humanistic ethos of Athenian society.

In Athens, it seems to have been an inviolable rule that citizenship was absolutely sacrosanct. Any breach could be treated with considerable severity – and this even applied to metics who were valuable members of the trading community. In 445 BC, there was a particular occasion – almost a cause célèbre – which highlights the citizens' response to presumptions of status. During the distribution of a special gift of grain imported from Egypt, it was discovered that a number of metics were posing as citizens. The disclosure must have precipitated something of a purge, and eventually a large body of metics – the number is given as a round 5,000 – were struck off the city's register and sold into slavery.[102] This affair raises several problems of interpretation. It is obvious that metics *wanted* to be citizens, at least for simple grain allocation reasons. But it is not certain if their imposture extended beyond the issue of rationing. If it did, how could so many have maintained this pretence in such a relatively small community without being discovered sooner? It is possible to draw the inference – perhaps quite wrongly – that despite the norms of citizenship, a 'blind-eye' situation had developed and had been allowed to continue until this particularly crucial economic issue had arisen. This threatened the privileges of citizenship and called forth the legally appropriate response. There is no evidence to suggest that this was any more than an isolated occasion, and it was certainly not part of a continuing policy of metic-oppression in any way analogous to the Spartan treatment of their helots.

At the lowest level of Athenian society were the slaves. Initially, this sounds like a statement of the obvious. But any analysis of Greek slavery will show that it is not as obvious as it appears, as there were gradations even within the slave category. These should be seen mainly in occupational terms, but they also necessarily involve questions of differential rights. Whatever the legal niceties, the de facto rights of a household slave or an unfree artisan were quite different from those of the chattel slave working in the mines.

M. I. Finley[103] shows that in Greece as a whole there were many shades of dependence within the status spectrum ranging from freeman to slave. These are exemplified by the types of servitude found in various kinds of Greek state. The oikeus (literally 'household servant') of Crete was actually nearer to what we understand as a serf. He was someone who was bound to the land by ties of obligation to a local lord, and had limited, but increasingly well-defined rights. The Gortyn Code c. 450 BC[104] which probably contains elements of earlier material, shows that Cretan slaves were liberally treated. They could be bought and sold, but they were allowed to own some property, and certain safeguards were operative in relation to their children.[105] By comparison, the helot of Sparta was not a slave by either purchase or capture in the normal sense, but a member of a subjugated people, those who had occupied Lacedaemonia when it was conquered by the Dorian Spartans in the eleventh century.[106] The Spartan ephorate gave their own people power of life and death over the helots, and there is evidence to show that periodic murder of helots was sometimes allowed, although this may only have been encouraged, according to Aristotle, as part of the young warriors' training.[107] Plutarch informs us[108] that the helots acted as serfs for the Spartans to whom they gave a share of their produce. There seems to be little doubt that the Spartiates, who were very much a powerful minority, feared possible uprisings among the helots, and not without cause; there had been a serious revolt of the helots in 464 BC which took five years to quell. Thucydides reports[109] that during the Peloponnesian War, some 2,000 helots were recruited for the Spartan army and quietly and peremptorily massacred by their masters as a precaution against incipient revolt. Yet helots were recruited in equal numbers with Spartans for overseas army service.[110]

The debt bondsman can also be classed with the unfree, although he was not a slave in the strict sense, but a person who could be eventually sold into slavery because he was unable to repay his debts. When this happened, it was common to sell the person abroad; certainly from the fourth century BC onwards, Greeks became increasingly reluctant to hold other Greeks as slaves. The 'opposite' of the debt-bondsman was the conditionally manumitted slave, that is a slave given conditional freedom by either deed or payment. At the extreme of the ranking order is the slave proper, the chattel-slave who had little or no hope of freedom.

All these types or categories were rarely, if ever, found in the same community. Generally speaking, debt-bondage and helotage were found in the more archaic Greek communities such as Crete, Sparta and Thessaly. Whilst slavery, per se, was more normally found in the politically and economically advanced societies such as Corinth and Athens. For example, Periander, tyrant of Corinth *c.* 600 BC, sent 300 youths from the Corinthian colony at Corcyra to Sardis where they were to be castrated and serve as eunuchs.[111] There were relatively few slaves, as such, engaged in agriculture; certainly there were no extensive slave-estates such as the later latifundia organised by the Romans. Most were involved in trade and manufacture, in household duties in the larger urban centres, and – most notoriously – in the silver mines at Laurium, near Athens.

The numbers of the slave populations of particular poleis are difficult to estimate, it is only possible to infer something of the dimensions of slavery from figures which are given in occasional references. It is almost certainly correct to assume that the majority of most slave populations were women and children. Men, trained at arms, were often difficult to keep enslaved under certain circumstances, so they were executed by their conquerors. A fairly typical example would be that of Thebes which attacked Plataea in 427 BC and, following the common practice in inter-poleis warfare, massacred 200 men and enslaved the women and children. The principal exceptions to this practice occurred where men had special and much-needed skills, or particularly where able-bodied males were required for heavy duties in mining and quarrying. During the campaign in Sicily, for instance, in 415–413 BC, after the rout of the Athenians, about 7,000 prisoners were made to work in the quarries where many of them soon perished, and the remainder were sold into slavery.

The slave population of Athens is uncertain. It was probably about 80,000–100,000, that is perhaps one-third of the total population. Many – possibly most – of the people did not own slaves although, by the fourth century BC, those who paid a war-tax, i.e. owners of 6–7 acres, would probably have an oikeus or household servant. Domestic slavery appears to have been quite common, and even families who did not have slaves working in their fields might well have a servant in the house. There was limited agricultural slavery; some slaves acted as overseers on the estates of the absentee aristocracy, and others were hired as casual labour during the harvest periods.

Slaves were relatively rare in the liberal professions – these were the particular province of the metics. But they worked as clerks and tutors, and even prison attendants and police, though not normally allowed to perform military duties – these were the privilege of free citizens.

Slaves were common in the manufacturing industries where they worked alongside freemen, but the worst excesses were probably to be seen in the mining industry. The silver mines at Laurium were being developed from *c*. 483 BC, and labour there was reserved for the 'lower class slave' or unwanted captured males. Silver had an international market, and by *c*. 427 BC under the impetus of the Peloponnesian War, the mines probably employed between 20,000 and 30,000 slaves – perhaps a quarter of the total slave population. They laboured there under the most primitive conditions. Only slaves worked underground; they were branded and chained, and worked day and night shifts in the 2,000 or so tiny shafts. It is hardly surprising that during the siege of Athens in 413 BC perhaps as many as 20,000 of them took advantage of the situation and deserted to the Spartans.

Some Delphic inscriptions indicate the slave's legal position; these can be summarised as follows:

(i) He was a non-citizen. He could not go where he pleased or live where he wished; he could not determine his polis or his affiliations. In having no political identity, he was virtually a non-person. He had, therefore, no independence. His will was that of his master, whose permission had to be sought for any activity.

(ii) In legal actions, he had to be represented by his owner or some other legally empowered person.

(iii) He was technically a chattel, and as such was subject to seizure as property, against which he had little, if any, recourse.

There were some compensations. To some extent, the slave was protected from undue violence. He was normally exempted from military service and therefore war duties. It was strictly illegal to strike a slave in Athens, although it is doubtful if this stricture applied to the owner.[112] It was a Spartan jibe that in Athens it was impossible from appearance to tell a slave from a citizen. This 'liberty' was extended to the practice of allowing slaves to buy their freedom, although the price for manumission was predictably in excess of the original purchase price – not surprising in those inflationary times. This was a great incentive for slaves who enjoyed the privilege of modest earnings. Some of these were actually able to form small security schemes (eranoi) which could make loans to fellow slaves – a rather novel feature of Athenian slavery. Although such rights were granted perhaps to the majority of Athenian slaves, it can be certain that the lower class slaves were virtually untouched by them. Those who toiled unremittingly and died prematurely in the silver mines would have known little of these benefits of Athenian social organisation.

Slavery was an accepted feature of the ancient world. When slaves were plentiful, and supply exceeded demand, life was very cheap, and the privations of the slave were at their worst. This was usually during expansionist phases when the market was glutted with captives. But during periods of consolidation, and especially retrenchment, the breeding of slaves might even be encouraged where supply could not keep pace with demand. In these circumstances, the lot of the slave might actually improve. This can be seen very clearly from the example of Roman slavery. Considerable changes took place between the first century BC the expansionist slave-estate period, and the second century AD when Rome was beginning to feel alien pressures on her frontiers.[113] Changes in slave conditions need not necessarily be seen in terms of compassion or morality – although kind masters obviously existed – but rather in terms of economic necessity. Whether or not slavery was the basis of the Athenian economy is still debated by scholars, and will be considered in the discussion on economic organisation (Chapter 9). But that it was a necessary factor – if not a sufficient factor – in the Athenian achievement is undeniable.

M. I. Finley has argued,[114] in answer to Marxist interpretations of Greek history,[115] that with a virtually unrestrained demos there was nothing approaching a working-class consciousness or class agitation. Marxists are inclined to take an 'interest' view of ideology – particularly the ideology of the dominant classes – and therefore tend to regard slavery simply as a contrivance for oppression. But far from being an exploitative institution devised by an unscrupulous aristocracy, the evidence shows that it was very much a given institution which was rarely questioned either by the intellectuals, reformers, or by the people themselves. Even slave revolts may not indicate any more than that the victims of slavery wanted to be free, *not* that they wanted to abolish the institution of slavery.[116] In fact, if revolution is defined as a violent attempt by one section of the state to effect social change, perhaps there were no slave revolts in Greece. This tends to support Parsons's view that there is an integrative consensus on values in society;[117] people share the same value-system, it's just that some – in this case the slaves – do not happen to like their allocated roles.

The question of class war presents similar problems – and perhaps admits of a similar analysis. There did occur in Greece what are described as Class Wars.[118] The incidents at Corcyra in the early phase of the Peloponnesian War (precisely between 427 and 425 BC) recorded by Thucydides could fall into this category. The Corcyraean aristocracy and the demos, partly out of principle and partly out of political opportunism, took opposing sides in the conflict. The result was disastrous; massacre, mass suicide and the wholesale enslavement of many of the women.[119] But, if we interpret 'class war' to mean an attempt not simply to reform, but actually to restructure society, the term may again be inapplicable. As in so many states, the desire was not to overthrow the existing system but merely to change the balance of power.

The position of Greek women, particularly upper-class women, has already been given some consideration (Chapter 7). In Homeric literature monogamy seems to be the rule and divorce is rarely mentioned. There appears to be little intensity indicated in men-women relationships.[120] This reflects the normative sexual mores of some warrior societies, and can be seen very clearly in the later military aristocracies of Thebes and Sparta.[121] Women were often held as captives and served as slaves, but the men were customarily slain. Sometimes they were elevated to the position of concubine which implies some regularisation of the sexual role. On this issue, Gouldner observes that 'while Greek homosexuality excludes the male slave, Greek heterosexuality includes the female slave ... low or slave status need not disqualify a woman as a bed-mate'.[122]

Although women in the *Iliad* and the *Odyssey* are obviously inferior to men, the poems do contain some enigmatic material. For example, would Penelope's marriage to one of the persistent suitors have conferred noble status on him as husband of a queen?[123] Was Helen desired for her fabled beauty or for her inherent transmission rights? And do both these problems indicate a vestigial matriarchalism in archaic times?

During the Classical period, the position of women in Athens is rather ambiguous. To begin with, most of our information concerns the womenfolk of citizens who were, by and large, the wealthier and more influential members of the community. Much has been inferred from limited available sources, namely, the dialogues of Plato, some histories, literature and plays in particular, and – to a lesser extent – pictorial art and inscriptions.

What we do know is that women were not enfranchised. They could not vote or hold political office; in fact, they were not even allowed to attend the Assembly. They had to occupy separate blocks of seats at the plays – normally at the back of the amphitheatre, and although they took a very full part in numerous religious festivals and had their own cults (see Chapter 12), married women were not allowed to attend the Olympic celebrations. They were permitted to carry on a limited trade, and could own property in a restricted sense.[124] They were always regarded as wards of a male guardian or relative, usually a parent or husband, and if a woman was divorced the dowry was returned not to her but to the guardian. The nearest male relative was entitled to marry an heiress (uncle-niece, and half-brother-half-sister unions were permitted) even if it meant having to divorce his own wife to do so. Adultery in Athens simply meant the union of a *married woman* and a man who was not

121

her husband. This was an offence against her husband – as rape or seduction were offences against the guardian. A married *man's* indiscretions were barely recognised.

This situation compares interestingly with Sparta, traditionally regarded as a more repressive society, where women appear to have enjoyed greater freedom and more equality. The fact that Spartan women exercised naked, often with men, was something of a byword among even the liberal Athenians[125] and was taken as one indication of their brashness and relative independence.[126] They married comparatively late, perhaps between eighteen and twenty,[127] but this could be an indirect consequence of the institutionalised pederasty which characterised the barrack lives of Spartan youths. The woman's primary task seems to have been to bear healthy sons for the state. The Spartan marriage ceremony involved no feast, but consisted of a mock abduction of the bride who cut her hair short and dressed as a man for the occasion. After marriage, the men continued to live in army quarters with their comrades, and visited their wives apparently by stealth and usually at night. Any children from these unions became the property of the state.[128]

Perhaps the Athenian practices were not so essentially different. The men appear not to have found their main companionship in the home, but in the company of comrades-in-arms (hetairoi), possibly in an age-set 'dining-club' (hetaireia) or in the arms of courtesans (hetairai) – an accepted and legitimate exercise.[129] The etymological connections are hardly accidental,[130] they express the sentiments and indicate the situational satisfactions of the Athenian male, as far as we know them.[131]

The ambiguous nature of our 'knowledge' of the woman's role in Classical Athens derives mainly from certain inferential correctives which may be applied to our interpretations.[132] One of the indices of relaxed attitudes towards women must surely be procedural mutuality in relation to divorce. Athenian women could institute divorce proceedings as well as men. In fact, the woman's parents might bring a case if there was no issue from the marriage. Such a move cast unfortunate doubts on the husband's capacity to produce children – an interesting situation in patriarchal societies where the failure to produce children was not uncommonly imputed to the wife's barrenness.[133] It follows too from the relative freedom of the hetairai that not all Athenian women were so repressed. Brothels enjoyed state patronage, certainly from the days of Solon; the porne or common prostitute was a readily available commodity – for a modest sum – for the general citizenry.[134] Prostitution was sometimes closely connected with religion. Strabo reported (VIII. 378) that Corinth had 1,000 sacred prostitutes who were also priestesses of the temple of Aphrodite. It was in fact they who offered up the sacrifices during the threatened Persian invasion. By comparison, the more expensive hetairai were virtually an upper-class institution. The texts and vase-paintings indicate[135] that their versatile charms were reserved primarily for the relaxation of tired orators and the leisured aristoi[136] and many of them became famous in Athens as the mistresses of eminent men.[137] Citizens' wives, by contrast, were supposed to live circumscribed lives which were assumed to be above reproach,[138] but what, for instance, did women make of the licentious Old Comedy which presumably they attended? Aristophanes' plays, for example, show a scant respect for that virtuous modesty (sophrosyne) which was regarded as a prime requirement for the well-bred Athenian woman.[139]

A nescient situation exists as far as the lower orders are concerned. So little is really known, and 'arguments from silence' are notoriously suspect. There is very little evidence of the daily lives of slaves – male or female – in any ancient societies. They were not the subjects of much concern, but some reasonable assumptions about them can be made, even if they do lack the desired detail. Little too is known about women of the lower strata, it may be – as M. I. Finley argues[140] – that poverty which gave less leisure to males gave females a greater measure of independence. The literature suggests that family life was essentially little different from our own. Vase-paintings depict homely scenes, and epitaphs often indicate a simple devotion within the family unit, binding both partners and children. Although virtually silent on the question of slavery, the intellectuals were sometimes more intrepid on the issue of women's rights; Socrates/Plato in the dialogues (particularly in *The Republic*) and especially the playwright Euripides in the *Medea*.[141] It may be significant though that the women of Greek literature, both real and legendary, Helen, Clytemnestra, Cassandra, Penelope, Phaedra, Sappho, Aspasia, etc., although figures of consequence, are also almost invariably seen as figures, and even occasions, of tragedy.

## Summary

<table>
<tr><td>

*Egypt*

1 Hierarchical and occupational gradings. Division between free and unfree. Mobility *within* classes. Limited meritocratic system between classes for literati, priests and military.

</td><td>

*Athens*

1 Property basis of class divisions. Some economic mobility. Divisions between: aristocracy and the people (demos); free and unfree citizen and non-citizen. Rotating political roles.

</td></tr>
</table>

2 Artisans mainly employed on state/temple projects.

2 Variety of occupational categories, but limited functional differentiation.

3 No emergent merchant class.

3 Emergent merchant class.

4 Slavery: Variety of occupational categories. Usually prisoners of war. Could be owned by state, temples or privately. No known clear codification of rights.

4 Slavery: Wide variety of occupational categories. Prisoners, debtors, slaves by purchase. All slaves privately owned – but sometimes leased to state. Clear legal status definitions.

5 Position of women: Similar rights to males. Some ambiguities. Matrilineal stress especially in property Some occupations, including religious functions.

5 Position of women: Unequal rights compared with males. Marked patrilineal stress, but some inconsistencies. Some occupations including institutional prostitution. Developed cultic functions.

6 New Kingdom toleration of non-citizens and foreigners.

6 Toleration of resident aliens (metics) who did not share political rights.

7 Ranking systems endorsed by religious sanctions.

7 Religious support of citizen-ship status which affected all other ranking issues.

# 9 Bases of economic organisation

Many early sociologists and economic historians proposed broad classifications of societies in economic terms. Bucher and Sombart were not significantly different in their approach from Marx who proposed a scheme consisting of five major types of society: Primitive society, Ancient society, Asiatic society, Feudal society and Capitalist society. These distinctions were not only made in terms of the level of technology and the mode of production, but also in terms of property and class relations.[1] Early in this century, there were attempts by Hobhouse, Wheeler and Ginsberg to refine this type of model by distinguishing a number of sub-types. They examined the different kinds of economic organisation of primitive societies, and tried to correlate these with their other social institutions.[2] More recently, the late Daryll Forde, in a comprehensive survey of simple societies, demonstrated that there was a wide variety of economic types when viewed from a socio-ecological perspective.[3] But much of the effort of sociologists since Marx has been concentrated on analyses of modern capitalism, its origins and its development,[4] and has largely ignored – or at least overlooked – the economic structures of traditional systems.[5]

Although the social consequences of economic growth, particularly of industrialisation and urbanisation, can be found in the writings of Adam Smith, Alfred Marshall and Theodore Veblen, the general development of formal economic theory has tended to exclude examinations of wider social variables. The rather simplistic notion entertained by fundamentalist Marxists that economic factors *determine* the forms of society has become modified by the notion that certain social and cultural forms may be necessary before economic growth can take place.[6] To reiterate the argument of Chapter 4, the economic order of society may itself be a function of the prevailing ideology.

125

There are, of course, exceptions to these general criticisms. Max Weber, despite his abiding preoccupation with the rise of capitalism in Europe, was attempting to demonstrate that ideology – in this case Calvinistic Protestantism – was an influential factor in a singular socio-economic order.[7] In Durkheim,[8] on the other hand, it is difficult to avoid the impression that his analysis of the social functions of labour in pre-industrial societies is merely a preamble to a treatment of industrial systems.

In the previous chapter, some effort was made to show that the bases of social stratification extend beyond the purely economic – if indeed such an unalloyed entity actually exists. But having established this point, it should not detract from the undoubted importance of economic factors in the makeup of historical societies especially in relation to their stratification systems. Any analysis must take account of 'who gets what, and how?'; the entire distributive process reflects the control structures of traditional systems. This is essentially the position taken by Gerhard Lenski.[9] For Lenski, privilege derives from having control of the surplus of goods and services in society, and this control, in turn, depends upon the power of the individual or group to be able to carry out their policies despite all possible opposition. It is Lenski's view that inequalities increase with the level of technology required to achieve the surplus. These, he maintains, reach their peak not in advanced technological societies, where large-scale production has an economically ameliorative effect, but in advanced agrarian societies,[10] that is the types of traditional society with which this study is primarily concerned.

This, of course, raises the rather subsidiary but necessary issue of what exactly is meant by an 'agrarian society'? Some scholars have argued for a careful differentiation between types of agrarian society, insisting that it is necessary to differentiate between 'simple' and 'advanced' stage agrarianism, the historical watershed being the first millennium BC. This is the view taken by Robert Bellah[11] who feels that the key developments were the great social and cultural inventions of that period, e.g. universal religions, alphabetic writing, bureaucracy, coinage etc. He argues for a breakdown into three sub-types of agrarian society, viz., city-states, bureaucratic empires and feudal regimes which cross cut the preliminary dichotomy between the 'simple' and 'advanced' types. In very general terms, this plea for the importance of careful distinctions would be supported by Talcott Parsons[12] and S. N. Eisenstadt,[13] and is obviously followed in the categorisations suggested in the present discussion. However, it is difficult seriously to disagree with Lenski's more generic approach when he insists that, 'When viewed in the perspective of *all* human societies, the similarities clearly outweigh the differences . . . (although) . . . this is not to deny the existence of internal variation or even the possibility that important sub-types exist.'[14]

Broadly speaking, agrarian societies do conform to a general pattern. They are usually very extensive, often based on conquest and characterised by severe internal and external pressures. They have monarchical tendencies and usually develop influential state religions. They are marked by increasing urbanism and a growing economic diversity and specialisation, which may be supported by a money system and high literacy – although special qualifications would have to be made in the case of Meso-American societies.

The general characteristics of complex pre-industrial societies are obviously very broad indeed, but the general characteristics of their economic systems can be delineated with reasonable accuracy. The directional influences too of these economic systems and their influence on power structures is not difficult to perceive, 'in pre-market societies, wealth tends to follow power, not until the market society will power tend to follow wealth'.[15] S. N. Eisenstadt shows in a study which is concentrated on Sassanid Persia, the Byzantine and Chinese Empires – with occasional glances elsewhere, particularly Spanish America and 'Absolutist Europe' – that 'the general characteristics of the economic systems of these societies are common to all of them'.[16] The most important difference factors to be noted in these areas which might well be applied to the analyses of other traditional societies were:

(i) the extent to which specific economic roles were differentiated;
(ii) the degree of development of specific units of production, exchange and consumption, in the major areas of the economy;
(iii) the relative importance of different types of exchange mechanisms.

Such conclusions bring into focus the underlying issue of how theorists see the relationships between economy and society and between economy and values. From which perspectives can these be most fruitfully examined? The tendency with economists such as Marshall was to see the term economy as somehow encompassing the whole of life. This involved the necessary assumption that all institutions have something to do with the acquisition or distribution of wealth.[17] This approach is rather limiting in that it makes any evaluation of the distinctive contributions of 'social' or 'economic' variables difficult to assess. But any strong reaction in the opposite direction tends instead to put undue stress on the formal 'separateness' of each, and this fails to give sufficient emphasis to the non-material forms of economic wealth. The more utilitarian

127

approach to wealth which emphasises its social usefulness, shifts the orientation towards the market and exchange as central features of an economy.[18] This can involve the distinctive and important factor of a money system. Money is a precise criterion, and will be a crucial variable in our analysis, but even here there must be some reservations in the context of pre-industrial systems where the distribution of rewards may have a social rather than an economic basis. The problem is simply that the utilitarian approach may overlook subjective considerations. Why any particular individual holds any particular commodity, object or activity to be useful may have nothing whatever to do with utility as it is customarily conceived, but may well be related – especially in traditional societies – to some aesthetic or religious value.

The relationship between systems of production, distribution and consumption may be held to delineate the specific spheres of economics.[19] This links with Parsons's view of the economy as an adaptive sub-system of society.[20] But in stressing production[21] rather than distribution (exchange), Parsons and Smelser appear to have some difficulty in making the economy a differentiated part of society, 'For it could be argued that all enduring social relations involve transactions which have an exchange aspect.'[22] The position taken by other theorists,[23] particularly in the context of pre-industrial societies, is that social and economic are not logically separable categories. Acts are neither economic nor non-economic. All acts have economic and social and cultural aspects. But not all acts can be seen as being manifestly rational. In categorising some social action as rational action, Max Weber was expressing a relationship of possible means to possible ends.[24] He was not suggesting that the ends themselves could be rationally chosen. Weber was well aware of the importance of other categories of social action, namely, affective or emotionally responsive action, and traditional or customary action which are particularly applicable to pre-industrial systems. Choices, whether ostensibly economic or otherwise, are determined by the traditional value-system of a society. How that value-system is itself determined may not admit of any final answers. Economic factors will almost certainly have played their part, but the evaluation of those choices or goals, however determined, may not be possible in terms of an economic theory which has been developed in modern, technological settings.[25]

Broadly speaking, then, it is possible to delineate the main features of traditional economic systems, although this must be done within the general framework of ideas which constitute at least part of what we now understand as economic theory. In any analysis, implicit notions of modern economic rationality are unavoidable.[26]

In *relative* terms, then we may identify the following characteristics:

(a) Limited technology. Superficially this may appear to be almost insulting in view of the incredible constructional achievements of many traditional societies. In fact, the opposite is the case. The wonder is that they achieved so much with so little. Even the pyramid and temple complexes of Egypt,[27] and the architectural marvels of Greece,[28] though the products of superlative engineering and artistic skills, were actually built with surprisingly little technology, as such. The block and tackle, the ramp and the plumb-line, are hardly machine technology, as we understand it. The traditional society was largely sustained by animate sources of energy; part of the achievement, therefore, lay in the ability to harness and control the necessary reserves of human effort. This relates particularly to public works which were commissioned either by the state or by religious organisations – which in many societies were substantially the same thing – and accomplished by a compulsory corvée.[29]

In the private sector, limited technology meant that manufacturing, in general, tended to be a small-scale affair. Workshops employing over 50 men, for example, would be rare in Athens. Production units were small because processing techniques did not require large concentrations of labour. These units were sometimes organised on a kinship basis although this did not necessarily preclude the existence of wage-relationships. Specialisation was in the product, e.g. types of pottery, rather than in the process. The work might be neither simple nor standardised, and a craftsman might well see the product through the entire process. The limited purchasing power of the masses in traditional societies meant that the luxury goods market, where high standards were required, became very specialised indeed.

(b) Limited economic specialisation. In traditional societies, developed commercial activity was not uncommon, but it was often only during periods of expansion and colonisation that there was the impetus for the creation of new demands. Entrepreneurs played a part in organising the flow of goods and services, but without a constantly expanding market for capital, there was only a qualified seeking for new avenues of investment. Overseas trade particularly was fraught with uncertainties, and it often took the promise of high profits to activate even the most intrepid of traders. The problems of storage and the preservation of goods, of communication and transport, and especially the limited ability to know the nature and strength of market demands, meant that by modern standards economic enterprise was necessarily limited. Though commercial activity was frequently well developed, formal and purposive planning was often lacking. With a limited degree of standardisation in goods and services, and especially in weights,

129

measures and currencies, the levels of economic integration were low and market synchronisation was difficult.

One key qualifying factor was the presence or otherwise of a money system.[30] This simplified enormously the process of rational planning and meant that the varied activities and accumulative interests of an economy could be calculated in common terms. Similarly, it greatly simplified the barter and exchange mechanisms of overseas trade by instituting interchangeable and mutually acceptable value systems.

(c) Limited capital formation. Banks were not a feature of pre-industrial societies, although forms of banking existed, for example, in China and in medieval Europe. Sometimes temples functioned as treasuries-cum-banking houses, as in Ancient Greece. The extending of credit was a risky venture. Few people had much collateral; morbidity and mortality rates were high, and credit was often consequently loaned at exorbitant figures. 'The rates of interest obtainable on credit extension for production or commercial ventures were substantially inflated by discounts for risk and uncertainty. . . . Among peasants, by far the most common form of debt was the consumption loan . . . this type were normally short-term. Interest rates charged on consumption loans might easily reach 100% or more. . . .'[31]

With limited credit facilities, both kinship groups and craft organisations sometimes played a conspicuous role in capital formation.[32] By pooling resources, a large extended kinship unit might raise appreciable amounts of capital which allowed members to develop common property or even expand their interests.[33] Craft organisations, particularly guilds, were also reservoirs of capital for their members. Guilds often transcended community boundaries, their memberships being partly but not entirely kin-based. They were frequently able to establish a monopoly of some salient economic activity, ensure the maintenance of standards and prices[34] and even act, when necessary, as a politico-economic counterweight to the traditional authority. Guild monies were often available for the financing of further guild interests.[35]

There were 'natural' limits to the scope and variety of such ventures, not least of all the slow and often unencouraged development of technological expertise. In fact, ideological factors played no small part in retarding the growth of economic innovation. The ban on usury in Jewish, Muslim[36] and – for a while – Christian communities inhibited economic investment, and the low premium put upon merchants and trade generally did little for the expansion of commercial activity in many traditional societies.[37]

In examining the broad economic arrangements of Ancient Egypt and Athens, some general criteria will be advanced as the bases of one kind of distinguishing analysis. In part, this incorporates Max Weber's useful theoretical distinction between formal and substantive rationality in economic systems.[38] In this way, Egypt and Athens can be seen as *types* of economies characterised by quite specific features.

Weber's 'formal rational' system is a construct of an ideal free market situation where there is a high level of market competition between autonomous economic units. This wide extension of economic freedom is aided by a money system which is an important – though not exactly indispensable – basis for rational accounting and exchange.[39] This necessarily involves conflicts of interest between competitors, the outcome of which can 'never be guaranteed to be strictly in accord with the standards of substantive rationality'. In very general terms, this represents the Athenian situation. By contrast, the Egyptian economy can be seen in terms of substantive rationality, that is a system where – again in general terms – there was a restriction of the area of market relations, where price levels were not determined simply by autonomous competition, and where there was a high degree of centralised planning and direction.

## Egypt

The Egyptian system was probably the nearest thing to a centralised economy in the ancient world. This conclusion is supported by both direct and indirect evidence and is particularly marked in the experience of the Old Kingdom. There seems to have been very little economic activity that was not either by royal command or – by extension – carried on with royal approval. On the other hand, we are not sure exactly how the system operated, whether it was always by direct control, or whether the state exercised its prerogatives by exacting dues and taxes in relation to certain forms of commercial enterprise. There were local markets which were not under the direct supervision of the state, but which obviously operated with the sanction of the requisite authorities. The great state and temple estates, which functioned like closed corporations, often sold their surplus produce to these markets. And there were a number of private producers who also supplied these markets.[40] Similarly, there were independent craftsmen who – on a small scale – manufactured articles, particularly in leather, wood and pottery, for the local markets, and petty merchants who organised the transactions. There is also evidence of foreign traders setting up stalls and selling their merchandise without any particular controls being exercised,[41] though presumably their business was noted by the diligent state officials and was therefore subject to the required taxes.

131

Certainly by the Empire period, the texts indicate that there was fairly extensive commerce with neighbouring peoples. By river or caravan, the principal imports were gold from Nubia, silver from the Middle East, perfumes and precious stones from South Arabia, ivory from Libya and the Sudan, ebony and scents from tropical Africa, and copper from Sinai. By sea came timber – especially cedar – from Lebanon, and other miscellaneous products, such as oil and wine from the Aegean. In exchange, Egypt's main exports were various manufactured linen goods, cereals, dried fish, papyrus, leather and glass.[42] These were obtained by trade and diplomacy, and – where necessary – by conquest. Otherwise, she was largely self-supporting. Each nome (province) produced for most of its own needs, each royal or priestly estate had its own craftsmen and workmen who were able to cater for their own employees and their dependants.

Each estate employed a labour force of serfs who appear to have owned cattle and cultivated small plots of land for themselves, and were subject to tax on the produce.[43] Tomb paintings often depict the peasants as contented souls toiling cheerfully for their masters; whether or not this gives an accurate picture of the peasants' lot is open to debate. What is certain is that the system, which was arguably a form of benevolent despotism, afforded the poor a meagre but assured income and some measure of security.[44]

The life of the skilled artisan, as might be expected, was appreciably better than that of the serf. New Kingdom paintings show craftsmen engaged in a range of diverse activities, carving, vase-making, leather and lapidary work, chariot and weapon making. Some were independent craftsmen, but in the main their workshops seem to have been housed on the large estates which supported them. Much of the work was routinised, and production was either for the markets or for the general maintenance of the estates. Some of the work, on the other hand, was of a very high order,[45] as the collections of Tutankhamun (Eighteenth Dynasty) and Psousennes (Twenty-first Dynasty) testify,[46] and was largely directed towards the comfort and aesthetic pleasure of the nobility. The skill of the craftsman was recognised and rewarded in Egyptian society, and grades of payment were made for various tasks.[47] The artist and sculptor were held in particularly high esteem and often commanded relatively high returns for their services.[48]

The state's capital consisted largely of produce and herds of cattle together with the wealth gathered from taxation and, during the Empire, from tribute from conquered neighbouring states. The economic system was based upon the annual production and the immediate consumption of food, apart from what was husbanded for the state granaries against failure of the harvest. The ruling

132

classes obtained their wealth from personal property which was originally given by the king and was possessed by inheritance, or assigned to them by virtue of their official positions in the state hierarchy whether as administrators, or priests on the temple estates. They did not capitalise their riches, but stored jewels and precious metals for their present and future lives, or left them as legacies to their families.[49]

Trade in Egypt was largely the monopoly of the king.[50] The available evidence suggests that trade was within the gift of the monarch, and there is no indication – certainly in Old Kingdom times – of any private enterprise outside the frontiers. The development of the turquoise and copper mines in Sinai and the gold mines in the eastern and southern deserts[51] which were manned by officials and policed by the army were likewise a royal prerogative. Egypt had exploited her copper deposits from the First Dynasty as excavations in tombs at Sakkarah have shown. From the Old Kingdom period, copper was the basic medium of exchange of the ancient world, and this continued until the early part of the thirteenth century BC. The abundance of copper gave Egypt a dominance in eastern Mediterranean affairs. It is probably no coincidence that her power began to wane with the ascendancy of the new iron-using nations, predominantly the Hittites.

The quarries from which the Egyptians cut stone for their obelisks, statues and sarcophagoi were exploited at the royal command. Very fine white limestone came from the quarries at Roiaou (Tura) and red quartzite from the 'red mountain' near On which appears to have been in full production by the Twelfth Dynasty. Granite came principally from the Aswan area, and diorite not very far to the west at Idahet. These quarries were not worked intensively all the time. When the king required stone, possibly to commemorate the triumphs of his reign, he would dispatch an expedition for the purpose. This too might then also rank as one of his main achievements. When Ramesses IV (1164–1157 BC) organised such a project, it was a huge-scale enterprise involving the practicalities of reconnaisance parties and the insurance of elaborate ritual preparations. He mobilised 9,368 men including the high priest of Amun and other high officials together with their cupbearers, and some twenty scribes. These were merely the headquarters staff, as it were, who were expected to master all manner of technical and logistical problems. The main body of the expedition included 91 masters of the horse, baggage train overseers, 50 police and 50 minor administrators, 5,000 soldiers, 2,000 temple staff, 800 foreign auxiliaries and 900 further officials of the central government. The particular craftsmen who were crucial to the entire undertaking, the draughtsmen, sculptors, stone-dressers and quarrymen, 140 in all, represented

133

a mere fraction of the total force.[52]

The ideological implications are all too evident. A high proportion of the personnel was composed of ritual experts, and the entire operation was dedicated to the gods, particularly Amun, without whose goodwill it was thought to be doomed to failure. And this was, of course, no singular instance. The whole burden of state economic activity was charged with ritual necessity.

Egypt was essentially a public sector economy, and for much of its history this was much the same as saying that it was a temple economy. Ritual served the state, and the state's requirements, in practice, were often inseparable from those of the king, especially in the earlier dynasties. For example, in First Dynasty times, a great hoard of copper – 75 rectangular slabs besides hosts of copper tools and weapons – was buried not in a separate state treasury but in a king's tomb for *his* specific use in the next life.[53] The prosperity of the land and its people was inextricably linked with the physical proximity and continued goodwill of the king. As evidence of how the Egyptians tended to see signs of divine intervention in everything and elevate these to the status of miracles, we should note the account of quarrymen looking for suitable stone for a sarcophagus lid for the Eleventh Dynasty king Mentuhotep (d. *c.* 2010 BC). They marked the route taken by a she-gazelle and attributed their eventual find to the intervention of the appropriate god – possibly Min, the ithyphallic lord of the desert – and made the required sacrifice. 'In earlier reigns soldiers had come and gone past where it lay, but no eye had ever seen it . . . it revealed itself only to His Majesty . . . people . . . shall learn of this (and) bow down to the ground and shall acclaim the perfection of His Majesty for ever and ever.'[54]

There were limits, of course, to the complete acceptance of these ideas, in which case they had to be rationalised by some form of theodicy. The Egyptian peasant – like his other ancient world counterparts – was often the victim of fearful pestilences and famines with which he could barely cope[55] and only partly explain. These were difficult to reconcile with the king's benevolence, but an anaesthetising amalgam of tradition and resignation usually did the job. Compliance is possibly simple and inevitable where the cognitive spectra are limited and alternative explanations are few.

Our knowledge of Egyptian economic priorities derives very largely from tomb paintings and temple engravings which are necessarily biased sources. They represent the interests of the king and the nobility who, in effect, *were* Egypt for practical politico-economic purposes. The interests of the king and nobility, and those of the state were virtually the same, although it is important to stress that they were not exactly identical. There were periods (as we have noted in Chapter 6) when there was some conflict between the king and the nobility, and there was certainly friction between the military and the government[56] and even more notably between the priesthoods and the government.[57] Nevertheless, these occurrences were relatively rare. In general, there was a mutuality of purpose in the higher orders of state. At the instrumental level, there was an enviable complementarity of function between the agencies of control.

The tombs and temples indicate that a pattern of enlightened patronage existed pre-eminently for the glorification of the god-king. Craftsmen and artists could manufacture for independent markets, but in general, these functionally specialised artisan groups operated with limited politico-economic autonomy. We are confidently informed that the ethics of the time 'forbade workmen or servants from being compelled to work unreasonably hard' (P. Montet quoting the 'Negative Confession' of *The Book of the Dead* where the deceased declares 'I have not compelled people, day by day, to work harder than they were able'). But during the reign of Ramesses III, for example, we find workers who normally received their allowances of food and clothing one to four times a month insisting, 'We are aching with hunger, and there are still eighteen days before next month.' A mob made for the warehouses, where one of their number outlined their grievances urging that the authorities 'Send to . . . Pharaoh, that he may give us the necessities of life.' This complaint was repeated before a magistrate, and they were eventually given the necessary rations. Perhaps this account is simply meant to reflect the beneficence of the king, but it also shows the system in operation.[58]

The system was not one of unending repression; labour relations of a rudimentary kind existed in the New Kingdom period, as the incidence of strikes and their resolution testifies. The fact that these could take place on state projects and be settled by negotiation shows that some degree of flexibility existed.[59] However, the energies of the masses, although manifestly directed towards the securing of a livelihood, were ultimately committed to the maintenance of king and state. There was really little alternative. Whether the allegiance was complete and unswerving must be open to doubt as records of proletarian protest barely exist, but such evidence as there is supports the view that there was a genuine and – in the main – unquestioning dedication to the traditional ideology.[60]

Foreign trade was very much a state-organised activity, although it was little developed until the Empire which was the great period of military and economic expansion. During the Old Kingdom, there was some trade with Phoenicia (even this broke down during the First Intermediate period), but archaeology has been unable to

135

trace any appreciable amount of Egyptian material on foreign soil until the New Kingdom.[61] In this period, the tribute wrested from conquered neighbours tends to be listed together with the wealth which flowed into Egypt as part of her normal commercial revenue.[62] Although they are not clearly differentiated, it can be reasonably assumed that economic activity was well advanced by this time. During the Eighteenth Dynasty, Egypt held an Empire which extended southwards to the Fourth Cataract. Her Asian territories included Palestine and certainly parts of Jordan, Phoenicia (Lebanon) and Syria. It may, if contemporary claims are to be believed, have even stretched as far as the Euphrates, although at the outer limits there may have been no resident Egyptian commissioners. Perhaps these areas were merely subject to occasional punitive raids to ensure continued contributions.

Not only was there a substantial influx of material wealth accruing from military conquest, there was also the exploitation of foreign slave captives for the further development of Egyptian economic resources – particularly the mines in Sinai. In addition, there were increased trading relations with countries as far afield as Crete, Mesopotamia and Punt (possibly Somaliland) from whence the Egyptian merchants brought back incense, ivory, apes and rare woods. Later, in the Ramesside period, Egypt became increasingly dependent on her Asian neighbours for wood and metals. She had always had to import silver, but iron – for which she had to trade – became the new and much coveted metal. Similarly, outlying areas, especially Nubia, were the source of slaves and the more exotic traffic in ostrich feathers, panthers and giraffes.

Such political and commercial expansion required the elaboration of an already extensive civil and religious bureaucracy, and, 'Most important from the Egyptian point of view', further expenditures because 'the gods had to be propitiated by buildings and new services'.[63] John A. Wilson argues[64] that the 'introduction of imperialism ended Egypt's formal isolationism', adding the unverifiable generalisation that it had a profound effect upon 'Egyptian psychology' and concluding that this 'ultimately brought the characteristic Egyptian culture to an end'.

Rather strangely, it is disputable whether Egypt can be said to have had a money system. Certainly in the Old Kingdom it was a barter economy, but as is customary in pre-industrial non-money systems, specific items or given weights assumed the role of money in as much as they became accepted as common means of exchange[65] although in some societies there was only minimal standardisation in this respect.[66] Under the New Kingdom, one of the measures of value was a spiral of copper wire called a uten. It is doubtful whether such spirals changed hands in the market, but other goods were often valued in terms of uten.[67] Another Egyptian unit was the deben, a word originally meaning 'ring', but which came to signify not the object itself, but its weight,[68] about 2½ oz. Its value varied according to the material in question, silver, gold, copper, etc. Usually the buyer was not in a position to pay in metal, especially precious metal, although the goods were calculated in these terms. The practice of actually settling transactions in precious metals seems to have developed under the Ramessides when more wealth was flowing into Egypt as the result of foreign tribute and trade, and the symptoms of inflation were making themselves felt. But these units were all notional media, merely referable standards whereby the economy could function with moderate efficiency. Egypt was essentially an exchange economy. A money system, in anything like the sense we have come to understand it, was not evolved until the declining years in the middle of the first millennium,[69] although a rudimentary temple banking system did evolve during the Empire.

Perhaps the absence of a money economy can be tenuously correlated with the absence of credit formation or entrepreneurial activity in Egypt. Such a relationship is at least plausible. What is not obvious is any link between a money system and the development of acquisitive tendencies as postulated by Max Weber – though Weber does stress that there is no lack of the acquisitive instinct in simple non-capitalistic structures.[70] Certainly there was no rational system of profit-making enterprise which is facilitated by a money system. But this was conditioned by structural constraints and – not least of all – by the prevailing god-king ideology and its concomitant expressions of state control.

The absence of a money economy in no way precluded the imposition of taxes. All classes were subject to taxation with the possible exception of the priests (this is a disputed issue and will be discussed below in connection with temple income and immunities). Taxes were assessed in terms of land and other capital possessions. Tax officials would note even gifts of slaves, wine, clothing, etc. given by the state in recognition of services rendered, but registered in the name of the recipient.[71] People simply paid their dues in produce which came either from the land or from small-scale, possibly household, manufacturing. It would appear from the records that people paid their taxes with no better grace than they do today. The documents contain numerous complaints of unfair assessment, injustice and even extortion. One text gives an account of an argument over the ownership of a donkey, and one of the disputants says, 'Behold . . . you have not sent it to me, and now they [the tax-collectors] demand from me the work of the donkey, year by year, while it has been with you.'[72]

137

Similarly, the Egyptian peasant was subject to payments which were institutionally exacted not only in terms of produce, but also physical labour. He was liable to be conscripted for the annual corvée, the mass mobilisation of labour for public works which might involve almost anything from digging ditches to building temples. There were certainly exemptions from these tasks for a range of higher order people including priests and literati.[73] There seems to be little doubt that the labouring masses were sometimes treated with severity, and even cruelty. A late text reads, '. . . the scribe lands on the embankment [to] register the harvest. The porters carry sticks and the Negroes palm-ribs. They say, "Give us corn". There is none . . . [replies the peasant]. He is stretched out and beaten; he is bound and thrown in the canal. His wife is bound . . . his children are put in fetters.'[74] Peasants worked almost entirely for others, with little chance of redress when they felt themselves to have been wronged. The Nauri decree of Seti I (c. 1300 BC) shows that those not specifically protected by royal decree could have their livestock confiscated and their persons conscripted arbitrarily – even indefinitely – for agricultural or military service.[75]

Some accounts may come from predjudiced sources, yet the general picture is clear that the Egyptian peasant was virtually a non-person whose interests were completely subordinated to those of the state. At the same time, it must be said that there is little evidence that he suffered excessive injustices *within the terms of his own system*, or that he seriously questioned the rightness of the established order of things.[76]

In one sense, the Egyptian conception of property was self-contradictory. On the one hand, all property belonged in theory to the god-king, that is, the state. On the other, private property, as we understand it, did exist. In principle, the king did administer the land as a personal possession. But, as we have seen, there was a real – if limited – measure of autonomy, especially for the intermediate orders of society.

The great dignitaries and royal officers, together with the king's relations, favourites and friends, had received presents from him (mainly as land). . . . Even greater were the gifts made to temples and priests who had collected very large estates in this way and had engaged bands of slaves and artisans to work them, independently of the king with immunity from taxation. Moreover, in addition to state commerce, private trade had started with foreigners, especially in the Delta, and new units of movable property had come into being. Other such property had originated in gifts made to mercenaries, and even in the essential needs of peasant life.[77]

Private property and the seeds of private enterprise certainly existed, then, during the Empire. We know that whilst land could be bequeathed to an owner's legatee, the transaction had to be ratified by royal decree.[78] Slave-owners were able to rent the services of their slaves to others,[79] owners could rent land to tenants and independent trade in other goods was possible,[80] but we are unable to define its limitations.[81] What can be asserted with some confidence is that very careful records were kept, certainly in Ramesside times, of both public and private wealth which was to be assessed for taxation purposes.[82] Perhaps there was little real wealth outside the public service.

In Weber's terms, therefore, the king enjoyed appropriated rights over all state property. These rights were inalienable and inheritable; they gave the monarchy both possession of tangible 'things', land, artifacts, etc., and control over their use,[83] although this system became modified in later practice. Tenure of land was, either directly or indirectly, the gift of the Pharaoh. This was the de jure system which became qualified by the de facto appropriation of land by both individuals and groups – especially the priesthoods.

Property, therefore, in Egypt was concentrated not so much in the public sector as the religious sector. There is overwhelming evidence that the vast public works were constructed from ideological motives, or were at least ideological in their inspiration. The classic example is the pyramids of the Old Kingdom. It is still generally accepted[84] that they were gigantic tombstones which were constructed to protect the Ka or living spirit of the king. The Great Pyramid, according to Herodotus, took 100,000 men twenty years to build, the causeway alone for the transportation of the stone blocks taking ten years.[85] More recent estimates have lowered or modified this figure, possibly to something like 35,000 men on a corvée basis working in shifts.[86] Whatever, it was an incredible undertaking involving the cutting, shaping, hauling and general erection of some 2,300,000 blocks weighing over two tons a piece.[87] But the pyramid building programme may have been simply a huge communal enterprise which was socio-economic rather than ritual in its intentions. Although such a view is not new,[88] it has been cogently argued by Kurt Mendelssohn,[89] that the main function of these projects was to generate a sense of national consciousness. Such a view hardly seems to answer the question, why pour incalculable resources into *this* particular form of economic activity? Were there no other possible forms of work-relief which would afford a similar sense of civic pride, and give the same degree of social unity? The Mendelssohn theory does not really answer this. It seems impossible to avoid the conclusion that the god-king ideology was the main motivating factor.

Similar interpretations must apply to the temples and their attached estates which enjoyed privileges not afforded other areas of the economy. The temples of the Old and Middle Kingdoms were relatively modest affairs compared with those of the New Kingdom. These acquired vast estates and were granted immunities which threw an extra burden on the rest of the economy. 'Egypt became top heavy with priests and specially privileged temple holdings.'[90] There were particular endowments, sometimes the gift of a grateful Pharaoh where a god had graciously lent his 'sword' to give victory in battle,[91] but these were far exceeded by the vast incomes which accrued from the continuing benefactions and exemptions granted by the monarchy.

Towards the end of the Empire, Ramesses III confirmed the temples in their property. The Great Papyrus Harris[92] gives an extraordinary picture of the wealth of the priesthoods, particularly that of Amon-Re at Karnak (Thebes). We have no idea how the temple revenues compared with those of the state at this time, but an annual income of 100 lb. Troy of silver and 1,100,000 bushels of grain must represent a considerable proportion of the nation's wealth. The temples owned 169 towns (nine of them in Syria), over 500 gardens, vineyards and orchards, more than 50 shipyards and 88 ships. On their estates, they also had about half a million head of cattle, over 400,000 of which were the sole property of Amon. It is estimated that the temples controlled about one-eighth of the arable land and employed a workforce of approximately 450,000, i.e. a tenth of the total population – but this is a very tentative overall figure.[93] The temple of Amon alone probably possessed one person in every fifteen and one acre in every eleven.[94] The doors of the sanctuaries of Thebes were either of gold or burnished copper; some of the statues wore garments of gold, and much of the temple's furniture and vessels were of silver. The temple of Atum at On like other temples, had its own treasury and, among other valuables, is said to have had thousands of statues of the Nile god. '13,568 . . . of pure lapis lazuli and turquoise, and half as many of gold and other materials. . . .'[95] Despite some dispute over the actual proportions of temple wealth and the debate as to whether they were always exempt from taxation,[96] the general impression seems inescapable that religious ideology had independent status as a motivating factor in the Egyptian economy.

## Athens

In the ancient world, the Athenian economy conformed, in broad terms, to Weber's ideal construct of a formal rational system. Compared with Egypt, there was a high level of market competition between independent economic units aided by money and banking systems which facilitated the extension of commercial enterprise. As in all traditional societies, the basis of the economy was essentially agricultural, but Athens also supported a small-scale yet flourishing industrial sector with functionally specialised economic groups of craftsmen and artisans with appreciable politico-economic autonomy.

As a preliminary to any examination of the Athenian economy, it is salutary to be reminded that the 'evidence for Greek economics will always remain too fragmentary for any kind of quantitative analysis. . . .'[97] Commerce and industry in Ancient Greece were very important, but in the absence of any statistics,[98] we are compelled to make inferences from a limited number of instances without being sure in what ways they may be typical or abnormal. Nevertheless, there is sufficient evidence to indicate the main orientations of Athenian economic activity.

The agrarian base of the Athenian economy had passed through an important period of change more than a hundred years before the Periclean period when Solon, one of Athens's traditional law-givers, had attempted a number of agricultural reforms including a redistribution of the land. Small-holders had apparently incurred huge debts due to the ruinous interest exactions of the rich land-owners, but Solon's insistence on the cancellation of these debts met with only partial success. Part of the problem was purely ecological. The soil of Attica was too thin to bear corn, yet it was well-suited to the olive and the vine. Solon tried to put Athenian agriculture on a new footing by encouraging diversification in agricultural products and more specialisation in industry.[99]

By the Periclean period, landed property was still the main basis of wealth especially for citizens, and Finley estimates that by the end of the fifth century BC, about three-quarters of the citizen families owned some landed property.[100] The rich were often rentiers, absentee landlords who were content to leave the oversight of their property to others. Pericles himself who was kept permanently busy with affairs of state, authorised his bailiff to sell the produce of his lands in order to defray the expenses of maintaining his town house in Athens. Really large estates were rare in Attica, and there was nothing approaching the vast temple lands of Egypt or the later Roman latifundia, which were often little more than slave-farms.[101] On the other hand, in other parts of the Greek world such as Thessaly and Boeotia, large estates seem to have been the rule from early times.[102] In Sparta, almost the opposite obtained. Each Spartan was given a medium-sized holding (kleros) from which he was entitled to keep the produce – about 100 bushels of corn for a man and his wife plus a proportionate quantity of fruit. But this

141

system does not appear to have been enforced consistently, and even in Sparta property became concentrated in the hands of a small number of citizens who continued to add to their domains.[103]

As is to be expected in peasant societies, there was a real attachment to the land. The notion that agriculture as a form of occupation necessarily produced the best citizens and soldiers is reflected in some of the literature. For example, Xenophon writes, 'When all is well with agriculture, everything else prospers.'[104] But there may be more than a hint of nostalgia here. These sentiments must be qualified by the' fact that many small-holders merely leased their modest holdings from the rich landowners who had numerous small farms scattered about the countryside rather than concentrated in any one area.[105] This tenancy system was obviously seen as the best way of giving them a good return from the land. Such tiny allotments could hardly sustain some families who became increasingly tempted to run themselves further into debt, and this put them at the mercy of land speculators.[106] The ownership of land was the main security for debt. The small-holder who negotiated a loan would remain in occupation, but would lose his property if he was unable to make repayment. Land and houses were bought and sold for cash; the credit system so common in our own society which provides mortgages for purchasers was still a thing of the future. Similarly, there was no official land register, although some people did keep records of land sales.[107]

In general, Greek tradition demanded that property ought to remain in the family. But strong sentiment is not the same as legal prohibition. There is no incontrovertible evidence that kinship holdings were inalienable, but property cases before the courts in Athens as late as the fourth century suggest that the prevailing norms and laws of inheritance favoured the retention of land within the family group.[108] This sentiment was bound up with the strict obligations to care for parents and maintain the family shrines.[109]

The popularity and qualified success of the small-holding system stems partly from having to make virtue of necessity, and partly from Greek attitudes to self-dependence. How such attitudes arose and how they came to be expressed in these particular forms are probably unanswerable questions. Only in highly qualified ways can they be said to have given rise to the democratic ethos which prevailed in certain states. The view that the Greeks despised manual labour has long been dispelled.[110] In both Homer and Hesiod physical work was not regarded as degrading. What was demeaning was that a man worked for somebody else. The banausos, the 'mere worker' tended to be despised in the old aristocratic tradition.[111] There was actually a supreme dignity in self-employment – although even this was circumscribed so as barely to include trade.

'There used to be a law in Thebes debarring all businessmen and traders from public office unless they had ceased their money-making activities at least ten years previously. . . .'[112]

Socrates, according to Xenophon, appears to deplore 'those occupations which are called handicrafts'. He maintained that 'they are quite rightly held of little repute in communities'. Again there are echoes of the old aristocratic-cum-martial tradition in the reasons given: 'they weaken the bodies of those who make their living at them by compelling them to sit and pass their days in-doors. . . .'[113] Although in another context,[114] the sage who himself was something of a stonemason, seems genuinely interested in craftsmanship. But then artists and sculptors enjoyed a more enviable reputation. The sources for such attitudes probably display a bias that was not always shared.

> the passages from ancient authors often cited to show . . .
> Athenian contempt for trade will not bear the weight that is
> put upon them. They show, as was to be expected, some
> upper-class bias against commercial life . . . the trader was
> (not) always a voteless alien – rather the reverse . . . the small
> trader was a regular component of the democratic assembly
> which the wealthy and the philosophers so much distrusted.[115]

The necessity for trade and industrial enterprise was gradually thrust upon the Athenians. The rising population and the shortage of alluvial soil meant that there was little hope of growing enough wheat to satisfy home consumption. The natural trend was to seek grain abroad, especially in southern Russia and Egypt, and turn from subsistence farming to a small-scale industrial import-export economy. Other factors helped to accelerate the decline of agriculture. Constant over-felling of trees for shipbuilding[116] and charcoal for fuel depleted the forests. This in turn led to soil erosion which did little for the agrarian communities.[117] Added to this, under the impetus of the Peloponnesian War, was the Periclean policy of abandoning the countryside to the invaders, and turning Athens and the Piraeus (its harbour area) into one vast fortress. The depredations of the Spartans during the initial invasion of Attica in the first year of the war (431 BC) affected the olive and grape harvests for several years to come. The polis became turned in upon itself, as it were, and needed industry and limited trade to maintain its viability. It became a political as well as an economic problem. 'A remarkable proportion of Greek (especially Athenian) foreign policy was dictated by the perennial need to secure grain, timber or precious metals in an area where natural resources were always inadequate.'[118] There is every reason to believe that land hunger was the primary stimulus behind the colonising movements which were well under way by the early part of the seventh century BC with the establishment of new poleis in Italy and Sicily. By the classical period, the colonies were important as both provisioning agencies and as readily available markets for Greek exports. In addition, they constituted suitable havens for immigrants from overcrowded parent cities.[119]

In the simple industry developed by the Athenians, production units were relatively small; only in a few cases can one speak of such things as rudimentary factories.[120] The main exception was the mining industry which was largely served by slaves (see Chapter 8). This included the silver mines at Laurium and the gold-bearing deposits in eastern Macedonia.[121] Apart from these, the largest known unit was one manufacturing shields in Athens. This was owned by a metic from Syracuse named Cephalus who employed 120 slaves. Normally a sizeable labour-force was no more than 50 men. For public works such as naval contracts or temple construction, the state usually supplied the raw materials and divided the work between several small firms who could supply the necessary specialists. It is to be assumed that on a much smaller scale, a similar pattern of operation would obtain for private contracts as well. The more common practice was that of a craftsman with one or two slaves manufacturing on his own premises producing goods which would be sold direct to the public.

Only with considerable charity can it be said that the Greeks were technically innovative. The oft-cited exception to the charge of Greek technological mediocrity is the much later Hero of Alexandria, but even he seemed content with his steam toys and did not seem to appreciate the incredible technical possibilities latent in his inventions. 'In the matter of production it is surprising to realise that the Greeks were not so inventive and ingenious as some of the peoples who had flourished earlier. Many Greek craftsmen had fine technique and wonderful ability in design and ornamentation, but they were not strong in improving technical procedures or inventing new ones.'[122] However, production was of a sufficiently high standard to satisfy not only home consumption but also to export enough to maintain much-needed supplies of timber and grain. By the middle of the fourth century BC, Athens was importing some 1,200,000 bushels of grain annually.[123] The maritime supremacy of the Greeks – despite the growing power of Carthage – ensured a minimum of piracy, and virtually untrammelled commerce in the Mediterranean world. In terms of returns, her overseas trade probably outstripped her shore-based activities. Jewellery, cotton and woollen articles, and even silk[124] were exported, besides the oil, wine and especially pottery for which the Greeks were well known. Greek artifacts have been discovered as far afield as Vix near

Châtillon and in Yugoslavia.[125] Quite large numbers of Athenian vases have been found abroad, many of them not intended as utensils, but as decorative amphorai often in the characteristic black glaze. Whether these were deliberately designed for the export trade is a matter of debate.[126] By contrast, some idea of the extent of Athens's dependence upon imports can be inferred from a contemporary comedy[127] which indicates that a wide range of goods was being received from Cyrene, the Hellespont, Thrace, Syracuse, Egypt,[128] Syria, Crete, Rhodes, Phrygia, Phoenicia and Carthage. Ten times a year the Athenian Assembly was presented with a report on the state of public provisioning. Extremely stringent laws defined the obligations of corn-merchants, and enforced the sanctions against hoarding or stockpiling which might produce a shortage.

The stratification system can be related to various levels of economic activity. Manual work done *for others* was associated with low status groups, particularly slaves, whilst trading was an area very largely dominated by the non-citizen metics.[129] The metics, who were prohibited from holding land but required to render military service to defend the lands of others, had very few civic rights and concentrated their energies on the originally suspect activity of trade. Citizens, on the other hand, predominated in olive- and grape-growing, hog- and sheep-breeding, activities associated with the land. But such generalisations must be qualified by evidence which shows different strata working together. The building accounts of Eleusis (329–328 BC) show that there were 21 citizens among the 94 craftsmen.[130] The nobility, too, can hardly be excluded from the field of commerce. The taste for imported luxuries led many to take advantage of the new opportunity structures and finance various kinds of trading venture. Perhaps in doing so they slowly undermined their previously unassailable position as aristoi. In order to finance commercial enterprise, many had to convert their frozen, land-based assets into liquid assets. Without fresh reinvestment in property, their wealth was subject to the vagaries of an uncertain commercial situation. But the potential gains were inviting and investment in trade and industry gradually rivalled land-based investment as counter-attractive possibilities. The state, however, did little to promote the interests of its citizens in foreign commerce. The search for export markets was no direct part of state policy.

The release of liquid capital became possible with the introduction of coinage to Greece c. 600 BC. A proverb, 'money makes the man' became the bitter slogan of déclassé reactionaries since wealth as opposed to breeding could in theory be acquired by anyone, and could lead – perhaps unintentionally – towards democracy.[131]

Iron objects (obolos = spit or nail) as a medium of exchange had

145

been used since the seventh century BC, but the actual minting of coins was a relatively late innovation for the Greeks. Until the Persian Wars, gold and silver coins were a rarity in Greece, although the stater (twice the weight of the Persian gold daric) was in wide currency among the Ionian Greeks in the early fifth century BC. In Athens coins were of silver, a practice which was accelerated by the discovery of rich seams in Thrace in 483 BC, and were either in multiples or fractions of the drachma (4·36 grammes). Comparative values are not easy to assess. For example, a slave sold at auction might fetch anything from about 70 to 300 drachmai. An inscription of 414 BC suggests an average of 168 drachmai for males and 147½ drachmai for females. These figures may be compared with those of a professional teacher offering a course on 'human and political virtue' at what was considered to be a quite modest fee of 500 drachmai.[132] Inflation was obviously a problem in the ancient world, but it had a differential impact on different commodities. A bushel of barley costing one drachma c. 590 BC had risen to only two drachmai by c. 390 BC, although the price of sheep had increased ten to twenty times.[133]

The money system and the gradual standardisation of values which Athens imposed upon her allies undoubtedly facilitated the ease of her commercial undertakings.[134] The state encouraged a free enterprise system – except in the grain market – but derived considerable benefits from others' trading activities by creaming off a healthy percentage for the city's revenues. Through a tax-farming syndicate it levied harbour dues of 1 per cent and later 2 per cent on the total value of all merchandise passing through the Piraeus.

The Periclean age saw the emergence of usury. Previously people had tended to hoard capital. Temples particularly had been used as treasuries,[135] a practice common in the Assyrian, neo-Babylonian and Hebrew kingdoms.[136] But with the development of trade, new avenues of investment presented themselves. A banking system developed and banking houses helped those whose commercial enterprise necessitated large capital outlays.[137] There were virtually no limits to the interest rates which could be as high as 200–300 per cent[138] although the norm was possibly nearer 12 per cent.[139]

The state was financed in several ways. Apart from the annual tax payable by non-citizens, direct taxes – eisphora or property tax – were only levied irregularly to deal with emergencies. For example, special funds were raised for the invasion of the island of Lesbos after her secession from the Delian league to become allies of the Spartans in 428 BC. It was the first levy of the war, and realised some 200 talents. Towards the end of the fifth century BC, such situations coalesced into one continuous emergency as the prosecution of the war became more desperate. There were, apart from

146

slaves and metics, four tax classes, the 500-bushel men, the knights, hoplites and thetes. Each had its civic rights and obligations, particularly as far as state offices were concerned, but for practical purposes the gradations were almost imperceptible. The real distinctions lay between citizens and non-citizens. In addition, the wealthy were expected to finance 'liturgies' (leitourgiai) or special public services such as plays and choruses, or even the outfitting of war vessels (triremes) of which they might be given command. This superogatory expenditure, though almost ruinous on some occasions, was apparently characteristic of the period. It was a quasi-voluntary system which, on the whole, seems to have worked rather well; some citizens actually contributed more than was 'normally' required.

Apart from the extra sources of revenue from taxes imposed on the importing and exporting of goods, there were also various tolls and fees for the use of market-places. Somewhat uncharacteristically, there was a tax on conjurors, fortune tellers, and members of what were considered other more or less 'dishonourable occupations'.[140] But there was no direct tax on trade or capital earnings.

By far the most important source of income for Athens was the tribute levied from her allies in the Delian league.[141] It is uncertain how many allies constituted the league, as the earliest tribute lists date from some twenty-five years after it was founded. At the outbreak of the Peloponnesian War it may have numbered between 100 and 200. Little, too, is known of its precise organisation in the formative years. We do know that the large island states provided ships which were a useful addition to the Athenian navy, whilst the smaller states were assessed a tribute (phoros), in lieu of service, totalling 460 talents. During the first phase of the war – known technically as the Archidamian War – this had more than trebled to 1,460 talents. Originally, the money was housed at the temple of Apollo at Delos – it was a common practice to secure money in temples which were technically sacrosanct – but later it was transferred to Athens. At its inception, the league, ostensibly founded as an alliance against the Persians, was a free federative union of states with all members having equal legal status. This relationship changed and the balance shifted in favour of the hegemonic power of Athens. When the war began, 6,000 talents had been accumulated in the Treasury of Athena; 9,700 talents was the highest level the reserves ever reached.[142]

The problem of whether Athenian prosperity was achieved at the cost of her allies – or subjects – is tenuously related to the other vexed question, was the Greek achievement only gained at the expense of her non-citizen population? Specifically, was the Athenian economy based on slave labour? It can be argued that Athenian

147

slave-keeping practices, even the abysmal treatment of those in the mines, was simply an extension of attitudes and practices which had been endemic in Greece since early times and which became particularly acute with the fratricidal strife which followed the development of polis organisation. So much is hardly in dispute. The relatively small proportion of free citizens undoubtedly benefited by the economic activities of the large unfree population. Similarly, the leisured upper classes could enjoy the privileges of relaxed philosophical discussion because the commercial life of the city was being carried on by others.

The relevance of a Marxist interpretation of this situation in terms of *modes* of production[143] is highly arguable. Whether slaves were employed in small-scale industry or in the more ambitious enterprises of mining and large-scale farming (as in later Rome) seems largely immaterial. The Ehrenberg-Westermann argument[144] that 'slave-based' simply turns on the quantitative assessment of the slave population's economic contribution is also an uncertain one. It is all rather like the problem of how much industry a society needs to be classified as an industrial society. In the absence of a machine technology, slave-labour must afford considerable advantages to a free population. All the more so in Athens where a large proportion of the unfree population was occupied in wresting the common exchange medium, silver, out of the ground to maintain the viability of a war-time economy. And many others were engaged in tasks which freed their superiors for duties which ensured the military and maritime supremacy which kept the tribute rolling in.

Certainly one of the most significant features of Athenian society was in the allocation of its revenues. After the depredations of the Persian Wars, the Periclean policy was to use a high proportion of the state's income to rebuild the temples and generally beautify the city.[145] But quite apart from this ambitious building-programme, state expenses were considerable. The payment of indemnities for service in the council, the magistracies, the jury courts, and even for citizen attendance in theatre, music-hall and stadion was a Periclean innovation.[146] Although such indemnities were nominal, they did tend to create a fluid class of salaried officials where formally no bureaucracy had existed. There were also the costs of games, festivals and other public occasions. Even in the midst of war, the celebration of the Greater Panathenaia festival (410 BC) cost six talents. In all, a significant proportion of the state's revenues was expended in creating architectural and artistic masterpieces[147] and this policy was pursued through virtually the entire period of the war.

From various sources we can form an incomplete composite impression of the range and distribution of wealth. Given that there were about 12,000 citizens in the lowest class (thetes), another 8,000 or so in the hoplite class, and about 1,000 in the two highest property classes, it has been reckoned[148] from the war-tax on property that some 90 per cent of them were in the 180–480 drachmai income bracket. We know that in the fourth century, a half drachma was the subsistence allowance paid for attendance at the Assembly or as a juror, an unskilled labourer got one and a half drachmai and a skilled labourer two drachmai a day – double the fifth-century rate.[149]

There was private wealth in the polis. In the year 378–377 BC, an assessment was made of the private property in Athens for tax purposes. The total estimate, excluding all state property and that of the thetes, was some 5,750 talents.[150] During this period, we know of particular instances from which we can make guarded assumptions about the previous century. A client of Isaios, a speech-writer, had 'houses in Athens worth 2,000 and 1,300 drachmai'[151] besides other wealth. But such fortunes seem to have been exceptional. Even allowing for inflation and changed circumstances, reasonable inferences can be made about the private wealth of the city during the fifth century BC. There seem to have been only a handful of really rich citizens. Possibly there were no more than about 1,200 who were expected to support the state by quasi-voluntary contributions (leitourgiai), and perhaps only a quarter of these were really wealthy, that is to say with incomes in excess of 3,000 drachmai. In the main, wealth was concentrated in the public sector. This is well expressed by Finley:

> Classical Greece was a world almost completely without
> palaces, and, on the whole, without private mansions. . . . Of
> the public buildings, the temple and later (to a lesser degree)
> the theatre, both directly and immediately connected with cult,
> outranked all others. . . . The State was therefore almost the sole
> patron of the monumental arts. Given the nature of the classical
> polis, this meant . . . the community acting through its usual
> instrumentalities, the assemblies, councils and magistrates. The
> same men who levied taxes . . . also ordered, supervised and
> maintained and paid for public works. Art was meshed with
> daily living . . . not set apart for the special enjoyment of rich
> collectors and aesthetes.[152]

It is sometimes argued[153] that the Athenian achievement was only made possible by forced payments to the Delian league. This must remain a matter of contention because, after the defeat of Athens and the temporary eclipse of the Delian league, similar state policies were pursued with greatly reduced revenues.[154] The crucial issue for the present discussion is not the quantitative one of how much all this was paid for by tribute exacted from the Athenian allies, but the qualitative one of how much this activity was the outcome of

149

ideological constraint. Many authorities tend to see the embellishment of the city in religious terms. For example, C. M. Bowra:

So Pericles set out to rebuild [the temples] of Athens on a magnificent scale . . . [but] he was moved by more than patriotism. In his supreme attention to Athene he showed what he wished men to think about her as the presiding goddess of Athens.[155]

Or T. B. Webster:

Religious patronage is general Greek rather than democratic Athenian. . . . The whole of Greek life is dominated by religion.[156]

Or yet again, M. I. Finley, though less categorically:

This is not to denigrate secular public buildings, for the Greeks lavished much care on them . . . but they had a scale of values which elevated the temple above other buildings.[157]

To what extent *were* the orientations of Athenian economic life really subject to religious determinants? The same authorities fully recognise the important political implications of the building-programme. For example, Bowra: 'the Parthenon was to surpass all other temples in size and splendour [and] proclaim the glory of Athens to ships sailing across the Saronic Gulf and strike awe and admiration into their crews.'[158] The social intentions too should not go unnoticed. Most citizens lived in very modest circumstances: the city was unhygienic, unlit at night, and with open sewers which were an invitation to epidemics,[159] and streets which were so poor and unpaved that they became seas of rutted mud in bad weather. A third-century BC traveller wrote, 'The city of Athens is very drought-ridden . . . the majority of the houses are extremely shabby . . . and being so ancient a town it is badly planned',[160] therefore, a fortiori, what was it like in Classical times? These salutary reminders of the great disparity between the living conditions of the populace and the grandeur of the public buildings may suggest that the people were so imbued with a religious spirit that nothing was too good for the gods. But there is much evidence to indicate, especially among the philosophers and playwrights,[161] that the gods were already in question – perhaps little more than forms of a 'noble lie' for the people. Possibly Plutarch has a point when he suggests that the money lavished on the Acropolis was really a large work-relief programme inaugurated by Pericles to reduce unemployment. It was a way of obviating the irregular hand-outs to the poor. 'As for the working population, Pericles did not want such people to go unpaid, but he was equally anxious that they should not get money for doing nothing. Consequently, he put a series of firm proposals before the Assembly involving large-scale construction projects ... which would keep numerous trades fully employed for some time to come. ...'[162] This, of course, does not really answer the question, why so much expenditure – the Acropolis cost in the order of 2,000 talents – on *religious* buildings? And what does 'religious' connote in this context? Peter Green summarises:

> Economically speaking, the amount invested in these elaborate non-functional buildings and the statues they contained ... was out of all proportion to a small city-state's standard of living, technical resources and available public funds. Why? Not, I think, religious fervour, except in the most generalised sense. The answer seems to be, rather, that this ... offered an infinitely rewarding medium for the expression of civic pride and propaganda. The conscious dignity and affluence of any polis could be measured by the splendour of its public (which meant, primarily, religious) architecture, thus satisfying those ... who sought some tangible expression for their unity of purpose and achievement.[163]

Perhaps the polis should be seen as an ideal which was physically actualised in the monumental symbols of its architectural and artistic creativity. Religious fervour was suffused – perhaps even confused – with civic pride. In a Durkheimian sense, possibly Olympianism was simply another term for Athenianism.

## Summary

In a chapter necessarily heavy with substantive material, it might be as well to summarise our findings in relation to the two economies concerned. This can be done on a simple point-by-point basis identifying the key similarities and dissimilarities of the systems.

| *Egypt* | *Athens* |
|---|---|
| 1 Economy characterised by substantive-type rationality. | 1 Systems characterised by formal-type rationality. |
| 2 High-level of bureau-cratically-organised central control of market operations. State-orientated economy. | 2 Non-bureaucratic low-level of central control of market operations. Entrepreneurial, market-economy. |
| 3 Centralised control and financing of extensive public works. | 3 Ostensible public control and financing of extensive public works. |
| 4 Limited private property. Extensive temple estates | 4 Extensive private property – mainly in possession of |

151

and state-holdings.

small-holders. Few large estates.

5 Wealth primarily invested in public sector.

5 Wealth primarily invested in public sector.

6 Qualified feudal 'base'.

6 Qualified slave 'base'.

7 Functionally specialised economic groups (artisans, etc.) with little/no politico-economic autonomy.

7 Functionally specialised economic groups (artisans, etc.) with considerable politico-economic autonomy.

8 Agrarian economy with low-level of exploitation of foreign markets.

8 Agrarian-maritime economy with high-level of exploitation of foreign markets.

9 Trade for scarce/essential goods.

9 Trade for scarce/essential goods but with range of colonial sources/markets.

10 Exchange-barter system.

10 Developed money-system.

11 Unambiguous ideological motivations.

11 Ambiguous ideological motivations.

# 10 Political and legal organisation

Some early sociologists tended to take an evolutionary approach to the study of political institutions. They were primarily concerned with the relationship between the state and civil society. With the growth of ethnographic knowledge, their interests centred largely on the origins and development of the state and the history and classification of political systems. They were influenced by contemporary developments in Western civilisation, and the typologies they advanced were really simple dichotomies such as the distinctions between primitive and archaic societies, city and feudal states and modern advanced states. In general, their explanations were of two main kinds. Spencer and Comte regarded the emergence of the state as a consequence of the increasing size and complexity of societies in which warfare was a major factor, whilst Marx argued that the state is a function of the differentiation of social classes which itself is related to the development of productive forces and disparities in the distribution of wealth.[1] On the other hand, anthropologists saw the growth of political forms in terms of rationalised kinship hierarchies.[2] '[Kinship is] the sole possible ground of community in political functions'[3] was contested by later theorists such as R. Lowie and I. Schapera who argued for a complementary emphasis upon territorial and other institutional considerations including religion.[4] A similar theme had been stressed earlier by Fustel de Coulanges who attributed the formation of the Greek and Roman cities to the elaboration of more inclusive religious systems.[5]

More sociologically sophisticated theorists concentrated not on typologies of political communities – valuable as that can be – but on analyses of political authority and the exercise of power. G. Mosca[6] maintained that the history of mankind could be reduced to conflicts which attend the attempt to control the operation of

153

judicial and executive systems. Political conflicts therefore arise because of opposing tendencies towards conservation and change; between the traditionalist 'old forces' and their possible replacement by other 'insurgent new forces'. The conflict is therefore one of rival factions in their attempt to monopolise political power. This can involve opposing groups striving for identical ends, a 'competition' situation, or groups striving for different ends, a 'conflict' situation. Both situations are familiar in the political process. Competition may, therefore, be regarded as an equilibrium concept with its associations of balanced social stability, whereas conflict may be seen as a processual concept with all the concomitant associations of disruption and change.[7]

Political power inevitably connotes the 'legitimate' use of coercion. In Max Weber's words, 'We wish to understand by politics . . . a state [or] human community that [successfully] claims the monopoly of the legitimate use of physical force within a given territory. . . . Hence politics for us means striving to share power or striving to influence the distribution of power, either among states or among groups within a state.'[8] Weber, in his well-known analysis of legitimate power, identified three main types of authority system:[9]

(a) Rational-legal: where an impersonal legal order obtains, and individual considerations are treated as applications of generalised rules which can only be changed by correct procedures. This type of authority system, Weber argued, involves organised administrative arrangements of a bureaucratic type, and is most characteristic of complex, advanced societies. Being 'rational' and technically efficient, it was the form of organisation best suited to modern societies.

(b) Traditional: in which authority rests upon the sanctity of norms and prescriptions of the traditional order. This type of authority system is characteristic of pre-industrial societies.

(c) Charismatic: in which authority is vested in the person of a leader rather than any particular mode of organisation. Such systems have strong ideological overtones; the leader is usually the founder or populariser of a cause[10] with which either a nucleus or a mass identify themselves.

There are many qualifications which can be made of Weber's illuminating analysis, especially his model of bureaucratic organisation. Coercion is not the only distinguishing feature of government, but Weber tends to stress *means* rather than ends in his categorisations. The implication being that the means of coercion constitute the main basis of political legitimacy and – what is probably just as important to rulers – operational effectiveness. Detailed critiques of his analysis are not lacking.[11] What is important, however, in any discussion of the political structures of complex pre-industrial

154

societies is that Weber's interest focused on the ways in which power was transformed into political authority. The term 'authority' implies some degree of acceptance and acceptability as opposed to sheer domination. This gives power its essential legitimacy. It is arguable whether power can be exercised without some regularisation of procedures to give it an operational base, and without some degree of popular concurrence to make those operations effective.

Limitations to the exercise of 'absolute' power have been voiced by a number of theorists,[12] notably S. N. Eisenstadt, 'the tendency to generalisation of power of the rulers in the historical bureaucratic empires was limited not only by the paucity of free resources and by the existence of many traditional forces. It was also restricted by internal regulative problems which emerged as a result of the growing differentiation of the social structure.'[13] So much, of course, depends upon how 'total' or 'absolute' is defined, particularly whether it is to be seen in terms of degree or extent – or both. Similarly, time-scales have to be taken into consideration. In actual cases, the specific periods of a society's life-cycle are important.[14] For example, throughout the whole span of Egyptian civilisation, a growing differentiation of the social structure was taking place, and the power of the Pharaoh was concomitantly reduced by both these internal as well as external factors. But there were also periods of Egyptian history, notably during the Old Kingdom and in the early years of the Empire, when the exercise of power was virtually unquestioned.[15]

Perhaps the most fruitful type of approach for our purposes is that suggested by Almond and Powell who direct their attention to the *capabilities* of political systems.[16] This is a General Systems Theory with Parsonian orientations[17] and involves the three basic ideas of input, what the system derives from the society; conversion, the internal utilisation of the resources; and output, the canalisation of those resources and the general contribution which the system makes to the society. Essentially, the theory examines the interactions between the system and its environment, and is primarily concerned with problems of system maintenance and adaptive functions. The principal capabilities of political organisations may be summarised as:

   (i) Extractive
   (ii) Regulative
   (iii) Distributive
   (iv) Symbolic
   (v) Responsive

Some elaboration of these factors is necessary before we can apply this general pattern of analysis to our examination of traditional societies.

155

The *Extractive* capabilities of the system concern its accumulation capacities. The emphasis is essentially quantitative, and involves the recruitment of manpower and the collection of funds as taxes and tribute, which are rarely given voluntarily,[18] in short, the overall mobilisation of resources. The notion of extractive capacity takes on a special significance when related to the exercise of power. In what we may broadly call 'non-democratic' systems, there are differences in the *degree* to which the decision-makers, whether they are aristocrats, oligarchs or autocratic rulers, are independent of the wishes of those they govern. As we have seen, no matter how arbitrary the dictates of the state may be, it can never be totally immune to the needs and aspirations of *all* its subjects.[19] Similarly, there are always differences in the status spectrum of the governed which qualify the *extent* of the state's jurisdiction and control. This particularly applies to its ability to mobilise and organise economic resources. But this, in turn, must be conditioned by the differences in the degree to which the decision-makers are independent of those who mediate their instructions, and those who have endorsed, passively or actively, their right to command.[20] In traditional and charismatic authority systems, the autonomy of the ruler(s) may be very considerable indeed. The restrictions on the realisation of their political and economic goals may be minimal.

The *Regulative* capabilities of the system concern its capacity to institute and operate effective controls. This involves the problem of what kind of mechanisms to employ and the frequency and intensity of their application. Broadly speaking, optimum control can be achieved in four main ways: by the exploitative use of force, or the threat of force; by compromise which necessitates some degree of decision-sharing; by a legal machinery which involves the institutionalisation of acceptable norms of conduct; and by general consensus which solicits support on a reciprocal-loyalty basis. No one of these can be completely effective by itself, and therefore all societies operate a composite which entails various shades of 'mix'. One of the differentiae of complex as opposed to simple (non-literate) pre-industrial societies is the development of some form of legal process. The presence of 'law'[21] both validates and reinforces other mechanisms of control.

The *Distributive* capabilities of a system not only concern the division of goods and services, but also the defining and allocation of statuses, honours and opportunities. In more autocratic systems such as Egypt where there was a minimal differentiation of roles, distribution had a strong ascriptive bias. By contrast, in societies with a qualified consensus such as Athens where roles were relatively highly differentiated, distribution had a marked achievement bias.

As far as the purely economic functions of the system are concerned, the principal aims of the state[22] are the regulation of available resources so as to ensure a constant flow of wealth. These can then be used to fulfil its obligations to its subjects, in terms of necessities and public works, and to discharge its protective duties by strengthening its own position *vis-à-vis* internal and external forces which may jeopardise its viability.

The *Symbolic* capabilities of a system are, by definition, concerned with the provision of ideological supports and legitimations. These may be credible and persuasive, or simply menacing. Where power is monopolised on an autocratic basis, it may be necessary to control effectively the 'symbolic flow' from rulers to people. Similarly in aristocracies, where a small number of ruling families often occupy virtually all the strategic seats of control, some kind of ideological legitimation is required to validate their position and justify their possession, even if it is simply an appeal to hereditary rights.[23]

Charismatic authority may well be expressed in symbolic terms. But personal charisma as opposed to charisma of office often has a social ephemerality which reduces its long-term effectiveness. This could easily be illustrated from the experience of Egypt and Athens. Greek tyrannies, which were frequently founded by discontented but ambitious aristocrats, rarely lasted more than two generations. Sons were not always as charismatically endowed as their fathers, and thus imposed more oppressive forms of rule which eventually undermined their authority.[24] By contrast, in Egypt where charisma was associated with the office as well as the person of the Pharaoh, dynasties were often of considerable duration. The Eighteenth Dynasty, for example, lasted some 260 years, and then the 'mandate' was merely transferred to the next ruling house. The essential nature of the authority did not change significantly until the later years of Egyptian history, i.e. from the Post-Empire period, when the rise of other powerful states threatened and ultimately destroyed the Egyptian power.

Symbolic and particularly charismatic capabilities are often rationalised and justified in terms of appeals to absolutes or to tradition. On the other hand, appeals to experts or to a mandate bestowed by the people is more commonly a feature of modern societies,[25] although there can be considerable overlapping on these issues. Athens, for instance, would constitute an appeal-to-the-people system, whilst ideologically-based modern régimes exemplify the appeal to absolutes-tradition-experts systems, although they too will make nominal democratic gestures of an appeal-to-the-people kind.[26] Whatever, symbolic mechanisms provide the ideological grounding upon which societies justify current policy and practice. Being value-based they constitute the unanswerable legitimations of the system.

157

The *Responsive* capabilities of a system simply concern its ability to elicit the necessary responses from society. This input capacity validates the normative structures of society whilst implicitly sanctioning the authority status quo. 'Ruling classes do not justify their power exclusively by the de facto possession of it, but try to find a moral and legal basis for it, representing it as the logical and necessary consequence of doctrines and beliefs that are generally recognised and accepted.'[27]

To summarise: a political system is an organisation of a territorial society which has the legitimate monopoly over the regulation and use of force.[28] This is authorised explicitly or implicitly by consensus acceptance. Thus political organisation has defined responsibilities in maintaining the system and implementing the society's collective goals. Any examination of political organisation must therefore take into consideration how political roles are differentiated and defined, and whether they are distributed in mainly ascriptive or achievement terms. It must also take into account the orientations and capabilities of the political process, and how these are both determined and achieved. And, finally, it must analyse the bases of legitimation which are held to explain the nature of the structure and sanction its operations.

## Egypt

The Egyptians had no word for 'state'. This conception so common to modern society with its connotations of consciously contrived political structures may well have been foreign to them. 'The Egyptian state was not a man-made alternative to other forms of political organisation. It was god-given, established when the world was created [and] part of the universal order' which, for Egyptians, 'involved the feeling of unalterable rightness'.[29] The word 'state' may have been absent from the language because all the significant aspects of the state were concentrated in the king. The monarchy was thought to be as old as the world; the creator himself having assumed the duties of kingship from the beginning of creation. So although for most of its history, Ancient Egypt was administered by a vast bureaucracy of officials, it is impossible to divorce the exercise of power from the position and authority of the Pharaoh. This was regarded as a function of his divine nature. 'There seems no doubt that Pharaoh's predicate "god" found its correlate in his absolute power over the land of Egypt and its inhabitants.'[30]

Private property appears early as a result of royal donations, although basically it seems to be little more than a transference of rights. This applies also to every personal liberty, personal status or rank which, in theory, the king could annul at any time. In principle, there was no autonomous justice or law outside that of the crown. But 'very few administrative and legal documents of Egypt have survived; and, as a result of this scarcity, our knowledge of the functioning of kingship in Egypt is of the vaguest.'[31] What is clear, however, is that the king's rule could not be entirely arbitrary. There was the perennial obligation to govern in accordance with 'ma'at', often translated as 'truth' or 'right order' but which actually expresses a cosmic principle of harmonious eternality.[32]

As god, the king alone could direct the state by virtue of the special divine attributes which only he possessed. These special qualities were 'hu', authoritative command, 'sia', perception, and 'ma'at'; all three were personalised, i.e. deified, by the Egyptians. 'Hu' represented the ability to recreate a situation by speech, and 'sia' the divine recognition and understanding of situations. These might be used for good or evil, so 'ma'at' was regarded as the most important as it imposed responsibilities on the ruler for just dealings with his subjects.[33] Only the god-king therefore had final authority in matters both sacred and secular – if such a distinction can be made in this context.

Henri Frankfort has argued that, although such a conception is largely alien to us, we must nevertheless not try to evade the difficulty by quasi-rational explanations. It was not an elaborate fraud con- trived and perpetrated by men who were anxious to retain and sanctify their claim to power. The Pharaoh 'ruled in the strictest sense by divine right; any attempt to describe the Egyptian state irrespective of the doctrine of [his] divinity could be fatuous. . . . The doctrine of divine kingship is only comparable to a religious creed.'[34] John A. Wilson, on the other hand, whilst recognising the theory and practice of the doctrine, admits that it must be qualified in view of the apparent inconsistencies involved.[35] The king, as god, though the sole source of law and authority, relied upon other gods for oracular direction. He also delegated responsibility to the vizier and other officials. This mediation of divine authority by humanly fallible agents may be presumed to both detract from the divine absolutism and even distort the intentions of the divine will, a paradoxical situation which continued throughout the history of ancient Egypt.

There were times when there was a marked diminution of royal power, e.g. the First Intermediate period, and others when the royal authority was confidently reasserted. The tendency was to idealise the king by emphasising in both art and literature not only his authority and beneficence, but also his exploits and warrior prowess.[36] The personal and political blemishes were often passed over in silence. Deviations from the sanctioned norms which can often only be inferred, were probably regarded as ephemeral in the overall economy of the divine order.

The officials who in the Old Kingdom period seem to have been mainly kinsmen of the king[37] may have been thought to share in some degree the mysterious essence which differentiated the king from other men.[38] As the bureaucracy expanded, especially under the Empire, this form of kin-based nepotism was necessarily modified. It is arguable whether such a quasi-nepotistic system actually ensured special qualities of loyalty. Kin-based political structures are not notably immune from dissension. Family schism and the pretensions to power of ambitious siblings can give rise to fratricidal strife within the royal houses, although there is actually very little evidence of this in the Egyptian monarchical tradition.[39] There were palace intrigues but, as far as we are aware, no popular uprisings. Occasionally 'godless' conspirators were prepared to seek ways of interrupting the royal succession. Towards the end of the reign of Ramesses III, one of his wives, Taia, schemed to secure the throne for her son and planned an unsuccessful coup d'état'.[40]

Legislation seems to have been a function of the king alone; there is no clear evidence that this was ever delegated to other groups or subordinates. The king's administrative and judicial work, however, was delegated to a large and elaborately organised body of officials[41] with such exotic titles as 'Chief Recitation – Priest of His Father' and 'Supervisor of All the Buildings of the King.[42]

Not too much is known about the actual operating of the state; 'actual information about how the Pharaonic government functioned and what effects it produced in the lives of its subjects, is unfortunately very scanty. Many of the relevant documents can be interpreted in more than one way, and the resulting picture necessarily includes much which is uncertain.'[43] We do know that the state was organised on a strictly hierarchical basis, and was authoritarian in structure. The government can be seen to be divided in two main ways, the central administration including control of the granaries, treasuries and so forth, and the government of the administrative districts (nomarchies) into which the country was divided. To these can, of course, be added the external provinces under the Empire. Every part and function of the state were de jure subject to the king and the central administration, although – as we have already seen – de facto shifts of power did take place. During the Old Kingdom, the principal officer of state was the vizier, 'the Steward of the Whole Land', the 'Councillor of All Orders of the King' who acted as the chief intermediary between the king and the bureaucracy. He reported to the king daily and sought divine approval on policy measures. 'He was exhorted to show no fear or favour, and to make himself available to receive and listen to all classes of petitioners with sympathy, patience and an open mind.'[44] In theory, the king was also open to the appeals of his people, but in practice it was extremely difficult to gain access to his presence.[45] It may be suspected that as the king was kept at one remove from the details of government, so the vizier too, as chief executive, was shielded from the burden of excessive legal-administrative trivia by an army of minor officials.

In his capacity as chief officer of state, the vizier concentrated his attentions on the 'secular' administration of the royal office. The religious functions were the special prerogative of the king who was also, by right, chief priest. The vizier was responsible for both internal and external affairs. It was his task to deal with district matters and – in later times – to cope with the extra burden of provincial administration. During the Empire, there were two viziers; one in Upper and another in Lower Egypt, where they presided over two 'Great Councils' in Thebes and Heliopolis respectively. As a rule, there was no single officer who exercised authority in all parts of the country and in all parts of the government at the same time. It may have been an intentional policy of the Pharaoh to prevent too much power falling into the hands of any one subordinate.

In each large town there were lesser councils which may not have had any specific administrative tasks, although they did have judicial functions and sat as courts of law in both civil and criminal cases. The men who comprised such councils appear to have been separately engaged in administrative work, so there was therefore no clear dividing line in practice between their administrative and judicial duties. The composition of the councils may have operated on an ad hoc basis, and been composed of different officials at different times[46] or they may have consisted of reservoirs of administrative talent whose variety of expertise could be drawn upon as and when the occasions demanded. The flexibility of the councils' composition is shown by the fact that they sometimes consisted entirely of priests, on other occasions entirely of lay-members, and sometimes both together.[47]

There is a 'catalogue' which lists the Egyptian hierarchy of New Kingdom times.[48] It is headed, predictably, by the various divinities, the royal family, followed by the vizier, magistrates and all those who had the good fortune to live near the 'Sun' i.e. the king, this included all those who participated in the central administration. Another list enumerates the king's representatives in the provinces and the foreign territories. It is clear that there was a highly differentiated bureaucracy whose members had their own specialised tasks. Each high official had his own personal entourage. The district governors maintained households which were often modelled, though on a much smaller scale, on that of the Pharaoh. The immense wealth of some of the temples, particularly those dedicated to Amun, generated a minutely graded body of priests and other

161

temple functionaries.[49] Even such a deity as the ithyphallic Min, Lord of Coptos and Ipou, less universally worshipped than Amun, possessed a large staff of priests, an administrative cadre of scribes, foremen of works, herdsmen, linen-masters, superintendents of transport, storekeepers and accountants.[50]

The temple priests should probably also be regarded as an integral part of the administrative machine. Theoretically, it was the king who was supposed to perform the daily rituals throughout the land. In practice, however, it was the priests who officiated in his stead. Perpetual service had to be offered to the royal ancestors and the other gods of the state. The Pharaoh, despite his divinity, was hardly omnipresent, and therefore rendered this service through the activities of the priesthood who were supported by generous royal endowments.

The Pharaoh appears to have been able to appoint and dismiss priests in much the same way as he could officials in other government departments. Removal from public office could have serious family repercussions for those involved as it was not uncommon for a son to follow his father into the public or priestly service. Bakenkhonson, a high priest of Amun during the New Kingdom, says, 'I assured a funeral for those who had none to succeed them and a coffin for him who was destitute. I gave protection to the orphan who . . . sought my help and I championed the cause of the widow. . . . I never snatched a baby from its mother. . . . I never deprived a son of his father's office. . . .'[51] Punishments for corrupt officials could be severe especially if their misdemeanours concerned temple property. Seti I in an address to officials and other state employees all the way down to the 'sunshade-bearers' warns of infringements and abuses of temple property. He announced that any official who appropriated goods would receive not less than a hundred blows with a cudgel, and would have to restore what he had stolen and pay a hundred times its value in penalty and interest. In severe cases, this could mean the cropping of a nose and ears and the humiliation of returning to the temple as a mere labourer.[52]

Although law was not carefully codified, as it was in some Asiatic states, there was a judicial machinery which operated throughout the state through duly convened courts. In principle, the king alone determined the law. The texts often relate how the king called his counsellors together to seek their advice, but this appears to have been rather a nominal procedure. It had no legislative force, and seems to have been little more than a sounding-board for the Pharaoh's ideas. Indeed, perhaps its reporting was a mere propagandistic device for emphasising the superhuman wisdom of the monarch.[53]

The highest magistrate was the vizier himself in his capacity as chief executive of the king. His theoretical function was to act in strict conformance with the will of the monarch who alone, for example, could confirm death sentences and exercise the royal pardon.[54] However, there is evidence which hints that within a tight procedural framework he had some independence of action.[55] His formal duties included listening to appellants in the audience hall, but he was also expected to walk in the streets so that poorer – and possibly less intrepid – supplicants too could seek his advice and present their petitions. The lesser magistrates in the numerous administrative districts seem to have enjoyed a considerable measure of autonomy in the legal sphere. But in working through the local councils, they too were expected to exercise their authority in keeping with the normative guide-lines of ma'at which, in theory at least, informed the administration of justice.

In Egypt, law came 'from the mouth of the Pharaoh'. In principle, therefore, it was constantly renewed by the divine beneficence of the sovereign. The precision which marked the codification of law in successive Mesopotamian societies,[56] was absent in Egypt. There is nothing known which was comparable with the explicit law-codes of, say, the Babylonians. In Egyptian, there was apparently no word for law as a principle, although there were terms for regulations which covered specific situations.[57] But these really relate to decrees rather than actual codes of law. Similarly, there are legal documents which refer to such matters as the transfer of property, together with abbreviated records of court proceedings,[58] but these only give us some indications about court procedure, and very little about the law itself. In fact, unlike the Greek situation where legal reformers were revered in both precedent and folk-memory, few Pharaohs had reputations as law-givers. Diodorus[59] lists only five such kings before the Persian conquest. The fourth and perhaps most eminent of these Bocchoris (c. 700 BC), appears to have concentrated his attention mainly on laws of commerce, loans and contracts.[60] This is a late period but it at least indicates the presence of practical legal procedures despite the textual insistence that law was impersonal and the sole prerogative of the Pharaoh.

Whether or not the noble sentiments expressed in the texts about the administration of justice were simply lofty idealisms, it is difficult to know. What evidence there is does not always support the view of the normative order which can be inferred from the texts, or the moral probity of officials as depicted in some of the literature. Various high officials wrote of their exemplary conduct and unimpeachable public service ostensibly to impress the gods. Viziers and magistrates were often quick to proclaim their unvarnished reputations especially in their tombs or on public stelae. Thus

163

Ptahmose says, 'I have done the things that men praise and the gods approve'; Rekhmire insists that he has always defended the weak against the strong; and Khaemhat, a royal scribe and superintendent of the granaries, maintains that he had never had any accusation levelled against him, and that he was guiltless before the gods.[61] One is tempted to ask if these catalogues of good works were really protestations of innocence in the face of either actual or anticipated accusations, or perhaps an insistence on singular exceptions amidst known corruption.

Officials were subject to severe penalties, particularly demotion, or even disfigurement, if found guilty of corruption or disloyalty.[62] In some actual cases, for example, the tomb-robbings during the reign of Ramesses IX (c. 1100 BC), we know that court proceedings took place, but we have no idea of the judgments that were given or what sentences were passed.[63] Records also show that for the lower orders particularly, debt and other infringements could bring harsh beatings and even the confiscation of their meagre property. The retired soldier, Horonemheb, who knew of the oppression by the tax-collectors and the general exploitation by the minor bureaucracy, warned his son against judges, 'You know that they never show mercy when they judge the unfortunate.'[64]

Punishments, especially beatings, were meted out to criminals, including some that might now be regarded as civil or moral offenders, on a carefully graded scale in proportion to their crimes. The cutting off of nose or ears or both was a common punishment for more serious offences, as was also deportation to the mines and quarries. The death penalty was reserved for rebellion and for adultery by women. This could take a number of forms, beheading, burning, or perhaps the 'voluntary' suicide which seems to have been the privilege of highly-placed dignitaries.[65]

The qualified autonomy which existed in the administrative districts and the increasing abuses of the later Ramesside period tend to support J. A. Wilson's contention that the 'Egyptians always shrank from carrying a series of concepts . . . or experiences . . . to their logical conclusions. They preferred to compromise or conciliate. . . . Crisis could be met with flexibility of action.'[66] In effect, the argument is that the dogma of the unique politico-legal authority of the king must have been qualified by practical exigencies. A pragmatic ethic prevailed. The perhaps too general principle of ma'at combined with the lack of precisely codified law, allowed a theoretically static system to adapt to a changing situation.

Obviously, the idea that the Pharaoh consulted only his own 'heart' was something of a fiction, and equally obviously precedent played a large part in the practical observation and detailed administration of ma'at. This is shown by the 'Instructions' which some kings gave for the benefit of their progeny, and the fact that decisions taken in earlier times were sometimes used as guide-lines for the present order.[67] But the weight of evidence is unequivocal that the king was regarded as the origin and fount of all law, and, as such, was the final court of appeal. This did not change throughout the dynastic system despite the questionings and upheavals of particular periods. There is little doubt that it reached its zenith during the Old Kingdom and was subsequently enunciated – and possibly regarded with reciprocal acceptability – during the periods of great socio-political renewal. What is important is that when the crises were past, the Egyptians did not look for – or apparently even *think* of looking for – another kind of system. They persistently returned to what they saw as the 'right' and eternal order. Despite its admitted practical deficiencies, this system exhibited high extractive and regulative capabilities with central control of the distributive processes. Its continuing viability over three millennia testify to its capacity to elicit the necessary response by means of an explicit and effective symbolic order.

## Athens

There was no accepted or unified system of Greek political organisation, any more than there was a really coherent body of Greek law.[68] There *were* elements of commonality. The various poleis had developed in sufficient isolation to allow for the gradual crystallisation of a wide spectrum of politico-legal systems.[69] As in Egypt, the political and the legal are difficult to separate, and to distinguish them in administrative terms has to be something of an academic fiction. This would be the case in most traditional societies, and Greece was certainly no exception. 'The doctrine of the separation of powers had no place in Greek constitutional theory or practice. The [political] councils and assemblies which passed the laws and took decision of policy . . . were also, for some purposes, courts of law.'[70]

More is known about the politico-legal arrangements of Athens and Sparta than any other Greek states, but even so the sources are limited.[71] Much of what we know about Athens is drawn, sometimes indirectly, from a few contemporary historians and philosophers particularly Thucydides, Xenophon and Plato. Important additional material can be taken from Aristotle[72] who was writing later in the fourth century BC in somewhat changed circumstances. Other than this, there are the inferences which can be made from contemporary playwrights, particularly Aristophanes whose insights tend to provide us with parodies – or at best caricatures – of the Athenian political situation and its personalities.[73]

It should always be borne in mind that these original sources may contain a good deal of bias. Thucydides[74] and Aristophanes were writing during and immediately after the war period, and had, in their different ways, particular axes to grind (or, perhaps in the case of Aristophanes – to blunt). Plato, writing after the war, expressed in *The Republic* and *The Laws* something of his disillusionment with the ineffectual cycles of Greek political arrangements. Whereas Aristotle, his pupil, writing later still, recaptured something of the earlier enthusiasm for the Athenian constitution.[75]

The actual details of development of the polis system are unclear. Perhaps the primary impetus was the need for defence. In Athens, the city proper was centred round the Acropolis which can be seen not only as a ceremonial area, but also as a defensible citadel. As a state, Attica was comparatively large, about 1,000 square miles, but the walled area of its controlling polis, Athens itself, was barely one square mile, and perhaps up to 30 per cent of this area was unoccupied in Classical times.[76] It has been estimated that about another 14 per cent made up the public places such as the Acropolis and other shrines together with the commercial area of the Agora, and the Pnyx where the Assembly met to discuss public issues.[77] The remainder consisted of the jumble of streets and houses comprising the residential and semi-industrial quarters, together with the port area of Piraeus which was carefully laid out in rectangles.

The essential framework of the Athenian constitution was established by Solon in the early sixth century BC, and was modified in certain important respects by Pericles a century later. As we have seen, Solon had divided the free citizens into four classes according to their income in terms of farm produce: the 500-bushel men, the 300-bushel men (the hippeis or knights), the 200-bushel men (zeugitai), and lastly the labourers (thetes). The thetes had no specified income and possibly no land; later they gravitated towards rudimentary industries and became an important element in the Athenian urban proletariat.

In earlier times, with the abolition of the monarchy and the reduction of the power of the nobility, the office of archon (regent) had been created, first for life, then for ten years, and afterwards for one year only. Under the economic class system of Solon, all four classes were allowed to vote at the Assembly of the citizens, although only the two upper classes were eligible for the archonship. This, in itself, was something of a political innovation in as much as men who were not of the nobility now qualified for high office in the state. When the archons had completed their term of office, they passed into the council of the Areopagus which consisted mainly of the heads of the most important families, in fact, a kind of House of Lords. The council exercised general supervisory powers of a

166

mainly legal nature, and ensured the smooth running of the existing social order. A second council or senate (Boule) was also set up consisting of 400 members drawn equally from the traditional four tribes.[78] These were chosen by lot, served for one year only, and their main task was to prepare the agendas for the general Assembly of the citizens. This limited control of the areas of debate gave them a form of administrative authority which presumably further undermined the power of the aristocracy.

During the Classical period, a number of important additional changes were instituted especially in relation to the matter of citizenship. The Athenians did not normally bestow citizenship very easily on outsiders,[79] and under Pericles (451 BC) they passed a law which restricted citizenship to those whose parents were both Athenian citizens. Citizenship and the threat of non-citizenship were used to great effect. Some offences against the state carried political penalties. They could result in a disqualification from speaking in the Assembly or being made ineligible to bring a case in the courts. Particularly serious offences such as cowardice or the avoidance of military service might result in a complete loss of civil rights (atimia).

Citizenship was based upon membership of the demes or villages which became the new political units after the legislation of Cleisthenes in 510 BC. In later times, there were 174 demes;[80] perhaps many of these also existed during the Classical period. They varied considerably in size, but each had its own local assembly, treasury and leading official, the demarchos, and each had modest religious as well as political functions. A father enrolled his son with his own deme, and at eighteen the boy was registered as a citizen of that deme, and always remained a member no matter where he lived.

The four traditional tribes of Attica were reconstituted as ten tribes (phylai), to which the demes were allocated. Under Cleisthenes, the phylai in turn were each allotted a city section (asty), an inland section (mesogaia) and a shore section (paralia). This ensured, to some extent at least, that the phylai were of comparable size, and – more importantly – that they represented a cross-section of the people. This reduced the preponderant influence of any one economic class, particularly the big landowners, and was designed to generate greater unity and participation at the local and national levels. Particular activities contributed to the ethoi of the new tribal entities. The tribal spirit was promoted and reinforced by such formal organised events as the chorus contests at the Great (City) Dionysia festivals. The intention to 'mix the people' (Aristotle) is reflected in Cleisthenes' own term isonomia, equal distribution and equality among citizens.[81] Membership of the re-formed phylai was hereditary and permanent. The phylai served as a framework for

167

the elections to practically all political institutions, especially to the Boule and the various boards of magistrates. Among its most important electoral functions was the election of its general (strategos) who commanded one of the ten tribal contingents of the army. To this extent the phylai performed an important function between the deme and the polis.

These reforms were achieved at the cost of disregarding traditional divisions and sentiments. The new mode of organisation, though given nominal approval by the oracular centre at Delphi, appears to have been governed almost exclusively by politico-rational considerations. 'The new phylae ... were never genuine sacred communities. The whole character of the new order was secular and rational.'[82]

The phylai supplied the membership of an enlarged Boule. Fifty men were chosen by ballot from the demes of each of the ten tribes to constitute the new council of 500. Each 50 or prytaneis[83] served in turn for one tenth of the year. No citizen could serve as a councillor (prytans) more than twice, and each prytany had a chairman, also chosen by ballot, who served for twenty-four hours only, during which time he was chairman of the Assembly and titular Head of State. There was, therefore, an overall and continuous turnover of personnel, and there were probably very few older citizens who had not served as prytans at least once. Athenian political procedures therefore had a strange contrapuntal quality where the same substantive themes were repetitively renewed in ways which brought variation and – sometimes – clarification to central issues.

Ostensibly, the Boule system was devised because a council of 500 was too unwieldy, and its changing composition made it unlikely that it would ever develop any corporate feeling. Operated in this way, the Boule provided 'a political school for the majority of Athenian citizens',[84] but it could not overshadow the ultimate power of the Assembly. There was the well-known incident towards the end of the war when Socrates, who was serving his one day as chairman of the Council, refused to allow a vote on a proposal of the Assembly that six strategoi (generals) should be impeached for failure to rescue the survivors of a naval battle of Arginusai (406 BC). This was an irregular action of the Assembly, trials being normally the province of the courts. Despite Socrates' resistance, in a 'mockery of justice' all six were condemned and executed.[85]

It was the task of the Boule to convene the Assembly, arrange its business and see that its decrees were carried out. It scrutinised the qualifications of officials and the allocation and use of their funds, and generally co-ordinated their activities. Its supervisory duties included all the state's concerns from the building of warships to the administration of state pension schemes. The membership of the Boule was full-time for the period of office during which time they were supported by state revenues.

Every male from the age of eighteen with the statutory birth qualifications had full citizenship rights and was allowed to participate in the work of the Assembly (ecclesia, literally, those who are called out). From the time of Cleisthenes, the ownership of land was no longer necessary as an eligibility factor. It was only late in the fifth century BC that citizens were compensated for attendance at the Assembly. During the Periclean period, they had to resign themselves to the loss of a day's pay if they wished to attend, although those required for jury service were reimbursed from public funds.

The Assembly met forty times a year, and some provision was made for extra or emergency war-time meetings when required. The forty meetings were held in ten groups of four; these corresponded with the ten 35- or 36-day periods of each prytany into which the Boule's year was divided. Each group of four meetings had a set format. The first considered whether the holders of offices were performing their duties satisfactorily, and also debated general matters such as the problems of corn-supply and defence, proposals for political prosecutions and property to be confiscated and – once a year only – the desirability of holding an ostracism. At the second meeting, any citizen might ask the Assembly to consider a motion on private or public affairs. And at the third and fourth meetings, the Assembly discussed and, if necessary, debated three proposals chosen by lot on religious affairs, three on secular affairs and three on foreign affairs.[86] It is not certain just how many people were present at the meetings of the Assembly, but a quorum at the regular meetings seems to have been 6,000.[87]

The Assembly appears to have had final authority in Athens. De jure, the Athenian citizenry was sovereign, and de facto no group or official could dictate to it, check it, and review or revise its actions. It could be influenced by trained rhetoricians and swayed by gifted demagogues and openly led by exceptional charismatic figures such as Pericles, but no person or group could order its policies. It could not be dominated, but it could be manipulated. There was the infamous incident in 416 BC when the entire population of the neutral island of Melos was condemned to death and slavery, possibly at the instigation of Alcibiades, an able and persuasive orator.[88] It was the people's system and there was apparently no written constitution which could inhibit its flexibility and adaptability, or guarantee an immunity against practised and opportunistic populists.

In addition to the membership of the Boule, a number of other officials were either elected or chosen by lot. Some 550 guards were

169

chosen by lot from the demes, and 277 further officials from the phylai. These included the commissioners of sacred places, officials to perform sacrifices (there were no religious functionaries in the customary sense), officials in charge of the market and the corn-supply, deme judges, police officers, guards of the dockyards and the Acropolis, besides members of miscellaneous other boards which worked closely with the Boule.[89] All of these held office for a single year except the archons in charge of the games who were elected every four years. The archonate, as such, had declined in influence and importance by the Classical period. Under Pericles, the third and fourth property classes, the zeugitai and the thetes, were eligible for the archonship. The duties of the archonate were divided according to areas of administration. The archon basileus was the general supervisor of the religious cults of the polis, and the polemarch was primarily concerned with legal dealings between citizens and non-citizens although formerly he had been commander of the army. In addition to these, there was also the eponymous archon who was generally in charge of jurisdiction. In all, with junior members (the thesmothetai) there were nine archons – all largely involved with the law and its applications – who comprised a college which, it has been argued, rarely exerted much influence as a group.[90] Complementing the archonate, there was the Areopagus – a kind of 'Upper House' – the former King's Council, of which all ex-archons were members. This judged cases of homicide, was guardian of the laws, and vetted those chosen for the archonate.

Elections were mainly confined to the appointments of the military. On the whole, these were the preserve of the rich, but among the sixty or so officers needed for any one year, including the ten-strong board of generals (strategoi), there were often exceptions.

There were probably more boards and committees than seems necessary to get things done; in total, some 700 officials, all paid by the state. Perhaps the idea was to distribute responsibility and reduce the opportunities for peculation. In naval matters, for example, the Assembly decided whether any new ships were to be built during the current year and then settled on the number. The Boule was responsible for the building of the ships, but worked through a board of ten, whilst another board of ten was in charge of the yards.[91] The income of the polis to finance these craft would itself be subject to further boards and possibly commissions, ostensibly to ensure a sharing of the task, but perhaps also to minimise the possibilities of corruption.

The ballot system for choosing officials may also have derived from similar motives. The vast majority of officials were chosen by lot; very few were elected. The Athenians felt that this ensured a fairer distribution of civic duties, but they also tended to view with

170

some suspicion those who actively sought office for its own sake. Some intellectuals disputed the wisdom and efficiency of the system,[92] and others actually despaired that it was open to demagogic manipulation.[93] The demagogos was, by definition, a leader of the people, and therefore a likely figure in any democratic system. The term became closely associated with the oratorical and emotional exploitation of populist feeling. The demagogue, therefore, came to connote a sinister and even heedless political opportunism which we now tend to regard with some apprehension.[94] In the war-time experience of Athens, this was linked particularly with Cleon who argued for the prosecution of what we would now call a 'total war'.[95]

Solon had instituted a single court of the people (heliaia) which had not been changed by Cleisthenes' reforms. In effect, this was a kind of sub-committee of the Assembly. It obviously could not deal with all court business, and in the mid fifth century, it was divided into a number of specialised 'benches' or dicasteries consisting of 201 jurors (dicasts) for civil cases and 501 for criminal cases. These were members of the total body of 6,000 jurors chosen by lot by the archonate who selected 600 names from each of the ten phylai. These candidates were, in turn, taken from lists submitted by the demes. The system was analogous to that used for the choosing of the membership of the Boule.[96] These huge panels of jurors which could even number 1,001, 1,501 or 2,001 were held to represent the whole people. The jury, whatever its constitution, took no vocal part in the proceedings of a trial; they simply listened to the evidence and made their decision, and this decision was final. There was no other body or court to which a further appeal could properly be made.[97]

The dicasteries were presided over by magistrates. These can hardly be regarded as judges in the currently understood sense, they were really only chairmen of the courts who ensured, as far as possible, the orderly conduct of affairs. A trial (agon) was fought out between the interested parties: the duties of the presiding magistrate – who was usually one of the archons – was confined to collecting sworn statements, recording the testimony, and generally acting as combined judge and jury foreman. Both magistrates and jurors were modestly paid for their services, another task arranged by the thesmothetai. Pay for jurors had been instituted by Pericles so that men with limited means were able to serve the state without undue loss of earnings, and perhaps no more than a fifth of the rich citizens actually did jury service.[98] Citizens under thirty were excluded from jury service,[99] and it may be that a high proportion of those who did serve were over forty-five – rather elderly by comparative standards. It was a conservative jibe that jury pay was a way of using the people's money to bribe the people. Aristophanes, in *The Wasps* for example, suggested – perhaps with some exaggeration – that the poor and elderly made pocket money by serving on juries.

The magistracy itself was not a career for aspiring legal experts. In fact, every citizen had the chance to become a magistrate at some time. No special qualifications were needed for candidature; it was simply required that the citizens in question had never themselves been condemned in court for any infamy.[100] There was no hierarchy of magistrates in Athens; all magistrates dealt directly with the Boule and the Assembly. This is in marked contrast to Sparta, where the special magistrates( ephors) were appointed with wide powers of supervision and control over the government and the administration of the laws. Any Athenian magistrate could be relieved of his office in the course of its term if his conduct was found to be unsatisfactory at a monthly review. On relinquishing his office, the magistrate had to give an account of his tenure, and if his administration was suspected of being dishonest, he could himself be subject to legal proceedings. At the completion of their year of service, principal magistrates passed to the Areopagus. Uncharacteristically, membership of this politically innocuous body was for life – an inexpensive and undemanding reward for service to the state.

Although the Areopagus had few effective political powers, it did retain certain important legal functions, notably in what might be broadly termed 'capital' cases,[101] including premeditated murder, wounding with intent to kill, arson (if the house was inhabited at the time) and poisoning. In cases of murder, it was entitled to impose the death penalty. Physical violence was normally punishable by exile and the confiscation of property.

The fifty-one criminal court judges (ephetai) were divided into three separate tribunals. At the first, the palladium, cases of incitement to murder and manslaughter were heard, and the maximum penalty was limited exile without confiscation of property. At the second, the delphinium, cases of homicide which were considered by the archon basileus (the examining magistrate) to be justified by way of mitigating circumstances were heard. A third tribunal dealt with cases of those already banished, possibly for manslaughter,[102] who had subsequently committed murder with intent. This 'court' was conducted by the sea; the accused – already in a state of banishment – had to conduct his defence from a boat while the judges sat on the shore.

It was the heliaia which dealt with most cases apart from homicide; this was the court of popular jurisdiction. Offences which involved men in public life were often brought before the Boule, and really serious cases – particularly those concerning the conduct of war – might actually be judged by the Assembly itself.[103]

Court procedures were conditioned not only by the nature of the offence but also the source of initiation of the charge. In private law-suits, only the injured party or their representative could bring the charge. A representative was essential in cases where minors, women, metics or slaves – that is technically, all non-citizens – were concerned. The plaintiff was allowed the assistance of a paid spokesman or advocate.

In criminal matters, however, anyone could prosecute. This included certain types of civil case, notably those of public indictment, where any citizen could regard himself as the injured party and bring a charge of unconstitutionality (graphe), a practice which encouraged public denunciations. This gave rise to public informers (sykophantai) who might well make allegations against the wealthy in the hope of extorting money to drop the prosecution. From different perspectives the same action can be seen as veiled blackmail or patriotic duty. Certainly it was a common feature of the Athenian political arena where ambition made it expedient to malign publicly one's personal enemies and political rivals.[104]

A prosecution was brought by summoning the defendant before the presiding magistrate. Both parties were allowed to interrogate one another and each other's witnesses. Speeches to the jury might be frank appeals to prejudice or exercises in flattery – especially in pleas for leniency. 'To bring one's wife and small children was a standard piece of stage setting [and] exchanging personal abuse of the most indecent kind was customary.'[105] In order to prevent the frivolous – or perhaps the malicious – multiplication of charges, in all private suits both parties were required to deposit a sum towards the defrayment of legal costs. In public hearings only the accuser had to make such a deposit. If he withdrew the charges, or did not obtain at least one-fifth of the votes when it came to the verdict,[106] he was liable to a fine of 1,000 drachmai. In a case where the state itself had incurred some material loss, the individuals who brought the prosecution were 'rewarded' with a proportion of the guilty person's fine which could amount to as much as three-quarters of the total sum.[107] By comparison, in the case of an acquittal, if the accuser did not obtain one-fifth of the votes cast, he was liable to pay a fine or even suffer a loss of civic rights (atimia). Paradoxically, this was considered necessary in order to curtail the activities of the public informers which the system encouraged.

Athens maintained a police force which was controlled by a group of magistrates called 'the eleven'. They were responsible for the state prisons, and brought those charges which necessitated preventative detention. They were also responsible for the summary executions of self-confessed murderers and those caught in flagrante

173

delicto.[108] Executions were carried out outside the walls of the city, and could take the form of chaining or tying to a plank or post and being left to die. This seems to have been reserved mainly for pirates and was really a variant of crucifixion.[109] Stoning to death was also practised. This had the doubtful virtue of being a participatory act which was sometimes considered appropriate for crimes which were an affront to the democratic system. Thus in 479 BC we find Lycidas stoned to death by his colleagues for proposing acceptance of the Persian peace terms.[110] There was also the drinking of hemlock as a form of privileged suicide, associated in the popular mind with the death of Socrates.[111] The term most used in Greek to denote capital punishment (apotympanismos) may refer to the exposure of criminals,[112] although some authorities maintain that it is impossible to know.[113]

When an accused person was found guilty by a majority of the votes, he was either sentenced according to a fixed penalty or there was an 'assessment of punishment' which called for another vote. Punishments varied according to the status of the offender. Imprisonment was normally restricted to non-citizens, and such niceties as confinement in the pillory, whipping on the wheel[114] and branding were reserved for slaves. Normally, punishments were either fines perhaps including the confiscation of property, or either temporary or permanent banishment, or perhaps loss of civil rights. A variant of these, and an institution peculiar to Athens, was the practice of ostracism.[115] This was a device – perhaps more political than judicial – whereby the Athenians sent one of their number into temporary banishment without bringing him to trial or even formulating a specific charge against him. Originally instituted by Cleisthenes to curb the possibility of tyranny, it was ostensibly intended as a preventative measure. The object was not to punish a crime, but to make its commission either impossible or unlikely by the banishment of those who were planning political subversion. Only one ostracism vote could be held each year, and only then if a preliminary committee of the Assembly decided that it had a prima facie case. The ostrakophoria, or extraordinary meeting of the Assembly to consider a possible ostracism, involved a secret vote, and was, in effect, a trial by presumption. Several names could be submitted for consideration, but only the person with the highest number of votes cast against him – and these must exceed 6,000 – was exiled, usually for ten years.[116] Unlike ordinary temporary banishment (phyge), the exile could retain control of his possessions and reside where he liked as long as he was well clear of Attica. He need be no further from Athens than Euboea or Argolis, that is about fifty miles from the city. He could even be recalled to civic service should the need arise, and be reinstated without obvious dishonour. There was, for instance, a general amnesty at the time of the threatened Persian invasion (480–479 BC) when those who had been ostracised were allowed to return. Ostracism was a common feature of the Classical period, but after the Peloponnesian War the practice tended to fall into disuse.[117]

In addition to this array of politico-legal penalties, there existed a number of religious and, presumably, archaic sanctions which could be invoked against the impious. These could range from the ritual condemnation or 'cursing' of offenders to the more serious deprivation of burial rights. It is difficult to know how effective these 'shaming' mechanisms were in the maintenance of public order in Athenian society.

A comparative analysis of the politico-legal machinery of Egypt and Athens involves the student in a set of seeming contradictions. One intriguing fact which emerges is that in Egypt, where law was theoretically the sole prerogative of the Pharaoh, the system was significantly less arbitrary than one might suppose. All was not subject to royal whim; monarchical capriciousness was largely contained by the force of tradition. Law and justice were deeply rooted in the unchanging principle of ma'at which, though variously interpreted and not entirely inflexible, ensured a relatively stable and enduring social order. Ma'at was the ideological continuity-principle which sustained an essentially homogeneous system. By contrast, the participatory system of Athens, with its carefully structured political constitution and its clearly defined legal administration, could be both arbitrary and inconsistent.

Athenian democracy was not a sham, even if it was confined only to those of citizen status. But the actual operation of the system was subject to a number of weaknesses,[118] some of which we have already identified. It was, to some extent, at the mercy of demagogues – perhaps a natural hazard of people's systems. Yet, in apparent contradiction of this, its procedures were so organised that ultimate power was vested in what has been termed the 'tyranny of the majority'.[119] A contemporary observer wrote:

> The Sovereign People recognise the fact that in foregoing the personal exercise of [such offices as sharing in the choice of actual military leadership] and leaving them to the control of the more competent citizens, they secure the balance of advantage for themselves. It is only in those departments of government which bring emolument and assist private households that the People care to keep in their own hands. . . . If any mischief should spring out of the deliberations of the assembly, the People charge that a handful of men acting against the interests of the citizens have ruined the state. But

175

if any good result ensue, they, the People, at once take the credit of that to themselves.[120]

Similar sentiments have been voiced by some modern commentators;[121] though others have advanced the complementary argument that power – particularly economic power – always really rested with the traditional middle classes who were even joined in their self-conscious civic superiority by the lower orders of citizens.[122]

The extractive capacity of Athens at the zenith of her power was considerable. The state grew rich from the autonomous entrepreneuralism of citizens and metics, and particularly from the wealth (or tribute?) contributed by her allies in the Delian league. This, of course, enhanced her distributive capacities; this is evidenced by her support of the arts and the financial maintenance of what can be seen as an extensive public bureaucracy. In regulative terms, the Athenian system was necessarily limited by the diffusion of authority, and its responsive capacities were circumscribed by the procedural mechanisms for the forming and mobilisation of opinion. In the symbolic sphere, there were limited practical applications. Religion was expressed mainly in terms of symbolic secular legitimations, and ritual observances were civic rather than metaphysical in emphasis.

## Summary analysis of political organisation

| *Egypt* | *Athens* |
|---|---|
| 1 Compulsory/high extractive capacities at both internal and external (Empire) levels. | 1 High external (League) extractive capacities. |
| 2 Centralised regulative capacities based on autocratic power. | 2 Diffused regulative capacities; authority based on consensus. |
| 3 Low differentiation of roles and relative paucity of autonomous groups. | 3 High differentiation of roles and relative proliferation of autonomous – especially economic – groups. |
| 4 State control of resource allocation. | 4 Market control of commercial activity with high level of control of public expenditure. |
| 5 Ascriptive status orientations. Narrowly graded ranking system within broad categories defined in terms of birth and wealth with mobility largely confined to military/priestly sphere. | 5 Achievement status orientations. Broadly defined ranking system based on wealth and citizenship, with mobility largely confined to the politico-economic sphere. |

| 6 Relatively unlimited capacity to elicit response and mobilise resources. | 6 Relatively limited capacity to elicit response and mobilise opinion. |
| 7 Strong ideological/symbolic legitimations. Cosmic orientations. | 7 Secular symbolic legitimations. Civic orientations. |

As a highly generalised distinction, the Egyptian system was theoretically arbitrary but controlled by precedent in practice, whereas the Athenian system was sometimes quite arbitrary in practice, although constitutional in theory.

# 11 Military organisation and expansionism

The contention that men are intrinsically warlike, and that war itself is a 'natural' activity has provoked a good deal of discussion among scholars. One view, that men are basically competitive and self-seeking, and therefore in need of less destructive ways in which to canalise their aggressive instincts has its proponents.[1] Alternatively, there are those who insist that war is a cultural invention not a biological necessity. 'It is like any other inventions in terms of which we order our lives, such as writing, marriage ... trial by jury or burial of the dead, and so on.'[2]

The further and probably more popular argument is that war is an inevitable concomitant of the development of the state, the struggle for land and natural resources which generates forms of class societies. This view sees war not so much as a product of man's nature as a product of social evolution; the problem being rooted in history rather than the human psyche. The 'answer' to war, therefore, is seen – perhaps simplistically – in terms of social change, in the outlawing of classes and the more equal distribution of goods.[3] Such structural arguments have been qualified by Mosca who contends that they confuse the 'struggle for existence' with the 'struggle for pre-eminence' which is characteristically human and 'a constant phenomenon which arises in all human societies from the most highly civilized down'.[4] This war-as-a-social-product view tends to be supported indirectly by those who not only correlate the incidence of war with the growth of urbanism and the fortress-towns but also with the rise of the new military-élites which were a concomitant of this development.[5]

A complementary argument is that the incidence of war has been associated with the growth of nationalism and the accompanying breakdown of the traditional moral order, and the liberating but disorganising influence of liberal social norms. It is held that the

178

older identities of estate, class, region and religion have been eroded by the emergence of the mass society, and that this, in turn, has precipitated the collapse of the stable moral order.[6]

There are additional hypotheses which – though more amorphous – have their own psychological plausibility. These relate more specifically to the question of values – to morality and rationality. Can all human differences be satisfactorily resolved by reason? G. H. Mead, for instance, insisted that there should be no situation which would not eventually yield to an intelligent analysis of the facts.[7]

The problem of why *men* go to war is really only peripheral to our main discussion, and detailed analyses of the types and occasions of human conflict are only marginally relevant. These have already merited competent treatment in specific texts.[8] On the other hand, the related problem of why *societies* go to war and the ways in which this is related to their respective forms of social order is important for our considerations of traditional systems.

Theories to account for the phenomenon of war proliferate, but the conclusion that aggression is in some way inimical to the human condition seems inescapable.[9] Regardless of the historicist implications, it has to be admitted that, in certain circumstances, men have persistently resorted to violent solutions to their politico-economic problems.[10] There have been exceptions, but these are extremely rare.[11] These traditional views have been reasserted by Stanislav Andreski who repudiates various kinds of popular explanation as naive and simplistic. He is particularly impatient with psychological theories and 'absurd ideas' which argue that all racial and ethnic animosity is pathological. He has considerable reservations about the entire question of war and cultural relativism. Instead, he maintains the validity of the demographic-economic position. Scarcity promotes war. Struggles for land, wealth, food, women, power and honours, are unavoidable. Struggle is omnipresent because resources are perennially scarce, and therefore war has a functional importance in ensuring the necessary balance of wealth over population.[12] These views should be compared with those, say, of Malinowski who has argued that war is often waged in primitive societies for status and ritualistic reasons, and that the politico-economic motive can be conspicuously absent.[13] Richard Lapiere has contended that the land-hunger theory of war is something of a myth. Many early migrations – including those of the Dorians into Greece – he maintains, were occasioned by social vacua rather than retreat from a deteriorating physical habitat.[14] To some extent, over-population and underpopulation are social evaluations. History is replete with instances of societies which have lived for centuries at near subsistence levels in areas which, in our terms, may be regarded

179

as overpopulated, without resorting to war on neighbouring peoples who were both weaker in numbers and in technology. The Egyptian Old Kingdom might well come into this category, although it must be admitted that in this and other cases, there was probably a complex of reasons why expansionist policies were abjured. In general, therefore, Andreski's arguments can still be maintained in terms of 'ophelimites', a neologism he employs to cover anything which is desired. In so far as men struggle to survive, and strive to possess either material goods or the intangibles of social esteem, then human conflict will continue indefinitely.

If war derives from the struggle for gain, it is probably useful to distinguish between conflicts which arise from 'position scarcity' and those which arise from 'resource scarcity'.[15] Position scarcity can be defined as the condition in which an object cannot occupy two places at the same time or fulfil two different functions simultaneously. Athens, as ostensible leader and benefactor of the Delian League, could not consistently perform the roles of both protector and oppressor – although she tried to do both. 'Resource scarcity' is much more straightforward. Conflict occurs when contending states cannot both have *all* they want. Different value judgments will almost certainly condition the demand or need for scarce resources and positions. Hence mutually exclusive and/or mutually incompatible values are the inevitable concomitants of conflict.

So for the sociologist, the key issue centres on the extent to which war is a function of social arrangements. Even if aggression is 'in-built', what determines its institutionalised expression as militarism? It is here that we must note the useful distinction between 'militarism' and the 'military way' made by Alfred Vagts.[16] For Vagts, the military way is 'marked by a primary concentration of men and materials on winning specific objectives of power with utmost efficiency . . . it is limited in scope [and] confined to one function. . . .' Militarism, on the other hand, 'presents a vast array of customs, interests, prestige and actions . . . it displays qualities of caste and cult, authority and belief.'[17] Militarism is seen, therefore, as something quite distinct from the military way, in as much as it is unlimited in scope, and consequently permeates the whole of society. In other words, war is different from militarism. Societies everywhere indulge in warfare, and some take the resigned and rational view that if war is necessary, it should be prosecuted with the utmost care and efficiency. By contrast, militarism is a way of life. It involves a complex of traditions and values which is integral to particular social orders. In model militaristic systems, war is regarded as a valorous game, an esteem-achieving enterprise, and aggression itself may be elevated to the rank of virtus – that which conduces to heroic manliness.

180

Perhaps distinctions should also be made in relation to different types of 'conquest', which may be classified as economic and cultural as well as that which is seen as unambiguously military.[18] As academic distinctions these seem to be legitimate, but whether they can always be clearly distinguished in practice is open to question. Certainly economic and cultural[19] exploitation have often followed in the wake of military success. The ancient world was virtually unanimous on this as a right, for example, Xenophon (*Cyropaedia* VII, 5, 73): 'it is a law established for all time among all men that when a city is taken in war, the persons and the property of the inhabitants belong to the captors.'

It can be argued that nothing is ever done out of a 'pure' motive, and this probably also applies to war. The initiative in particular cases was obviously not blatant and unadulterated greed, as with, say, the predatory adventures of the Assyrians in the first half of the first millennium.[20] Conquest for ideological reasons would tend to support this.[21] Ideologies represent conceptions of the desirable, and can be regarded as alien or opposed depending on the extent to which values and beliefs can be accommodated or absorbed. In this sense, ideological conquest – that is, conquest to perpetuate or universalise the ideology – was something of a rarity in the ancient world.[22]

The reasons or ostensible motives for militaristic activity in different societies are complicated by the apparent or declared intentions of politico–military rulers.[23] The aims of leaders were often very diversified. Not infrequently, they used their rule – and even more commonly, their success – to enrich themselves and secure favourable positions for their families and friends. But this could usually only be achieved by using success to tighten their hold on the existing bureaucracy and extending their control of the aristocratic élite.[24] Where the military leaders were not themselves political rulers, the military vocation could be a source of mobility for the ambitious careerist. Military leaders were often members of the traditional nobility as, for instance, the samurai in Tokugawa Japan[25] or the war-chiefs in many pre-Columbian American societies.[26] But this was by no means always the case.[27] The power of some military echelons could rival that of both the established literati and the priesthood, as in the Egyptian New Kingdom. And where they were not drawn from the aristocracy, they might even threaten the existing hierarchical structure itself, a situation exemplified – on one interpretation – during the rule of Marius in the later days of the Roman Republic.[28]

Again, politico–military leaders in traditional societies seem rarely to have been impelled by ideological considerations,[29] although ideological *justifications* have always been very much in evidence to

181

rationalize or explain official actions, as we shall see exemplified in different ways in the experience of the Egyptians and the Greeks.

## Egypt

The Egyptian military machine can only really be discussed in relation to particular periods of Egyptian history. The forces of the Old and Middle Kingdoms had a thoroughly amateur appearance beside the large armies of the New Kingdom with their chariotry, mercenary stiffened infantry and marines. Similarly, expansionist motivations – in so far as they can be ascertained – varied with both period and monarch. These often appear as responses to the external pressures which were first seriously experienced during the Hyksos invasions and occupation[30] (c. 1730–c. 1570), and much later in the Hittite threat and the incursions of the so-called 'Sea-peoples' during the New Kingdom period.

Egyptian military organisation, therefore, can only be described in general terms. As is to be expected, it changed with the centuries, so any description must have a rather contrived synchronic 'look' which cannot do justice either to actual circumstances or the passage of time. More problematically, Egyptian expansionist policies can be related to structural factors, and yet more tenuously to those ideological imperatives which undoubtedly informed the system.

During the Old Kingdom, the government does not appear to have maintained any uniform or compact military organisation. The evidence[31] suggests that each nome or administrative district possessed its own militia commanded by civil officials who were not necessarily trained professional soldiers. The various temple properties also supported bodies of troops who were mainly engaged in the seemingly unending task of mining and quarrying besides acting as guards to the estates themselves. In the event of serious hostilities, these motley militia, perhaps together with some Nubian auxiliaries, were mobilised as quickly as possible and put in the command of some responsible official nominated by the king. The king had no standing army other than a royal corps or bodyguard which probably outnumbered any other local force.[32] It comprised both Egyptians and Nubians whose primary task was that of policing the capital and protecting the king. Having to rely on this specialist corps was both a strength and a weakness for the monarch. It meant that there was no separate class of military professionals to usurp power. But it also meant that his military strength was vested on the goodwill and loyalty of nomarchs and priests. This decentralisation of authority into the hands of numbers of local officials may have contributed to the upheavals of the First Intermediate period which was marked by the growing independence of the nomes.

182

The relative isolation of Egypt in Old Kingdom times is thought to have generated such a sense of security from external aggression that possibly a permanent force was felt to be unnecessary. This is not to argue for some form of spatial determination[33] but it can be reasonably hypothesised that this comparative seclusion gave rise to a kind of passivity which was entirely foreign to the later Empire period. This would have to be qualified in the case of the Old Kingdom invasions of Nubia and Canaan. In one campaign in Nubia, Pepi I (Sixth Dynasty) exacted tribute of negro levies, and in Canaan he pursued and attacked the border Bedouin.[34] The generalisation of non-aggressiveness would seem to apply but only with some reservations.

The Middle Kingdom was marked by the increasing influence of the nobility and the inevitable frictions which this generated between these powerful officials and the king. There is evidence of the usurpation of inordinate powers by commanders in outlying territories, and at least one attempted regicide during the Twelfth Dynasty.[35] As a reassertion of authority, it is not surprising that the monarchy increased the strength of its special military attendants.

It is during this period that there appear the first professional soldiers, apart from the royal guard, of whom we have any knowledge in Ancient Egypt. In companies of 100 men they garrisoned various strongholds from Nubia to the Asiatic frontier; they campaigned regularly and also participated in quarrying expeditions. They comprised the nucleus of a standing army which was supplemented for specific purposes by local levies, possibly of free-born citizens of the middle classes. These contigents were commanded by high-born officials who owed direct allegiance to the monarch on a quasi-feudal basis. The overall size of the army is unknown, but the local militia may have numbered as many as 500–1,000 for each district.[36]

All free citizens were organised and enrolled in a form of age-set system, and became generationally liable to military and public service. Large-scale hostilities were still largely unknown and war – in the main – consisted of little more than loosely organised forays into the territories of immediate neighbours and punitive expeditions into Nubia where fortresses have been excavated as far south as the Third Cataract.[37]

The Middle Kingdom effectively closed with the appearance of the Hyksos or so-called 'Shepherd-Kings' who should perhaps be known as the 'rulers of foreign lands'. Their origins are uncertain, but they probably combined some West Semitic peoples with groups of Hurrians who descended on Mesopotamia as well as Syria–Canaan and Egypt.[38] They may have arrived initially as predatory nomads, but stayed to share power with their reluctant Egyptian

183

hosts. The conquered learned a great deal about warfare from the invaders, especially in the use of chariots and the composite bow. A few of their fortified camps have survived in Egypt and Asia, of which some are up to 1,000 yards square. In fact, it has been estimated that one large enclosure in the Delta may have housed as many as 10,000 men and their horses.[39] Similar beaten earth structures have been located as far east as Iran and the Caucasus, and are evidence of the widespread influence of the Hyksos at this time.[40] The Egyptians, however, were manifestly superior at sea. Naval tactics were obviously unfamiliar to the Hyksos who were much more at home in the saddle.[41] Hyksos power was finally broken by an Egyptian army led by a Theban military aristocracy which had gained considerable expertise in its engagements with the enemy.[42] The army, tempered by its continual campaigning against invaders, was now ready for more ambitious enterprises. And so the embryonic Empire began to take shape.

This was to be the new era of Egyptian military organisation and expansionism. Until this time, as we have seen, warfare had been a periodic rather than a relatively permanent state of affairs. Army recruitment had not always been easy, and ordinary soldiers appear to have enjoyed comparatively little social prestige.[43] Campaigning had, therefore, required special mobilisation, and defensive measures were sometimes no more than hurried ad hoc arrangements.[44] Basically, all this changed with the new martial emphasis of the Empire.

Under the Empire, two large armies in four divisions named after the gods, Amun, Ptah, Ra and Seth were permanently stationed in Upper and Lower Egypt. There was also a form of police force composed chiefly of Nubians. The actual numbers and composition of the army are uncertain. Each division may have consisted of about 5,000 men; quite a force to be supported by the Egyptian economy. It is certainly unlikely that the Egyptians ever invaded Asia with more than 25,000–30,000 men,[45] and these usually included troops who had been recruited from neighbouring territories. For example, at the battle of Kadesh, c. 1295 BC, Ramesses II had a contingent of Sardinians who had been captured in previous wars. Nubians and Libyans were allowed to win their freedom by taking service with the army which in later periods came to contain more and more mercenaries.

The supreme commander of the army was the Pharaoh himself, though some executive functions were often delegated to the crown prince. There was a war council of high army officers and state officials which was nominally consulted before the initiation of any particular campaign. The plan and its execution – particularly when successful – were attributed to the inner esoteric knowledge of the divine ruler. The Pharaoh's due glory was not to be eclipsed by the strategic inspirations of ambitious subordinates.

The executive command of the army was the responsibility of a general staff who were primarily concerned with logistics and organisation, tasks which in earlier days were often among the duties of the vizier or chief treasurer.[46] It can be no coincidence that members of the general staff were regarded as the best people to take over kingship at various critical periods of pharaonic vacua. A number of trained staff officers succeeded to the throne at different times including Ay who followed Tutankhamun because no direct royal succession was possible.

Army officers were usually educated men who were drawn from the ranks of minor scribes or those who had been educated for the forces since boyhood. It was, however, possible to be promoted from the ranks, and a career in the army was possibly 'the only opportunity for an adventurous and uneducated man, either Egyptian or alien to achieve a position of importance or affluence'.[47] The actual desirability of the army as a career can be questioned in the light of contemporary records. It is clear that some scribes did not view the prospect of military life as anything to be coveted: 'Listen to . . . his campaigns in Syria, and his marches over mountains. He carries his water on his shoulder like an ass's burden; his spine is dislocated. He drinks brackish water and sleeps with one eye open. When he encounters the enemy . . . there is no strength left in his limbs [and] when the time comes for him to return to Egypt he is like a worm-eaten piece of wood.'[48] This, of course, may be construed as the reactionary pique of petty teachers and administrators who led drab, inconsequential and relatively sheltered lives at home – but it is probably not without a measure of truth. A different situation obtained for higher officers who were served by numbers of orderlies for whom they were in part financially responsible.

But the military life could also be profitable. As early as the Middle Kingdom, there is evidence of rewards for service. Ahmes, a naval officer (see note 41) who was a hero of the successful onslaught upon the Hyksos at Avaris received the 'gold of valour', women, slaves and a tract of land. And for similar services, another member of the same family was awarded 'amulets, bangles, rings, sceptres, two golden axes, two silver axes and further decorations in the shape of six flies and three lions of gold'.[49] It is a reasonable assumption that those who were more highly placed were in a better position to secure such benefits, but the evidence suggests that the perks of the profession were available to all who were commended for valour. A soldier not only had a fixed wage, he might also be rewarded with a grant of land in his own town, and with a distribution of the booty which had been confiscated from the conquered.

Discipline was strict. Superior officers could sentence their juniors to be beaten for a variety of offences. There is an account of a soldier who was given a hundred blows for abandoning a chariot which he had purchased himself at a cost of eight deben of silver.[50] But alongside this must be read other accounts such as the sack of Arrad in Phoenicia by Tuthmosis III where we are told 'the army of his Majesty was drunk and anointed with oil every day'[51] – presumably on the confiscated fruits of victory. This indicates that even in rigorously supervised military units, some indiscipline is inevitable in given circumstances.

The weaponry of the Egyptians became much more sophisticated after the Hyksos interlude. In preparation for war, troops were equipped with weapons from the royal armoury, and classified according to their armed functions. Spearmen carried long spears with copper or bronze points, and large shields covered with leather. Archers were provided with bows and arrows, and both spearmen and archers also carried an assortment of axes, daggers, short swords, and sometimes slings. Weapons were normally of copper or bronze; iron was introduced late in the Ramesside period from Anatolia, and was one of the factors in Hittite military supremacy.[52] Uniform was simple and hardly protective, consisting of a short linen skirt and a narrow leather guard which acted as a kind of rudimentary 'jock-strap'.[53] Officers were mainly distinguished from the men by their axe or mace, and by the ceremonial fan which was an emblem of rank.

The most important innovation in the army of the Empire was the introduction of the chariot. Although used sometimes for peaceful purposes, it was essentially a war chariot drawn by a span of horses and manned by a driver and his partner who was armed with a spear, and a bow and arrow. There is now evidence that the horse was introduced into Egypt from Asia as early as the Middle Kingdom and before the Hyksos invasions.[54] What seems strange from a modern historical perspective is that the Egyptians had no cavalry until a much later period, and it may be that the actual practice of riding horses was repulsive to the Egyptians.[55]

By the Ramesside period, soldiering had become a hereditary profession supported largely by a long-suffering peasantry. Herodotus' comments on the army of the Twenty-sixth Dynasty are probably appropriate: that son succeeded father in families which learned no other trade. They all owned property, and members of the royal bodyguard were entitled to extra rations of corn, wine and beef.[56]

With time the Egyptian army came more and more to rely upon the services of mercenaries. They were recruited from many parts of the Empire which were garrisoned by army personnel. Nubia supplied negro auxiliaries, and Libya provided yet further contingents sometimes as a form of tribute to the state. Later still, mercenaries from non-controlled territories were employed including Sardinians and troops from the Aegean. Arguably these territories were within the Egyptian sphere of influence, but this became decreasingly the case as the first millennium wore on, and other states successively eroded the power and authority of Egypt.

It can be reasonably inferred that with military success and the influx of new wealth, the Egyptians themselves became less willing to undergo the rigours of months of hard campaigning on foreign soil. The thirst for conquest was abated by growing affluence. Others could do the fighting, captives could serve as soldiers. The Egyptians wanted to enjoy the fruits of their victories, and re-occupy themselves with local concerns. So by the fourteenth century BC, we find that Akhenaten actually preferred foreigners in his army, especially in his bodyguard.[57] Later, in the reign of Ramesses IV, we find a body of 5,000 troops in which there was not a single Egyptian, being sent to the quarries at Hammamat.[58] Perhaps the material and status benefits of hewing stone were rather marginal for the front-line professionals of a warrior-Pharaoh.

Retrospectively, we can see how inherently dangerous this expansionist policy was. When their military service was ended, these professionals were pensioned with small grants of land. They were expected to settle, however uneasily, for a peaceful retirement, but they may well have become a persistent source of anxiety to the government.[59] Eventually, they developed into a military class. Their relations vis-à-vis the state became increasingly uncertain. In time, they gained such power and influence that they became, in effect, a state within the state which alternatively both supported and threatened the native dynasties.[60]

Campaigns were both parades of power and predatory expeditions. They began at much the same time of year, after the Egyptian spring harvest but a little before the Asiatics harvested their own produce – a time when, economically, they were at their most vulnerable. One campaign text for Phoenicia records that, 'their orchards were filled with their fruit. Their wines were found lying in their vats . . . and their grain was on the threshing floors . . . more plentiful than the sands of the shore. . . .'[61]

The treatment of conquered peoples varied, and it is sometimes difficult to distinguish between state policy and the capriciousness of individual Pharaohs. Usually, the land was plundered and put under tribute, frequently in the form of an obligation to supply Egypt with priority goods such as coniferous woods, including the much-prized 'cedars of Lebanon'. Towns were not always razed, nor the people massacred or enslaved. For example, we find that Tuthmosis III

187

spared Megiddo even after a seven months' siege, and the exaggerated official claim that he 'destroyed' Kadesh in his thirtieth year did not obviate the necessity of reconquering it yet again in his final campaign twelve years later.[62] On the other hand, slaughter was by no means unknown. Amenophis II does not hesitate to inform posterity that he personally crushed the skulls of seven Asiatic princes and hanged their bodies on a city wall to discourage further rebellion.[63] Nor are we spared the details of his exploits in Syria when single-handedly he drove into the town of Khashabu and returned with sixteen of the enemy, still alive, tied to the two sides of his chariot, and twenty severed hands hanging from the foreheads of his horses.[64]

Captives were sometimes killed for accepted ideological reasons. Enemy massacre was enemy sacrifice as a thanksgiving to the gods who had granted the victory. So we read of the battles of Ramesses III against the 'Sea-peoples'; how he crushed their army and scattered their ships with enormous losses, 'over 12,500 slain upon the field and at least a 1,000 captives . . . taken.' There was then the usual triumph at the royal residence when the king viewed the captives and the trophies from the balcony while his nobles 'rejoiced below'. The significant point is that we are told that 'Amon, who had granted the great victory, did not fail to receive his accustomed sacrifice of living victims, and all Egypt rejoiced in restored security.'[65] Similarly, we find that before his Libyan campaign, Merneptah, the successor of Ramesses II, saw a vision of the god Ptah who held a sword before him and commanded him not to be afraid. The result was an inspired and innovatory use of his archers, 'the bowmen of his Majesty spent six hours of destruction among them [the Libyans], then they were delivered to the sword'.[66]

The religious overtones of military activity can also be seen in lesser ways. The cursing of enemies in the texts[67] appears to reflect a quasi-mystical approach to the problems of state – and perhaps more specifically – pharaonic security. Real and potential foes were sometimes castigated in terms which covered most contingencies. Perhaps it was done on the assumption that to name a thing gave power over that which was named.[68] On the other hand, it may simply have been an elementary exercise in intimidation. The triumph-songs also found in Egyptian literature appear to have a similar mystical basis. As early as the Sixth Dynasty, we read:

The army returned in safety
It had destroyed the land of the Sand-dwellers . . .
It overturned their strongholds.
It cut down their figs and vines . . .
It had slain tens of thousands of soldiers . . .
It had seized multitudes of living captives.[69]

Allowing for a measure of customary hyperbole, the sentiments are transparently clear. Later during the Empire, with the accession of the warrior-kings, the attribution of victory to the gods is much less ambiguous. The poet of Amenophis III puts words into the mouth of the god, Amun:

> When I turn my face to the South, I work a wonder for thee
> I cause the chiefs of the miserable Kush to turn to thee
> Bearing their tribute on their backs . . .
> When I turn my face to the West I work a wonder for thee,
> I cause thee to capture the Tehennu, none are left. . . .[70]

The campaigns are not described, they are merely paeans of praise to the triumphant Pharaoh. But in the later triumph-songs of Ramesses II, there is certainly a 'feel' of the battle itself. He prays to Amun in his plight at Kadesh in his struggle against the Hittites. The style is loquacious and self-extolling, and purports to reaffirm his divine capabilities when deserted by his troops:

> At the cry of my despair swiftly the god came to me
> Took my hand and gave me strength
> Till my might was as the might of a hundred thousand men
> With the rapid onward sweep of a fierce consuming flame
> I destroyed their serried ranks . . .
> Slew and wearied not to slay.
> In terror they did flee to the water's edge . . .
> Rotted were their hearts with fear as they tasted of my hand
> And amazed they shrieked aloud,
> . . . No mortal man is he![71]

Egyptian kings sometimes took enemy hostages, but this policy was only marginally prompted by ideological motives. Certain Pharaohs such as Tuthmosis III[72] combined the holding of hostages with the practice of egyptianising foreign princes. The holding of hostages was obviously a form of insurance against possible future insurrection. But it also facilitated a kind of ideological inculcation of Egyptian values which sometimes paid dividends in times of crisis. Presumably the 'sons of princes' were quite young, and this new experience was, in effect, a type of secondary socialisation.[73]

The surrender of tribute, too, had its ideological implications. The simple acknowledgment of the Egyptian gods by non-Egyptians can be interpreted as almost anything from token acts of obeisance to diplomatic tolerance. We find Asiatic slave-workers in the early fifteenth century BC making images of their own Semitic gods in Egyptian forms, and subject nobles 'giving praise to the Lord of the Two Lands [i.e. Upper and Lower Egypt], kissing the ground to the

189

good god . . . as they extol [his] victories with tribute upon their backs . . . seeking that there be given to them the breath of life.'[74] Yet during the next Dynasty, the Nineteenth, there are what appear to be genuine acceptances of the Egyptian deities by traditional enemies. The Egyptian scribe, admittedly a biased source, causes the Hittite king, Hattusilis, to attribute the current drought to the anger and, by implication, supremacy – of the Egyptian god, Seth, and to send 'gifts of fealty to the good god . . . that [the Hittites] might live'.[75] Similarly, alliances and peace treaties were contracted with religious solemnisation. The gods were dutifully called upon to witness the good intentions of the participants (see Chapter 3). It will always be arguable whether this was authentic supplicancy or customary ritual gestures.

To summarise: the Old Kingdom was marked by a singular lack of military expansionism. It may, therefore, be somewhat ironic if – as has been argued[76] – the only really successful peasant revolt in the history of ancient Egypt which effectively brought the Old King-dom to a close, occurred when the peasants were still eligible for military service. This was, in all probability, actually a rebellion of the nomarchs, but this must have had appreciable peasant support. By contrast, the New Kingdom operated an extensive expansionist policy with a highly trained professional army increasingly supple-mented by mercenaries. This is analogous to the transition from the military state to the militaristic state.

From early times, military success was seen as a primary task of the monarch, but this received increasing emphasis under the Empire. To some extent this is represented in the pictorial art of Egypt depicting the victories of her forces. Even as early as the First Dynasty, the king is shown destroying his defeated enemies (on the so-called Narmer Palette). By the time of the expansionist Eight-eenth Dynasty, the Karnak inscriptions show a gigantic figure of Tuthmosis III defeating dwarf-like Syrians. It may be that the texts emphasised the traditional at the expense of the historical. The army itself, is not really depicted until the Nineteenth Dynasty and then only in a rather subsidiary position as in the victory reliefs of Ramesses III at Medinet Habu. 'The king [appears] as the . . . sole agent of victory. But . . . [in this] . . . as in every other deed of his reign, the king acts out and realizes a pre-figured course of events.'[77] A stylised Pharaoh was depicted by the temple artists in classic victory poses of supreme military confidence and ability supported by an anonymous and often invisible army.

It can be hypothesised that the insistent emphasis in the Empire upon the invincibility and prowess of the monarch was, in fact, a compensation for the almost imperceptible diminution of acceptance of the Pharaoh's divinity. The militaristic Pharaoh succeeded the remotely god-like king of the Old Kingdom. Could the prowess-emphasis have been a reaction to status-uncertainty? Military assertiveness can possibly be correlated with diminishing charisma. Alternatively, military success may be seen as a physical proof of divinity and of heterodeistic approval.[78] Perhaps mundane achievement reflected supramundane validations.

It might further be hypothesised that, under given circumstances,[79] there might even be an inverse relationship between militarism and ideology in that where militarism is strong, ideology may be weak. At its most effective, as in the Old Kingdom, ideology does not need militaristic assertiveness to bring political cohesion. When the potency of ideology is maximised, the coercive action of the state may not be necessary – a supportive military presence is enough. In fact, the development of the military ethos in Egyptian society may even be construed as a revolutionary ideology to counter the growing power of the traditional priesthoods with whom the Pharaoh had ambiguous relations. He both supported the temples by his benefactions, and feared the divisive potentialities inherent in their increasing wealth and prestige. He needed their aid in containing the new class of military experts which the Empire had produced, and who now constituted a new challenge to the divine authority.

Although the capacities of the gods to bring benefits to their respective adherents was thought to be reflected in military success and failure, there were no overt ideological conflicts which impelled expansionist activities. The militaristic Pharaohs were not intent on spreading a new faith. The gods of Egypt were seen very much as Egypt's gods although, during the Empire, there was some recognition of the idea that they might be identified with the gods of other nations.

The militaristic operations of the Empire were expressions of resource rather than position scarcity. There were no obvious conflicts of role or ambiguities of function. Given the pressures and imperatives, the activities of the state followed a consistent line. On the other hand, certain prized goods, particularly wood and metals, were scarce and the possibility of ensuring a monopolisation of supply must have been a very real incentive to the warrior kings. The prescriptions for royal reassertiveness were militarism and expansionism which were justified in ideological terms. The maintenance of the state involved traditional measures, but these economic and defensive requirements were inextricably bound up with imperial ambition and the validation of a unique divinity.

## Athens

The art of war seems to have been something which was temporarily lost to the Greeks of the so-called Dark Ages. Vestigial memories of

191

the elaborate military organisation of the Mycenaean period remained in the writings of Homer. These reflect the time when the power of the army was concentrated in the persons of the king and his companions and retainers. These are depicted as possessing horses and shield-bearers and chariots which merely conveyed warriors to and from the battlefield. They are shown as clothed in full body armour together with large shields of wood and hide. This contrasts with the equipment of the Classical period where the cavalry generally was given a subordinate role and heavily-armed hoplites were the norm. In the Homeric writings, the kings' subjects follow as rather ill-armed foot soldiers whose confused encounters are only a backcloth for the main action. The valorous but often indecisive combats between princely contestants were the foci of the poems.[80]

The next phase of military development is also reflected in the poems. The masses were given a form of tactical organisation based upon kinship groupings.[81] The Myrmidon battalions, for example, consisted of 500 men each,[82] and in battle the army was arranged in three lines, the chariots, the inferior infantry and lastly the best reserve troops.[83] The developmental phase which most closely approximated to the fifth-century pattern is also anticipated in the poems, namely, the formation of the phalanx the compact group of heavily armed troops or hoplites.[84] These wore leather and metal armour, were equipped with lances and smaller bronze shields, and their superiority lay in their ability to maintain an unbroken line in the face of an enemy charge.[85] Evidence shows that this type of infantry was evolved a considerable time before the Classical period; hoplite formations were depicted in vase paintings from the early seventh century BC,[86] and Gyges, tyrant of Lydia, was certainly using hoplites at about this time.[87]

In earlier times, the cavalry had dominated the battlefield, as the aristocratic arm of any Greek force. Aristotle had maintained that during this early period, the Greek states had relied on the cavalry for the main military strength. This had meant a reliance on the aristocratic classes who could afford to keep horses. But when the military strength of the city came to rely on hoplites, the basis of the constitution was necessarily widened.[88] This cannot be verified from present sources, but it has a ring of authenticity. The change to highly organised infantry formations almost certainly represents a decline in the political as well as the military pre-eminence of the aristocracy, and the new ascendency of the Greek middle classes.[89] It also reflects the emergence of the autonomous city-state mentality. The hoplite armies were citizen armies. Individual combat between nobles or heroes gave way to tight formations of mutually dependent troops. The cavalry was largely relegated to light skirmishing

192

operations, often on the peripheries of an engagement. The Greeks had never made any marked contribution to the art of warfare, but the development of the hoplite armies was a tactical innovation of real consequence which influenced military thinking for centuries.[90]

The hoplite was equipped with body armour (cuirass or thorax) which was usually made of bronze strips backed with leather and which covered the upper torso but failed to protect the loins. The armour was completed by a helmet, almost always surmounted by a crest, and a set of metal greaves for the legs – a practice which had been largely abandoned by the fourth century BC. For defence, he also had a shield made of bronze or leather which was fitted with a double grip device so that it could be held firmly with both arm and hand. For offence he had a spear which was designed for thrusting rather than throwing, and a reserve weapon which was either a dagger or a short sword.

Hoplites attacked in lines of perhaps eight deep, a phalanx of human armour which pushed forwards until either they or the opposing line broke. Once this happened, it was usually difficult to reform. Exceptionally, the Spartan hoplites[91] were greatly praised for their ability to regroup,[92] and this was seen as a product of their rigorous and superior training.[93]

As we have seen (Chapter 7), it was normal for the young Athenian male to exercise in the palaistra; gymnastic training was part of the preparation for military service, and this continued in adult life. In fact, it is difficult to see how the non-professional Athenian army could have survived without this constant emphasis on physical fitness after the initial period of military training between eighteen and twenty.

Every Athenian was liable for military service between the ages of eighteen and sixty. A period of initial training was customary for epheboi (males between eighteen and twenty), but it is not certain whether those of the lowest tax class (thetes) who mainly served as rowers in the Athenian navy were exempt from this obligation.[94] During this period of training, epheboi – although technically citizens – were exempt from political duties and even legal prosecution.[95]

From twenty to fifty, Athenians remained members of the regular forces, and between fifty and sixty they were classed as veterans. In peace time, the bulk of the army remained on reserve; the veterans, with the epheboi and the metics formed a kind of territorial army which guarded frontiers and strong-points, as required. This was a necessary contingency when it is realised that from the Persian Wars in 490 BC until the battle of Chaeronea in 338 BC, Athens was at war more than two years out of every three, and never had ten consecutive years of peace.

The tribal basis of recruitment still obtained in Classical times. Epheboi were registered for military training within their fathers' demes at the beginning of the Attic year. The total annual enrolment involved 700 or so recruits. The deme-assembly checked their physical aptitudes and their ages and credentials to ensure that they were legitimate and freeborn. Special cases were brought before the court of heliaia,[96] and any youth found guilty of imposture was immediately sold into slavery. There was also a second scrutiny by the Boule; again the question of status was the special concern of those who conducted the screening. The officers in charge of the epheboi were chosen from the tribes by which they were paid on a per capita basis[97] for the upkeep of their recruits. In addition, special instructors for gymnastics, combat techniques, etc., were nominated, and an overall director was elected, who had final authority for the group and their welfare. At the end of the first year of training, the epheboi were paraded before the Assembly in the public theatre, and the state presented them each with a spear and shield in recognition of their military graduation. During the second year, they carried out patrols and garrison duties in certain key areas,[98] and the towns where they were stationed sometimes made financial contributions towards the cost of their training.[99]

In 431 BC, at the opening of the Peloponnesian War, Athens had a regular army of 13,000 hoplites and 1,000 cavalry together with a territorial reserve which included 1,400 epheboi, 2,500 veterans and 9,500 metics.[100] The supreme command of the army was in the hands of the polemarchos (the war archon) and the strategoi who, as already indicated (Chapter 10), were elected and not chosen by lot. Even the Athenians – with their penchant for participation – were reluctant to leave such a vital issue as national security to chance.

In broad terms, the army comprised cavalry, hoplites, light armed troops such as archers and slingers, and other auxiliary groups for liaison, medical and even ritual purposes. Horses were not supplied by the state, so the cavalry represented the aristocratic minority which could afford to breed and maintain its own steeds. Youths who were experienced in horsemanship were drafted into the cavalry after the completion of their initial training. The commander of the cavalry division (hipparchos), who was elected for a year by the Assembly, recruited suitable epheboi, but his choice had to be ratified by the Boule. As supernumeraries, he had ten squadron commanders each from a particular tribe. In action, the cavalry man wore only a minimum of protective clothing; he carried two spears and a sword, and rode bareback without saddle or stirrups.[101] The cavalry considered themselves to be something of an élite, and bore themselves with a certain aristocratic hauteur, although popular opinion may again be reflected obliquely by Aristophanes[102] when he depicts them as upholders of a commendable but outdated patriotism.

The hoplites, who also had to supply their own equipment, were similarly divided into ten units on a tribal basis. These were commanded by ten officers (taxiarchos) elected by the people, but these had the privilege of appointing their own company commanders. The light-armed troops usually wore no protective armour. They consisted of slingers and javelin-throwers (the javelin or short spear was also hurled using a propulsive thong), and both mounted and infantry archers who normally carried no other defensive weapons. Archers were usually recruited from the thetes and, during the Peloponnesian War, they had an effective strength of about 1,600.[103] These must be distinguished from the Scythian archer mercenaries who numbered about 1,000. These were brought in not to strengthen the army, but to act as a kind of police force, mainly in the lower part of the city. Originally the Scythian archers had been slaves who were purchased by Athens about the time of the inception of the Delian league, about 477 BC.

The general strategy in Greek warfare was quite simple. The object was primarily to dominate the enemy's agricultural plain. Few states could survive the devastation of their crops for more than two years running.[104] One of the most significant features of Athenian strategy during the early stages of the Peloponnesian War was the decision to encourage the citizens of Attica to retire within the city walls, allow the Spartans to ravage the countryside, and rely on supplies of essentials coming from overseas protected by the Athenian fleet. This policy of Pericles came in for a great deal of criticism but, ruinous as it eventually proved to be, it successfully avoided a direct confrontation with the superior force of the Spartan hoplites. Siegecraft was not as highly developed by the Greeks as it had been in some other ancient societies; the Assyrians had already set the standards, and this was later developed by the Macedonians[105] and their successors, the Romans.[106] It is perhaps significant that in the entire thirty years of the Peloponnesian War, the Spartans and their allies never once tried to storm the fortress of Athens and its Long Walls to the port of Piraeus. If a city was determined to withstand a siege, there was little the enemy could do short of treachery to bring about its collapse. Starvation or the cutting off of the water supply were perhaps the most common reasons for the city's surrender. It is rather interesting in view of the ferocity with which wars were often fought that the deprivation of water was banned as 'unfair' by the Amphictyonic League of Delphi.[107]

The battle tactics of the Greek armies were even more rudimentary than their general strategies. The basic principle was for each side to draw up their hoplites against one another, and to cut

195

and thrust until one line broke. In the meantime, skirmishers and cavalry would do their work to weaken the flanks. Victory went to those who could stand their ground more tenaciously. Given the traditions, and the limited range of weaponry at the disposal of ancient armies, there were few possible variations on this familiar theme. One innovation, used with great success by the Thebans against the Spartans at the battle of Leuctra in 371 BC, was to weaken one wing and the centre, and increase the other wing from the customary eight-man line to an extraordinary depth of fifty men.[108] The heavy-armed infantryman gave the Greek armies their particular invincibility as mercenaries in later years,[109] but they were at their most effective when the enemy was prepared to meet them in similar array on level ground. Where the terrain was more uncertain, and the opposition was more enterprising, the cut-and-run tactics of lightly-armed troops could be devastating.[110] There would probably be little serious dispute that the Greek art of war reached its zenith under the Macedonians in the fourth century BC. Philip, and later his son, Alexander, showed what ruthless but imaginative leadership could achieve against often numerically daunting opposition.[111]

Unlike Egypt, Athens was a significant naval power. Except for the Carthaginians – who were only just emerging at the time of Greek pre-eminence – Athens, in the early years of the Peloponnesian War, had possibly the most powerful fleet in the ancient world. It had been built up during the pre-war period, largely at the expense of allies in the Delian league, ostensibly to counter the continuing Persian threat. The eventual ability of Athens to import enough food from overseas to offset the devastation of her crops by invading Spartan armies all but won the war. And ironically, it was the destruction of a large part of that fleet in the Syracuse expedition (415–413 BC) in a fruitless attempt to ensure corn supplies, which arguably lost her the war. The 'Sicilian adventure' was catastrophic for Athens and was possibly the turning point of the war. She lost some 200 triremes and, perhaps as many as 50,000 men including 10,000 hoplites, a force that was really irreplaceable.[112]

The build-up of Athenian naval power is usually attributed to the foresight of Themistocles who is said to have persuaded the citizens to invest the newly found wealth of the Laurium silver mines in the construction of a fleet. Enormous strides were made between the Persian invasions of 490 and 480 BC, the building programme including not only ships but also the attendant harbour facilities. This was so accelerated that by the time of the war, Athens probably had between 300 and 400 triremes on active commission. In addition to these, there were the naval contingents of the allies, especially Chios and Lesbos, in all a formidable maritime force which dominated the Aegean.

196

The trireme, the most common type of warship during the Classical period, was some 150 feet long and about 20 feet in the beam. It was usually made of pine and oak and the seams caulked with tow and wax, the hull being coated with pitch. Its finish traditionally included emblems which were embodied either in the basic design or in the painting; whether these were purely decorative or vaguely totemic or talismanic in nature is not really known. The trireme had only one mast, and normally only travelled under sail when not engaged with the enemy. There were three banks of oars necessitating some 170 rowers, a further dozen or so men engaged in general duties, some marines and the commander and his staff, perhaps 200 men in all.[113]

The trierarchoi[114] or commanders of triremes were nominated annually by the board of generals (strategoi). Names were taken from a list of wealthy citizens who had contributed to the building of these craft and who would now be financially responsible for keeping them in good repair.[115] 'Wealth, rather than naval skill or experience', was a principle eligibility factor in the appointment of naval commanders,[116] although they had always had seasoned naval staff to assist them. The rowers were usually either poorer citizens (thetes), metics, or – when the manpower shortage became really acute – slaves who were promised their freedom on the completion of their service. The rate of pay was between three obols and one drachma, a modest income for the servicemen, but burdensome for the state who were employing some 60,000 naval personnel.

The overall strategy of the Athenians during the war was initially established by Pericles. This was simply to contain the enemy on land by a defensive policy of interrupted attrition, whilst seizing the initiative at sea, and unsettling the Spartans with surprise landings on their coasts. At sea, tactical variety was again rather limited: ramming the enemy ships, shearing off enemy oars, and generally crippling enemy vessels, involved manoeuvres which were both crude and skilful. Few ancient fleets mastered these arts as well as the Athenians.

As the pursuit of military solutions is rooted in human fallibility, so the practice of war is plagued by moral uncertainties and political inconsistencies in which class factors have played their part. Even when tension was growing between Athens and Sparta in the pre-war period, it was possible for the Athenians to help the Spartans to suppress a slave revolt.[117] Similarly, as a prelude to the Peloponnesian War, Corcyra – an island polis off the western coast of Greece – acceded to the request of the ousted oligarchs of their nearby colony of Epidamnus to help in their reinstatement as the rightful leaders of the polis. The oligarchs had first asked their barbarian neighbours, against their own class interests, and had been

197

refused. Corcyra was itself a colony of Corinth, an ally of Sparta and an ostensible enemy of oligarchy. But probably out of economic self-interest and contrary to her political ideology, she was drawn into conflict with her mother city of Corinth.[118] This relatively minor incident precipitated the war which eventually involved almost all the Greek states. For Athens, it brought to a close its most creative and influential period.

Attenuated and often fragile relationships between states frequently dissolved into rigid alignments. In the Peloponnesian conflict, this meant the effective division of the entire Greek world. This may have been the inevitable outcome of the city-state ethos rather than anything inherent in the Greek mentality. Admittedly, the tradition of arete, or excellence,[119] was extremely potent in Greece. It was certainly an important term of commendation from Homeric times onwards and strongly connoted military prowess.[120] Arete reflected the contest morality of an achievement-oriented society 'in which the objective was not simply to improve on one's own past performance, but to put the other man down. The "glory that was Greece" was, in some important measure, born of this violent competitiveness.'[121]

It is interesting to ask to what extent this competitiveness derives – at least in part – from the autonomous nature of city-state existence. Of course, the emergence of the poleis themselves may be one physio-political manifestation of this same competitiveness. But this may be to ignore the significant historical and geographical factors attending their development. To seek the origins of attitudes is probably a fruitless exercise, but to identify the conditions in which these attitudes find categorisable expressions, is another matter. Impressionistically, one can hardly doubt that the struggle for independent recognition at least encouraged, if it did not actually crystallise, the contest morality in the city-states. And given the assumptions of such a code, the infrastructures of individual poleis would always be susceptible to disruption from discontented citizens. The authority system would be open to the challenge of enterprising contenders for power. Between states, ambition could only effectively be realised in military terms, hence the interminable internecine warfare which characterised the ancient Greek world.

Inter-poleis differences were often resolved at terrible cost. The legacy of archaic practice where towns were sacked, men of military age killed, and women and children taken as slaves[122] still existed in Classical times.[123] There were, of course, variants and refinements. Conquering states might put the defeated under tribute, and where women and children were taken, they might not be kept as slaves, but sold *into* slavery and similarly swell the coffers of the state. The Corcyran episode, which took place in the opening phases of the

Peloponnesian War (427 BC) heralded some of the horrors which were to come. Later, with Athenian help, the Corcyran proletariat defeated the aristocracy in the 'class war'.[124] Their prisoners, who had been confined in a large building, were being led out in batches for execution, when the remainder decided to put up further resistance. This could only be a token gesture. Realising that the situation was hopeless, they picked up Athenian arrows and committed suicide by thrusting them down their own throats, whilst others hanged themselves with cords taken from some stored bedding. In Thucydides' words, 'these scenes of horror continued through the greater part of the night . . . with the return of daylight, the corpses were piled in layers upon wagons by the Corcyreans and carted out of the city, while all the women who had been captured in the fort were sold into slavery. This is how the Corcyreans . . . were exterminated by the proletariat. . . .'[125]

The merciless treatment of the defeated was by no means uncommon in Greek warfare. Following their victory over the Persians, the Athenians captured Eion in Thrace and sold the inhabitants into slavery. They then sailed to Skyros, enslaved the inhabitants and replaced them with planters from Athens. During the same period, Gelon tyrant of Syracuse, captured two Greek colonies in Sicily, and sold its 'common people'. During the war itself, such practices were rife on both sides. For instance, in 421 BC, the Athenians captured Torone and Skione: in Torone they took the men to Athens and enslaved the women and children, and in Skione, they massacred the men and again enslaved the women and children. Later, in 416 BC, they did the same on the island of Melos, and again the area was resettled by land-seeking Athenian planters. But when the Athenians were routed during their catastrophic campaign in Sicily (413 BC), some 7,000 Athenian and allied prisoners were either thrown into the stone quarries of Syracuse, where many of them died, or were sold into slavery.[126] In their inhuman treatment of the defeated, the Spartans were little – if anything – better than the Athenians. During the final stages of the war (405 BC) their naval commander, Lysander, surprised and destroyed some beached Athenian ships on the Thracian Chersonese (Gallipoli), and executed 3,000 prisoners, ostensibly as retribution for Athenian atrocities.[127]

Within the conventions of the ancient world, there were only three things the victors could do with their prisoners: put them to death, enslave them or release them gratuitously. Prisoners were sometimes exchanged when an armistice was arranged on mutually compromising terms but, where the result was decisive, the vanquished literally became the property of the victors.[128] In fact, there was no status for prisoners corresponding to that of the modern prisoner-of-war, and no specific word to designate them. They were simply 'goods' to be disposed of as the victors saw fit. A similar state of affairs obtained among the Romans until c. 264 BC when a fourth alternative was introduced, namely that of giving able warriors the chance to be gladiators.[129] This not only institutionalised but also trivialised the slaughter as a form of entertainment.

The specific relationship between militarism and ideology in Greek society in general, and Athenian society in particular, is fascinatingly ambiguous. The term citizen connoted the warrior function. Young citizens, epheboi, took oaths at various sanctuaries before embarking on their military service. Greek armies performed numerous rituals both at the outset and during the course of their military campaigns. Hostilities did not even commence until a herald – whose person was sacrosanct – had formally announced the severing of relations between the states in contention. This declaration had a legal force, in the same way that the herald's proclamation that hostilities had ceased formally concluded the war.

The use made of the Pythian oracle at Delphi to seek advice, and perhaps even settlement in some cases of inter-poleis rivalry, suggests that religion was important to the Greeks. But the actual pronouncements of these oracles[130] opens up the whole question of exactly what their function was. Were they ideological oases in a desert of unending disputation, or were they mere pawns in a lucrative political game? Certainly, the Greeks paid lip-service to the importance of ritual requirements as a concomitant of military enterprise.

When opposing armies were drawn up for battle, both commanders, possibly with the aid of ritual assistants, would offer prayers to the gods, and 'dedicate' to them the persons and property of their enemies. In Archaic times, this might involve the sacrifice of prisoners, but by Classical times, there was little attempt to sacrilise the carnage in terms of ritual offerings. Even the dedication of the booty had, by this time, been reduced from the sum total of the spoils to a mere tenth,[131] although the despoliation of enemy crops and the destruction of their property might still be accompanied by formulaic oaths.[132] Similarly, the burial of the war dead was celebrated by rituals and funeral orations which both honoured the deceased and encouraged the living to a greater dedication to the city's cause.[133]

The observance of the religious festivals was also important. Ostensibly, a festival prevented the bulk of the Spartan army being present at Thermopylae during the second Persian campaign. This was virtually a repeat performance of their response to the first Persian invasion ten years earlier. Then, they were also celebrating the Carneia, and maintained that they were unable to send their promised help until the full moon, which was probably six days away.[134] How crucial was this religious factor? Were these celebrations of the Carneia and the Olympics *that* essential, or were there obvious political gains? Scholars are divided on this issue.[135] Much as one might be tempted to doubt a religious cover for Spartan motives, it is attested[136] that at the battle of Plataea, the Spartan army actually stood motionless, shields at their feet, amidst a hail of arrows, waiting for the gods to direct them.

The victory of Marathon, won by such a relatively small force – mainly of Athenians – seemed little short of a miracle which merited the appropriate ritual thanksgivings and dedications to the gods.[137] Similarly, after the victories over the Persians in their second campaign, rich offerings were made to many of the temples.[138] When the Athenians besieged and took Thebes which had been the main ally of the Persians, the Theban leaders surrendered themselves for mandatory punishment, but there was no suggestion that their execution was some form of ritual sacrifice. In fact, it is impossible in all these acts to disentangle motivations of genuine piety and those of civic pride.

A further complicating factor was superstition. Academically, this may be distinguished from religion,[139] but in practice, it often operates in very similar ways. The Sicilian expedition (413 BC), the major 'second front' campaign of the Peloponnesian War, set out on what was considered an ill-omened day. And it could be argued that the conclusive factor in the Athenian defeat was the refusal of the commander, Nicias, to withdraw for a month on the advice of some soothsayers.[140] The result was disastrous. This was the greatest military enterprise the Athenians had ever mounted, and its failure was greeted first by incomprehension, and then by an almost unreasoning fury against generals, orators and soothsayers, 'as though they had not voted . . . for the expedition . . . themselves'.[141]

This apparent incapacity to see their responsibility for situations, and the convenient transference of that responsibility to others was a recurrent feature of the Athenian demos. In a system where responsibility was ostensibly shared between participating members, the apportioning of blame could be undemocratically selective. This tendency was, in turn, exploited by opportunistic populists who saw in the persecutions of social scapegoats the stepping-stones to political advancement. The manipulation of the demos became a cultivated art in Athens. The endorsements of the people were seen as a strength of the democratic system, but may in fact have been one of its most subtle weaknesses, especially where those endorsements were regarded as ipso facto unquestionable.

In this kind of situation, religion is more likely to give way to socio-political expediency. Thucydides writes of party-leaders who 'invented high-sounding catchwords and posed as the champions of

201

political equality' who stopped at nothing to gain personal power. As a contemporary, he argues that they were prepared to ignore both national interest and moral right. 'They did not shrink from bringing themselves into power by verdicts obtained immorally against their opponents, if not by naked force. . . . In fact, religion lost its hold . . . and they relied upon . . . powers of misrepresentation.'[142] In general, it is arguable whether religion ever played more than a subordinate and reactive role to the militaristic and civic ideology of Athens.

It can hardly be argued that the surprising success of Athenian arms against the vastly superior Persian forces in the early part of the fifth century BC precipitated the militarism which was to come, although it did inspire the Athenians to realise their military-naval potential. The martial spirit had been present from early years, and was by no means confined to Athens, but was partly a function of the autonomy ethos. The need for larger armies to defend political independence and win control in a competitive inter-poleis situation called for some democratisation of the military machine. The predominance of the aristocratic cavalry[143] gave way to the hoplite formations of the higher citizenry, and finally – with the Persian threat – to the proletarian power of the maritime forces.[144]

Military imperatives had derived partly from resource scarcity. There was a need to secure certain essential supplies, particularly of grain, and to establish overseas markets. These and demographic factors gave rise to the intermittent phases of colonial expansion. It could be hypothesised that, in the absence of any very distinctive Greek ideology, expansionism created forms of socially acceptable diversions from the awareness of internal weaknesses, and increased the sense of cohesiveness in individual states. In Athens, there was ambiguity of control over the process of decision-making. At different levels, on the various councils and committees, the democratic process was both extended and circumscribed. Control was therefore diffused, and the inherent instability of the system exacerbated. In the Classical period, the need for coherence took an imperialistic form, the attempt to establish hegemonic control in particular areas of the mainland and the Aegean. Military prowess was extolled as a virtue. The Athenians made necessity of that virtue, unlike the Egyptians who – if anything – made a virtue of military necessity. All the Greek world loved a hero, and military prowess and valour were among the most clearly appreciated expressions of the contest system.

Position scarcity was more applicable to the Athenian situation than resource scarcity.[145] The Peloponnesian War represents the conflict between mutually exclusive and mutually incompatible values. But what Athens and Sparta had in common was mutuality of ambition. Their means of government were very different, but the goals were unsurprisingly similar. Each wanted control, each wanted national esteem, and each both feared and envied the influence of the other. Religion, as such, played little part in all this. It was very much a conflict of opposing ideologies.

Perhaps the true irony in Athens was that the military pursuit of imperialistic objectives symbolised a division in her own thinking. There was a kind of dualism in the Greek world,[146] which was reflected in the internal thinking of the Athenians. The dichotomy could not be resolved. The conflict persisted between the substantive ambition and the normative idealism of its citizens. Alexis de Tocqueville has pointed out, in a quite different context, that this is not an unfamiliar paradox. 'We arrive at this singular consequence: that of all armies, those most ardently desirous of war are democratic armies, and, of all nations, those most fond of peace are democratic nations. And what makes these facts still more extraordinary is that these contrary effects are produced at the same time by the principle of equality.'[147]

## Summary of comparative military systems

### Egypt

1 State-religious ideology strong and militarism weak (Old Kingdom). Military charisma as remedy for possible status uncertainty of Pharaoh (New Kingdom).

2 Effective authoritarian control over the decision-making process. Specificity correlates with social stability.

3 Militaristic spur has economic basis.
Resource scarcity problems.

4 Militarism gives rise to new class of experts to challenge divine authority.

5 Militarism: necessity becomes virtue.

6 Religious ideology as mechanism for militarism.

### Athens

1 Militarism/expansionism give internal coherence where religious ideology is weak.

2 Ambiguity of control in democratic decision-making process.
Diffuseness correlates with social instability.

3 Expansionist spur has economic/demographic basis but primarily political problem of position scarcity.

4 Militarism/maritime activity gives rise to proletarian participation in state process.

5 Militarism: virtue becomes necessity.

6 Religious ideology in justificatory ambiguous relationship with military activity.

# 12   Systems of ideation

All discussion of ideational or religious systems is both vitiated and complicated by problems of definition. Weber insisted that any study of religion must begin with a definition.[1] But much of the controversy about the meaning of the term religion[2] is really disputation about delineations of the range of phenomena which are held to constitute legitimate areas for enquiry.

There are a number of ways in which this may be approached, but, broadly speaking, definitions can be classified as being either Nominal or Real.[3] Nominal definitions are those in which meanings are arbitrarily assigned to the properties or phenomenon in question. Thus the term 'marriage' is merely a convenient linguistic symbol which denotes empirically identifiable sets of contractual relations between the sexes. Real definitions, on the other hand, are concerned with a 'true knowledge' of the phenomenon in question; so a real definition of 'marriage' suggests an understanding of what marriage really is. There is the implication that marriage is more than seen sets of contractual relations, and that it has an 'essence' which is more than the sum total of its social expressions. By extension, therefore, Real definitions go further. They imply, first, that the phenomenon at issue has some kind of universal status or applicability having properties which are common to most if not all societies,[4] and, second, that these properties also have an indefinable ontological status.

Historically, the Nominalist–Essentialist controversy has been largely confined to issues in moral philosophy: is 'goodness' a property we ascribe to certain actions, or is it possible to know something of the quality of 'goodness' in itself?[5] Such issues have intangibilities which have obvious affinities with those of religion. It is for this reason that many sociologists and anthropologists have tended to limit their investigations to the rather circumscribed area

204

of the behavioural expressions of religion. Their conclusions – whilst not exactly banal – have those unsurprising and predictable qualities which one has come to associate with those studies which are 'firmly dedicated to proving the indubitable',[6] exhibiting what Morris Janowitz has called 'the dead hand of competence'.[7]

As a necessary preliminary it is important to note that there are several levels at which the phenomena which we collectively term religion can be usefully discussed. Analyses can be offered in terms of:

(i) Typologies of religious systems. These include broad classifications such as polytheistic, henotheistic and monotheistic systems through to quite sophisticated categorisations in terms of particular differentiae.

(ii) Historical approaches which sometimes hypothesise the 'origins' of religious systems. This is a somewhat passé procedure, but still necessary for an appreciation of the history of the study of religion.[8]

(iii) Developmentalist categories which contain marked evolutionary implications. These analyses which are commonly associated with such theorists as Comte, Frazer and Spencer have much in common with the origin-seekers. They represent an outmoded stages-theory approach to social classification which was restated by L. T. Hobhouse[9] in the present century who contended that the forms and development of social structures could be correlated with religious and moral evolution.

(iv) Functionalist approaches which are largely reactions to the earlier origin-seeking schools, and tend to stress the role of religion in maintaining the social structure of societies. Functionalist orientations have been developed particularly in social anthropology, a discipline which has been concerned almost exclusively with pre-literate societies where a 'knowledge' of the system has to be inferred from current institutional practice.[10]

(v) The instrumental or activist expressions of religion. The view here is that ritual 'announces' social relationships. Belief and myth are seen as necessarily subject to distortion and misinterpretation: cultic practice alone really conveys the traditional meanings of the system.[11] Both the historical and the functionalist schools may offer causal explanations about either the general existence of religion or the presence of a particular form of religion in a specific society. But historical explanations are frustratingly conjectural, and function should never be confused with cause.[12]

For our present discussion of traditional societies, it might be more helpful to analyse religious systems in terms of reflective cosmologies. This is neither better nor worse than other kinds of

205

analysis, it may simply be more useful in the context of the ancient world. To examine the ways in which the social order is held to reflect the cosmic order complements other forms of analysis. Religious symbols formulate a basic congruence between a particular ethos and an implicit metaphysic – each supporting and sustaining the other.

> The notion that religion tunes human actions to an envisaged cosmic order and projects images of cosmic order onto the plane of human experience is hardly novel. But it is hardly investigated either, so we have very little idea of how, in empirical terms, this particular miracle is accomplished . . . [although] we have an enormous ethnographic literature to demonstrate it.[13]

At one level, therefore, the emphasis of this discussion is substantive and phenomenological.[14] It is concerned with the empirical nature of Egyptian and Athenian religions whilst, at the same time, attempting some evaluation of their practical and cognitive importance for the members of those societies. Religion has psychological as well as sociological dimensions, and must, therefore, be seen from the perspective of the adherent as well as that of the system. It is hardly presumptuous to assume that most people do not make analytic distinctions in this respect and are content to deal with their everyday concerns pragmatically, without any conscious attempt to construct a comprehensive system. Yet cognitive problems persist; certain ubiquitous facts need to be explained, especially injustice, suffering and death. In all societies, the fundamental question of meaning is answered – however inadequately – by theological explanations. No other kinds of ideological speculation seriously compete at this level.[15] All beings are vulnerable, and the very permeability of the psycho-social experience has generated the apparent need for various kinds of expressive protective rituals.

There are several ways in which men tend to interpret reality. They may advance positivistic and rational interpretations which are characteristic of modern societies, or they may espouse magico-religious ideas which range from beliefs in the ability to manipulate cosmic forces to complete resignation before the gods. But the view that men are *either* rational, magical, fatalistic or religious[16] involves purely academic distinctions. In practice, all these orientations may co-exist not only in the same culture but also in the same individual.[17] A similar point is made by Henri Frankfort in the context of pre-industrial societies; he argues that the ancients did not regard reality as something to be apprehended by different modes of cognition because the mythic nature of their traditions indicated that for them 'the realm of nature and the realm of man were not distinguished'.[18] The need to 'see' religion in multiple perspectives is also made by some philosophers[19] who maintain that symbols and concepts do not represent parallel lines of approach, but have their own complementarity.

At an instrumental level, ancient societies differ in the extent to which there is a fusion between religion and the institutional complex. In some, such as Athens, a separate political organisation, for example, can be identified. In others, such as Egypt, there appears to be no such clear distinction. In practice, religious values and symbols were common to the cultural orientations of all strata, and permeated all forms of institutional structures, kinship, education, the economy, the military, and pre-eminently the arts. Rulers defined their policies and objectives in religious terms, and bureaucratic élites often legitimised their activities with the necessary obsequies in relation to the prescriptive system.

Particular religious orientations are consonant not so much with particular social structures – as though there were some functional one-to-one correspondence – as with particular kinds of social order. In putting the emphasis, therefore, on reflective cosmologies, we are simply asking in what ways do the cosmologies of societies reflect the social order. It is a conceptual angle which requires a formal typology to indicate the range of possible relationships between religion and society.

The following typology is suggested:

(a) Concrescent systems: those where the cosmic and social orders are regarded as growing together. The emphasis is existential. In some schools of Christianity,[20] for example, God is seen as realising himself in his creation. The gradual triumph of the Kingdom of God may be viewed as a form of 'realised eschatology'. This has a universal application and is not regarded as confined to any one society.

(b) Congruent systems: are systems of ultimate explanation. They can take two main forms, one open and the other closed. The open, by definition, has universal applications, the closed has specific applications. In the open form, the social order and the cosmos itself are seen as one and indivisible. The emphasis is pantheistic as in traditional Buddhism. In the closed form the cosmic order is coterminous with a *particular* social order. In general, Ancient Egypt can be placed in this category, as may also some other ancient societies at specific periods, notably China and Inca Peru.

(c) Contingent systems: where the relationship between the social and cosmic orders is one of ritualised dependency. The land is the possession of the gods, and men are their servants whose primary task is the maintenance of the cultus. It is a system of selective explanation. In general terms, this would be the position of various Mesopotamian societies.[21]

207

(d) Constituent systems: where the cosmic order comprises only part of the social order. That part is the chosen or favoured community. Its place in that order may have been challenged but never carefully defined, and individual members of that order will have differential comprehensions of its nature and role. But its minimal effectiveness may constitute a kind of institutionalised isolation. Israel in both its formative Jahwist stage[22] where God is thought of as unique to a particular people, and in its later history as randomly dispersed ethnic communities, might be classified under this heading. This situation is also typical of deviant, sect-type religious groups with a totalising ethic who seek to survive as minorities in an alien society.

(e) Contiguous systems: indicate systems of adjacency where the boundaries of the cosmic and social orders touch. There is a proximity relationship only; effective contact may no longer be either operative or enjoined. These, therefore, are systems of marginal explanation: a situation largely characteristic of modern, highly secularised societies.

It must be emphasised that this typology simply represents a spectrum of generalised possibilities. Some actual societies and belief-systems can be classified within this framework with relative ease, but this is not the case with Egypt and Athens. The Old Kingdom certainly seems to fit the Congruent category, but 'true' congruency is relatively rare. The New Kingdom, however, presents difficulties. During the Empire, there was an increasing willingness to recognise non-Egyptian gods, in fact it was virtually essential for alliance purposes. Similarly, Egyptian gods were 'exported' to the provinces, either in a relatively pure form or as syncretised versions of existent foreign deities. But the Egyptians never really succumbed to the temptation actually to universalise their belief-system or to see the Pharaoh as someone with a mandate for world rule. Any attempt, therefore, to 'place' Egypt in this way, must be related to the period in question. Egypt was a Congruent system in so far as religion was the source of ultimate explanation, but this categorisation must be qualified in practice.

Athens, too, is a problem. The city shared its gods with the rest of Greece, indeed, in barely disguised forms, they appear in a number of quite different societies. But the identification of, say, the love-goddess, Aphrodite, as a hellenised version of her Mesopotamian counterpart, Ishtar, in no way implies an attempted universalisation by either society. Athenian religion also throws into relief the common problem of differential apprehensions. There is no serious dispute that there was a generalised decline in the status of the gods during the Classical period, and that this was not unnaturally reflected in the writings of the intellectuals. Whether they led the way in the process of 'spiritual' disenchantment is unclear; after all, theirs are the only voices we hear. We cannot know to what extent their writings expressed a public mood. But the appeal of the gods still seems to have had some resonance among the populace. Witness, for example, the general indignation occasioned by the violation of the Herms in 415 BC at the time of the departure of the ill-fated expedition to Syracuse. These stylised figures of Hermes[23] were mutilated, mainly by being deprived of their generous phallic characteristics, perhaps as the result of drunken vandalism.[24] Citizens who presumably took occasional inspiration from their unflagging tumescence were outraged. Whether this was an affront to their spiritual sensitivity, their superstitions or their civic pride is still a matter of debate. Theoretically, it was sacrilege and therefore an act of impiety which deserved to be punished.

Particular factors, therefore, make Athens difficult to classify. There was a pervasive nominal acknowledgment of the gods. The actual 'spirituality' of the Athenians is impossible to gauge – even if such a quality were measurable. We are not even sure as to just how assiduous they were in their ritual observances. On the evidence available, therefore, the Athenian system can probably be located in the Contiguous rather than the Contingent category.

## Egypt

No examination of ancient Egyptian history and culture is possible without a serious consideration of the religious system. Religion is a persistently refluent theme in Egyptian studies and it impinges upon every aspect of the institutional complex. About many aspects of Egyptian life, for example, family and kinship arrangements, we know relatively little, but on the subject of religion we are in danger of knowing just enough to be completely confused. These uncertainties have given rise to some diversity of opinion among the scholars.

Some authorities regard Egyptian religion as being not one system but many. These sometimes overlap and occasionally conflict especially in the contradictory statements of their respective supportive myths. The differences seem never to have been carefully thought through or satisfactorily reconciled, and therefore as a complex of systems, they carry very little conviction. This position was taken by some earlier scholars such as W. Flinders Petrie[25] who did a great deal of very important preliminary work in this area, and would be followed – to a greater or lesser degree – by perhaps the majority of modern Egyptologists.[26] Alternatively, there is the work stemming indirectly from the Chicago school of J. H. Breasted[27] which is sometimes more sympathetic to the apparent inconsistencies of Egyptian religion. Among the more articulate apologists for the essential internal coherence of Egyptian religion is the late Henri Frankfort[28] and – in a less extreme form – J. A. Wilson.[29] The task in this section of the discussion is not to evaluate the particular contributions of these and other theorists,[30] but to indicate that any study of the substantive nature of Egyptian religion must be informed by these separate academic traditions.

If we include the local deities and the foreign gods who in later times were welcomed to the pantheon, something in the order of 2,000 gods were probably worshipped in Egypt at one time or another.[31] The traditions from which they appear to have derived are historically uncertain. Perhaps in the pre-dynastic period, even the principal deities were local gods who were believed to preside over the fortunes of different agricultural settlements and perform specific fertility functions. The mysteries of fecundity and reproduction were probably centres of reverential concern. In time, particular deities might then follow the success of the more aggressive and expansionist communities, and be elevated to district – and eventually – national gods.

But this is all hypothetical and conventional reconstruction. What, however, is quite certain is that from very early times there were several clearly distinguishable traditions, although the view that they were necessarily developments of existing local or tutelary systems is contested.[32] These traditions can be conveniently categorised in a number of possible ways. A dichotomy in terms of aristocratic and popular deities[33] has much to commend it. The principal gods are always *theologically* related to the king. It is through him that their good offices appear to be extended to the people. Perhaps this helps to explain the 'host of minor deities who people the supramundane world of the 'ordinary' Egyptians.

Any classification criteria are somewhat contrived, but they can indicate possible determinatives in the emergence of these separate yet related systems.

(i) The 'first' group of gods, who were primarily nature deities, were associated with the city of On, better known as Heliopolis (the city of the Sun). These may represent the oldest known religious tradition in Egypt. The foundation myth relates how from Nun, the primordial waters, came Atum or Re-Atum the sky-god who with self-generating masturbatory techniques produced the air-god Shu and the moisture-goddess, Tefnut. These, in turn, gave birth to Geb, the earth-god and Nut the goddess of the sky who was also sometimes identified with the cow-headed goddess, Hathor. From these came the popularly contrasted brother-sister unions of Seth and Nebhet, and Osiris and Isis. There are other versions of this creation-myth: one in the Pyramid texts speaks of Atum creating

Shu and Tefnut by spitting them out of his mouth, whilst *The Book of the Dead* more loftily records how the sun-god created his family pantheon by naming them as parts of his 'body'. Whatever the version, it normally includes the same dramatis personae who are usually referred to as the Great Nine or Great Ennead. The first five gods are clearly cosmological, whilst the second four have ill-defined intermediary functions between men and the gods.

The Egyptians apparently saw no real inconsistency in accepting that the same gods might take many forms and assume numerous titles and functions simultaneously.[34] Thus Re-Atum was simply *one* representation of the sun-god, Ra or Re, who occupied a perennial place in Egyptian cosmology. There were others: Khepra, the sacred scarab-beetle, symbolised the youthful sun journeying in his Ship-of-Millions-of-Years across the heavens; Re was the re-vitalising fully-grown sun; and finally the elderly Atum who wearily disappeared over the horizon at sunset. At night, the sun-god sailed in a second ship through the underworld and fought an unfailingly successful battle with the serpent-monster, Apep (apophis), and emerged again to recommence his daily routine at dawn.

In the developed form of the myth, this dramatic ritual journey of Re and his retinue of fellow deities, became linked with the solar god Hor (Horus) who, in one persistent form of the tradition, was the son of Isis and Osiris. As such, Re-Horus or Re-Harakhte was depicted as a falcon-headed man wearing the solar-disc and uraeus.

Sun-worship was probably introduced in or about the Second Dynasty, and seems to have been fully established by the Fifth Dynasty when, as one later account suggests, the sons of the high-priestess of Re became kings and included among their titles that of 'Son of Re'. Perhaps the earliest sun temple also belongs to this period and was built in connection with the royal pyramids at Abusir.[35] At death, the king, as an embodiment of the sun, joined his father in the sky where he continued to reign as an aspect of the cycle of eternal recurrence.

The forms and names of Re seem innumerable, and the Litanies of the Sun, engraved at the entrance of the royal tombs, list no fewer than seventy-five.[36] Efforts were made to distinguish various sun-gods from one another, but they seem to possess little coherence and even less credibility. One remarkable myth tells of how Re sent down his own divine Eye in the form of the goddess Hathor, to massacre his rebellious subjects, but some were saved from extermination when Hathor became drunk and confused by beer, prepared by her fellow deities, which was made to resemble blood. This diversity of myths was perpetuated by tradition; 'the inevitable

211

result was a bewildering confusion of tangled and often self-contradictory ideas. . . .[37] Nevertheless it does not appear that the learned priesthood ever succeeded in drawing up a comprehensive system of Egyptian Theology.'[38]

(ii) Other centres in the Delta were also associated with the initial act of creation. Their priesthood promoted the worship of Thoth who was depicted as a man with the head of an ibis or baboon sometimes surmounted by a crescent-moon, and was later identified with his Greek counterpart Hermes, the spokesman of the gods. Thoth was said to have called the other gods into being, which were originally conceived as primeval snakes and frogs. He is also said to have enjoyed solar pre-existence, for as the universal Demiurge – the divine ibis – he was able to hatch the sun from the appropriate egg at Hermopolis Magna a companion cult centre in Middle Egypt. Thoth was regarded as a nature deity to the extent that he was thought to control the moon, the stars and the seasons. But he was also regarded as the patron of learning, the inventor of writing and the fount of wisdom and knowledge. These cultural functions suggest that Thoth should be thought of primarily in societal terms.

The Pyramid Texts contain a separate set of traditions which refer to Thoth variously as the son of Re, as the brother of Osiris and sometimes merely as the vizier of Osiris during his mythical reign.[39] One suspects that here was a procrustean attempt by either the Heliopolitan or the Hermopolitan theologians to reconcile cultic practices in favour of the widely-accepted Horus-Isis-Osiris tradition.

(iii) The god Amun seems to have been a rather obscure deity in early times, and is mentioned only four times in the Heliopolitan texts of the pyramids. The traditions, perhaps reflecting some political upheaval, suggest that Amun, the solar god of the North, superseded Montu, the solar-god of the South, and became generally recognised in his co-regal form as Amon-Re, the 'king of the gods'. He was sometimes depicted – like so many of the Egyptian deities – in animal or composite human-animal form, in this case as a man with a ram's head. Also like some other warrior deities Amun had fertility associations, and he is sometimes represented with human features posed in an ithyphallic manner.

Amun was adopted by the military rulers of Thebes, and became – as Amon-Re – perhaps the most redoubtable of the Egyptian gods. Certainly the temples and priesthoods of Amun, primarily at Thebes (Luxor and Karnak) became extremely rich and influential, mainly from the benefactions of grateful warrior-Pharaohs.

The king was regarded as the physical son of Re. As early as the Fifth Dynasty, there are references to the wife of a priest being pregnant with 'three children of Re',[40] although this might well be a theological justification for the founding of a new dynasty from the Re priesthood. A similar theological foundation can be seen in the unusual case of the female Pharaoh, Hatshepsut (c. 1486–c. 1468 BC) of the Eighteenth Dynasty. The records claim that her true progenitor was Amon-Re who is said to have masqueraded as her father, Tuthmosis I, in order to produce a divine child. Amun took the 'form [of his] majesty . . . her husband, the king. . . . Then he went to [her mother] immediately . . . had intercourse with her. . . . The majesty of this god did all that he desired with her [and said]. . . . Now . . . Hatshepsut is the name of the daughter whom I have placed in thy body. . . . She is to exercise . . . [king]ship in this entire land.'[41] Whilst enhancing the importance of the religious underpinnings of the system, this kind of rationale tends to minimise the male role in procreation and implicitly reinforce the matrilineal principle.

Amon-Re should possibly be seen primarily in political terms. He was the protector of the monarchy, the great national god who led Egypt to her greatest military triumphs in Libya and Asia, and who lingered on as patron of a declining culture. It is interesting that even Alexander paid his respects at the temple of Amun as late as 332 BC when the oracle diplomatically saluted him too as the 'Son of Amun'.

In mythopoeic terms,[42] the king was also linked with the Isis-Osiris-Horus triad myths which can be reconstructed from allusions in the Pyramid Texts. These relate how an ancient king Osiris is killed by his brother Seth but revivified by his wife Isis. Osiris becomes ruler of the next world and is succeeded in his earthly kingdom by his son, Horus. Similarly, by a mystical process, each Pharaoh at death became Osiris only to be succeeded by his son, the new Horus. This corpus of myths became the basis of the mortuary rituals which were performed on behalf of the dead king.[43]

(iv) Importantly but unchronologically, any consideration of the principal Egyptian religious traditions must include some reference to the celebrated and very ancient Memphite theology. The existing text dates from c. 700 BC, but there is reason to believe – as the inscription claims – that these traditions go back to the early dynasties centred at Memphis.[44] These relate how the god Ptah, the Creator of All, the self-conceived and self-existent mind of the Universe, made all the other gods by simple verbal authority.[45] He was normally depicted not as an animal, but as a mummified human figure holding a sceptre with the emblems of life, stability and omnipotence. The Memphite theology is not entirely free from the often crude anthropomorphisms of the other Egyptian cults, but it may represent an uncharacteristic philosophical tradition which

213

both antedates them – in their more developed forms – and super-sedes them in theological coherence. It is possible that it was instituted to reconcile the disparate interests involved in the merger of the Two Kingdoms at the beginning of Egyptian dynastic history. But despite its undoubted all-embracing political advantages, it does express a near-monotheism which was not approached again in Egypt until the transient Aten worship instituted by the late Eighteenth Dynasty Pharaoh Akhenaten. It may be that its rather abstruse and elevated nature precluded its popular acceptance, and with time it degenerated into a Ptah-cult concerned with patronage of the arts and simple industry.

Egyptian religion was peopled by innumerable subsidiary deities. Some of them were local refractions of the major gods; some were peculiar to minor cults; whilst yet others were imported from neighbouring states to join the already overcrowded realms of the Egyptian pantheon. There were yet further metaphysical mantissae in the form of magic (hike) and ghosts; occult practices too are re-corded in connection with an attempt to influence the guardians of the royal harem.[46]

Whether one should make a distinction between worship and reverence in this context is difficult to determine. But as objects of religious attention, the Egyptians *recognised* cult-figures which ranged from human to animal to vegetable forms.[47] Representa-tionally, the principal deities were mainly to be found at the 'human' end of the spectrum. Although many of the older and popular deities, which may have been legacies of a pre-historic phase, were totally animal in type such as Sebek, the crocodile god, and Bast, the cat. Indeed, during the New Kingdom, Apis bulls, as living reincarnations of Ptah[48] were ceremoniously interred in a necropolis at Saqqara, and Ramesses II provided the sacred bulls with a subterranean gallery some 350 feet in length cut from solid rock, the Serapeum, to house their stone sarcophagoi.[49] Falcons were sacred, and ibis birds were also revered and often mummified with special honours especially at a later period.[50]

The complex of rituals which attended the worship of the deities centred on acts of purification and the physical care of the images. The nexus of most cultic activity was the Pharaoh himself. The king performed daily rites which appear to have been fairly standard-ised from the Middle Kingdom onwards. These included acts of identity with the primordial gods; acts of humility which necessitated the 'waking' of the gods with the appropriate prostrations and recitations, and acts of dependency which involved the clothing and 'feeding' of the statue(s). All rituals throughout the state were nominally the prerogative of the king, but being a non-omnipresent immortal he required others to deputise for him.[51] Priests vicariously carried out similar ceremonies in the temples at the king's expense. These were performed in secret; the mystery of the rites could not be the property of the laity, although the people were permitted to share in certain annual festivals when the gods were paraded publicly.[52]

Each temple was a self-contained unit with its own officials, artists, police, craftsmen and peasants. Precise knowledge of the priesthoods is lacking, but a composite picture is possible from partial evidence which has come down to us from specific temples. We know that priests were trained for their vocations, normally from the age of five, and that it was often a family tradition, if not an actual profession. The priesthoods themselves were organised on an hierarchical basis, and their duties were arranged so as to maintain the perpetual care and supplication of the gods, and ensure their continued benevolence. Temples were not always dedicated to the worship of any one deity, and similarly priests were not necessarily bound by indelible vows to any particular god. Women too participated in cult practices usually as instrumentalists or singers.

Temple prostitution was a common practice in a number of ancient societies, notably India and Mesopotamia. It could also take an 'amateur' form. For example, in later times at the Canaanite town of Byblos, women were required to give themselves to strangers during the feast of Adonis and give the profits to the temple treasury. It is not certain whether temple prostitution, as such, was practised in Egypt. A Turin Papyrus does suggest that the singers of Amun were not always too particular about their forms of service.

Although there was no one coherent theology, other than the divinity of the king, there were certain beliefs which were esteemed throughout the cults. These pre-eminently concerned the nature and survival of the soul or Ba which could assume many forms, a bird or fish, and which left its owner at the moment of death and possibly became a star. There was a companion belief in the Ka – a rather more difficult concept which is subject to interpretation. The Ka seems to have been regarded as a kind of protean life-essence or alter ego with which the individual became fully united at death, but which had to be attended and fed with offerings if immortality was to be fully enjoyed. The Ka-concept was closely associated with the practice of mummification. It was important that the form of the dead person was preserved either in body or by statue, and that it could be 'animated' by the requisite ceremonials. Mortuary-cults were therefore endowed by prosperous families for the permanent care of the deceased. A son might be designated Ka-priest to act as both supervisor of the funerary rituals and executor of the estates.[53] The living were consequently kept in permanent touch with the dead and made more aware of their own future states. Priests

215

were required to contract themselves on a prebendal basis to the fulfilment of these specific tasks, but the poor who could not afford consecrated officials had to rely on their families not to overlook their ritual duties. There was obviously neglect of the tombs, as in our own times relatives soon cease to bring fresh flowers to the grave. During the upheavals of the First Intermediate period, for instance, even occasional passers-by were enjoined to make small offerings to the deceased.[54]

These institutionalised contacts with the dead do not seem to have allayed anxieties about the nature and consequences of death. In contrast to the situation in modern societies, the problem of death seems to have been ethical rather than cognitive. The doubts about survival which assail scientific man presumably existed, but the main fears seem to have centred on the judgment and destiny of the soul. The *fact* of survival was not in serious dispute, but its nature for the individual concerned was altogether another matter. Perhaps not all Egyptians quite accepted that life in the Land of the Dead was a modified continuation of life on earth as many tomb paintings depict.[55] As one religious text puts it, 'O Atum, what does this mean that I must go into the desert? It has no water, it has no air, it is very deep, very dark, boundless.' The questioner, Osiris, is assured that Atum will nevertheless sustain him with alternative spiritual benefits.[56]

We probably know as much – if not more – about Egyptian ideas on religion than any other intellectual area, and yet, in a sense, we know very little at all. It is not so much a matter of coping with the volume of physical evidence, the texts and inscriptions, or even the complexities of dating and translation. About these, there is at least some consensus. It is really a question of interpretation. We know, more or less, what the texts *say* – it's what they *mean* that presents problems. For example, although it is argued that the Egyptians – unlike the Greeks – never really developed myth, epic or drama as art forms,[57] they did have elaborate esoterica which took the form of dramatic rituals. The rites for the dead, especially for the king and nobility, were particularly complex, and their theological implications are often far from clear. For instance, mummification procedures sometimes included a chant which reads, '. . . the west wind blows straight . . . into thy nostrils. . . . For thy pleasure the south wind changes and blows from the north. Thy mouth is laid against the udder of the cow Hesat. Thou becomest pure in order to gaze upon the sun. . . . Thou art justified in the presence of Re. . . .'[58] What is clear is that the symbolic universe of the Egyptians was completely different from almost anything we know in the modern world, although the basic cognitive principles involved are not entirely unfamiliar.

216

The concentration on animal figures, the almost naive anthropomorphic imagery, and the inconsistencies of the multi-strand traditions all tend to detract from the obvious attempts to arrive at intuitive insights. To depict Seth as stupid and lecherous, and Horus as sulky,[59] does little for the gods either as authentic beings or as mythical exemplars. Whereas explaining the daily appearance of the sun as its birth, or the disappearance of the night as the ritual triumph of Re over the serpent of darkness, if not intellectual is at least imaginative. Such accounts should not be seen as allegories; the one-to-one correspondence which allegorical interpretations involve, would hardly explain, for example, the waning of the moon as the ailing eye of Horus. On the other hand, it may be possible to see them as poetic and picturesque *analogies*. Perhaps men without the assurances of revelation must resort to analogical insights. Anthropomorphic symbols may then substitute for visual certainty. Divinity can always be imputed to persons, animals and even inanimate things. In the case of Egyptian society, these assurances were supplied in the physical presence of the god-king. Where the gods are imperceptible, the deification of man is always a possible solution. Mythic coherence was therefore almost unnecessary. There was little need to rationalise or reconcile the traditions. Theology was actualised in a living myth – the ineluctable authority of an immanent divinity.

But how impregnable *was* the Pharaoh? And just how unquestioned was his divinity? Doubts must be raised, for instance, when we find that of the eighty or so known tombs of these god-kings, all had been violated *in antiquity*.[60] The sanctions against such sacrilege were presumably enough to deter the most intrepid thieves, yet neither this-worldly penalties nor other-worldly curses[61] saved the Pharaohs from these indignities.[62] Such possibilities were realised at the time, and officials were known to take intricate precautions in order to protect the bodies and the Ka-spirits of the kings.[63]

The invincibility of the Pharaoh is brought into question by the palace intrigues which were designed to depose and even assassinate him, as in the famous case of Ramesses III (see Chapter 10). Coups were comparatively few, and plots intended to establish a new rule seem to have been rare but not exactly unknown during the period in question. As we have seen, priests occasionally succeeded to royal office, and sometimes military leaders took over the throne.

The power of the priests in relation to the Pharaoh can be evidenced by the resolution of the Amarna 'revolt'. The attempted religious reforms of Akhenaten in the mid-fourteenth century BC eventually foundered, and his immediate successors capitulated to the demands of the Amun priesthood for a restoration of the traditional system. The final humiliation was that of Tutankhamun who was obliged to redress the damage done to the temples of Amun. 'His majesty deliberated . . . searching for any beneficial deed . . . for his father Amon . . . fashioning his august image in genuine gold [surpassing all that] had been done previously. . . .' We are told further that the property of the temples was 'doubled, trebled, and quadrupled in silver, [gold], lapis lazuli, and turquoise'.[64]

Such qualifications to pharaonic authority suggest that Weber's distinction between charisma of office and personal charisma may be relevant to the Egyptian situation. The person of the king was nominally sacrosanct, but not entirely inviolable. What was perhaps more important was his *office*. He who occupied the seat of power was also endowed with divinity. He upheld ma'at; he was the son of Re; if he died or was deposed, the mandate merely passed to his successor. Authority and power were vested in the institution rather than the incumbent; the monarchy rather than the monarch.

This might also explain why the king could be held up to ridicule. Certainly at a late period stories circulated about how he was incapable of taking personal responsibility, or was cuckolded by his wives; others suggested that he was subject to the control of his counsellors and magicians, and the dupe of his architects.[65] The kings, like the gods, were sometimes shown to be capable of the failings and vices which beset their mortal subjects.

The ethico-religious ethos of Egypt is not easy to determine. Some authorities see the ancient Egyptian as a reasonably easy-going moral pragmatist, a man with an individualistic zest for the good life and worldly success.[66] Others are quick to stress that quite different inferences might be made, even from the same basic texts.[67] It is argued that it may be an error to regard the Egyptian ethic as simply opportunistic and materialistic.[68] It also had a refluent other-worldly quality which qualified this-worldly ambitions. Perhaps the paradox is that it was something of both. It is necessary to reconcile the immanent and the transcendent elements of Egyptian religion. These different modes of thinking were not merely characteristic of different historical *periods*, the one aggressive and optimistic, and the other submissive but hopeful,[69] but represent a perennial duality in Egyptian thought which was expressed with different emphases at different periods. This parallelism of values was not peculiar to Egypt, and is found in a different guise in Athenian society. Indeed, in one form or another value-inconsistencies are found in all societies.[70]

This study has attempted to show, first, that both kinds of orientation can and do exist side by side and are not mutually exclusive. And, second, it has tried to indicate something of the nature of the interaction between them in institutional terms. We have seen how ideological imperatives have informed every facet of Egyptian life, particularly government and law, the economy and the military demands of the New Kingdom. Religion provided the stimuli, the supportive philosophy and the justifications for the Empire. This is borne out – if further evidence were needed – by the recently translated inscription on the Second Pylon of Tuthmosis III at Karnak which speaks of the Pharaoh's benefactions to the temple in gratitude for 'the first campaign of victory which [my father] Amon had commanded. . . .'[71]

Writers on Egyptian religion do not necessarily distinguish between cosmology and theology. For the society itself, it did not really matter that a cosmology had never been clearly formulated, what did matter was that a reasonably coherent *theology of rule* was operative within the state. The former was open to question and interpretation on the tacit assumption that the gods might not answer back, but the latter – being politically enforceable – admitted of very limited debate.[72]

The consubstantial cosmologies of Egypt can be synthesised so that their divergencies are of no practical significance. Their essential import was that the gods were beneficent, they favoured the good land and personally directed its affairs through the divine-king. They decreed its changeless order which was laid down at creation. Historical events were ephemeral, mere sequential disturbances within an essential regularity. Fundamentally, the universe was imperturbably static, and its order was governed by the eternal principle of ma'at.

Moral action was action which did not violate ma'at. In practice, this meant that which did not contravene traditional norms. This was reflected in the papyri which were placed in the tombs of the dead to justify their earthly actions. Their lives had to be evaluated. At the supreme judgment by the gods, and the 'weighing of the heart' (the seat of intelligence and will), the deceased was required to recite the ritual formula, 'I have committed no injustice against men, I have not maltreated animals, I have not killed anyone. . . . I did not deny bread to the hungry, or drink to the thirsty, or neglect to console the widow and orphan. . . .' If the heart then balanced ma'at, and the judges were satisfied, the deceased was then admitted to the Kingdom of Osiris.[73]

Within the theoretical frameworks suggested (Chapter 3), Egyptian religion can be classified as a cosmic ideology. We have seen that despite its acknowledged amorphousness, it was a potent and practical force within a highly centralised theobasilic system. Yet it had a marked other-worldly quality which appears to have been pervasive and enduring. As a mechanism of control, it possessed

219

totalising characteristics which were effective in both degree and extent, and which operated through the spiritual and politico-economic influences of well-endowed priesthoods. By the Empire period, Amun was coming to be seen as a singular deity with possible universal applications,[74] but Egypt offered no universalising message. There was toleration of other non-Egyptian deities, but the Egyptian system itself was not for export either by proclamation or conquest.

Ancient Egyptian religion was essentially introverted, and peculiar to the 'beloved land'. The evidence points to a qualified but active acceptance of the authority of a supramundane dimension mediated through the divine being of the Pharaoh. A congruent system of ultimate explanation in which the social order was seen as a reflection of its cosmic counterpart.

## Athens

Greek religion presents us with a number of interesting issues and – for our immediate purposes – one salient problem. If the Greeks were the first people, as such, to subject religious ideas to rational-istic scrutiny, can we meaningfully speak of them as 'religious'? And to what extent was this passion for critical enquiry the pre-occupation – or indulgence – of a leisured intellectual minority whose views were largely unrepresentative of the uncritically religious majority? This issue may never be resolved[75] but it can be elucidated by an examination of the way in which Greek belief-systems operated in Athenian society.

Primitive Greek religion may have had its origins in the early invasions of the Chalcolithic period which, in turn, affected the Asiatic coast and the Aegean during the Mycenaean Age, c. 1400– c. 1200 BC. The decipherment of the Linear B tablets of this period shows that many of the major Greek gods, including Dionysos whose cult was very influential during the Classical period, were being worshipped with sacrifices and offerings as early as the fifteenth century BC.[76] The religion of Classical Athens, therefore, had at least 1,000 years of history behind it, although the actual develop-ment of these ideas is difficult to trace. Perhaps the most crucial changes during this time reflect a diminution in the authority and functions of the Mycenaean king and the centrality of the palace shrine. These were broadened and democratised so that in Classical Athens there was a king archon chosen by the citizen body, and city temples which were public property.

In the formative period, there appear to have been strong animistic elements in proto-Greek religion; the veneration of natural phenomena such as springs, caves and mountains; of meteoric phenomena such as winds and rain; and cosmic phenomena

220

of sun, moon and stars, so common to most ancient peoples.[77] The Greek pantheon of later times consisted of a plurality of groups or families of gods which may be distinguished etymologically into those who came with the original invaders, those which belonged to the indigenous peoples of the peninsula,[78] those which were subsequent importations, and those which seem to have been products of the emergent Greek culture.

During the developmental period, regions presented their own peculiarities, and differentiated between the gods in their own ways. But inevitably the uncertain federative nature of the Greek states demanded some degree of identification, selection and syncretism in the formation of the pantheon. The Greeks began to express their commonality in hegemonies and politico-cultural leagues which favoured religious ground-rules.

The writers Homer and Hesiod were both influential in shaping religious ideas. In the *Iliad* and the *Odyssey*, Homer presented a graphic Dark Age image of the Olympian family which provided – albeit unintentionally and haphazardly – a kind of proto-theology for the Greeks which became the main literary bases of their education. Hesiod, writing some time after Homer, attempted a systemisation of ideas about the Olympian gods. In his *Theogony* (*Birth of the Gods*), the myths which linked with current rituals were given some semblance of order and unity. This advanced the processes of religious conceptualisation which were taking place in Greek society.[79]

Well before Classical times, the Greek pantheon had crystallised around the following principal deities. The list is not exhaustive but it does indicate the major areas of concern.

  (i) Ancient gods related to the gods of Olympus: Ouranos and his consort Ge (earth), Kronos (time) and his sister-wife Rhea, the parents of Zeus.

 (ii) The gods of Olympus: Zeus (sky), Hera (marriage), Poseidon (sea), Demeter (corn), Apollo (law), Artemis (hunting), Hermes (commerce), Athene (learning), Hephaistos (handicrafts), Aphrodite (procreation), Ares (war), and Dionysos (wine).

(iii) Subsidiary deities: Hestia (home), Eros (love), Helios (sun), Selene (moon), Pan (flocks), Persephone (springtime), and Hades (underworld).

(iv) Mortals who became gods: Herakles (labour), Asklepios (healing).

In broad terms, the religious observances of Classical Greeks exhibit a well-attested dichotomy. There was the state religion represented by the official Olympianism and its attendant cults, and there were other recognised mystery cults which encouraged

221

divination and sundry magico-religious practices, and – above all – satisfied the apparent need for individual spiritual assurance as well as mere ecstatic curiosity. Initially, the Olympian pantheon looks impressively coherent with the relationships and respective functions of its gods well established. But on closer inspection we find that the goddesses do not even have Greek names and the 'keystone to the whole arch', the marriage between Zeus and Hera looks like a dynastic union[80] and may reflect the syncretistic processes which took place in early Greece.

Olympianism derived from the cults of family and tribe, and by extension became the religion of the state. It was pre-eminently the religion of the citizens, although non-citizens were allowed to participate in some of the festivals. In earlier times, Olympianism had had certain explanatory functions. In the seventh century the war against Troy was attributed to the competitive vanities of Hera, Athene and Aphrodite[81] but, in the Classical period, Olympianism did not actually *teach* anything except an implicit civic responsibility. Its emphasis was essentially prodemic.[82] It evolved as a rational agency for the reinforcement of community consciousness. The protective capacities of Olympianism related specifically to the socio-political organism and, within this framework, it tended to be catholic in its applications.

There seems to be no direct evidence that some people turned to the mystery religions for class reasons, in fact, differential status and occupational positions were, to some extent, catered for within the Olympian system. For example, married women had their own festivals such as the Thesmophoria, from which men were rigorously barred. The festival had obvious fertility emphases, and was held in honour of Demeter. It was conspicuously phallic; pastries shaped like sexual organs were displayed and possibly manipulated.[83] Artisans too, as an occupational group, also celebrated their crafts with specific rituals.[84]

The mystic cults, on the other hand, appear to have had marked didactic and inspirational functions. If anything, they tended to be ademic in emphasis. Their concern was not so much the community as the individual or, at best, the esoteric group. And their psyche-centric teaching[85] appears to have been principally directed towards purification and spiritual initiation, and to the personal assurance of immortality.[86] A soteriological element was introduced which had no necessary connotations of sinful or meritorious conduct. It was a factor which was absent from state Olympianism. Except for the continuing psychecentric thread which persisted from early times in Greek philosophy, notably that of the Pythagoreans and the Orphics,[87] and is just detectable in Socrates,[88] it seems to have been otherwise foreign to Greek thought.

The distinction between Olympianism and the mystery cults[89] tends to break down at the operational level. There were movements within the state system which had unmistakable mystery-cult characteristics. Secret initiations, group consumption of the raw flesh of sacrificed animals, and symbolic liturgical drama, were all features of the Greater Mysteries of Eleusis which were celebrated in September in honour of Demeter with the state's sanction and support. All, except unpurified murderers, were eligible as candidates, even slaves and barbaroi, as long as they were Greek-speaking and could therefore repeat the ritual formulae.[90] Other mystery ingredients were to be found in the related but very different cults of Dionysos and Orpheus, a possibly mythical Thracian poet and prophet of Dionysos whose movements flourished mainly in Western (Italian) Greece. In the cathartic Dionysian rites, devotees were promised communion with the god through an induced ecstatic experience. Alternatively, Orphism enjoined its followers to lead disciplined lives of renunciation and abstinence as a way of salvation. It purged Dionysianism of its orgiastic aspects, and substituted an ascetic emphasis on respect for living creatures, expressed as vegetarianism, and a belief in the transmigration of souls.[91] Little is known about it during the Classical period, although something of its influence can be inferred from the contemporary writings of others. Plato, for one, certainly had ambivalent attitudes towards it; he was possibly influenced by the self-disciplinary emphasis of Orphism, yet was quite prepared to be critical of its more suspect practitioners.[92]

Generally speaking, Greek philosophy of the Classical period had been considerably influenced by earlier Ionian thinkers whose anticipatory probings had displayed an unusual intellectual daring. This gave way in the second half of the sixth century BC to the more mystical approaches of men such as Pythagoras and Xenophanes of Colophon, a wandering teacher. Xenophanes, for example, made the subversive observation that different peoples make their gods in their own images. He defended his anti-Olympian scepticism by mocking the ludicrous and criminal antics of the gods, as described by Homer and Hesiod. This was the legacy of the Classical philosophers, many of the Sophist tradition, and most notably of such figures as Parmenides of Elea, 'the first Greek philosopher who reasons',[93] of Socrates and later of Plato, all of whom tended to be rather idiosyncratic and guardedly rationalistic in their attitudes towards orthodox religion.[94]

The uncertainties for the individual Greek who may have been seeking some kind of spiritual assurance in an age of religio-philosophical pluralism is highlighted by the confusing responses which were given on just one key cosmological theme, namely, what happens to the soul (psyche) at death? Olympianism taught that the souls of the departed joined the shades which tenuously existed in the underworld realm of Hades. Whether such views were convincing to the ordinary Greek are disputable. Apart from the Eleusinian and, particularly, Orphic cults, there seems to have been no 'larger hope'. Certainly the more cerebral doctrines of immortality of the Pythagoreans and of Plato made little impression on the majority. The Thracian Getae, who did believe in the possibility of immortal life, were reported as a curiosity.[95] Perhaps most Greeks only really expected to live on in the memories of their successors, but at the same time remained apprehensively optimistic.

A problem arises in trying to reconcile the apparent scepticism about immortality and the well-attested Greek fear of the ghosts of the dead. Whatever theological contradictions are involved in these conflicting attitudes, it was a sine qua non of Greek kinship obligation that the rites of burial were carried out according to prescribed customs. There is little doubt that this was associated in the Greek mind with the need to be protected from the post-mortal powers of the departed.[96] Combined with this, there may also have been the desire for a quiet and uneventful future existence which, in turn, required the correct burial rituals. Plutarch relates the instance of how, after the battle of Plataea, the Plataeans agreed to bring the slain who were buried on the battlefield offerings of food, wine and perfumes every year. This was apparently done conscientiously with great ceremony and invocations that the dead would take part in the feast.[97] These views were not peculiar to the Greeks, but with them they assume an interestingly ironic form in the light of the increasingly rationalistic attitudes which were current in some other areas of activity, particularly politics.

Similar contradictions obtained on the subject of fate (moira). Divination, mainly for telling the future, was common in numerous forms ranging from the 'reading' of animal entrails (hieroskopia), often used before battle – a known practice among the Spartans, which seems to have been highly respected by Xenophon[98] – to the interpretation of dreams (oneirokrisa). These deductive and intuitive practices were closely bound up with religious ideas, and it may be that the highest form of divination was mediumship, the ability to receive a direct message from the gods whilst in a trance-like state. What evidence there is[99] suggests that the Pythia – usually referred to as a priestess – at Delphi, perhaps the most influential oracle in Greece, operated on this basis. This shrine to Apollo which was only one of some thirty or so oracular temples, was the centre of a panhellenic consultancy service which had become thoroughly institutionalised by Classical times.[100] But the vagueness and ambiguities of its predictions had prompted some sceptical spirits to question its inspirations.[101]

224

The wide spectrum of divinatory practices (mantike) were also associated with retribution (nemesis), arguably another kind of 'fate'. In the classical mind, this was often connected with hubris, an overweening pride which was regarded as a source of conflict with other men, and an affront to the gods. Nemesis was interpreted in a number of ways. As an impersonal causal agency; as the direct retribution of the gods; or perhaps as the malevolent acts of shadowy, little understood daemonic forces which even the gods could not completely control.[102] For Herodotus, who represents a more conservative strain in Greek thought, it was a philosophical axiom of history that 'God suffers no one to be proud except himself'.[103] But for later pragmatic politicians such as Critias, one of the Thirty Tyrants who controlled Athens after the Peloponnesian War, the Homeric-Hesiodic belief that Zeus punishes human crime with, say, agricultural disaster, was just a device for keeping the subjects in order. The Greeks differentiated between nomos, law or custom, which reflected man-made conventions, and physis which reflected the natural order. Religion could therefore be seen as part of the nomoic superstructure of society; politics dealt with hard realities, and should be conducted by the only law visible in the natural world, the law of the jungle.[104]

The organisation of Athenian ritual observance was graduated through various levels from the oikos to the state temples. Greek temples were not places of worship, but merely sanctuaries in which the gods were housed. Originally they were of wood, but stone temples are known from c. 700 BC. From this time they became more numerous and increasingly elaborate, and the finest artists and sculptors were employed in their construction, particularly by city tyrants.[105] The rituals themselves required no temples; the processions and even the sacrifices were performed in the open-air. Altars were to be found everywhere, but rarely inside temples, so a man could make his own sacrifices, perhaps no more than a meal of meat, without the intercessory aid of a priest. The figures of the gods themselves were sometimes brought from the temples for religious celebrations at the stadium or the theatre, but very little took place within the temple itself.[106]

The priesthood was very different from its Egyptian counterpart. In fact, the term 'priest' is, in one sense, something of a misnomer when applied to Greek religious functionaries. They were simply lay people who were appointed in much the same way as other deme and city officials to carry out the appropriate cultic observances. Like most other Athenian officials, they did not have what we regard as professional status, and were not able to develop into an influential priestly class. No special training was required, and priests were not expected to lay claims to a prerequisite vocational experience or

225

sense of calling. There were no charismatic expectations, except where certain mediumistic qualities were called for in the illuminati of the mystery cults. The priest was just another conscientious layman whose amateurism was not even dignified by prophetic presumptions; his religious duties were simply his civic duties.

The offering of sacrifice, prayer and libations are the accepted ingredients of most religious rituals; what we find in Greek religious practice which was not so usual was the inclusion of games and drama.

There were four great panhellenic festivals of games: the Pythian (Delphic), Isthmian, Nemean and – the best known – the Olympian. The Olympian games traditionally began in 776 BC, perhaps one of the most reliable dates in early Greek history. It was held at the sanctuary of Zeus at Olympia, and celebrated, like the modern Olympics, every four years. The festival lasted seven days in all. The first two days were largely devoted to preliminary formalities which included the prescribed religious rituals at the seven altars. The next four days were mainly taken up with sporting events, and the last day to a banquet and procession. Essentially, it was the occasion for a limited variety of male athletics together with some chariot racing. Singing by trained choruses and public readings by writers and poets gave it some additional artistic trimmings. There was probably also a choice of various not-so-cultural amusements in the fairground atmosphere of the festivals. Prizes consisted simply of crowns of wild olive which carried tremendous prestige. An olympionikos – a victor at the games – could virtually command the freedom of the city.[107]

The games were primarily religious festivals. A truce was declared between warring poleis, and a state of temporary peace was observed. The celebrations were times when hostilities were ostensibly forgotten. Yet there was the tacit reaffirmation of inter-poleis rivalry with every competitive act. For the individual contestants, who sometimes found a kind of idealised literary immortality,[108] the games may well have been simply forms of uncomplicated autotelicism.[109] But the differential quality of the representative teams must have reflected something of the size and recruitment potential of the wealthier cities. Perhaps, despite this, the games manifested the underlying cultural unity of the Greeks which in the chequered Classical period found all too infrequent expression.

The theory that games and sociability are really playforms of sociation,[110] is particularly relevant to the matter of Greek drama. In the retelling of myths, the tragedies mirrored the serious concerns of human existence. The plays themselves often give the impression of short courses of ethical-history masquerading as entertainment.

The Greeks apparently welcomed the reiteration of these refluent moral themes, which were cast into sharper relief by the value problems posed by the Peloponnesian War. The war was possibly the most prolific period for writers and artists in Athens, and a challenge to the intellectuals who sometimes tended to adopt a rational but uncomfortable neutrality.

Little is known about the origins of Greek drama, but the choral lyric which often comprised an exchange between the chorus and the leader had been developed into an art form by the middle of the sixth century BC. Later, by c. 500 BC – perhaps at the inspiration of Thespis of Athens – a third element, the answerer (hypocrites) was introduced.[111] Thus the unfolding of the tragedy became something of a moral debate. During the fifth century BC, tragedy was normally presented as a religious ceremony in honour of Dionysos. There were three main festivals in the year, the Rural Dionysia in December, the Lenae in January and the Great (or City) Dionysia in March. As with the games, celebrations began with religious invocations, sacrifices and gifts to the temple of Dionysos. Besides the performances of tragedies and comedies at the theatre, which usually commenced a little after dawn, there were choral contests and general revelries which lasted several days. The entire occasion was presided over by the priest of Dionysos, but it was organised by the civic authorities who were themselves present at the festivals.

There were no Athenian impresarios, as such; the expense of the play was customarily borne as a 'liturgy' by one of the wealthier citizens, and it was usually produced and directed by the author who might also act as tragedos. The actors in Greek drama were all males. Women's parts were played by men or boys, and masks were worn to give identity to the various characters. After Classical times, the entire production operation became more professionalised at every level. Payment was introduced (theorikon) so that citizens could attend the plays. This encouraged the spread of culture and, at the same time, fostered the inculcation of the civic ideal.

There is still some doubt about the actual cultural standards of the audiences. It may be that the ordinary Athenian was not the 'walking handbook of mythology and legend'[112] that posterity has sometimes assumed. Certainly the playwrights themselves did not necessarily assume it: for example, in Sophocles' play *Oedipus Rex* it can be seen how the author skilfully imparts information to an audience which was obviously not au fait with the background of the plot.

If the standards and extent of mass literacy are in question, the matter of moral standards can be dimly illuminated by drama – after all, what people were *really* like or what they really did, is something which constantly eludes us. Given that these festivals

227

were ostensibly the expressions of an ill-defined religiosity, drama highlights some of the apparent inconsistencies in Athenian normative structures. This is, of course, not unique to Athenian society. In other societies – our own included – drama does not *exactly* reflect everyday usages; conventions are observed which are believed either to set examples to the public,[113] or at least command general respect. On the Athenian stage, especially in the Old Comedy, virtually any obscenity of gesture or word was permissible, yet no violence was shown or blasphemy allowed. Blasphemy, in this context, did not mean swearing in the name of a deity, or disparagement of the gods – this was being done all the time especially in the caustic comedies of Aristophanes. In fact, abusive and indecent language may have sometimes been used quite deliberately for apotropaic purposes, that is to avert the ill-will of possible unseen powers. Blasphemy was much more concerned with what the Athenians understood by atheism and impiety.

During the Classical period, there were several cases of eminent people – usually artists or intellectuals – who were hounded for their alleged 'impiety': Pheidias, the principal sculptor of the Parthenon and the superintendent of the design work of the Acropolis; Protagoras, Anaxagoras and Diogenes who were philosopher-teachers, and, of course, the unclassifiable Socrates. We also gain the impression that certain groups, namely the Sophists, sometimes had to teach privately for fear of informers.[114] Aristophanes, who appears to be extremely liberal, but who, in fact, adhered very much to traditional values, may have directly pointed the finger at Socrates long before the famous trial of 399 BC when Socrates was condemned to death. He accused him of teaching the young to argue in new and irresponsible ways, and associating these practices with an interest in 'things in the heavens and below the earth', that is, astronomy which, together with meteorology, was indictable as a form of atheism.[115]

Not enough is known of these impiety trials, or just how many there were. Perhaps they can be dismissed as exceptional manifestations of the suspicions and anxieties of a people under siege; certainly they were all part of the general backwash of the war. It may be that they were not essentially religious at all, and that impiety actually implied an unacceptable disbelief in the special place of Athens in the Greek world, and therefore – by extension – a rejection of Athena as the patron tutelary goddess and also her fellow divinities. Whatever, they do call into question the vaunted parrhesia of the Athenian system. Was the freedom of thought and expression any more than a romantic myth?[116] Or is the 'lesson' of Athens simply that repression and democracy were not – and never have been – mutually incompatible in practice?

The entire panoply of Olympianism was underpinned by a body of myths which can be variously interpreted. Myths are not exclusively about the gods, although this is a position which has been taken by some scholars.[117] After all, the stories of the Trojan Wars, which may be forms of poetic history, or, say, Perseus and Medusa, are myths about heroes rather than gods. But they do have the kind of religious associations which seem to be inextricably interwoven with myths. It is probably also too circumscribed to treat myths as though they were no more than functional validations of existing institutions,[118] or alternatively to emphasise simply their speculative and problem-reflecting properties.[119] The confident attempts to formulate graduated theories of religious development from the study of myths is now regarded as ill-considered,[120] and in many respects positively mistaken.[121] 'What is wrong with such attempts is not merely their arbitrary quality and lack of supporting evidence, but also, and even more serious, their unspoken assumption that myths are all of one kind.'[122] Myths – and this is almost certainly the case with Greek myths – have a multi-dimensional quality which cannot easily be reduced to single explanatory variables. To complicate matters still further, the relatively unrestrained licence of the poets gave rise to regional variations[123] with their rhapsodic elaborations of mythical events. But in all this, the religious element was not far away. The Greek myths both validate and speculate; they can act as explanatory mechanisms, but at the same time – mundane as it may seem – they are probably also just entertaining narratives.

Greek religion, despite its obvious and confusing heterogeneities, has been praised by writers for its liberal and tolerant orientations, but this must be open to dispute.[124] Others,[125] in an attempt to resolve or, at least, understand the existing contradictions, have taken up the distinction made by Nietzsche[126] between Apollonian and Dionysian religious orientations. Greek culture is seen as an ongoing tension between the Apollonian aristocratic virtues of individualism and self-assertion and the Dionysian classless values of mystical collectivism.[127] But this distinction between rational Apollonianism and irrational Dionysianism is regarded as another source of confusion by some Greek scholars. It is viewed as a simplistic dichotomy which ignores actual cases and disregards historical specificities, although it may be a 'rough, though useful tool for the analysis of Greek religion as a whole'.[128]

The social significance of Greek religion is something of a problem. It is extremely difficult to assess to what extent it really *counted* in Athenian society. It appears as both a dependent and an independent variable in different social situations and – what is more perplexing – in similar social situations. And the rationality of these differential responses is not easy to identify.

Athenian religion was hardly totalising either in degree or extent, although it was always pervasive. Contrary to the advocation of the dominant nature of middle-class ideologies, it can be seen that, for the Athenian middle classes and certainly the intellectuals, religion was, if anything, in decline, yet it could be invoked for and by the proletariat for whom it still had a measure of emotional resonance. A case in point is the incident of the generals who after their naval victory at Arginusai had neglected to bury their dead and were therefore accused of impiety and condemned to death. It was the relatives of the dead – members of the public – who came to the tribunal and asked for vengeance. But whether the people's indignation was aroused because the souls of the dead were in jeopardy,[129] or simply because there had been an act of alleged criminal negligence – with hints of cowardice – is difficult to say. Similar questions arise in relation to the desecration of the Herms on the eve of the Sicilian expedition. Theoretically, this was an act of religious impiety which may have been superstitiously associated with the subsequent failure of the military operation. In practice, it may also have been seen as an act of vandalism which was directed – almost traitorously – at the city itself. In analytical terms, therefore, Athenian religious beliefs and practices, in so far as they can be discerned, comprised a contiguous system of marginal/ selective explanation. But it was a system which was plagued with ambiguities.

One conceptually alien factor was the extroverted – one might almost say universalising – nature of the general Athenian ideology. It was not so much the gods, but the Athenian way of life which was thought to be superior to others, and therefore worthy of emulation. The cult of the city is what really seems to have mattered. Perhaps the 'real' religion of the Athenians was not so much Olympianism as Athenianism.

## Summary of systems of ideation

| *Egypt* | *Athens* |
|---|---|
| 1 Plurality of syncretistically related religious traditions. | 1 Coherent corpus of related religious traditions with mystery cult and rationalistic philosophical school additions. |
| 2 Operative congruent theo-basilic system of ultimate explanation closely harnessed to the interests of the state. | 2 Contiguous polytheistic system of marginal/selective explanation enjoying state patronage but not closely harnessed to state interests. |

230

3 Cosmic totalising ideology with supranaturalist orientations.

4 Non-universalising and ademic (non-participatory).

5 Psychecentric in emphasis.

6 Hierarchically organised professional priesthood.

7 Differentiation separation of esoteric (nobility) and public observances.

8 High investment in religious sector.

9 Marginal occult practices.

10 High effectiveness as agent of social control.

3 Civic totalising ideology with humanistic orientations.

4 Qualified universalising emphasis and highly prodemic (participatory).

5 Psychecentric emphasis confined to some (Orphic) cults and philosophers.

6 Democratically organised non-professional priesthood.

7 Non-differentiation and separation of cultic practices.

8 High investment in civic-religious sector.

9 Marginal occult practices.

10 Ambiguous effectiveness as agent of social control.

# 13   Conclusions

In the foregoing analysis, we have identified a number of features in the development of two traditional societies. These features may only be sequential; it is not possible to say with any finality if they were causally related. We have also examined certain cardinal institutional areas which functioned as mechanisms of control and shown that they can be plausibly linked with the prevailing ideologies. With some qualifications, these societies, Egypt and Athens, approximate to the ideal types of traditional society designated Archaic and Seminal (Chapter 5). These may be summarily compared as follows:

| *Egypt* | *Athens* |
|---|---|
| 1 Theocratic ethic. | 1 Ethoic ethic. |
| 2 Centralised politico-economic control. | 2 Diffused politico-economic control. |
| 3 Scholar-literacy. | 3 High literacy. |
| 4 Limited inter-stratum mobility. | 4 Rigid stratification with considerable citizen strata mobility. |
| 5 Qualified socio-cultural exclusivity. | 5 Qualified socio-cultural exclusivity. |
| 6 Non-participatory (ademic) political organisation. | 6 Participatory (prodemic) political organisation. |
| 7 Central control of military system with expansionist ambitions. | 7 Ecclesian (assembly) control of military systems with hegemonic ambitions. |
| 8 Cosmic ideology as source of ultimate explanation. Philosophically unreflective. | 8 Civic ideology as source of selective explanation. Philosophically reflective. |
| 9 Retrospective orientations. | 9 Ambiguity of orientation. |

232

These features were accompanied by certain concomitant social features which may be causally related.

| Egypt | Athens |
|---|---|
| (i) Social stasis: an adaptive 'unchangingness'. | (i) Social astasis: inherently subject to disruption and change. |
| (ii) Cultural homogeneity. | (ii) Limited cultural homogeneity. |
| (iii) Qualified eunomia: 'good order'. | (iii) Qualified anomia: in a nominally ordered society. |
| (iv) Societal longevity. | (iv) Instability and impermanence. |

The hypothesis underlying our entire discussion has been that there is a direct correlation in any given society between the forms and effectiveness of social control and the nature of the prevailing ideology. Such a hypothesis can never be more than persuasive. There is no way in which this kind of relationship can be measured. It has, therefore, only been possible to attempt an institutional analysis of representative societies, and on this basis to advance a plausible case. Despite great advances in scholarship, not enough is known about the actual workings of either Ancient Egypt or Classical Athens to be able to make definitive statements. And even if it were, we are dealing with incommensurable phenomena which are not susceptible to quantification.

As we have seen (Chapter 1), complex pre-industrial societies can be classified in a number of ways. Existing typologies have usually concentrated on socio-political organisation, and are venerated by tradition for their sociological utility. They are valuable but necessarily deficient for any balanced analysis of this kind of society because they concentrate too exclusively on stratificatory and economic variables. In the explication of the model dichotomy proposed here certain constructions were suggested for the types designated Archaic and Seminal in which ideology is an important variable.

Egypt and Athens were chosen not because they were seen as ideal-type Archaic and Seminal societies, but because they represented a polarity which approximated to those types. In comparing them with these societal constructs, we shall see that although any ideas of synonymity are impossible, a clear identification can be made.

Ancient Egypt, especially in its Old Kingdom phase, fits the Archaic type in most respects. The society was organised as a strict hierarchy of occupational gradings with the main divisions between the nobility, the administrative echelon and the peasants. It was ruled autocratically, and centrally controlled by an hereditary divine-king whose will was mediated through a small body of chief ministers. The will of the king was law; there were no codified legal prescriptions, only precedent. This, in turn, was based upon the expert interpretation of ma'at (justice) which was implemented by a cadre of trained officials. This bureaucracy constituted the literati in a society where learning was the prerogative of a class of craft specialists. Social positions were ascriptively defined at the higher nobility levels, but in qualification of the Archaic model, status achievement was possible on a meritocratic basis within the ranks of the scribes, the priests and the military.

The economy was highly centralised with very limited autonomous market operations. There was no effective or emergent merchant class. State revenues were mainly directed towards the financing of large-scale public works which were largely co-extensive with religious interests. Building programmes were made possible not, in the main, by slaves, but by a huge reservoir of feudal labour which was mobilised on an annual corvée basis. There were functionally specialised artisan groups but these had little or no politico-economic autonomy. It was a barter-exchange system which, because of its high grain production, was relatively independent of foreign markets. The need to import certain scarce goods, especially woods, necessitated a limited overseas trade. This encouraged a degree of ethnicity which was gradually eroded with the expansion which took place under the Empire.

The miscellany of polytheistic religious beliefs of Egypt were contained and harnessed by the state in the worship of the Pharaoh. Regardless of the heterogeneity of supernaturalistic ideas, ideological praxis centred on the authority of the king. This focus on the theobasilic nature of a person actualised and expressed the concern for the traditional gods. Control was legitimised with the necessary mythic validations, and institutionalised in elaborate cultic practices performed by highly trained ritual specialists. The conflicts between priesthoods, and the power struggles between the various temple complexes and the nobility were among the most important forces for change in a comparatively static society.

Egypt remained culturally homogeneous for about 3,000 years. Adaptations did take place, but, in general, it was a eunomic and, relatively stable society, particularly during the early period. It is notable, in keeping with the Archaic type, that when disruption did occur, as in the First and Second Intermediate periods,[1] movements for reform and consolidation were persistently retrospective in their orientations.

By contrast, the Athenian system approximates to the Seminal society model. It was organised as an hierarchy of economic classes with clear legal divisions between the citizen and the non-citizen, the free and the unfree. The society was democratically governed and diffusely controlled by a citizen body with rotating political roles. No bureaucracy was necessary; the Assembly of the citizens was the executive.[2] All the subsidiary boards and committees had limited independence of action; they were directly responsible to the Assembly which had final political, military and legal authority. Law was administered through a series of courts with differential powers and clear legal precedents.[3]

Learning was not confined to a cultured and literary élite. There was an independent educational system which favoured the higher classes at the more advanced levels. The actual operation of the political system did not necessitate literacy, but it could hardly have functioned without *informed* citizens.

Except for the financing of extensive public works, the state economy was not highly centralised and there was a low level of control of market operations. The developed money system facilitated autonomous entrepreneurial activity and an emergent merchant class.[4] There was a variety of occupational categories, but limited functional differentiation of status which tended towards achievement rather than ascription valuations. Colonisation was comparatively small-scale for a predominantly maritime people, but overseas trade was well developed, and foreign markets exploited. There must be some doubt whether the Athenian achievement would have been possible at all in an economy of small farmers and rudimentary industry had it not been supported by the labour of a large slave population.

Greek religion, though pervasive, was not integrally harnessed to the needs of the state. Cults proliferated, and were administered mainly by non-professionals as part of their occasional duties for the state. However, the role of religion in Athenian society is not clear. There was a great deal of ritual activity, and vast amounts were expended on temples and festivals, but ambiguities arise because of the uncertainty of the values which these were supposed to represent.

The Athenian social order was characterised by instability and anomia. For a society which had so much law, it appeared at times to have very little. It was given to constitutional experimentation and artistic innovation. It was both brilliant and transient, democratic and violent. Its intellectuals tried – perhaps in vain – to find satisfying legitimations for the system, and were ultimately divided between radical and traditional solutions for its structural weaknesses and its institutional dilemmas.

Anomalies vitiated both societies. Egypt, the theoretically autocratic society, could be very flexible on certain issues. The attitudes to women and the rearing of children; the comparatively reasonable treatment of slaves and prisoners of war, a tolerance of other religious systems,[5] and a capacity for adaptation within a virtually unchanging socio-cultural framework. There was a singular devotion and obedience to the person – and particularly the office – of the Pharaoh. But flaws were evident. The system had its weaknesses. The dynasties changed and the mandate transferred; reigns were not without question or incident. But despite its imperfections, it survived – largely through the unholy alliance of the military and the priesthoods – into an unprecedented cultural old-age.

Athens presents a quite different picture. As part of Greece, it was one of a number of potentially coalescent states which could never satisfactorily unite except in hegemonic leagues which were renowned for their dissension and fragility. It had upwardly mobile economic groups, and a strong middle class which in themselves suggest an atypical traditional society. But, at the same time, there was a clear and indelible demarcation between citizen and non-citizen. Democratic privileges were for citizens only, although the non-citizens were possibly better-off in Athens than in other Greek states.

Corresponding ambiguities obtained in other areas. Women were unenfranchised and subject to certain social and legal restraints, yet *some* women – notably the prostitutes and courtesans – were not subject to so many restrictions. Slavery, too, suffered from similar anomalies. The evidence shows that the very best *and* possibly the very worst forms of slavery were to be found in this one state. Athens was ostensibly a liberal society, encouraging political participation and promoting artistic expression. Yet allies were oppressed, intellectuals and political enemies proscribed, and public denunciations encouraged.

Both societies were to a greater or lesser extent conditioned by the nature and foci of their internal struggles. In Egypt, the conflict was between the influential echelons of state – variously the nomarchs and the king or the priests and the military – the people were relatively untouched by these rivalries. In Athens, virtually the opposite was the case. The conflict was between the hereditary holders of power, the aristocracy, and the emergent demos straining for greater recognition in an increasingly participatory society. In comparing the two societies, therefore, we find ourselves confronted by contradictions and antinomies which may not be entirely atypical of autocracies and people's systems. For example, it is interesting to observe that autocracies can produce artistic cultures which equal those of so-called free systems: Egypt matched Athens architecturally but not in the broad range of philosophic and artistic achievement. Artistic expression is not necessarily dependent

236

on the type of political process. Autocracy need not retard cultural achievement providing certain conventions are observed.[6]

Both autocracies and people's systems, as this study shows, can be equally ambitious in their expansionist intentions and military practices. But a more cynical and unsurprising fact which emerges is that the 'people' can be as tyrannical[7] as any autocrat whose capriciousness is most likely to affect those of his immediate entourage. Despots can often be beneficent without obvious advantages to themselves. They can be – and have been – prodigal with resources in, say, the beautification of a city or the honour of the gods despite the fact that the returns in terms of prestige are of a diminishing order. In comparison, one of the ironies of democratic systems is that those who normally have most to fear from the people are usually the people themselves.

It is a sociological truism that the organisational patterns of societies are related to the control mechanisms which operate to maintain their structural viability. The discussion of the social systems of Egypt and Athens demonstrates this connection in a number of integral institutional areas, the family, the differentiation systems, the economic and political arrangements and their military implications, together with the supportive role of religion. In both societies, the agencies of control were much the same, although they operated in different ways. Both societies recognised the value of custom and moral precepts, but differed profoundly on the matter of law. In Egypt, authority was vested in the Pharaoh and the esoteric interpretation of ma'at, the eternal principle of justice. In practice, this probably meant the application of precedent and was less arbitrary than might be supposed. In Athens, authority lay with the citizens who also theoretically applied traditional normative principles but whose decisions could sometimes be both arbitrary and unpredictable.

This raises the crucial issue of legitimation. The manner in which societies ensure the appropriate responses is inseparably related to the ways in which their actions are justified and implemented. Indeed, the desired responses themselves may be determined by the nature of the legitimating traditions. This problem is central to this entire discussion. It is a contention of this study that the legitimating traditions are functions of the prevailing ideology and that, important as the socio-economic 'realities' may be, they are often, in practice, subordinated to ideological considerations. Whether these ideological considerations can, in turn, be reduced to non-ideological values depends, first, on how ideology is defined and, second, whether the values in question merit the term. Ideology can obviously be seen in non-religious terms. Therefore, ideological values do not have to be interpreted as being primarily religious – as the value of

237

honour or merit in Athens demonstrates. On the other hand, this does not mean that *all* ideological values are basically non-religious. It can hardly be seriously argued, for instance, that the ideological imperatives behind the mobilisation of vast revenues to build the pyramid and temple complexes of Egypt can simply be dismissed in terms of, say, the need to reinforce social solidarity. Reductionism of this kind simply results in a diffuse and meaningless regression.

Every society is confronted with the problem of meaning and the cognitive functions of ideology are most clearly seen in the experiences of Egypt and Athens. How does a society explain itself to itself? To argue that ideology is itself culturally determined is really to say very little. Such a statement could have a rather irritating circularity. So much depends upon the interpretation of 'cultural'; this can be so broadly defined as conveniently to subsume almost anything. On the other hand, to try to establish some kind of chronological precedence for ideology may be equally mistaken. The origination of a value or genesis of a tradition should be regarded as quite separate from their subsequent observance by citizens or their implementation by the state. It is not chronological precedence which is so functionally important, but rather *situational* precedence in specific circumstances.

The difficulty with ideology is that it has an almost ethereal intangibility. In given contexts, it is perceived but not seen – an influence rather than an identifiable variable. As religion, it has cultic manifestations, but its essential nature is not contained by ritual. It is not, strictly, a 'fact' – but then it has long been known that facts can be poor servants of truth. The extent and nature of the reciprocally interactive role of ideology in society presents something of a dialectical dilemma, but it can be evaluated in qualified terms,[8] although this provides a form of diagnosis rather than an explanation.

In Egypt, belief in the god-king took intricate forms of ceremonial expression but these were largely confined to the priesthood and the nobility. There were limited opportunities for the mass of the people to share the ritual exercise which presumably had a cathartic value and promoted a sense of communal well-being. There may have been some attenuated satisfactions derived from seeing the king carefully preserving good order by being safely interred in his tomb or pyramid, or some vicarious pleasure at his victories against the non-peoples of the surrounding territories. But it is difficult to detect, in such occasions, that class-surmounting empathy which is the theoretical pre-requisite of social solidarity.

In a sense, Egypt was essentially an ademic society.[9] It almost encouraged a non-participatory quality which precluded free communication and that overt sense of community which were found in Athens. In all societies, and especially traditional societies, there is a gulf between the esotericism of the illuminati and the religion of the people, but this seems to be particularly marked in Egypt. The very nature of Egyptian religion demanded trained interpreters of the mysteries, and this in turn produced a hierocratic system of authority which automatically ruled out participatory procedures. Catharsis may have been an individual rather than a social experience. The presence of magical and quasi-occult beliefs and practices in this kind of society can therefore be seen as a spiritual palliative in the face of social anonymity, a reactive form of personalised religious activity for the achievement of lower-order goals.

In Athens, the situation was very different. In general, religion and its rituals had a public quality.[10] The cultus was not confined to temples, the worship was in the open air, and the officiating priests were simply lay functionaries. The rites were relatively simple and uncomplicated, and performances required a minimum of training. Such a system hardly encouraged the emergence of a priestly literati who alone could interpret the mysteries.

The prodemic nature of Athenian society was expressed by a range of participatory procedures which theoretically maintained morale and fostered a sense of social solidarity. Rituals to inaugurate various political activities, rituals for warfare, and the broadly-based ethoic festivals of the games and the theatre.

Despite the absence of a hierocracy, Athens also had its philosophical esotericism – or agnosticism – of the intellectuals and its religion of the people. The dichotomy was not as instrumentally effective as in Egypt but, in its own way, it was much more socially divisive. For those seeking either salvation or just sheer diversion, there were, of course, exotic and orgiastic mystery cults as well as soteriologically-oriented movements. These too can perhaps be interpreted as forms of reactive individualism in the face of an insistent collectivism. It was probably only in these movements that personal charisma had a chance to flourish. Prodemic societies may not always be the best proving grounds for prophets, but participatory systems are usually quick to validate or otherwise the charismatic pretensions of would-be religious functionaries. It is in non-participatory systems, where the people are not in a position to question openly the beliefs and practices of the prevailing order that charisma attaches more to the office than to the official who occupies it, and religion is more a source of mystification than enlightenment. This is not an unexceptional rule, but it has general applications.[11] Personal charisma tends to be transient and socially 'unstable', whereas charisma of office, as in Egypt, is perpetuated regardless of the competency of the incumbent, and therefore helps the society to weather the lean periods in its own historical process.

Assuming that there is, therefore, a plausible relationship between ideology and social order, we must take the argument a stage further and ask if the *type* of ideology is a determinative factor in the type of social order which evolves. It must be stressed again that, in the nature of the case, this cannot be demonstrated scientifically. Connections are apparent even if they are merely adventitious. What is not so apparent are the ways in which ideology acts as an independent variable in given situations. Not only is it sometimes possible to identify the dominant or subordinate role of ideology in specific situations, it is also theoretically useful to delineate types of systems in which ideology interacts in these ways. Ideology can be evaluated in terms of its theoretical roles. The common distinction between Interest and Strain theories may be useful but somewhat artificial. They actually complement one another. Interest theories reflect the instrumental and regulative aspects of ideology, whereas Strain theories reflect the responsive aspect; the former emphasise the active manipulation of the system, and the latter indicate the modes of passive receptivity and acceptance. Interest theories of ideology can certainly be applied to Egypt, which was concerned to maintain the viability of its own social order. But this hardly applies to Athens. Any kind of conspiracy theory would be difficult to sustain where the conspiratorial group could only be the people themselves. The ideology of Egypt was essentially conservative, whilst that of Athens was the product of an unresolved clash between the conservative values of the aristocracy and the revolutionary values of the demos. Strain theories also have some relevance, particularly in the case of Egypt which for much of the latter part of its history was creaking under the weight of its own administrative complexity, and needed the unifying force of ideology to sustain it. However, in this study it has been thought more appropriate to employ the model dichotomy which has already been proposed (Chapter 3) between Cosmic and Civic ideologies; this can now be applied to the comparative analysis of Egypt and Athens.

The ideological orientations of Egypt can be seen as Cosmic in type. Therefore, on the basis of our definitions, we can speak of these orientations as the *religion* of Egypt. Religion, within the definitional framework, does not simply mean an operative value-system, but a belief-system which has unambiguous supernaturalist orientations.[12] Egyptian religion was introverted and totalising, and the imperatives of the ideology, though questioned, were pervasive and persistent. The congruency between the theological structures and the observed values of society[13] were never perfect, but it did inform every aspect of Egyptian life.

By comparison, the ideology of Athens cannot be neatly classified. The institutional religion together with the complementary and sometimes conflicting cults were not exactly peripheral to Athenian life, but then they were hardly integral either. Athenian religion was pervasive but it was certainly not totalising. Admittedly, the Acropolis and the temples were there, and the rites were dutifully performed by the priests. But in all this, the possibility is inescapable that these were ritual marginalia. Offerings before the Assembly, sacrifices before the games, libations before an expedition, all give the *impression* of religion, and yet there is the recurrent suspicion that these were simply the obligatory preliminaries to the real business on hand. What really mattered was the polis and its affairs. The gods were acknowledged by deferential gestures, but in general, there was a lack of that sense of real *dependence* on them which is so common in other traditional societies. It is even arguable whether Athena was the tutelary goddess of the city or whether she was merely a convenient symbolisation of the state.

Athens was secular in tone. Its emphases were materialistic and self-consciously political. While its intellectuals were eroding the old traditions, Athenians were thinking and living in terms of a framework of reality and values which were remote from religious beliefs. There was a doubtful congruency between the theological structures and the practical imperatives of city life. If the operational religion of Egypt was the cult of the god-king, the operational religion of Athens was Athenianism.[14] In effect, a Civic ideology. All that civic pride represents seems to have been the focal point of Athenian attention. The beautification of the city, the admiration and reputation which it duly acquired; these are the things which commanded the loyalty of its citizens. The subsidiary concerns for the individual soul and its destiny were either subsumed under a general care for the city and its patron goddess or they were left to the more esoteric comforts of the peripheral cults.

This appreciation of the civic nature of Athenian ideology is really Durkheimian in emphasis. From his study of primitive rituals, Durkheim concluded that religion was simply a product of the group mind, an institutionalised process whereby society reaffirms its own values.[15] These views have been rehearsed and ably criticised in seemingly countless texts.[16] But although they are subject to a great deal of qualification, they do contain valuable insights which are particularly pertinent to the Athenian situation where religion was becoming supplanted by a ritualised humanism.

From a different perspective, the Weberian emphasis on the determinative nature of religious ideology is more relevant to the Egyptian situation. Here religion can be seen as an independent variable which really does influence social arrangements. There seems to have been no significant aspect of Egyptian life which was not touched either by the nomoic or political implications of

241

religion whose cosmic nature – despite the questionings and qualifications – endowed it with a certain ultimacy for those concerned. Perhaps these complementary emphases of Durkheim and Weber are neatly reconciled by Parsons's insistence on the essentiality of shared values. And shared values which have become crystallised as ideologies can be determinative whether they are cosmic or civic in their orientations. The *nature* of the ideology is important, but the mere *existence* of a coherent ideology can be crucial.

Both Cosmic and Civic ideologies are conditioned by exigencies of a practical nature. Cosmic ideologies do not invariably produce stable, long-lived social systems, neither do Civic ideologies necessarily allow or generate systems of anomic instability. The importance of the environment-ideology interactive process can be seen in the orientations of the different religious systems.[17] Do men infer the nature of their gods from the nature of their experiences? Or do men interpret their experiences in terms of the believed natures of their gods? For instance, in Egypt, where the Nile inundations occurred with reassuring predictability, the gods – in general – were regarded as austere but beneficent beings. The geographical isolation, the protection afforded by the seas and the deserts, all increased her sense of being favoured by the gods, particularly in Old Kingdom times.[18] The social experience of fifth-century Greeks was very different. Not especially rich in natural resources, increasingly dependent on others for even staple commodities, and lumbered with a history of fratricidal strife, the Greeks saw the gods increasingly as capricious and even frivolous beings. Ultimately, these attitudes gave rise to the schools of enquiry which often questioned whether the gods existed at all. Experimental and experiential uncertainties in the pursuit of truth can lead to either complete resignation or a gnawing scepticism. But doubt need not be the solvent of faith; it can act as the catalyst of change.

Ideologies are not only conditioned by developmental contexts, they also crucially affect – and are affected by – the modes of implementation. This has been demonstrated in the foregoing institutional analysis. In general terms, there appear to have been significant discontinuities between the normative and substantive structures in Athens, although fewer inconsistencies are detectable in the Egyptian situation. This can be related to the forms and mediation of the ideologies, and to the nature and patterns of their implementation.

This study began with the assumption that belief was important, with or without an external referent. Both Cosmic and Civic ideologies contribute to the maintenance of subjective and objective structures and legitimate their social orders. What is important is that whatever the ideology, it should have the necessary authoritative imprimatur and the means to implement its imperatives. Civic ideologies suffer the disadvantage of visibly emanating from a mortal source which can be seen and therefore challenged, whereas Cosmic ideologies are, by definition, ultimately indisputable – only their interpretations are subject to debate. Both supranatural-istic and humanistic ideologies are capable of evoking dedicated responses, but supernaturalism, when fully espoused, offers ad-herents a final and irrevocable authority. Its potency lies in its unquestioned inviolability. Ideology which can be indelibly in-culcated and suitably implemented, if necessary by coercive sanctions, is the most effective – and certainly the least expensive – mechanism of social control.

Human society is riddled with behavioural inconsistencies and moral contradictions. Any attempt to analyse it or impose coherent patterns upon it must be content with approximations. For this reason, it has been necessary in this study to resort to convenient neologisms, typologies and generalisations. It remains a matter of debate whether values have an autonomous status or whether they are reducible to non-normative explanations. This may even apply where coagulative social exigencies harden belief into set ideological patterns. Does belief affect action, or is it merely the intellectualisa-tion of the need for action? This study has shown that there are occasions when ideology is a dependent variable, and therefore subordinate to other determinative factors in the institutional complex. But there are also circumstances in which ideological imperatives appear to be superordinate and influential in their own right. Specific indices for the resolution of the society-ideology dialectic may actually be impossible. The dependent-independent variable problem admits of no ultimate or unilateral solution.

# Notes

Chapter 1    Methods of analysis

1  T. Bottomore, *Sociology*, 1962.
2  Ibid., p. 29.
3  Note, for example, the assumptions of Emile Durkheim about primitive religion in *The Elementary Forms of the Religious Life* (1915), 1968.
4  The number of simple societies untouched by scholarship is now rapidly running out, and anthropologists have been reduced to studies of kinship in East London and Liverpool, and the investigation of quaintly anachronistic fishing villages in Western Ireland. See P. Willmott and M. Young, *Family and Kinship in East London*, Penguin, 1965; M. Kerr, *The People of Ship Street*, Routledge & Kegan Paul, 1958; K. Connell, *Irish Peasant Society*, Clarendon Press, 1968.
5  See P. Sorokin, *Fads and Foibles of Sociology*, 1956.
6  H. J. Eysenck, *Uses and Abuses of Psychology*, Penguin, 1958.
7  R. Lipsey, *Introduction to Positive Economics*, 1965, pp. 4–5.
8  T. Bottomore, op. cit., p. 25.
9  D. Downes, *The Delinquent Solution*, Routledge & Kegan Paul, 1966.
10  See the excellent treatment of causality in A. Ryan, *The Philosophy of the Social Sciences*, 1970.
11  K. Popper, *The Poverty of Historicism*, 1960; also T. Bottomore, op. cit., p. 26 on the work of Max Weber.
12  A. Richardson, *Christian Apologetics*, 1947, p. 42.
13  C. Wright Mills, *The Sociological Imagination*, 1967.
14  S. Andreski, *Social Sciences as Sorcery*, 1972.
15  Note, for example, Peter Calvert, *Revolution*, 1970.
16  Note the method employed in C. E. Rolph, *Women of the Streets*, Secker & Warburg, 1955.
17  See Clyde Mitchell in Peter Worsley *et al.*, *Introducing Sociology*, 1970.
18  E. Gellner, in article in J. Gould and W. Kolb (eds), *Dictionary of the Social Sciences*, 1964.
19  B. de Jouvenel, writing primarily of economic models in *The Art of Conjecture*, 1967.

20 M. Weber, *Theory of Social and Economic Organisation*, 1966.
21 H. Gerth and C. Wright Mills, *From Max Weber*, 1948.
22 This is particularly the case in E. Durkheim, op. cit.
23 See D. Lockwood, article on 'Ideal-Type Analysis' in Gould and Kolb (eds), op. cit.
24 See P. Cohen, *Modern Social Theory*, 1968, p. 15.
25 E. Durkheim, *The Rules of Sociological Method*, 1964.
26 For a critical appraisal, see J. Rex, *Key Problems of Sociological Theory*, 1961.
27 De Jouvenel, op. cit., p. 63.
28 Note the treatment which is particularly critical of Parsonian schemata in A. R. Louch, *Explanation and Human Action*, 1966, Chapter 2.
29 For a brief summary see T. Bottomore, op. cit., pp. 113ff.
30 L. T. Hobhouse, *Morals in Evolution*, 1906.
31 For example, F. Toennies' *Gemeinschaft and Gesellschaft* and E. Durkheim's Mechanical Solidarity and Organic Solidarity.
32 For a philosophical treatment of the subject, see E. Gellner, *Thought and Change*, 1963.
33 For an excellent review of such theories, see J. Littlejohn, *Social Stratification*, 1972.
34 Note, for instance, the work of some modern Deviancy theorists e.g. Ian Taylor's interpretation of soccer hooliganism in terms of 'embourgeoisification'.
35 See S. Cotgrove, *The Science of Society*, 1967, pp. 210–11.
36 Ibid., pp. 214–15; and H. Bredemeier and R. Stephenson, *The Analysis of Social Systems*, 1970, pp. 318ff.
37 See G. Thomson, 'Slavery in Ancient Greece' in Jill Claster (ed.), *Athenian Democracy*, 1967.
38 A distinction made by R. Firth who argues that the term 'social organisation' should be used to denote the 'working parts' of a society as opposed to its structural elements. See *Elements of Social Organisation*, 1951.
39 This can be seen particularly in the works of A. Comte, K. Marx and V. Pareto.
40 See A. Etzioni, *Studies in Social Change*, 1966; W. Moore, *Social Change*, Prentice-Hall, 1963; R. Applebaum, *Theories of Social Change*, Markham, 1971; P. Cohen, *Modern Social Theory*; S. N. Eisenstadt (ed.), *Readings in Social Evolution and Development*, 1970.
41 The term stasis in common classical usage implied political or social conflict. It is not being used here in that way, but rather in its original and more literal sense of 'standing' or 'standing still'.

### Chapter 2 Functions of social control

1 This may not have been characteristic of all periods of Roman history, but it certainly seems to have functioned in this way in the early Imperial age when Augustus tried to encourage a semblance of outward patrician respectability despite the sexual waywardness of his own family. See Otto Kiefer, *Sexual Life in Ancient Rome*, 1971.
2 T. Bottomore, *Sociology*, 1962, p. 211.

3 H. Bredemeier and R. Stephenson, *The Analysis of Social Systems*, 1970, p. 146.
4 Compare the somewhat different emphasis of G. Abcarian and M. Palmer, *The Human Arena*, 1971: 'Social control refers to the vast system of expectations and restraints, including socialisation, through which deviant behaviour is either prevented or restrained' (p. 5).
5 Ibid., p. 5.
6 E.g. Ivan Illich, *Deschooling Society* and *Celebration of Awareness*, 1971.
7 See Paulo Freire, *Pedagogy of the Oppressed*, 1973, for an equally radical, but more balanced approach to the functions of education.
8 Talcott Parsons, *The Social System*, 1951, pp. 297ff.
9 See particularly J. A. Wilson, *The Culture of Ancient Egypt*, 1956 and C. Aldred, *The Egyptians*, 1956.
10 Although there were exceptions to this, e.g. Akhenaten, the so-called heretic Pharaoh of the Amarna period (c.1375–1353 BC) and his sister-wife, Nefertiti.
11 For a brief review, see H. Wood Jarvis, *Pharaoh to Farouk*, Murray, 1955.
12 Actually, a Mameluke general, Baibars, established the dynasty after murdering the Sultan of Baghdad who had defeated the Mongols just prior to his death.
13 See Thubten Norbu, *Tibet is My Country*, 1960.
14 See R. Dawson, *Imperial China*, 1972.
15 Eric Carlton, *Patterns of Belief*, vol. 1, 1973.
16 Alan Moorehead, *The White Nile*, 1962.
17 Lesley Blanch, *Pavilions of the Heart*, 1974.
18 Plato, *The Republic*, translated by H. D. P. Lee, 1964.
19 See particularly Max Marwick (ed.), *Readings in Witchcraft and Sorcery*, 1972.
20 Robert Payne, *The Roman Triumph*, 1962.
21 Michael Grant, *The Gladiators*, 1971.
22 H. D. Kitto, *The Greeks*, 1951.
23 C. Seltman, *Women in Antiquity*, 1956.
24 For a more developed discussion of these themes see Chapter 9.
25 H. Bengtson (ed.), *The Greeks and the Persians*, 1969.
26 C. Ryecroft (ed.), *Psycho Analysis Observed*, 1966; T. Szasz, *The Myth of Madness*, Paladin, 1972.
27 J. Brown, *Techniques of Persuasion*, 1964; W. Sargent, *Battle for the Mind*, 1959.
28 Max Weber, *Theory of Social and Economic Organisation*, 1964.
29 Talcott Parsons, *Societies: Evolutionary and Comparative Perspectives*, 1966, pp. 11–12.
30 W. O. E. Oesterley, *A History of Israel*, Clarendon Press, 1957.
31 See D. G. Macrae, *Ideology and Society*, 1961.
32 For a more elaborate exception, see Richard Lapiere, *A Theory of Social Control*, 1954.
33 Elizabeth Nottingham, *Religion and Society*, 1964, p. 42.
34 Emile Durkheim, *The Elementary Forms of the Religious Life*, 1968.

NOTES TO PAGES 21-4

35 See, for instance, E. Evans-Pritchard, *Theories of Primitive Religion*, 1965, and M. Ginsberg, *On the Diversity of Morals*, 1956.

36 L. Cottrell, *The Penguin Book of Lost Worlds*, vol. 1, 1966.

37 Georges Contenau, *Everyday Life in Babylon and Assyria*, 1969.

38 Is not Contenau mistaken when he writes (ibid., p. 142) 'ideological factors have taken the place of "the will of Ashur"'? Surely practical policy, in this case warfare, is being justified in ideological terms. This point is taken up again in Chapter 12.

39 In this context, Hannah Arendt is particularly concerned with modern totalitarianisms which have been grounded in ideological modes of thought. See C. Friedrich (ed.), *Totalitarianism*, 1954.

**Chapter 3  The problem of ideology**

1 For a detailed discussion of these issues, see J. Plamenatz, *Ideologies*, 1971; and compare Nigel Harris, *Beliefs and Society*, 1971 with special reference to the applications of Marxist and nationalist ideology in south-east Asia.

2 Parsons gives this as a system of empirically-oriented ideas which give men 'an interpretation of the empirical nature of the collectivity and of the situation in which it is placed, the processes by which it has developed to its given state, the goals to which its members are collectively oriented, and their relation to the future course of events'. Talcott Parsons, *The Social System*, 1951, p. 349.

3 J. Plamenatz, op. cit., p. 15.

4 H. Bredemeier and R. Stephenson, *The Analysis of Social Systems*, 1970, p. 310.

5 Note, for example, Arnold Toynbee (see also Chapter 4) who argues that 'civilisations' – as he defines them – have specific identifiable characteristics. For a critical analysis of Toynbee's central theses, see Patrick Gardiner (ed.), *Theories of History*, 1959.

6 Julius Gould, article on 'Ideology' in J. Gould and W. Kolb (eds), *Dictionary of the Social Sciences*, 1964.

7 A view probably best reflected in the work of Vilfredo Pareto, *The Mind and Society*, 1935.

8 Marx distinguished between the material substructure of society and its ideological superstructure, hence his insistence that social consciousness was conditioned by social existence. In attributing primacy to the material order it follows that the ideological order is consequently reduced to a dependent variable in the social process.

For a critique of Marx's uncertainties on this point, see particularly Plamenatz, op. cit. See also Karl Marx and Friedrich Engels, *The German Ideology*, 1965.

9 K. Mannheim, *Ideology and Utopia*, 1955, pp. 238-9. See also writings of: G. Sorel, *Reflections on Violence*, 1950; V. Pareto, *Sociological Writings* (ed. S. E. Finer), 1966.

10 This is not meant to imply that ideological pronouncements are patently false, and are only calculated to deceive. There is evidence to suggest that underneath the 'party line' of some modern movements

247

there is a believed ideology. See S. Bloom, *The Peasant Caesar*, Commentary, 1957; H. R. Trevor-Roper, *The Last Days of Hitler*, 1947.

11 See particularly David Apter (ed.), *Ideology and Discontent*, 1964.

12 R. Southern, *The Making of the Middle Ages*, 1967.

13 William Dale Morris, *The Christian Origins of Social Revolt*, 1949.

14 See Francis Sutton *et al.*, *The American Business Creed*, Harvard University Press, 1956.

15 E. A. Gellner, *Thought and Change*, 1963.

16 See William Douglas, *Points of Rebellion*, Random House, 1970.

17 See Ralph Conant on the 'Urban Crisis' in *The American Scholar* vol. 37, 1968 and *Report of the National Advisory Commission on Civil Disorders*, Bantam, 1968.

18 That this was a preoccupation of some ancient political theorists is well attested by Plato in his analyses of the just society in *The Republic* and *The Laws*.

19 M. I. Finley, *Slavery in Classical Antiquity*, 1964, p. 72.

20 The phrase is David Apter's (*Ideology and Discontent*).

21 Perhaps, in Ernest Gellner's words, by 'a good dose of absurdity . . . (which) . . . blocks the understanding'. 'Is Belief Really Necessary?', *Hibbert Journal*, 1957.

22 Closely related to this type of strains theory is the cognitive insufficiency view often associated with Talcott Parsons. This stresses the idea that ideologies either result from deviations from scientific truth, or derive from discrepancies in an understanding of scientific facts. See Talcott Parsons, op. cit.

23 See Norman Birnbaum, *The Sociological Study of Ideology 1940–1960*, 1962.

24 There can, of course, in modern societies be non-ideological responses of an 'unscientific' non-rational kind, to certain kinds of stress, e.g. alcohol and drugs.

25 Talcott Parsons, 'The Sociology of Modern Anti-Semitism' in I. Graeber and G. H. Britt (eds), *Jews in a Gentile World*, Macmillan, 1942.

26 Sutton *et al.*, op. cit.

27 Talcott Parsons, see Introduction to *Essays in Sociological Theory*, 1954.

28 Gilbert Murray, *Five Stages of Greek Religion*, Watts, 1946.

29 Robert Merton, 'Priorities in Scientific Discovery', *American Sociological Review*, XXII, 1957, and particularly 'Science, Technology and Society in Seventeenth Century England' in *Osiris* (ed. G. Seaton), 1938.

30 C. Friedrich and Z. Brzezinski, *Totalitarian Dictatorship and Autocracy*, 1965.

31 A. Inkeles, *Public Opinion in Soviet Russia: A Study in Mass Persuasion*, Cambridge University Press, 1950.

32 Apter, op. cit.

33 This can be very graphically illustrated, for example, by witchcraft practices among the Zulu for covert political reasons. See Donald Morris, *The Washing of the Spears*, 1968, and E. E. Ritter, *Shaka, Zulu*, 1967.

34 There has been a proliferation of excellent literature on this subject particularly from the Columbus Centre. Also see T. Adorno *et al.*, *The Authoritarian Personality*, 1950; G. Reitlinger, *The Final Solution*, 1953.
35 Philip Converse, 'The Nature of Belief Systems in Mass Publics' in Apter, op. cit., pp. 210–11.
36 Michel Leiris, *Race and Culture*, 1951.
37 J. Baker, *Race*, 1974.
38 M. Ashley Montague, *Man's Most Dangerous Myth*, 1970.
39 See *The Larousse Dictionary of the Ancient World*, 1963.
40 S. Kramer, *The Sumerians*, 1973.
41 M. I. Finley, *The Ancient Greeks*, 1963.
42 R. Dawson, *Imperial China*, 1972.
43 The Spartan infantry was acknowledged as the finest in Greece for something like 400 years.
44 It had some affinities in Crete, and strangely enough in early nineteenth-century Zulu society. See H. Michell, *Sparta*, 1952; and Donald Morris, op. cit.
45 Peter Berger, *The Social Reality of Religion*, 1967, pp. 33–4.
46 Emile Durkheim, *The Elementary Forms of the Religious Life*, 1968.
47 John Collier, *Indians of the Americas*, 1956, p. 52.
48 See also the classic of William Prescott, *The History of the Conquest of Mexico* (abridged by C. H. Gardiner), 1966.
49 See Bernal Diaz del Castillo, *The First Spanish Contact with the Aztecs of Mexico in the Americas on the Eve of Discovery* (ed. H. E. Driver), Spectrum (Prentice-Hall), 1964.
50 A view particularly associated with B. Malinowski. See (a) *Man and Culture* (ed. R. Firth), Routledge & Kegan Paul, 1963; (b) Percy Cohen, 'Theories of Myth', *Man*, September 1969.
51 Mircea Eliade, *Myth and Reality*, 1963.
52 E. R. Leach, *The Political Systems of Highland Burma*, 1964.
53 See the excellent account of the meaning and functions of myth in G. S. Kirk, *Myth*, 1973.
54 Eric Carlton, *Patterns of Belief*, vol. 2, 1973, p. 23.
55 Michell, op. cit., especially Chapters IV and V. This has been the occasion of some debate among scholars. Both Plutarch and Aristotle *seem* to suggest that the ecclesia had no say in affairs – but the weight of evidence now favours participation.
56 Note the possible motives for the voting behaviour of particular groups, e.g. farmers and industrialists in relation to the Nazis in Germany in the 1930s. William Shirer, *The Rise and Fall of the Third Reich*, 1965.
57 There was even limited participation during periods of tyranny. See A. Andrewes, *The Greek Tyrants*, 1956.
58 Robert Merton, *Social Theory and Social Structure*, 1957.
59 Talcott Parsons, *The Social System*.
60 'As for these words, a thousand gods of the male gods and of the female gods of them of Hatti, together with a thousand gods of the male gods and the female gods of them of the land of Egypt are with me as witnesses. . . .' Any violation would therefore be seen as an affront to

the honour of both earthly and cosmic forces. See J. A. Wilson, *The Culture of Ancient Egypt*, 1956, pp. 247–9.

61 W. K. C. Guthrie, *The Greek Philosophers*, 1950.

62 For a critical treatment of the influence of Plato and his teachings, see K. Popper, *The Open Society*, Vol. I, 1965; and B. Russell, *A History of Western Philosophy*, 1948.

63 For example, C. E. M. Joad, *Philosophy*, 1960.

64 G. C. Field, *Plato and His Contemporaries*, 1967.

65 For a general appraisal, see A. H. Armstrong, *An Introduction to Ancient Philosophy*, 1968.

66 V. Ehrenberg, *From Solon to Socrates*, 1968.

67 H. Scullard, *From the Gracchi to Nero*, 1965.

68 Note the argument of J. A. Wilson (op. cit., p. 223) that Aten worship was the peculiar prerogative of the royal family, and that the operative religion of the laity was a re-emphasised Pharaoh-worship.

69 L. Cottrell, *The Lost Pharaohs*, 1956.

70 H. Johnson argues that 'reactionary' is merely a form of revolutionary, but it seems much more relevant to see it as a revivified conservative ideology. *Sociology: a Systematic Introduction*, 1965, p. 588.

71 See H. Frankfort *et al.*, *Before Philosophy*, 1954.

72 Admittedly, there are degrees of instability, but these are impossible to measure. The problem lies in identifying the nature of particular situations and relate them to the proliferation of ideologies and counter-movements. Note the similar argument that social instability facilitates the emergence of messiahs and millennial movements. T. Hoult, *The Sociology of Religion*, 1958.

73 See Mannheim, *Ideology and Utopia*.

74 For instance, J. Milton Yinger, *Religion, Society and the Individual*, 1957.

75 Bredemeier and Stephenson, op. cit., p. 316.

76 For example, Stephen Cotgrove, *The Science of Society*, 1967, p. 206: 'Political ideologies, then, can be functional alternatives to religion.'

77 See particularly R. Robertson, *The Sociological Interpretation of Religion*, 1970.

78 P. Worsley, 'Religion as a Category' in R. Robertson (ed.), *Readings in the Sociology of Religion*, 1969.

79 R. Bendix, 'The Age of Ideology' in Apter, op. cit.

80 This would approximate to the view of ideologies held by Michael Oakeshott. See *Rationalism and Other Essays*, 1962.

81 For an excellent discussion of causation models, see D. Lerner, *Cause and Effect*, The Hayden Colloquium on Scientific Method and Concept.

82 See particularly Popper, op. cit., vol. II, Chapter 25.

83 This is not to imply that an *understanding* of the ideology is essential, in fact, it might be argued (in a similar vein to Gellner, 'Is Belief Really Necessary?') that the degree of acceptance should be seen as being in inverse ratio to the degree of understanding.

## Chapter 4 Theories of cultural development

1 For a more eleborate treatment of this theme, see E. Carlton, *Patterns of Belief*, 1973, vol. 2, Chapter 1.

2 See the analytical distinctions between history and sociology made by R. Bierstedt (following W. Dilthey) in *British Journal of Sociology*, June 1959.
3 The 'Nutcracker Man' skull uncovered at Olduvai by Dr L. Leakey was radio-carbon tested at 1,750,000 years.
4 The entire field of pre-history and palaeontology is studded with chronological and physiological uncertainties. New species are said to 'appear' or 'emerge' – very little more than this can be said. For example, Cromagnon Man and his contemporary, the more negroid Grimaldi Man (or some very similar type) left skeletal remains in North and East Africa, Israel, France and China, and may have come from Africa or Asia – or both.
5 For a detailed appraisal, see Carleton Coon, *The History of Man*, 1962.
6 This is suggested by the presence of crude figurines with exaggerated sexual characteristics.
7 Glyn Daniel, *Lascaux and Carnac*, Lutterworth, 1955.
8 V. Gordon Childe, *Man Makes Himself*, 1948.
9 Perhaps the best examples are still Jarmo in north-east Iraq (from *c.* 6750 BC) excavated by Robert Braidwood of the University of Chicago Oriental Institute, and Jericho (from *c.* 7800) excavated by Kathleen Kenyon.
10 See Kathleen Kenyon, *Archaeology in the Holy Land*, 1960.
11 For a fairly straightforward treatment, see Creighton Gabel (ed.), *Man Before History*, 1964.
12 An archaeological term to express the situation where a Stone Age culture was gradually passing into a metal culture.
13 Milton Covensky, *The Ancient Near Eastern Tradition*, 1966, p. 8.
14 In Heine-Geldern's 'The Origin of Ancient Civilizations and Toynbee's Theories', he derives all civilisations from an early Mesopotamian centre.
15 For a brief survey of some of the arguments, see Gideon Sjoberg, *The Pre-Industrial City*, 1965, Chapter 2.
16 Gideon Sjoberg, for example, defines three main types of societies, folk, feudal and urban/industrial, in terms of the technological variable. Ibid.
17 The principal difficulty with any investigation of the Indus valley cultures is that no one, as yet, has been able to decipher the script – an almost insuperable problem without a bi-lingual text.
18 See E. Thompson, *The Maya*, Penguin, 1970.
19 See H. E. Driver (ed.), *The Americas on the Eve of Discovery*, 1964.
20 Sjoberg, op. cit., p. 26.
21 For an able though hardly impartial presentation of the case for Old World – possibly Carthaginian – influences, see, Constance Irwin, *Fair Gods and Stone Faces*, W. H. Allen, 1964.
22 Covensky, op. cit., p. 8.
23 Henri Frankfort, *The Birth of Civilization in the Near East*, 1956.
24 E. Huntingdon, *Mainsprings of Civilization*, Mentor, 1959.
25 R. Braidwood *et al.*, *Courses Toward Urban Life* (Harvard Symposium), 1962.

26 See particularly V. Gordon Childe, *What Happened in History*, Penguin, 1960.

27 Note the similar division made by the anthropologist, Darryl Forde, in his classification of simple societies into:
   (i) Hunting
   (ii) Collecting
   (iii) Fishing
   (iv) Stock rearing/stock keeping
   (v) Cultivating
   Darryl Forde, *Habitat, Economy and Society*, Methuen, 1968.

28 For amplification of this point see the chapter on Systems of Ideation. Also G. Contenau, *Everyday Life in Babylon and Assyria*, 1969.

29 Sjoberg, op. cit., p. 65.

30 For a rather unorthodox interpretation of the functions of the pyramid and temple structures, see P. Tompkins, *The Secrets of the Great Pyramid*, 1973.

31 Sjoberg argues (op. cit., p. 76) for a de-emphasis on the correlation between commerce and urbanisation, but this must be treated with some caution in the light of the increasing dependence of some states on external sources of supply. See particularly J. Boardman, *The Greeks Overseas*, 1964.

32 Note H. Bengtson (ed.), *The Greeks and the Persians*, 1969; and F. Millar, *The Romans and Their Neighbours*, 1970.

33 This is reminiscent of the Greeks who often seemed to be on the brink of a technological breakthrough. For example, Hero, in the first century AD was experimenting with steam toys, but never seems to have appreciated the applicational possibilities. See particularly Hugh Lloyd-Jones (ed.), *The Greek World*, 1965.

34 Thompson, op. cit.

35 J. Alden Mason, *The Ancient Civilizations of Peru*, Penguin, 1964.

36 See R. LeMay, *The Culture of South-East Asia*, Allen & Unwin, 1954; and C. Pym, *The Ancient Civilization of Angkor*, Mentor, 1968.

37 Karl Wittfogel, *Oriental Despotism*, 1957.

38 Max Weber, *The Protestant Ethic and the Spirit of Capitalism*, 1930.

39 Stanislav Andreski agrees with this point about the subordinate position of merchants, this was certainly the state of affairs in, say, Imperial China. But he suggests that such systems also lacked a stable nobility and that they allowed the consolidation of autocratic power. This would be difficult to sustain in relation to both Egypt and China at particular periods, and especially Peru where the members of the political hierarchy were all related to the ruling Inca. See article 'Despotism' in J. Gould and W. Kolb (eds), *Dictionary of the Social Sciences*, 1964.

40 S. N. Eisenstadt in his critique of Wittfogel is probably a little unfair on this point. Wittfogel does not say that other institutions *will* not develop, but he does insist that they will never be allowed to jeopardise the authority of the state. S. N. Eisenstadt, in *Journal of Asian Studies*, 1957–8, pp. 435–46.

41 A disregard of this 'law' has obviously been the downfall of a number of conquerors, e.g. the fragmentation of the unwieldy Empire of the Mongol Khans in the thirteenth and fourteenth centuries AD.

42 See the critique by D. G. Macrae in *Man*, June 1959.

43 'Wittfogel's hydraulic determinism – though appealing in its simplicity – is grossly oversimplified . . . urban centres . . . could never have arisen and been sustained were not an elite to manage and control a relatively wide range of human activities. . . .' Sjoberg, op. cit., p. 117.

44 W. Eberhard, *A History of China*, 1950.

45 Eisenstadt, op. cit.

46 He did compete unsuccessfully in Greece with his poems, although he on one occasion won a prize for tragedy. See A. Andrewes, *The Greek Tyrants*, 1956.

47 Peter Green, *Alexander the Great*, 1973.

48 Sjoberg, op. cit. Note particularly Chapters 2 and 3.

49 Ibid., p. 69.

50 Paradoxically, aggression and the bringing of cultural benefits may well go hand in hand. This is particularly evidenced for the British by the Roman conquest and occupation. See Sheppard Frere, *Britannia*, 1967.

51 Talcott Parsons, *Societies: Evolutionary and Comparative Perspectives*, 1966.

52 They can hardly be classed as Parsons's 'advanced intermediate' societies which possess upper-class literacy and an historical religion.

53 In context, Parsons concentrates on Ancient Egypt and Mesopotamia, thus giving support to this particular assumption.

54 V. Gordon Childe, 'Civilization, Cities and Towns', *Antiquity* XXXI, 1957.

55 Sir Mortimer Wheeler, 'The First Towns', *Antiquity* XXX, 1956.

56 See particularly Max Weber, *The Religion of China*, 1964.

57 Arnold Toynbee, *A Study of History*, 1970.

58 See Covensky, op. cit.

59 These implications are probably more apparent in relation to Toynbee's five 'arrested' civilisations, and additional 'abortive' ones.

60 For appraisals of the arguments, see: P. Geyl, *Debates with Historians*, Fontana, 1962; P. Gardiner (ed.), *Theories of History*, 1959 and Ved Mehta, *The Fly and the Fly-bottle*, Penguin, 1965.

61 Gardiner, op. cit., pp. 308–11.

62 P. Sorokin, *Social Philosophies of an Age of Crisis*, Dover, 1964.

63 To be fair to Toynbee, he does not actually say civilisations are *totally* integrated, merely that they have a kind of organic unity.

64 This is, of course, impossible to quantify – an influence is difficult to calculate. One immediately thinks of Roman law and modern European legal codes; the Phoenician–Greek alphabet; the Sumerian sexagesimal system which we still use in the calculation of time and in navigation. The debt to the past is incalculable.

65 R. Redfield, *The Primitive World and its Transformations*, 1953.

66 Ibid.

67 According to Childe, these characteristics apply to all civilised communities. They may be summarised as follows:

253

   (i) Increase in the size and complexity of settlements
  (ii) The institution of tribute or taxation and central treasuries
 (iii) Monumental public works
 (iv) The art of writing
  (v) The beginnings of exact and predictive science, mathematics, etc.
 (vi) Developed economic institutions and perhaps foreign trade
(vii) Full-time technical specialists
(viii) A privileged ruling class
 (ix) A state organisation
  (x) The reappearance of naturalistic art

See R. Redfield, 'On the Nature of Civilization' in Gabel, op. cit., p. 178.

68 Henri Frankfort et al., Before Philosophy, 1954, p. 12.

69 M. Eliade, Myth and Reality, 1963.

70 E. O. James, The Beginnings of Religion, 1948.

71 Braidwood, op. cit.

72 Sjoberg, op. cit., pp. 281–2.

73 It is interesting that Toynbee also stresses the uniformities of man's religious experience, and contends that a declining civilisation's only way of salvation may be by means of a religious 'transfiguration'. This will not so much preserve as restore it by preparing the way for a new and more value-conscious future.

74 Parsons, op. cit., p. 68.

75 Rushton Coulborn, The Origins of Civilized Societies, Princeton University Press, 1959.

76 Andrew Tomas, We Are Not The First, Sphere, 1972.

77 Brother Philip, Secret of the Andes, Spearman, 1961.

78 The extra-terrestrial-Mu-Atlantis theories can all be linked as one overall explanation. See ibid.

79 See, for example, Erich von Daniken, Chariots of the Gods, Souvenir Press, 1969.

80 Note the views of Crick and Watson, who won the Nobel prize for their work on the genetic code, who have hypothesised that life on Earth had an extra-terrestrial source.

81 For an amusing yet scholarly refutation of many of these theories, see R. Wauchope, Lost Tribes and Sunken Continents, Chicago, 1970.

### Chapter 5   Comparative typologies: Egypt and Athens

1 Note Durkheim's treatment of religion as the basis for social relations in traditional societies: 'Originally, religion blankets everything; what is social is their religions; the two words are then synonymous.' E. Durkheim, The Division of Labour in Society, 1933, pp. 152ff.

2 When is a civilisation 'born' and when does it 'die'? This is the basis of one of P. Sorokin's most pungent criticisms of Arnold Toynbee. See P. Gardiner, Theories of History, 1959.

3 Talcott Parsons, Societies: Evolutionary and Comparative Perspectives, 1966.

4 Ibid., pp. 51–62; 103–8.

5 'We shall distinguish two principal substages of intermediate society, the archaic and the "advanced intermediate". By archaic, we mean the first major stage in the evolution of intermediate society. The advanced stage is characterised by full upper-class literacy and . . . historic religion, one which has broken through to philosophical levels of generalization and systematization.' Ibid., p. 51.

6 Parsons does not categorise China as an Archaic society, but as an 'historic intermediate Empire' (ibid., pp. 71ff).

7 See Parson's brief preamble in ibid., p. 96.

8 On this point of singularity, Parsons appears to come very close to Toynbee's position (see Chapter 4) of arguing that civilisations have identifiable distinguishing characteristics.

9 The polis of Greece certainly had its anticipations in the city-state systems of early Mesopotamia (see G. Roux, *Ancient Iraq*, 1964). And, in some respects, the uniqueness of Israelite religion – especially in its developmental phases – can certainly be questioned (see Sir Frederick Kenyon, *The Bible and Archaeology*, 1940).

10 Parsons, on the other hand, appears to suggest that position by appointment is a characteristic of the 'historic intermediate empire'.

11 Where there is ostensible open competition for official positions, it is not unusual for sons of the aristocracy to obtain the appointments. This may even happen where there is a form of civil service examination system as in China. See L. Eberhardt, *Social Mobility in Traditional China*, Brill, 1962 also W. Eberhard, *A History of China*, 1950.

12 See J. A. Wilson, *The Culture of Ancient Egypt*, 1950, pp. 91–3.

13 Quoted from some of the writings of the First Intermediate period, *c*. 2200–*c*. 2050 BC, after the breakdown of the Old Kingdom. See ibid., pp. 106–9.

14 On this issue of religious functionaries, this typology obviously differs considerably from that of Parsons who sees such a hierocratic society as Ancient Israel as a 'seed-bed' type.

15 'Ethoically' is used here as an adjectival form of ethos, i.e. the spirit of a people or society. 'Ethical' – which derives from the same Greek root would now have entirely the wrong connotations. It is not to be confused, of course, with 'ethology' as used by Konrad Lorenz (*On Aggression*, Methuen, 1966) to denote genetically inherited patterns of behaviour in vertebrates.

16 H. D. Kitto, *The Greeks*, 1951.

17 M. I. Finley, *The Ancient Greeks*, 1963, p. 58.

18 A. Andrewes, *Greek Society*, 1967, p. 144.

19 E. B. Castle, *Ancient Education and Today*, 1961.

20 Alvin Gouldner, *Enter Plato*, 1967, p. 71.

21 Gilbert Murray, *Five Stages of Greek Religion*, Watts, 1946.

22 For example, such classic texts as A. Zimmern, *The Greek Commonwealth*, 1911 and G. Glotz, *The Greek City and Its Institutions*, 1929.

## Chapter 6 Patterns of historical development

1 The Palermo Stone (so named because it is housed in the museum in Palermo) records – perhaps authentically – what purports to be some-

thing of the early history of Egypt up to the Fifth Dynasty *c*. 2500 BC. This is recounted not in political but economic terms, the historian(s) involved being particularly careful to note the height of the Nile from year to year. Apparently a rise of less than 25 feet or more than 30 feet might be disastrous, bringing either drought or floods.

2  J. Finegan, *Light from the Ancient Near East*, 1969.

3  Scholars customarily use the system of dynasties which is ascribed to the work of Manetho, a Greek-speaking Egyptian priest who wrote in the third century BC. According to this system Egypt had thirty dynasties down to the Greek conquest in 332 BC, thereafter there were three additional Greek (Ptolemaic) dynasties. His work is very late for our purposes, and survives only in quotations from Greek and Roman authors.

4  The Archaic period has been very ably documented, see particularly W. Emery, *Archaic Egypt*, 1972.

5  W. Flinders Petrie, *Prehistoric Egypt*, 1920.

6  Some tombs were approximately 200 feet by 100 feet and consisted of several rooms around a central chamber. See Emery, op. cit.

7  See E. Weech, 'Civilizations of the Near East' in W. Weech (ed.), *History of the World*, 1946, p. 37.

8  The symbols of the two Kingdoms were the vulture and the uraeus serpent. (Upper Egypt acknowledged Horus, the falcon-god, and took the symbol of the vulture-goddess, Nekhebet.) Sometimes the unification of Egypt was also represented by ties of lotus (south) and papyrus (north).

9  In the Royal Cemetery of Ur, the remains of some 76 attendants were discovered. Whether they were killed or went willingly to their deaths as a form of ritual mass suicide is uncertain. See L. Woolley, *Ur of the Chaldees*, Penguin, 1950 edn.

10  An interesting comparison may be drawn between the familial nepotism in Egyptian society and the similar but more highly institutionalised system of the Incas of Peru. See J. Hemming, *The Conquest of the Incas*, Macmillan, 1970.

11  Osiris represents the dying and re-living god whose adventures may have enjoyed some popularity because they appealed to a wider class spectrum – a fact that may have been prudently exploited by respective priesthoods.

12  The Pyramid Texts were – as the term suggests – writings put in the chambers of the pyramids, and were primarily ritualistic in content.

13  That they were *simply* tombs has been questioned. There is a minority view that they may have originally been ancient observatories. See P. Tompkins, *Secrets of the Great Pyramid*, 1973.

14  What little is known about the First Intermediate period has been graphically interpreted by J. A. Wilson in *The Culture of Ancient Egypt*, 1956, Chapter 5.

15  The Egyptians had early developed the practice of mummification to preserve bodies. This process was expensive and was used only for kings and nobles. Because it was possible that despite all the efforts of the embalmers the body might still decay, figures or paintings were also

put in the tomb as lasting symbolic representations – perhaps even as substitutes – of the physical body.

16 Some writers, e.g. Tompkins (op. cit.), insist that the geodetic insights of Egyptian pyramid and temple construction show that in the mathematical and astronomical sciences they were very advanced indeed although this has been contested by other commentators, for example, K. Mendelssohn, *The Riddle of the Pyramids*, 1974.

17 The Hyksos probably came from north-east Syria. They may in fact have been Mitanni, but this is uncertain. When they were eventually driven from Egypt, they were pursued into southern Canaan, which suggests that the main areas of their suzerainty extended northwards.

18 J. A. Wilson allows for a period of consolidation and reconquest, and prefers to date the Empire from the later Eighteenth Dynasty, i.e. from the reign of Queen Hatshepsut *c.* 1465 BC.

19 As yet, the Hebrews (designated by Talcott Parsons as a 'seed-bed' society) – whose influence was to outlive their fleeting moments of power during the reigns of David and Solomon *c.* 1000 BC – had not arrived on the scene in Canaan. Their Exodus from Egypt is usually dated from the reign of Ramesses II, but this is uncertain. For a discussion see, e.g., Sir Frederic Kenyon, *The Bible and Archaeology*, 1940.

20 The term Pharaoh which comes from 'pero' meaning Great House or palace has its first known recorded use during the Eighteenth Dynasty in a letter to the 'heretic' king Amenophis IV (Akhenaten).

21 See particularly the authoritative work of J. H. Breasted, *A History of Egypt*, 1946.

22 The Egyptians referred to the 'Sea-peoples' as the 'northerners in their islands'. The period of their invasions also coincides with the fabled siege of Troy by the Achaeans *c.* 1190 BC, as recounted by Homer in the *Iliad*. The collapse of Mycenaean civilisation in Greece also dates from about this time which again indicates the restless movements of migratory northern tribes.

23 See R. M. Haywood, *The Ancient World*, 1971, p. 60.

24 Regarding Crete, see R. Willetts, *Ancient Crete*, 1969.

25 See M. I. Finley, *Early Greece: The Bronze and Archaic Ages*, 1970 and L. Cottrell, *The Lion Gate*, 1963.

26 Intellectual enquiry flourished, for example, at the school at Miletus which boasted the services of such teachers as Anaximander and Anaximenes who enjoyed the reputations of highly-respected polymaths in the ancient Mediterranean world.

27 The city-state was hardly a Greek invention; similar political forms had existed in much earlier times in Ancient Mesopotamia (see G. Roux, *Ancient Iraq*, 1964) but in Greece their development was often linked with democratic traditions.

28 The word polis is usually translated 'city-state', but it is arguable whether this really conveys the meaning which it had for the Greeks themselves. It connotes both an ideal and a practical political experiment. See H. D. Kitto, *The Greeks*, 1951.

29 J. Revill, *World History*, Longmans, 1962, p. 54. Expansion in the west was largely inhibited by the presence and sometimes hostile activities

of the Carthaginians. These people, who may have originated in Phoenicia, controlled by *c.* 500 BC the Straits of Gibraltar, the metal trade from Spain, the whole coast of North Africa from Cyrene to Morocco, the Balearic Islands, Malta, Sardinia, Corsica, and western Sicily.

30 For a very thorough treatment of Greek colonisation, see J. Boardman, *The Greeks Overseas*, 1964; and also R. Carpenter, *Beyond the Pillars of Hercules*, 1973.

31 N. G. L. Hammond, *A History of Greece to 322 BC*, 1967.

32 Coinage which was developed by the Lydian kings in Asia Minor, spread to the Ionian cities – particularly Miletus and Ephesus which produced coins of electrum. From here, the practice rapidly extended to the islands and the Greek mainland.

33 See particularly, V. Ehrenberg, *From Solon to Socrates*, 1968.

34 H. Bengtson (ed.), *The Greeks and the Persians*, 1969.

35 The Athenian historian Thucydides, towards the end of the fifth century, in his *History of the Peloponnesian War*, remarks that posterity, seeing the humble ruins of Sparta, would never think them appropriate to the power of Sparta at the zenith of her military achievement.

36 For a treatment of some of the lesser poleis, see K. Freeman, *Greek City States*, 1963.

37 Names which end in the patronymic –dae denote 'the children of' or 'the descendants of'. It was a common practice for clans to group themselves around the memory of a distinguished earlier member by calling themselves his descendants.

38 On the injustices of the Aristocratic period, see Hesiod, *Works and Days*.

39 For a very thorough analysis of tyranny in Greece, see A. Andrewes, *The Greek Tyrants*, 1956.

40 Some tyrannies were relatively long-lasting, for example that of Orthagoras of Sicyon from *c.* 650 BC.

41 Perhaps the classic father-son syndrome can be seen in the case of the Athenian tyrant, Peisistratus (d. 527 BC) whose sons were quite incapable of continuing his rule. A contrary case, however, is provided by the successful father-son tyranny in Corinth of Cypselus (from *c.* 650 BC) and Periander (from *c.* 627 BC).

42 Periander of Corinth, for instance, made rich allowances to the cultic centres of Delphi and Olympia, and instituted the Isthmian games.

43 A generation after Zeleucus, a similar code was drawn up by Charondas for Catania in Sicily. It was written in verse so that it could be repeated and memorised. Chester Starr, *The Origins of Greek Civilization*, 1961.

44 Note Ehrenberg, op. cit.

45 See H. Olmstead, *History of Persia*, 1948.

46 For a thorough treatment of this theme, see Bengtson, op. cit.

47 The designation Delian was used about the Athenian Confederation because the monies held ostensibly in common – though controlled by Athens – were housed in the treasury at Delos.

48 See C. M. Bowra, *Periclean Athens*, 1971.

49 By this time, the term 'allies' may have been little more than a thinly disguised euphemism for dependants. See W. S. Ferguson, *Greek Imperialism*, 1913.
50 Sir R. Livingstone, *The Legacy of Greece*, 1969.
51 One of the most infamous examples of the outworking of Athenian frustration can be seen in the massacre of all males of military age on the island of Melos as a punitive act because Melos refused to join the Delian league.

## Chapter 7 Agencies of socialisation

1 For a fascinating discussion of these issues see particularly Konrad Lorenz, *On Aggression*, Methuen, 1966.
2 For the development of this line of argument, see G. H. Mead, *Mind, Self and Society*, University of Chicago Press, 1934.
3 A. Kardiner and Ralph Linton, *The Individual and His Society*, 1939.
4 H. Bredemeier and R. Stephenson, *The Analysis of Social Systems*, 1970, p. 61.
5 H. Johnson, *Sociology: a Systematic Introduction*, 1965, p. 110.
6 See, for example, Kingsley Davis, *Human Society*, 1966.
7 T. Adorno *et al.*, *The Authoritarian Personality*, 1950, pp. 5ff.
8 There have been philosophical appreciations of this problem at least since Plato. The Empiricists, Locke and Hume, and the Idealists Butler and Kant were very much concerned with it. For a general treatment see, Kardiner and Linton, op. cit. and for an attempt to reconcile the perspectives of psychology and sociology, see H. Gerth and C. Wright Mills, *Character and Social Structure*, 1954.
9 Frederic Le Play, *Organisation of the Family*, 1871.
10 Ralph Linton, *The Study of Man*, Appleton-Century, 1936.
11 For a personal view of upper-class urban Chinese society in the pre-revolutionary period, see Christiana Tsai, *Queen of the Dark Chamber*, Moody Press, 1953.
12 Gideon Sjoberg, *The Pre-Industrial City*, 1965, pp. 157-9.
13 In a more particular context, it has been argued that authoritarian fathers thwart their sons' efforts to be autonomous and self-reliant (Bernard Rosen in a study on Brazil in W. Goode, *Readings on the Family and Society*, 1964). This is hardly borne out by the experience of many simple and complex pre-industrial systems, for example, among military aristocracies such as those in Sparta and Thebes.
14 See also William Goode, *The Family*, 1965.
15 This becomes arguable in the case of, say, Sparta, where a boy left his mother at the age of six, and for the next six years was in a paidion class leading a barrack-life existence supervised by state officials. See H. Mitchell, *Sparta*, 1952, pp. 166-8.
16 See particularly Fustel De Coulanges, *The Ancient City*, 1864.
17 Sabatino Moscati, *The Face of the Ancient Orient*, 1962.
18 Pierre Montet, *Everyday Life in Egypt*, 1958, p. 57.
19 Ibid., p. 48.
20 Georges Contenau, *Everyday Life in Babylon and Assyria*, 1969, pp. 15-19.

21 Montet, op. cit., pp. 45–6 quoting G. Maspéro, *Études Egyptiennes I*, Paris, 1879.

22 See particularly, Robert Graves, *The Greek Myths*, 1966.

23 J. A. Wilson, *The Culture of Ancient Egypt*, 1956, p. 4.

24 Herodotus II. 82.

25 J. Cerny, 'Consanguineous Marriages in Pharaonic Egypt', *Journal of Egyptian Archaeology*, XL (1954), quoted by Montet, op. cit., p. 48.

26 Contenau, op. cit., pp. 15–16.

27 An intense preoccupation with female chastity could be found, for example, in traditional Islamic societies. See D. Lerner, *The Passing of Traditional Society*, 1958.

28 Sjoberg, op. cit., p. 150.

29 The argument is put forward by Sjoberg (ibid., p. 151) that in traditional or – in his terms – feudal society, there was a de-emphasis on physical attractiveness in a wife, and a premium on reputation. In high-status families particularly, a man could always resort to concubinage or courtesans.

30 See A. Leo Oppenheim, *Ancient Mesopotamia*, 1964, and Contenau, op. cit. A concubine was given the privilege of the veil when she accompanied the legal wife out of doors. See Contenau, op. cit., p. 17.

31 Sjoberg, op. cit., p. 160.

32 Strabo XVII. 2, 5. And Diodorus (I. 80, 5–6) suggests that this was because the Egyptian child could be fed and clothed for practically nothing.

33 Wilson, op. cit., pp. 128–30.

34 This compares with the powers of the paterfamilias in Roman society. See Coulanges, op. cit.

35 On the issue of adoption contracts, see the highly-praised text by Oppenheim, op. cit.

36 Montet, op. cit., p. 46.

37 Ibid., p. 50.

38 Herodotus II. 82.

39 A medical treatise known as the Ebers Papyrus gives some examples, for instance that a child whose cry resembled the creaking of pines could expect a future fraught with evil.

40 H. Ringgren, *Religions of the Ancient Near East*, SPCK, 1973.

41 For example, we do not know the status of children born to an Athenian man and woman who merely lived together without a formal wedding ceremony. See W. Lacey, *The Family in Classical Greece*, 1968, p. 104.

42 The term used in a mainly architectural context by J. Stobart, *The Glory that was Greece*, 1964.

43 For a survey of Greek literature covering such topics as law and causation, social evolution, and the philosophy of history generally, see Arnold Toynbee, *Greek Historical Thought*, 1952.

44 Aristotle, *Politics* I.

45 For the earlier writer, Hesiod, this might include animals which served man, e.g. the plough-ox, but for Aristotle's citizen – or political man – the household slave is implied.

46 Lacey, op. cit., p. 16.

47 The oikoi were also associated with phratries – the origins of which are obscure – which appear to have been blood-brotherhoods perhaps originally based upon military considerations, as in the *Iliad*. The implication in Homer is that the phratry was the sub-division of the tribe, but the tribal system was breaking down by Classical times under the pressure of developing urbanisation.

48 The anchisteia was also the limit chosen by Plato in *The Republic* in cases of homicide. It may have been general throughout the Greek world. See Lacey, op. cit., p. 29.

49 Until after the death of Pericles (429 BC), the only significant exception was probably Themistocles.

50 On the aristocracy, see N. G. L. Hammond, *A History of Greece to 323 BC*, 1967.

51 If the child was rescued before it died of exposure or starvation, it might be reared as a slave. Oedipus is just one of many 'heroes' who are said to have been rescued in this way.

52 See R. Flaceliere, *Daily Life in Greece*, 1965, p. 65.

53 Perhaps best translated as courtesan, or more colloquially 'call-girl'. Hetairai who often began life as slaves were not exactly 'common' prostitutes. In fact, at least some seem to have had artistic or musical accomplishments. Whether these approached the level of, say, the traditional Japanese Geisha is open to question.

54 This may be the main reason why such odium surrounded the relationship between the Athenian leader, Pericles, and his mistress, Aspasia, who to make things even more difficult was foreign-born.

55 This is quoted by the fourth-century BC Demosthenes from the speech of a prosecuting counsel, Apollodorus, in a case against the courtesan, Neaira, who had – he claimed – 'cohabited with her husband, pretending she was a citizen'.

56 Flaceliere op. cit., pp. 65–6. Although Lacey (op. cit., p. 108) quoting Demosthenes suggests that women had a good deal more freedom than this, and that even divorce by mutual consent was possible.

57 By comparison, the relative freedom of Spartan women was something of a byword in Athens.

58 For a general treatment see T. B. L. Webster, *Everyday Life in Classical Athens*, 1969.

59 For example, it is said – as if it were a somewhat uncommon occurrence – that the tyrant Peisistratus' daughter married for love and even kissed her fiancé openly in the street. See Lacey, op. cit., p. 69.

60 Flaceliere, op. cit., p. 58.

61 See M. I. Finley, *Aspects of Antiquity*, 1972.

62 Particularly Aristophanes in *Lysistrata* (411 BC). The 'Old Comedy' was given to caricature and exaggeration, but these plays undoubtedly reflect some reappraisal of sexual roles. See Doros Alastos (ed.), *Aristophanes: Two Plays*, 1953.

63 See Mitchell, op. cit.

64 M. I. Finley, *The Ancient Greeks*, 1963, p. 146.

65 Even Plato who has been called the apologist for 'ideal pederasty' (Flaceliere, op. cit., p. 58) inveighed against sodomy, especially in *The Laws*.
66 Note, for instance, how this incurs the wrath of the gods in Sophocles' *Oedipus Rex*.
67 Note that Plato in *The Laws* considers one boy and one girl per union adequate by law. This contrasts with his earlier view of the ideal state in *The Republic* where marriage is to give way to periodic mating festivals between specially state-approved couples. This, it was held, would 'naturally' limit the birth-rate.
68 See Hesiod, *Works and Days*.
69 See Flaceliere, op. cit., p. 77.
70 See W. Forrest, *A History of Sparta*, 1968.
71 Quoted by Lacey, op. cit., p. 231.
72 See, for example Mircea Eliade, *Myth and Reality*, 1963.
73 Note the Israelite injunction to 'honour your father and mother that your days may be long in the land'. Exodus 20:12 (RSV).
74 This is the point made most forcibly by Coulanges, op. cit.
75 Lacey, op. cit., p. 27.
76 Weddings were particularly frequent in January (Gamelion – the wedding month – the seventh month of the Athenian year) which was sacred to Hera, the goddess of marriage. Although as R. Flaceliere points out, no rites connected with marriage appear 'intended to consecrate, in some visible and tangible form, the personal union of two betrothed individuals. Everything seems rather aimed at, ensuring the prosperity of the Oikos.' (op. cit., p. 64.)
77 This may be compared with the ancestor cults of simple societies, e.g. the African Lugbara peoples. Here the recent dead are feared and the task of the living is to placate the dead ghost so that misfortune might be avoided. This is the duty of the senior male and it gives him considerable authority within the group. This is continued until he too dies and becomes a much feared ghost. Seniors are respected in this life and hope to be honoured in the next. J. Middleton, *Lugbara Religion*, International African Institute, 1960.
78 E. Durkheim, *Education and Sociology*, 1956.
79 See also G. D. Mitchell, *Sociology*, 1959, pp. 140–2.
80 For example, pedagogy was one of the preoccupations of Plato and his friends.
81 See T. B. Bottomore, *Sociology*, 1962, p. 254, who argues that in pre-industrial societies, more emphasis was laid upon moral training for social life than upon learning and instruction.
82 See R. de Vaux, *Ancient Israel*, 1961.
83 A point made forcibly by Talcott Parsons in *Societies: Evolutionary and Comparative Perspectives*, 1966.
84 Sjoberg, op. cit., p. 290.
85 Max Weber, 'The Chinese Literati' in H. Gerth and C. Wright Mills, *From Max Weber*, 1948.
86 The classical written language has remained essentially the same since about the tenth century AD. Estimates vary, but even after the pai-hua

revisions of the Republic, the writer had to know about 6,000 characters.

87 N. Kramer, *The Sumerians*, 1973.

88 The Phoenicians may, in turn, have derived alphabetical forms from the Canaanites. At least the Ras Shamra tablets indicate as much. See D. Harden, *The Phoenicians*, 1971.

89 Some critics have argued that the relatively low pay of teachers in Greece and Rome reflects their relatively low status in the social pyramid, but this seems doubtful sociologically. See M. Cary and T. Haarhof, *Life and Thought in the Greek and Roman World*, 1957.

90 Memorisation was central to the learning process in many ancient societies. See, e.g., J. Carcopino, *Daily Life in Ancient Rome*, 1970.

91 Sjoberg, op. cit., Chapter 10.

92 R. Dawson, *Imperial China*, 1972.

93 Among the innumerable texts which eulogise the achievements of the past see, e.g. Stobart, op. cit. M. Sullivan, *The Arts of China*, Cardinal Books, 1973; M. Murray, *The Splendour that was Egypt*, 1963.

94 See the Old Kingdom records of Ptah-shepses, A. Erman, *The Literature of the Ancient Egyptians*, 1927.

95 See L. Cottrell, *Life under the Pharaohs*, 1955, Chapter 8.

96 Montet, op. cit., p. 254.

97 Murray, op. cit., p. 73.

98 Ibid.

99 Montet, op. cit., p. 256.

100 Kramer, op. cit.

101 H. Marrou, *A History of Education in Antiquity* (trans. G. Lamb), 1956.

102 For example, Flaceliere, op. cit., p. 93.

103 Plato, *Protagoras*, 326 C.

104 Demosthenes, *On the Crown*, 258.

105 E. B. Castle, *Ancient Education and Today*, 1961, p. 64.

106 See E. Gardiner, *Athletics of the Ancient World*, 1930.

107 Flaceliere, op. cit., pp. 96–7.

108 Plato, *Against the Sophists*.

109 See W. K. C. Guthrie, *A History of Greek Philosophy*, vol. I, 1962.

110 Castle, op. cit., p. 61.

111 F. Beck, *Greek Education*, 1964, pp. 85ff.

112 See Lacey, op. cit., Chapter 8.

113 Harold Nicolson, *Good Behaviour*, Constable, 1955, p. 40.

114 Marrou, op. cit., p. 43.

115 To be fair, the Homeric ideal of arete could also carry more 'practical' connotations as evidenced by the warrior skills of the Homeric heroes.

116 See, for example, G. Lowes Dickinson, *The Greek View of Life*, 1957.

117 Castle, op. cit., p. 35.

118 Gilbert Murray, *Five Stages of Greek Religion*, Watts, 1946, p. 75.

119 Euripides' views can be contrasted with those of Aeschylus whose attitude is one of resignation before the gods.

120 Plato, *The Republic*.

121 C. M. Bowra, *The Greek Experience*, 1957, Chapter. 5.

122  Milton Covensky, *The Ancient Near Eastern Tradition*, 1966, p. 136.
123  Leonard Woolley, *Ur of the Chaldees*, Penguin, 1952 edn. See also G. Roux, *Ancient Iraq*, 1964; Kramer, op. cit., Oppenheim, op. cit.
124  L. Cottrell, *The Penguin Book of Lost Worlds*, vol. 1, 1966, p. 136.

## Chapter 8  Systems of social differentiation

 1  The market is probably already overstocked with some very competent analyses of stratification theories, for example: R. Dahrendorf, *Class and Class Conflict in an Industrial Society*, 1959; T. Bottomore, *Classes in Modern Society*, 1965; K. Mayer, *Class and Society*, 1955; R. Bendix and S. M. Lipset, *Class, Status and Power*, 1966; G. Lenski, *Power and Privilege*, 1966; J. Jackson (ed.), *Social Stratification*, Cambridge University Press, 1968; S. Ossowski, *Class Structure in the Social Consciousness*, Free Press, 1963.
 2  A. Beteille, *Social Inequality*, 1969, pp. 12–13.
 3  T. Parsons, *Essays in Sociological Theory, Pure and Applied*, rev. edn., 1954, p. 166.
 4  So writes Gideon Sjoberg in *The Pre-Industrial City*, 1965, p. 109, adapting the general framework laid down by Talcott Parsons, op. cit., pp. 171–2.
 5  M. Tumin, article on Social Class in J. Gould and W. Kolb (eds), *Dictionary of the Social Sciences*, 1964.
 6  J. Littlejohn, *Social Stratification*, 1972, p. 11.
 7  This was really the basis of Weber's qualifications of Marx's view of classes in society. For important appraisals, see Bottomore, op. cit. and Dahrendorf, op. cit. For a brief but excellent summary of the Marx–Weber argument, see Littlejohn, op. cit., Chap. 1: 'It was to this levelling of the uniqueness of previous epochs and of other existent civilizations that Weber objected, and to the view that the past could be interpreted in the terms most relevant to the interpretation of the present' (p. 25).
 8  A translation of Weber in R. Bendix, *Max Weber: an Intellectual Portrait*, 1960.
 9  See, for example R. Zaehner, *Hinduism*, 1962 (especially Chapter 6).
10  M. Weber, *Essays in Sociology*, trans. H. Gerth and C. Wright Mills, 1948, p. 301.
11  This was noted by Champollion, one of the pioneers of Egyptology in the early nineteenth century. See also J. A. Wilson (joint editor) in H. Frankfort *et al.*, *Before Philosophy*, 1954, p. 41.
12  The question of universal values is a fascinating one which, in one form, has been taken up by the Structuralists following ideas that were earlier popularised by Kant. See, for example, C. Lévi-Strauss, *The Savage Mind*, 1966 and as perhaps a necessary astringent E. R. Leach, *Lévi-Strauss*, 1970.
13  M. Weber, *The Theory of Social and Economic Organisation*, 1964.
14  This is a point suggested by Parsons contra Marx. For Parsons, norms and values have some effective force in shaping social structure, especially the stratification aspect, whereas Marx derived norms and values from the social structure and treated them as features of

ideology. Talcott Parsons, *Societies: Evolutionary and Comparative Perspectives*, 1966.

15 It is certainly possible to construct separate model hierarchies of status and class for hypothetical situations. See W. G. Runciman, 'Nature and Types of Social Inequality' in Beteille, op. cit., pp. 48–50.

16 For a general treatment, see M. Smith, 'Pre-Industrial Stratification Systems' in N. Smelser and S. Lipset (eds), *Social Structure and Mobility in Economic Development*, 1966.

17 Frankfort *et al.*, op. cit.

18 A Confucian monopoly was established in 141 BC and its doctrines were proclaimed as state dogma in 136 BC. From then on its scholars began to organise state institutions and founded the first state university in 129 BC. Eventually Confucius was canonised and the writings codified, but with increasing acceptance came an increasing syncretisation of the ethic as it absorbed various cult elements.

19 S. Kellett, *A Short History of Religions*, 1960.

20 S. N. Eisenstadt, *The Political Systems of Empires*, Free Press, 1969, p. 56. This gives an extensive analysis of the structural arrangements of complex pre-industrial societies in relation to the political variable.

21 Sjoberg, op. cit., p. 108.

22 Eisenstadt, op. cit., pp. 85–7.

23 The peasantry often formed different types of associations. For example the secret cults and Tongs in China, and the quite distinctive eranoi or mutual-aid societies which were formed in fourth-century Athens.

24 The Vatican particularly accommodated such practices during the Borgia period. Cesare Borgia, the 'nephew' or natural son of Pope Alexander VI, was so honoured – but this was by no means an exceptional case. See Michael Mallett, *The Borgias*, 1969.

25 R. de Vaux, *Ancient Israel*, 1961.

26 Max Weber, *The Religion of India*, 1955.

27 'Protological' – in contradistinction to eschatological – is used here to denote a doctrine of the 'first things' i.e. the original or pristine 'truth'.

28 For very thorough analyses of the priestly, and prophetic functions, see Max Weber, *The Sociology of Religion*, 1965 and Joachim Wach, *The Sociology of Religion*, 1945.

29 What applies to revelation-based systems also must apply to rationality-based systems which breed newer and perhaps more extreme rationalities. See Eric Carlton, 'The Unitarian Movement in England', 1972.

30 The socio-cultural compatibility thesis beloved of some functionalist theorists (as T. Hoult, *Sociology of Religion*, 1958) is by no means an invariable rule. It has a general applicability only. For serious reservations, see Carlton, op. cit.

31 Barbara Sewell, *Egypt Under the Pharaohs*, 1968, p. 79.

32 For example, Kurt Mendelssohn, *The Riddle of the Pyramids*, 1974.

33 H. Frankfort, *Kingship and the Gods*, 1948. According to Plato (*Timaeus* 24A, B) there were five classes; Diodorus gives six hereditary

divisions, and Herodotus (II. 164) cites seven professional castes. But these relate to a late period. (See C. D. Darlington, *The Evolution of Man and Society*, 1969, p. 120.) H. Frankfort (following E. Meyer, 1928) notes that these divisions into castes which classical authors claimed for Egypt were part of the disintegration of the traditional social order following the usurpation of the crown by the High Priest of Amon after the decline of the Empire (Twenty-first Dynasty).

34 See H. Frankfort, *Ancient Egyptian Religion*, 1961.
35 J. A. Wilson, *The Culture of Ancient Egypt*, 1956, p. 257.
36 See P. Montet, *Everyday Life in Egypt*, 1958, p. 134.
37 M. Covensky, *The Ancient Near Eastern Tradition*, 1966, p. 62.
38 T. Parsons, *Societies: Evolutionary and Comparative Perspectives*, 1966, p. 55.
39 W. Emery, *Archaic Egypt*, 1972, p. 111.
40 What may be a biased account records: 'the scribe landeth on the embankment and will register the harvest; the peasant who is unable to supply corn for taxes is beaten and his wife and children put in fetters. But the scribe, he directeth the work of all people. For him there are no taxes, for he payeth in writing, and there are no dues for him.' Quoted by L. Cottrell, *The Penguin Book of Lost Worlds*, vol. 1, 1966, pp. 52–3.
41 'We reiterate that throughout the preindustrial civilized world the upper class, and above all the society's ruling stratum, is urban in nature.' Sjoberg, op. cit., p. 113.
42 Lenski, op. cit., p. 257.
43 A. Erman, *Life in Ancient Egypt*, 1894, pp. 299–305.
44 M. I. Finley, *Slavery in Classical Antiquity*, 1960, p. 164.
45 See Mendelssohn, op. cit., p. 147.
46 Wilson, op. cit., p. 191.
47 Ibid., p. 201.
48 J. A. Wilson, *American Journal of Semitic Language and Literature*, XLIX (1933), pp. 275ff.
49 A. H. Gardiner, 'Lawsuit arising from the Purchase of Slaves', *Journal of Egyptian Archaeology*, XXI (1935), pp. 140–6.
50 A. L. Oppenheim, *Ancient Mesopotamia*, 1964, pp. 74ff.
51 What evidence there is suggests that fugitive slaves were relentlessly pursued by their owners. For laws relating to runaway slaves, see W. C. Hayes, *The Brooklyn Papyrus*, New York, 1956.
52 See A. Olmstead, *History of Assyria*, 1960.
53 A. Gardiner, *The Wilbour Papyrus*, 1941, 1948–52.
54 Sewell, op. cit., p. 80.
55 Although slaves might be allowed to earn their own livings in Mesopotamia – providing their masters took a percentage – in some regions, slaves had to wear fetters outside the household as a sign of bondage.
56 Oppenheim, op. cit., pp. 75–6.
57 Erman, op. cit., p. 128.
58 Slave status for the captive was almost certainly preferable to capture for ritual slaughter as in, say, Aztec society in the fifteenth century AD. See E. O. James, *Sacrifice and Sacrament*, 1962.

59 Slavery by debt – of oneself or one's family – was common in many societies, for example, Imperial China, see A. Bullock (ed.), *Asia: the Dawn of History*, 1968.

60 L. Cottrell (*Life Under the Pharaohs*, 1955, p. 78) argues for the equal desirability of male or female children mainly on the uncertain evidence of child-names whereas P. Montet (op. cit., p. 57) insists that male children were preferred. But this is not an unambiguous yardstick as to the status of women in Egyptian society.

61 For example, the story of the unhappy widower in the Leyden Papyrus.

62 Note the scenes depicted in the Hypostyle Hall at Karnak.

63 W. Flinders Petrie, *Social Life in Ancient Egypt*, 1930.

64 Margaret Murray, *The Splendour that was Egypt*, 1963.

65 It may be that eventually the widow, Ankhesenamun actually married the vizier, Ay, in order to confer upon him the right to the throne – but the facts are very much in dispute. See Christine Desroches–Noblecourt, *Tutankhamun*, 1972, Chap. 9.

66 Wilson, *The Culture of Ancient Egypt*, pp. 96–7.

67 It should be added that J. A. Wilson in this same context goes on to say that brother-sister marriage among the Pharaohs also had the 'derivative purpose of cutting down on the number of pretenders to the throne'. See Chapter 2 in this book on the Functions of Social Control.

68 Cottrell, op. cit., p. 80.

69 Petrie, op. cit.

70 This is suggested by Petrie (ibid.) but the sources quoted are very late, *c.* 442 BC, and concern contracts between Jews living at Elephantine in Upper Egypt.

71 Cottrell, op. cit., p. 84.

72 See H. Krich and A. Greenwald, *The Prostitute in Literature*, 1960. Also F. Henriques, *Prostitution and Society*, 1962–8.

73 J. A. Wilson maintains that 'ancient Egypt survived "unchanged" for long centuries by changing constantly and ignoring such change.' *The Culture of Ancient Egypt*, p. 76.

74 Ibid., p. 86.

75 The term 'Homeric society' is really ambiguous. It could refer to the society of which Homer writes, i.e. twelfth-century late Mycenaean society, or the society of Homer's own time i.e. eighth-century 'Dark Age' society, or, as has been argued, twelfth-century characters and incidents dressed unwittingly in an eighth-century guise. Compare sixth-century AD Arthur and his knights in medieval trappings. For a discussion of the Homeric problem, see M. I. Finley, *The World of Odysseus*, 1958.

76 For a general treatment of the period, see H. Michell, *The Economics of Ancient Greece*, 1940.

77 Finley, *The World of Odysseus*.

78 For a detailed analysis of this absorption process in the eighth and seventh centuries BC, see A. French, 'The Economic Background to Solon's Reforms', *Classical Quarterly*, 1 and 2 (1956).

79 Contemporary evidence i.e. from the eighth century BC can be seen in Hesiod, *Works and Days*.
80 M. I. Finley, *The Ancient Greeks*, 1963, p. 43.
81 This applies particularly to the archonship. Archons ('rulers') were elected annually by the Assembly from among the aristocracy with property qualifications. After their period of office, they became members of the ancient Council of the Areopagus, a body which in some ways was analogous to the Roman Senate (see H. D. Kitto, *The Greeks*, 1951, p. 101). Solon became archon in 594 BC and after he had completed his work he left Athens for ten years so that the city could 'test' his programme without prejudice. It can never be known whether the discontentment which attended his efforts would have been so evident had he stayed.
82 G. Glotz, *Ancient Greece at Work*, 1926, p. 169.
83 A. Gouldner, *Enter Plato*, 1967, p. 19. The definitive work of social analysis on the philosophy and organisation of the polis.
84 Ibid., p. 23.
85 See A. W. H. Adkins, *Merit and Responsibility: a Study in Greek Values*, 1960.
86 Littlejohn, op. cit., p. 56.
87 The 'voteless alien(s)' were not the only people interested in trade by any means, although it is probably incorrect to think of merchants as a class before the fourth century BC. What is evident is that there was a certain contempt for trade among the Athenian upper classes, although they undoubtedly benefited from its operations. See A. Andrewes, *Greek Society*, 1967, pp. 143–5.
88 Finley, *The Ancient Greeks*, p. 71.
89 Some slave-owners held slaves in considerable numbers. Nicias, the leader of the ill-fated Sicilian expedition which was destroyed in 413 BC – perhaps the turning point of the Peloponnesian War – is said to have owned 1,000 slaves which he hired at a daily rate. This may have given him an annual return of 'at least 35 per cent'. See G. Thomson, *Studies in Ancient Greek Society*, Lawrence & Wishart, 1955, pp. 196–205.
90 Cimon, who according to Aristotle (*Constitution of Athens* XXVII. 3) 'possessed the fortune of a tyrant' was an eminent political opponent of Pericles, and used his wealth to further his political ambitions.
91 Andrewes, op. cit., p. 241.
92 R. Flaceliere, *Daily Life in Greece*, 1965, p. 52.
93 Kitto, op. cit., p. 66.
94 H. Bengtson (ed.), *The Greeks and the Persians*, 1969, p. 112.
95 These figures for citizenship are large by Greek standards. Only three poleis had more than 20,000 citizens, Syracuse and Acragas in Sicily, and Athens.
96 Finley, *The Ancient Greeks*, pp. 55 and 73. He argues that army figures are almost certainly accurate unlike the estimated population figures. As far as we know, the Greeks conducted no actual censuses.
97 See Thomson, op. cit., pp. 196–205.
98 See R. Flaceliere, *Love in Ancient Greece*, 1973.

99 On the position of metics, see particularly Flaceliere, *Daily Life in Greece*, pp. 41–5.
100 Thucydides II. 39.
101 The thiasoi or religious associations included such foreign deities as the Thracian goddess Bendis and the Great Mother cult from Phrygia.
102 Gouldner, op. cit., p. 22.
103 Finley, *Slavery in Classical Antiquity*.
104 The Law Code of Gortyn in Crete is the chief source of our knowledge of the social history of Ancient Crete. It is the only complete law code we have from Ancient Greece. See R. Willetts, *Ancient Greece*, 1969, pp. 22ff.
105 The fact that slave and freeman unions were the subject of legislation shows that they did take place, but almost certainly gave rise to some legal problems, if not actual disquiet.
106 It is not known for certain whether Spartans held slaves by purchase or capture, but the helot and similar systems was not peculiar to Lacedaemonia. Compare the Penestes of Thessaly and the helot-like subjection of conquered Messenia.
107 The periodic murder of helots may have been the work of the Spartan 'secret police', the krypteia. Myron of Priene also writes of the annual floggings of helots, but he is regarded as a doubtful source, and anyway the Spartans were extremely harsh to their own kind, especially youths in training who could be flogged for relatively trivial offences. See H. Michell, *Sparta*, 1952, pp. 75ff.
108 Plutarch, *Inst. Lac.*, 239E.
109 Thucydides IV. 80.
110 Andrewes, op. cit., p. 153.
111 See Thomson, op. cit. It should also be noted that Chios had the oldest slave market in Greece, yet from *c.* 600 BC its constitution was democratic. One particular individual, Panionios, is said to have made a fortune *c.* 500 BC, by castrating Greek boys and selling them at Ephesus and Sardis.
112 In Rome, a master had the power of life and death over his slaves, and in other societies, e.g. early Assyria, the master had the authority to maim, especially runaway slaves. Deformity was a seen punishment which might deter other would-be malcontents.
113 See particularly Morton Chambers (ed.), *The Fall of Rome*, 1970.
114 Finley, *Slavery in Classical Antiquity*.
115 For example, the Marxist historian, Thomson, op. cit.
116 Slave revolts were much more a feature of Roman society, particularly in the first century BC. They needed the organisational skills which were sometimes found in large aggregations of slaves. In the Sicilian slave war, it is interesting that those in revolt succeeded in enslaving those who opposed them. P. Green, 'The First Sicilian Slave War', *Past and Present*, XX, November 1961.
117 See Littlejohn, op. cit., pp. 59–61.
118 See Arnold Toynbee, *Greek Civilization and Character*, 1953, in which he writes of the First and Second Phases of the Class War (pp. 44–53 and pp. 74–80).

119 Thucydides III. 70–85 and IV. 46–8.
120 Finley, *The World of Odysseus*, pp. 148ff.
121 Flaceliere, *Love in Ancient Greece.*
122 Gouldner, op. cit., p. 63.
123 C. Seltman, *Women in Antiquity*, Pan, 1956.
124 See Bengtson, op. cit., pp. 149–51.
125 V. Ehrenberg, *From Solon to Socrates*, 1968.
126 Note, for example, the character attributed to Spartan women in the *Lysistrata* of Aristophanes.
127 Seltman, op. cit.
128 See J. Stobart, *The Glory that was Greece*, 1964, p. 71.
129 The hetaira or courtesan is used here in distinction to the porne (prostitute).
130 Finley, *The Ancient Greeks*, p. 146.
131 H. Licht, *Sexual Life in Ancient Greece*, 1935.
132 For a detailed exposition of the view that women in Athens enjoyed more liberal treatment, see Kitto, op. cit., pp. 219–36, and particularly A. W. Gomme, *Essays in History and Literature*, 1937.
133 In antiquity, many semitic societies, for example, Hebrew society, believed barrenness in the wife could constitute grounds for divorce or justification for polygamy or concubinage.
134 Licht, op. cit., pp. 329ff.
135 Flaceliere, *Love in Ancient Greece*, Chapter 5.
136 There is a much-quoted passage from Demosthenes to the effect that hetairai are for pleasure, female slaves for the care of the person, and wives to bear legitimate children and manage the household.
137 In the fourth century, for example, Phryne (Mnesarete) was the mistress of the orator Hyperides and the sculptor Praxiteles, and posed for his *Aphrodite*. In the later Hellenistic age, some courtesans even managed to become queens.
138 Athenian wives were not above taking lovers and even entertaining them under their husbands' roofs. See, for example, Lysias (*On the Murder of Eratosthenes* 9–10) who writes of an Athenian woman who took her lover on the ground floor while her husband slept upstairs.
139 Flaceliere, *Daily Life in Greece*, p. 71.
140 Finley, *The Ancient Greeks*, p. 147. An argument which he develops in greater detail in the case of lower class Roman women in 'The Silent Women of Rome' (*Aspects of Antiquity*, 1972, pp. 159ff.).
141 For the *Medea*, Euripides may have drawn upon the character of Aspasia, the mistress of Pericles, but this is conjectural, and her position anyway was exceptional. See Bengtson, op. cit., p. 150.

**Chapter 9 Bases of economic organisation**

1 For a general discussion of these issues, see T. Bottomore, *Sociology*, 1962, Chapter 8.
2 L. T. Hobhouse, J. Wheeler and M. Ginsberg, *The Material Culture and Social Institutions of Simpler Peoples*, LSE Monographs, 1915.
3 D. Forde, *Habitat, Economy and Society*, 1968.
4 See Bottomore, op. cit., p. 139.

5 This even applies to historians. See, for example, H. Pirenne, 'The Stages in the Social History of Capitalism', *American Historical Review* XIX (3), 1929.

6 See Cyril Belshaw, *Traditional Exchange and Modern Markets*, 1965, pp. 2ff.

7 Max Weber, *The Protestant Ethic and the Spirit of Capitalism*, 1930.

8 Emile Durkheim, *The Division of Labour in Society*, 1933.

9 G. Lenski, *Power and Privilege*, 1966.

10 For an outline of Lenski's position together with some criticism, see J. Littlejohn, *Social Stratification*, 1972, pp. 36-9, who maintains that Lenski, in effect, has attempted a stimulating – though not entirely successful – reconciliation of the Marxist and functionalist approaches to social stratification.

11 Quoted by Lenski as criticisms of the first draft of his book, op. cit., pp. 191.

12 T. Parsons, *Societies: Evolutionary and Comparative Perspective*, 1966.

13 S. N. Eisenstadt, *The Political Systems of Empires*, Free Press, 1969.

14 Lenski, op. cit., p. 191. See also the elaboration of the argument, pp. 194-209.

15 R. Heilbroner, *The Making of Economic Society*, 1962, p. 27.

16 Eisenstadt, op. cit., p. 49.

17 A. Marshall, *Principles of Economics*, Macmillan, 1898.

18 Market and exchange orientations are emphasised by Belshaw, op. cit.

19 See Kenneth Boulding, *Economic Analysis*, 1941.

20 T. Parsons and N. Smelser, *Economy and Society*, 1956.

21 Whereas Boulding tends to emphasise distribution (exchange), Parsons and Smelser put much more stress on production factors.

22 Belshaw, op. cit., p. 4.

23 See, for example, Raymond Firth, *Elements of Social Organisation*, 1961 and *Essays on Social Organisation and Values*, Athlone Press, 1964.

24 Max Weber, *The Theory of Social and Economic Organisation*, 1964.

25 For a very illuminating general discussion of the main themes, see Alan Wells, *Social Institutions*, 1970, pp. 43ff.

26 Note the argument in relation to primitive societies between M. Herskovits and R. Firth (*Elements of Social Organisation*, p. 122).
   Herskovits: acknowledging the importance of machine technology, etc., as features which distinguish the modern world, writes, 'practically every economic mechanism and institution known to us, is found somewhere in the non-literate world. . . .'
   Firth: on the other hand, insists that 'the principles of economics which are truly general . . . in their application, are few. Most of those which purport to be general, have been constructed primarily within the framework of ideas of an industrial capitalist system with its machine technology, monetary exchange, and elaborate credit system.'

27 I. S. Edwards, *The Pyramids of Egypt*, 1972.

28 Among the many books on this subject, see Sir R. Livingstone (ed.), *The Legacy of Greece*, 1969.

29 Jacques Gernet (*Les Aspects économiques de Buddhisme dans la société chinoise du V<sup>e</sup> au X<sup>e</sup> siècle*, 1956) maintains that the corvèe exacted from the peasantry and others in fifth-century China by Buddhist leaders for the construction of monasteries was so excessive that many farmers could not raise their crops and had to sell members of their families into slavery in order to survive. Quoted by G. Sjoberg, *The Pre-Industrial City*, 1965, p. 199.

30 Note the considerable importance which Weber ascribes to money systems. Max Weber, *The Theory of Social and Economic Organisation*, pp. 158ff.

31 Richard Roehl, *Patterns and Structure of Demand 1000-1500 AD*, 1970, p. 35.

32 Sjoberg, op. cit., pp. 215-16.

33 E. T. Williams, *China, Yesterday and Today*, Crowell, 1932.

34 See Sylvia Thrupp, *Medieval Industry 1000-1500*, 1970, pp. 29-35.

35 Sylvia Thrupp, *The Merchant Class of Medieval London*, University of Michigan Press, 1962.

36 For a discussion of trading in Muslim societies, see H. A. R. Gibb and H. Bowen, *Islamic Society and the West*, 1950, I. Part I.

37 See Chung-Li-Chang, *The Chinese Gentry*, 1955.

38 Max Weber, *The Theory of Social and Economic Organisation*, particularly pp. 32-9 and Part II.

39 For Weber, the highest degree of formal rationality took the form of *capital* accounting; and is more appropriate to advanced technological systems than to pre-industrial societies.

40 See P. Montet, *Everyday Life in Egypt*, 1958, pp. 165ff.

41 N. de G. Davies and R. D. Faulkner, 'A Syrian Trading Venture to Egypt', *Journal of Egyptian Archaeology*, XXXIII (1947), p. 40.

42 See Luigi Pareti *et al.*, *The Ancient World*, 1965, vol. 2, p. 134.

43 Tax-gatherers seem to have been very unpopular and even feared. They could be very persuasive with recalcitrant payers; beatings were not unknown as a method of exacting payment. See the wall-carvings from the tomb of Mereruka.

44 Compare the benevolent despotism of the Incas in Hammond Innes, *The Conquistadors*, 1969.

45 See the *Introductory Guide to the Egyptian Collections in the British Museum*, 1964.

46 For a general treatment, see J. Harris, *Egyptian Art*, 1966.

47 A cemetery found at Deir el-Medina on the west bank of the Nile near the Valley of the Kings probably houses the inhabitants of a village who served the funerary temple as artists, masons, etc. They lived in virtual isolation and called themselves the 'Servants of the Place of Truth' and seem to have been directly responsible to the vizier himself. These New Kingdom artisans left some record of their work in the royal necropolis including reference to differential scales for seniority. See Barbara Sewell, *Egypt Under the Pharaohs*, 1968.

48 As early as the Old Kingdom, a chief steward, Menna, prided himself on the rewards to his workmen, 'No man who took part . . . shall ever

regret it, be he artist or stone-cutter, I have given him his reward.' Montet, op. cit., p. 159.

49 Sewell, op. cit., p. 80.

50 'Foreign commerce was probably a royal monopoly, although our evidence is slight and comes from texts which express attachment to the King.' J. A. Wilson, *The Culture of Ancient Egypt*, 1956, p. 81.

51 There were rich deposits of gold in the desert between the Nile and the Red Sea; the Harris Papyrus particularly makes reference to the gold of the Coptos mountains.

52 Quoted by Montet, op. cit., pp. 135–6.

53 W. B. Emery, *Archaic Egypt*, 1972.

54 J. Couyat and P. Montet, *Hieroglyphic and Hieratic Inscriptions at Hammamat*, 1912.

55 There is an Old Kingdom relief depicting emaciated peasants in a famine. See *Illustrated London News*, 26 February 1944, p. 249.

56 During the Amarna revolution, a general Haremhab was able to seize the throne even though he was a non-royal person, and reign as Pharaoh from 1342 BC.

57 One of the most notable instances of priesthood-government conflict is again associated with the problems of the Amarna period, although the revolution had strong politico–military overtones. See C. Aldred, *Akhenaten*, 1968.

58 W. Edgerton, 'The Strike in Rameses III's 29th Year', *Journal of Near Eastern Studies*, X, 1951.

59 Some craftsmen, like traders, were itinerant operatives. For instance, barbers – who flourished in a society where so many men shaved and had their heads shaven – set up 'shop' in the open wherever a group of customers seemed likely. Those who catered for a more prosperous clientèle often also doubled as doctors. Predictably, there was a barber-god in the Egyptian pantheon.

60 W. Flinders Petrie, *Social Life of Ancient Egypt*, 1930.

61 Wilson, op. cit., quoting A. Rowe, *A Catalogue of Egyptian Scarabs*, 1936.

62 For example, the records of the warrior-king, Tuthmosis III are not clear in this respect. Wilson, op. cit.

63 Ibid., p. 169.

64 Ibid., p. 174.

65 Montet, op. cit., maintains that a referable medium of exchange from as early as the Fourth Dynasty was the shat literally a 'seal' which was an entirely imaginary value calculated at one-twelfth of a deben i.e. about $\frac{5}{24}$ oz. It seems not have been much used in the later New Kingdom. Perhaps inflation had overtaken it.

66 Sjoberg, op. cit., pp. 211–14.

67 For example, Adolf Erman (*Life in Ancient Egypt*, 1894) mentions a transaction in which 119 uten of copper was paid for an ox.

68 L. Cottrell, *Life Under the Pharaohs*, 1955, p. 169.

69 There is the argument of K. Polanyi that markets were largely absent in Babylonia, early Assyria and Ptolemaic Egypt, because the lack of coinage as a medium of exchange made price negotiation of the market

type virtually impossible. This seems to take a rather narrow view of what passes as money. See K. Polanyi *et al.* (eds), *Trade and Market in the Early Empires*, Free Press, 1957, pp. 38–63.

70 Weber attributes enormous significance to the role of money. It extends the range of possible exchange relationships, it facilitates acquisitive orientations, and it provides a systematic basis for budgeting and rational economic calculation. Weber, *The Theory of Social and Economic Organisation.*

71 Cottrell, op. cit., p. 173.

72 Erman, op. cit.

73 A school exercise of late period records, 'Be a scribe, who is freed from forced labour, and protected from all work.' A Erman, *The Literature of the Ancient Egyptians*, 1927.

74 Ibid.

75 See W. Edgerton, 'The Government and the Governed in the Egyptian Empires' (1947), reprinted in S. N. Eisenstadt, *The Decline of Empires*, 1967, p. 43.

76 See L. Cottrell, *The Penguin Book of Lost Worlds*, vol. 1, 1966, p. 53.

77 Pareti *et al.*, op. cit., p. 179.

78 C. Aldred, *The Egyptians*, 1956, p. 171.

79 There are records of slave rental during the reign of Amenophis III (Eighteenth Dynasty). See W. Edgerton, 'The Government and the Governed', p. 45.

80 Papyrus Harris 46.2.

81 Edgerton, 'The Government and the Governed'.

82 A. H. Gardiner (ed.), *The Wilbour Papyrus*, 1941, 1948–52.

83 It may be, as Weber argues, that 'Centralized control over the process as a whole is functionally essential to efficiency [and that] this control cannot exist without what we consider property rights', *The Theory of Social and Economic Organisation*, p. 45.

84 See, however Chapter 6, note 13 regarding the theory that their *primary* purpose may have been that of ancient observatories. P. Tompkins, *Secrets of the Great Pyramid*, 1973.

85 Herodotus writing some 2,200 years after the building of the Great Pyramid was mistaken about other dimensions and may have been wrong about this although he claimed to have got his information from Egyptian priests who had preserved the tradition.

86 C. W. Ceram, *A Picture History of Archaeology*, 1957, Chap. 6.

87 I. S. Edwards, *The Pyramids of Egypt*, 1972.

88 For a criticism of the view that pyramid building may have been a kind of work-relief operation, see Wilson, op. cit., p. 83.

89 Kurt Mendelssohn, *The Riddle of the Pyramids*, 1974.

90 Wilson, op. cit., pp. 185–6.

91 After a campaign against the Western Libyans, Ramesses III gave 28,337 animals to Amun, i.e. two-thirds of his total booty in cattle.

92 See A. H. Gardiner, *Journal of Egyptian Archaeology*, XXVII (1941).

93 Wilson, op. cit., pp. 269–71.

94 Estimates – or guesses – have varied. They range from 2 per cent of the people and 15 per cent of the land to 15–20 per cent of the people

and 30 per cent of the land. See J. H. Breasted, *Ancient Records of Egypt, 1906–7*, vol. 4.
95 Montet, op. cit., p. 148.
96 There is evidence that in the period of Ramesses V (*c.* 1150 BC) – rather late for our purposes – such immunities did not exist. Gardiner, *The Wilbour Papyrus*.
97 A. Andrewes, *Greek Society*, 1967, p. 160.
98 Ibid., p. 130. Professor Andrewes goes on to argue that in the past there has been an unfortunate and misleading tendency to try to apply concepts which are more appropriate to modern business than an analysis of Greek economics.
99 H. Kitto, *The Greeks*, 1951, p. 100. Hesiod (*Works and Days*), a small-holder, complains of the big landowners who are even referred to as 'kings'.
100 M. I. Finley, *The Ancient Greeks*, 1963, p. 71.
101 The latifundia increased considerably in size and wealth after the Roman wars of conquest from the middle of the third century BC. In one campaign alone in 167 BC, the Romans are said to have made 150,000 slaves in Epirus, and in 176 BC another 80,000 in Sardinia: '[this] exercised a strong economic effect, especially in the growth of large country estates.' J. P. V. D. Balsdon (ed.), *Roman Civilization*, 1965, pp. 28, 174.
102 Andrewes, op. cit., p. 101.
103 See A. H. M. Jones, *Sparta*, 1968.
104 Xenophon, *Oeconomica*, V. 4–17.
105 Andrewes, op. cit., p. 120.
106 R. Flaceliere, *Daily Life in Greece*, 1965, p. 120.
107 For a specialised discussion of these and related issues see M. I. Finley, *Land and Credit in Ancient Athens*, Rutgers, 1952 and *The Ancient Economy*, 1973.
108 Andrewes, op. cit., p. 106.
109 Fustel de Coulanges, *The Ancient City*, 1864.
110 A. Zimmern, *The Greek Commonwealth*, 1911.
111 In the middle of the fourth century, Aristotle wrote that 'the title of citizen should be withheld from those on whom the city depends for its livelihood. . . the perfect city will not enfranchise the mere worker . . . it is not possible to practise the civic virtues while leading the life of a worker with a pay-packet . . . by "banausic" . . . we mean [that which robs] the mind of all freedom, all aspirations to higher things.' Aristotle, *Politics*, III.3, 2–4. Both Plato and Xenophon express very similar sentiments. Plato, *Gorgias*, 512 and Xenophon, *Oeconomica*, IV, 2–3.
112 Aristotle, *Politics*.
113 Xenophon, *Oeconomica*, IV, 3.
114 See Kitto, op. cit., pp. 240–1 and Xenophon, *Memorabilia*, III, 10.
115 Andrewes, op. cit., p. 144.
116 Shipbuilding increased enormously after Marathon, 490 BC in the wake of the threat of a further Persian invasion, and was continued with the onset of the Peloponnesian War in 431 BC.

117 See Plato, *Critias*.
118 Peter Green, *Ancient Greece*, 1973, p. 23.
119 J. Boardman, *The Greeks Overseas*, 1964.
120 The term 'factory' is sometimes reserved for slave-based operations. For example, the father of Isocrates the rhetorician owned a flute 'factory', but these were actually made by slaves, the father simply directed their activities. See Flaceliere, op. cit., p. 119.
121 Theophrastus says that in 415 BC the Athenian Callias made a fortune by working Spanish cinnabar (from Almaden) from which mercury is obtained. Later – according to Pliny – these mines were heavily exploited by the Romans. Pareti *et al.*, op. cit., p. 387.
122 R. M. Haywood, *The Ancient World*, 1971, p. 220.
123 H. Bengtson (ed.), *The Greeks and the Persians*, 1969, p. 112.
124 The first mention of Greek cotton is found in the Assyrian cuneiform texts, and later in Herodotus and Ctesias. Aristotle reports that silk from cocoons of larvae was invented at Cos by a woman named Pamphile. Pareti *et al.*, op. cit., p. 388.
125 Andrewes, op. cit., pp. 126–7.
126 See T. B. L. Webster, *Athenian Culture and Society*, 1973, p. 130.
127 Hermippus, *Phormophoroi* (*The Basket-Carriers*) dating from *c.* 431–425 BC, i.e. early in the Peloponnesian War.
128 As part of contemporary diplomacy, Egypt sent a gift of 50,000 bushels of grain in 445 BC which gives some impression of her enormous potential in cereals.
129 See Chapter 8.
130 H. Michell, *The Economics of Ancient Greece*, 1940, p. 126.
131 See particularly Green, op. cit., pp. 58, 102–3.
132 G. Thomson,*Studies in Ancient Greek Society*, 1955, vol. 2, pp. 196ff.
133 Bengtson, op. cit., p. 113.
134 C. M. Bowra, *Periclean Athens*, 1971, pp. 83–4.
135 Pareti *et al.*, op. cit., p. 184.
136 Herodotus II, 150.
137 For a presumably typical account of banking in operation in the fourth century BC see C. Mossé, *Athens in Decline*, Routledge & Kegan Paul, 1973, pp. 47–8, who writes of a banker, Pasion, who started with nothing and after thirty years in business was worth 20 talents.
138 J. Hasebroek (trans. L. Fisher and D. MacGregor), *Trade and Politics in Ancient Greece*, 1933, p. 96.
139 This development should more accurately be attributed to the fourth century when the normal rate was 12 per cent, but could rise to something like 25 per cent during wartime.
140 Bengtson, op. cit., p. 116.
141 The Delian–Attic maritime league is sometimes technically designated a plural-symmachy, i.e. an organisation with Athens on one side and a mass of allies on the other.
142 For a general treatment, see J. Bury, *A History of Greece to the Death of Alexander the Great*, 3rd ed. revised by R. Meiggs, 1974. The standard work on the Tribute Lists is by B. Merritt, H. Wade-Gery and M.

McGregor, *The Athenian Tribute Lists*, vol. 3, Princeton, University Press, 1950.

143 Thomson, op. cit.

144 See W. Westermann, *The Slave Systems of Greek and Roman Antiquity*, University of Philadelphia Press, 1955. For a more balanced, though somewhat generous approach, see A. H. M. Jones on 'The Economic Basis of Athenian Democracy' in his *Athenian Democracy*, 1957.

145 The decision on the form the rebuilding of Athens should take may have been a joint one. Pericles called a meeting of the states *c.* 449 BC for discussion purposes. Bowra, op. cit., p. 98.

146 For an interesting and critical treatment of public responsibility in Athens, see W. S. Ferguson, *Greek Imperialism*, 1913.

147 For a general view of architectural and artistic achievements, see G. M. A. Richter, *A Handbook of Greek Art*, Phaidon, 1968; J. D. Beazley and B. Ashmole, *Greek Sculpture and Painting*, 1966.

148 Jones, *Athenian Democracy*, pp. 83ff.

149 Webster, op. cit., pp. 42–3.

150 Bengtson, op. cit., p. 271.

151 Webster, op. cit.

152 Finley, *The Ancient Greeks*, p. 152. See also C. A. Robinson Jnr, *Athens in the Age of Pericles*, University of Oklahoma Press, 1959. Reproduced in J. Claster (ed.), *Athenian Democracy*, 1967.

153 Ferguson, op. cit.

154 Webster, op. cit., p. 106. A point also forcibly made by Jones.

155 Bowra, op. cit., p. 98.

156 Webster, op. cit., pp. 260–1.

157 Finley, *The Ancient Greeks*, p. 152.

158 Bowra, op. cit., pp. 98–9.

159 The Great Plague of Athens (429 BC) spread with incredible rapidity in the absence of elementary sanitation.

160 Pseudo–Dicaearchus, *On the Cities of Greece*, quoted by Flaceliere, op. cit., pp. 6–24.

161 See W. K. C. Guthrie, *A History of Greek Philosophy*, vol. 2, 1965. K. Dover, *Aristophanic Comedy*, Batsford, 1972.

162 Plutarch, *Pericles*, 12.

163 Green, op. cit., p. 67.

**Chapter 10  Political and legal organisation**

1 T. B. Bottomore, *Sociology*, 1962, p. 147.

2 For example L. H. Morgan's *Ancient City* (1877) upon which Engels may have relied for *The Origins of the Family, Private Property and the State* (1884). Note too, L. T. Hobhouse, J. Wheeler and M. Ginsberg, *The Material Culture and Social Institutions of Simpler Peoples*, LSE Monographs, 1915.

3 Sir H. Maine, *Ancient Law*, 1906.

4 R. Lowie, *Social Organisation*, Holt, 1950 and Isaac Schapera, *Government and Politics in Tribal Societies*, Watts, 1956.

5 Fustel de Coulanges, *The Ancient City*, 1864.

6 G. Mosca, *The Ruling Class*, McGraw–Hill, 1939.

7 For a further discussion of these themes, see A. Wells, *Social Institutions*, 1970, pp. 133–67.

8 H. Gerth and C. Wright Mills, *From Max Weber*, 1948, pp. 77–8.

9 Max Weber, *The Theory of Social and Economic Organisation*, 1964, pp. 324–72. Note also the summary by Talcott Parsons in his Introduction, pp. 57–77.

10 See Joachim Wach, *Sociology of Religion*, 1945, for a typology of religious leadership, and an elaboration of the distinction between the originator and the innovator.

11 Among those who have reservations with the Weber analysis and who are especially concerned with institutional factors, note: Talcott Parsons's critique in his Introduction to *The Theory of Social Economic Organisation*. Also Wells, op. cit., pp. 159–62 and G. Sjoberg, *The Pre-Industrial City*, 1965, pp. 224–38.

12 Note, for instance R. Lapiere (*A Theory of Social Control*, 1954) who writes, 'No one has ever attempted to ascertain quantitatively the extent to which and the specific conditions under which determined government action can through coercion bring about changes in the norms of any community of persons' (pp. 318–19).

13 S. N. Eisenstadt, *The Political Systems of Empires*, 1969, p. 367.

14 Note the problems raised by the phase categorisation methods of some cyclical theorists, notably Pitirim Sorokin, *Social and Cultural Dynamics*, 1962.

15 See particularly, G. Steindorff and K. Seele, *When Egypt Ruled the East*, 1957.

16 G. Almond and O. Powell, *Comparative Politics: a Developmental Approach*, 1966.

17 Talcott Parsons, *The Social System*, 1951, or, for an outline of the basic concepts, *Societies: Evolutionary and Comparative Perspectives*, 1966.

18 Lapiere argues (op. cit., p. 317) that non-voluntary payment of taxes, etc. is a characteristic of societies 'in general', but this discounts the leitourgiai of Classical Athens.

19 See the very helpful analyses in H. Bredemeier and R. Stephenson, *The Analysis of Social Systems*, 1970, pp. 373–5.

20 Historically, there are innumerable instances of the failure of rulers' policies due to their disregard or inability to judge the mood of the people. The Roman Emperor Diocletian (AD 245–313), for instance, failed in an attempt to secure the distribution of basic commodities such as cereals, wine, etc. by fixing prices. The price-control programme did not work even though the punishment for overcharging was death or deportation. M. Rostovtzeff, *Social and Economic History of the Roman Empire*, 1957.

21 This is not entirely to ignore the argument among anthropologists as to whether all societies have 'law' in some form, or merely have custom. So much depends upon how law is defined. Should it be defined in terms of the offence, or in terms of the *process* which follows the offence? And how important are the circumstances and the person(s) by whom that process is initiated? Alternatively, perhaps law

can only exist where there is a separate judiciary to administer it. See particularly: Schapera, op. cit.

22 Note Eisenstadt, op. cit., pp. 121–30.

23 In Tibet, for example, a small hereditary nobility of some 200 families supported the nominal rule of the god-king. Their authority actually derived by extension from the purported divinity of the Dalai Lama, a commoner, whom they reared and educated from childhood. See Heinrich Harper, *Seven Years in Tibet*, Hart–Davis, 1953, p. 175.

24 A. Andrewes, *The Greek Tyrants*, 1956.

25 Sjoberg, op. cit., pp. 224–31.

26 See, for example, J. Weiss, *The Fascist Tradition*, Harper & Row, 1967.

27 Mosca, op. cit., p. 70.

28 See Eisenstadt, op. cit., pp. 5–9 following D. Apter, 'A Comparative Method for the Study of Politics', *American Journal of Sociology*, LXIV (1958).

29 See H. Frankfort, *Ancient Egyptian Religion*, 1961, p. 30.

30 H. Frankfort, *Kingship and the Gods*, seventh impression, 1971, p. 51.

31 Ibid., p. 51.

32 Any consideration of 'ma'at' necessarily recalls the much later (sixth-century BC) Pythagorean doctrine of harmonia which expresses similar ideas of the cosmic order. See A. H. Armstrong, *An Introduction to Ancient Philosophy*, 1968, pp. 6–8.

33 See J. A. Wilson, 'Authority and Law in Ancient Egypt' in S. N. Eisenstadt (ed.), *The Decline of Empires*, 1967, p. 13.

34 Frankfort, *Ancient Egyptian Religion*, pp. 31–2.

35 Wilson, 'Authority and Law in Ancient Egypt', p. 12.

36 Note the feats of bowmanship of the Eighteenth Dynasty warrior-king, Tuthmosis III and his son Amenophis II which far exceeded the abilities of ordinary mortals. Or the claimed invincibility of Ramesses II in his various campaigns against his enemies. See P. Montet, *Everyday Life in Egypt*, 1958, especially pp. 210–11.

37 This was certainly the case during the Fourth Dynasty when the vizier and the high priests of the great cult centres were sons or cousins of the king.

38 Frankfort, *Kingship and the Gods*, p. 52.

39 The death of the young Smenkhkare (c. 1352 BC), the advent of Tutankhamun and his somewhat mysterious demise, at least suggest palace intrigue. See Christine Desroches-Noblecourt, *Tutankhamun*, 1972.

40 See Montet, op. cit., pp. 216–18.

41 For an outline of the organisational structure of the Egyptian state, this section is particularly indebted to the article by W. Edgerton, 'The Government and the Governed in the Egyptian Empires' (1947), reprinted in Eisenstadt (ed.), op. cit., pp. 35–47.

42 These titles are mentioned particularly in connection with the Fourth Dynasty when, according to Henri Frankfort, there was a 'purity of structure of the officialdom' (*Kingship and the Gods*, p. 360).

43 Edgerton, op. cit.

44 B. Sewell, *Egypt Under the Pharaohs*, 1968, p. 109.

45 Frankfort, *Kingship and the Gods*, p. 53.
46 When council members were listed, the list was often headed 'the council of this date'. Edgerton (op. cit., p. 41) concluded that this may indicate that the composition 'changed from day to day'.
47 A judicial hearing possibly in connection with the interests of the Temple of Mut at Karnak was presided over by the high priest of Amun and except for the scribe-recorder consisted entirely of priests of the Karnak temples.
48 See A. Gardiner, *Ancient Egyptian Onomastica*, 1952.
49 The staff of the First Prophet of Amun, for example, included a chief assistant, a head steward, a guard of the chamber, a body of scribes, a commander of sailors and numerous servants. His deputy also had his own personal staff.
50 See Montet, op. cit., pp. 252–3.
51 From G. Lefeuvre, *History of the High-priests of Amun at Karnak*, Paris, 1929.
52 The Nauri Decree: see W. Edgerton in *Journal of Near Eastern Studies*, VI (1947).
53 See Wilson, 'Authority and Law in Ancient Egypt', pp. 14–15.
54 C. Aldred, *The Egyptians*, 1956, p. 169.
55 Wilson, 'Authority and Law in Ancient Egypt', on the autobiography of the eighteenth-century vizier, Rekhmire.
56 See particularly A. L. Oppenheim, *Ancient Mesopotamia*, 1964.
57 Wilson, 'Authority and Law in Ancient Egypt', pp. 16–17.
58 Ibid.
59 Diodorus I. 74ff.
60 See also L. Pareti *et al.*, *The Ancient World*, 1965, vol. 2, p. 202.
61 Montet, op. cit., p. 258.
62 Ibid., pp. 258–9.
63 Ibid., pp. 261–9, where the account of the tomb-robbing enquiry is given in some detail.
64 Ibid., p. 258.
65 Sewell, op. cit., pp. 109–10.
66 'It is impossible to claim that ancient Egypt formulated any ethical basis for government and law.' Wilson, 'Authority and Law in Ancient Egypt', pp. 17–18.
67 Tuthmosis III is said to have recalled decisions taken by a vizier who lived five centuries earlier. See Aldred, op. cit., p. 169.
68 See T. A. Sinclair, *History of Greek Political Thought*, 1961.
69 See C. Hignett, *History of the Athenian Constitution*, Oxford University Press, 1953.
70 A. Andrewes, *Greek Society*, 1967, p. 184.
71 Stephen Usher, *The Historians of Greece and Rome*, 1969.
72 Aristotle, *The Constitution of Athens* (Hafner, 1950, edn).
73 See V. Ehrenberg, *The People of Aristophanes*, 1951.
74 See J. de Romilly, *Thucydides and Athenian Imperialism*, 1942.
75 A. Lesky, *History of Greek Literature*, 1966.
76 See T. B. L. Webster, *Athenian Culture and Society*, 1973, Chapter 3.
77 See T. B. L. Webster, *Everyday Life in Classical Athens*, 1969.

NOTES TO PAGES 167–71

78 Some modern scholars do not accept that the Boule was created by Solon, but came into being some hundred years later. See V. Ehrenberg, *From Solon to Socrates*, 1968, pp. 66–7 and note 41 (p. 395). For a highly specialised discussion of the Boule, see P. Rhodes, *The Athenian Boule*, 1972.

79 Sparta too did not easily extend citizenship to others, but sometimes it was done as a reward to both helots and perioikoi (literally, the 'living-around ones' i.e. the non-Dorian people of Sparta).

80 Strabo, IX, 396.

81 The democratic intentions of Cleisthenes have been contested. Some have argued that his underlying aim was to put more power into the hands of the influential Alcmaeonid family. See W. Forrest, *The Emergence of Greek Democracy: The Character of Greek Politics 800–400 BC*, Hutchinson, 1966.

82 Ehrenberg, *From Solon to Socrates*, pp. 89–90.

83 This term which is usually rendered 'prytany' can be used to denote the period of time, one-tenth of the year, or the group of 50 in session on the council.

84 Ehrenberg, *From Solon to Socrates*, p. 93.

85 See H. Bengtson (ed.), *The Greeks and the Persians*, 1969, p. 193.

86 See Webster, *Athenian Culture and Society*, Chap. 6.

87 R. M. Haywood, *The Ancient World*, 1971, p. 205.

88 See V. Ehrenberg, *From Solon to Socrates*, pp. 285–6.

89 There were five main Boards: the treasurers of Athena, the sellers of public properties, receivers of public monies, scrutineers of official accounts, and examiners of official conduct.

90 See Haywood, op. cit., p. 206.

91 Ibid.

92 Socrates seriously questioned the lot system maintaining that if people want a pilot, they do not subject their choice to the uncertainties of the ballot. A fortiori, how much more hazardous this is in affairs of state. See J. Ferguson, *Socrates*, 1970.

93 Plato's devastating critique of democracy in *The Republic* may well stem in part from the Assembly's condemnation of his mentor, Socrates, in 399 BC on what appears in retrospect to be a valid but unnecessary charge.

94 Compare the article by M. I. Finley in *Past & Present* (1962), p. 3.

95 Cleon has excited both admiration and hostile criticism from commentators. See, for opposite points of view, E. M. Walker, 'The Periclean Democracy' in *Cambridge Ancient History*, vol. 5 and A. G. Woodhead in *Mnemosyne*, 13 (1960), p. 289.

96 For a comparative approach to voting procedures in Classical societies, see, E. S. Staveley, *Greek and Roman Voting and Elections*, 1975.

97 There was some uncertainty about the details of the ways in which the system actually worked until the 1930s excavations of the Agora which uncovered fragments of the lot-drawing machines. See Sterling Dow, 'Allotment Machines', *Hesperia*, Supplement I (1937).

98 Webster, *Athenian Culture and Society*, p. 102.

NOTES TO PAGES 171–5

99 6,000 jurors would certainly represent over half the number of Athenian citizens eligible to vote, but there is some uncertainty about this. Webster in ibid.
100 See entries in Pierre Devambez et al., The Praeger Encyclopedia of Ancient Greek Civilization, 1967.
101 For a discussion of 'capital' cases, see D. Macdowell, Athenian Homicide Law, 1963.
102 There was also a 'blood-tribunal' which 'condemned unidentified murders in absentia, and pronounced a solemn judgement upon the animal or object, be it of wood, metal or stone which had occasioned the death in question'. G. Glotz, The Greek City and its Institutions, 1929, p. 275.
103 For a definitive discussion of Athenian legal systems, see R. Harrison, The Law of Athens, Oxford University Press, 1969, vols 1 and 2 and J. L. Jones, The Law and Legal Theory of the Greeks, 1956.
104 See Haywood, op. cit., p. 208.
105 Ibid.
106 Although juries had no official vocal part in the proceedings, they were known to demonstrate their sympathies by 'murmuring'.
107 R. Flaceliere, Daily Life in Greece, 1965, p. 229.
108 Macdowell, op. cit.
109 Crucifixion – often as a form of impalement – was a type of punishment traditionally associated with the Persians. See H. Olmstead, A History of Persia, 1948.
110 See Herodotus, IX, 5.
111 There is evidence that Socrates could, with the connivance of friends – and perhaps even magistrates – have got out of prison and gone into exile instead of taking the hemlock. See G. Lowes Dickinson, Plato and his Dialogues, 1947.
112 Peter Green, for example, maintains that all references in Liddel–Scott-Jones indicate some form of exposure or crucifixion.
113 Some of the tragedians make references to execution of other kinds. For example in the pursuit of Orestes – who had murdered his mother Clytemnestra and her lover Aegisthus – Apollo tells the avenging Erinyes, 'Your place is where justice is executed with beheadings and eye-gougings and slit-throats . . . .' Aeschylus, Eumenides, line 185–90.
114 A reference to whipping as a punishment can be seen in Aristophanes, Peace, line 452.
115 Ostracism is named after the practice of voting with potsherds (ostraka).
116 Plutarch, Aristides. There is some uncertainty whether the figure of 6,000 refers to the number of votes cast or to the quorum of voters at the ostrakphorioa. See Jérôme Carcopino, The Athenian Ostracism, 1935, p. 5.
117 For a general survey, see R. Bonner and G. Smith, The Administration of Justice from Homer to Aristotle, University of Chicago Press, 1930.
118 What Arnold Toynbee has called 'the poisonous ingredients with which it had been contaminated at the outset'. A. Toynbee, A Study of History, 1970.

119 For a devastating critique of 'People's Systems', see B. de Jouvenel, *On Power*.
120 This obviously biased but rather ironically clever argument is taken from an anonymous source usually designated as the 'Old Oligarch'. See E. G. Sihler, *Hellenic Civilization*, 1920.
121 Note particularly the work of Rostovtzeff, especially his *History of the Ancient World*.
122 See, for example, F. W. Walbank, 'The Causes of Greek Decline', *Journal of Hellenic Studies*, 64 (1944), pp. 10–20.

## Chapter 11 Military organisation and expansionism

1 See, for example, William James's essay on 'The Moral Equivalent of War'. Also B. Malinowski, 'An Anthropological Analysis of War' in L. Bramson and G. Goethals (eds), *War*, 1968.
2 Margaret Mead in ibid., p. 270.
3 See, for instance, K. Marx and F. Engels, *The Communist Manifesto*, 1967.
4 G. Mosca, *The Ruling Class*, McGraw-Hill, 1939, p. 29.
5 See Gideon Sjoberg, *The Pre-Industrial City*, 1965, p. 58. Also the more qualified analysis of G. Lenski, *Power and Privilege*, 1966, pp. 68–9.
6 For a discussion on war, nationalism and the mass society, see L. Bramson, *The Political Context of Sociology*, 1961.
7 G. H. Mead, 'National Mindedness and International Mindedness' quoted by R. Park, 'The Social Function of War', *American Journal of Sociology*, XLVI (1941).
8 Among the considerable body of literature devoted to analyses of war are a number of helpful general texts including: K. Waltz, *Man, War and the State*, 1959; Q. Wright, *A Study of War*, 1942; R. Aron, *On War*, 1963; A. Toynbee, *War and Civilization*, 1950.
9 For persuasive discussions of the 'aggressive instinct' thesis, see K. Lorenz, *On Aggression*, Methuen, 1966 and R. Ardrey, *African Genesis*, Collins, 1963.
10 See M. Harris, M. Fried and R. Murphy (eds), *War: the Anthropology of Armed Conflict and Aggression*, 1968.
11 The phenomenon of seeking *peaceful* solutions to politico–economic situations is itself in need of explanation. One account of the Lepchas of Sikkim, for example, insists that they do not understand war – even defensive war. See G. Gorer, *Himalayan Village*, Michael Joseph, 1938.
12 S. Andreski, *Military Organisation and Society*, 1968.
13 Malinowski in Bramson and Goethals, op. cit., pp. 258–9.
14 R. Lapiere, *A Theory of Social Control*, 1954, pp. 450–1.
15 See article by Raymond Mack and Richard Snyder, 'The Analysis of Social Conflict', in A. Etzioni and M. Wenglinsky (eds), *War and its Prevention*, 1970.
16 A. Vagts, *A History of Militarism*, 1959. See especially the Introduction.
17 Ibid., p. 13.
18 The distinction between military, economic and cultural conquest is emphasised by Lapiere, op. cit., Chaps. 16 and 17.

19 'Cultural Conflict' must, in some ways, be rather an unsatisfactory term because when used in the broad sense it conveniently subsumes all that can be generally regarded as 'social'.

20 H. T. Olmstead, *History of Assyria*, 3rd imp., 1968.

21 Ideological conflict may be defined as 'a clash . . . of the prescriptive norms and beliefs who do or should govern particular behaviours'. Mack and Snyder, op. cit.

22 Within the general ambit of our discussion, Sparta – with qualifications – might just prove an exception to this. In the *pre-industrial* world, as distinct from the ancient world, the expansionist activities of Islam from the sixth to the ninth centuries AD would probably best exemplify the ideological position. Although possibly the Muslims themselves would have been hard put to it to disentangle the priorities of their respective motives. See Bernard Lewis, *A History of the Arabs*, 1956.

23 It has been argued that the armies of these politico-military leaders, which derive from religious orders or which have a strong ideological identification, tend to evince a more sustained interest in political issues. S. N. Eisenstadt, *The Political Systems of Empires*, Free Press, 1969, p. 174.

24 See the discussion, though from a somewhat different perspective, in ibid., pp. 172–5.

25 See R. Bellah, *Tokugawa Religion: the Values of Pre-industrial Japan*, 1957.

26 See J. Hemming, *The Conquest of the Incas*, Macmillan, 1970.

27 Traditional China is a case in point: there is some dispute between Sinologists on this issue. See D. Bodde, *China's Cultural Tradition*, 1957, pp. 58ff.

28 Marius helped to precipitate change in the Roman system, particularly in so far as he showed that, with an ostensibly consular constitution which favoured the patrician order, a form of plebeian autocracy was possible. See M. Rostovtzeff, *Rome*, 1963.

29 It has been argued in connection with revolution that the military are frequently the leaders of palace-revolutions, but it is the intellectuals who articulate the ideology who are almost invariably the leaders of *social* revolutions. See Lenski, op. cit., p. 70.

30 Regarding the origins and organisation of the Hyksos, see particularly G. Steindorff and K. Steele, *When Egypt Ruled the East*, 1957, Chap. 3.

31 J. H. Breasted, *A History of Egypt*, 1946, pp. 83–4.

32 See C. Aldred, *The Egyptians*, 1956, p. 171.

33 It is an instructive exercise to compare the experience of the Egyptians during the Old Kingdom with their contemporaries in Mesopotamia. Here there was relative *non*-isolation; the frequent incursions of foreign invaders consequently gave rise to a martial ethos which became more marked with time. See A. Leo Oppenheim, *Ancient Mesopotamia*, 1964.

34 Breasted, op. cit., pp. 134–5. Campaigns in Nubia and Libya were known since the Fourth Dynasty.

NOTES TO PAGES 183–6

35 In Nubia, the local commander appointed by King Sesostris I made himself so prominent on the triumphal monuments that the king had his figure erased, and possibly the commander was dismissed in disgrace. J. Breasted *Ancient Records of Egypt*, 1906–7, vol. 1 (514).
36 J. E. Manchip White, *Ancient Egypt*, 1970, p. 56.
37 Note the archaeological work of the American, G. Reisner, at Kerma south of the Third Cataract, mentioned in Sir A. Gardiner, *Egypt of the Pharaohs*, 1961, p. 136.
38 Siegfried Herrmann, *A History of Israel in Old Testament Times*, SCM, 1973, pp. 19–20.
39 J. A. Wilson, *The Culture of Ancient Egypt*, 1956, pp. 159–61.
40 Note the work of M. Gimbutas and R. Schmitt in articles in *Journal of Indo-European Studies*, vol. 2, no. 3, 1974.
41 In the tomb of a naval officer named Ahmes, there is an account of an engagement at Avaris which finally helped to dislodge the Hyksos from Egypt during the reign of the first Eighteenth Dynasty Pharaoh, Ahmose I. Manchip White, op. cit., p. 56.
42 For a specialist study, see H. E. Winlock, *The Rise and Fall of the Middle Kingdom in Thebes*, 1947. Wilson (op. cit., p. 161n) takes the view that Winlock spoils his argument regarding the influence of the Hyksos and the importance of their importations by overstating his case.
43 L. Pareti *et al.*, *The Ancient World*, 1965, vol. 2, p. 207.
44 Middle Kingdom defensive measures were difficult in Libya and Sinai partly because of the nature of the terrain, but they were particularly well organised in Nubia. The French Archaeological Mission has unearthed the remains of established fortress-towns near the Second Cataract at Mirgissa, and the late Professor Emery, an expert on the Archaic period, found similar structures at Buhen. Manchip White, op. cit., pp. xiv–xv.
45 Breasted on the basis of Ramesses II's campaign at Kadesh, the date of which is disputed, estimates that the army was probably nearer 20,000. Breasted, *A History of Egypt*, p. 285.
46 There is an account of Henu, the Chief Treasurer of the Middle Kingdom ruler Mentuhotep, who was responsible for the provisioning of a contingent of 3,000 men on a quarrying expedition to the Hammamat area of the Red Sea. His task was to ensure that each man received two jars of water and twenty small biscuit-loaves daily. Ibid., p. 153.
47 Aldred, op. cit., p. 172.
48 P. Montet, *Everyday Life in Egypt*, 1958, p. 222, quoting the *Bibliotheca aegyptiaca*, VII. 26.
49 Manchip White, op. cit., p. 56.
50 *Bibliotheca aegyptiaca*, VII. 27.
51 Breasted, *A History of Egypt*, p. 299.
52 See O. R. Gurney, *The Hittites*, 1964.
53 See Steindorff and Seele, op. cit., pp. 89–91.
54 A horse skeleton has been found by the British expedition at Buhen which indicates that the horse may have been known in Egypt a

285

hundred years or more before the Hyksos. Manchip White, op. cit., pp. xiv–xv.
55 Suggested by Steindorff and Seele, op. cit., p. 91.
56 Herodotus II. 164–8.
57 See Montet, op. cit., p. 227, quoting N. de G. Davies, 'The Rock Tombs of El Amarna', *Egyptian Exploration Society* III (1903–8).
58 Breasted, *A History of Egypt*, p. 449.
59 It is the view of Steindorff and Seele (op. cit., p. 93) that restless mercenaries may well have periodically pillaged and oppressed the villages where they were settled, especially during times of scarcity or when payments were delayed.
60 The position of the mercenaries in the post-Empire period became somewhat analogous to that of the Mamelukes in the Middle Ages.
61 Breasted, *Ancient Records of Egypt*, vol. 2, 461–2.
62 See Wilson, op. cit., p. 180.
63 Breasted, *Ancient Records of Egypt*, vol. 2, 797.
64 Wilson, op. cit., p. 200.
65 Breasted, *A History of Egypt*, p. 478. The view that there were sacrificial victims may simply be an inference of Breasted's for which evidence is rather flimsy.
66 Margaret Murray, *The Splendour that was Egypt*, 1963, p. 44.
67 This practice of 'destroying' an enemy by curse appears to go back to the 'breaking of the red jars' ceremony of the Old and Middle Kingdoms, where names of enemies were inscribed on pottery which was then ritually smashed. See Wilson, op. cit., p. 156.
68 The belief that the power to name gives also the power to control is well known in ancient Hebrew literature. See R. H. Pfeiffer, *Introduction to the Old Testament*, Black, 1952.
69 Murray, op. cit., p. 207.
70 Ibid., p. 208.
71 Quoted by Murray, op. cit., p. 209.
72 Of Tuthmosis' sixth campaign it is recorded that '... the sons of the princes and their brothers were brought away to be hostages in Egypt.... List of the sons of princes carried off this year: thirty-six men.' Breasted, *Ancient Records of Egypt*, vol. 2, 467.
73 Some Asiatic princes showed 'almost fanatical loyalty' to the state during the Amarna crisis when the influence of the Akhenaten and the Aten priesthood were being seriously tested. See Wilson, op. cit., p. 221.
74 Ibid., p. 191.
75 Ibid., p. 250. It should be noted that this was a traditional scribal. format in keeping with pharaonic interests – it is doubtful whether the Hittites interpreted events this way.
76 Andreski, op. cit., p. 43.
77 Note H. Frankfort, *Ancient Egyptian Religion*, 1961, p. 49.
78 Heterodeistic is here meant to refer to 'other or other kinds of gods'.
79 An inverse relationship between militarism and ideology would have to be seriously qualified in historical cases. The *type* of ideology is important, and the circumstances in which it operates. Where the

ideology is universalistic, as for example, Islam, militarism and expansionism may be seen as adjuncts which are necessary to its acceptance and realisation.

80 See Pareti *et al.*, op. cit., p. 208.
81 Homer, *Iliad*, II. 362.
82 Ibid., II. 168ff.
83 Ibid., IV. 297ff.
84 Ibid., XIII. 130ff.
85 Tyrtaeus *c.* 660–640 BC describes hoplite infantry in a poem of a contemporary battle between Sparta and Messenia during the 'Second Messenian War'.
86 M. I. Finley, *The Ancient Greeks*, 1963, p. 36.
87 Pareti *et al.*, op. cit., p. 212.
88 Aristotle, *Politics*, 1297b.
89 A. Andrewes, *The Greek Tyrants*, 1956, pp. 34ff.
90 A. Andrewes, *Greek Society*, 1967, p. 161.
91 Spartan hoplites could be distinguished immediately by their all purple tunics, which were thought to disguise bloodstains, and their long hair – something of an anachronism in the Classical period – which they are said (Herodotus VII. 208) to have ritually combed before battle. Athenian officers wore tunics with a purple stripe, whereas epheboi apparently always wore black.
92 Xenophon referred to the Spartans as the 'technicians of war' in contrast to the impoverished militia of many other Greek states. Andrewes, *Greek Society*, p. 164, quoting Xenophon's possible idealisation of Sparta in his *Polity of the Lacedaemonians*.
93 For a general treatment of Greek armour, see A. Snodgrass, *Early Greek Armour and Weapons*, 1964.
94 Much of what we know of Athenian military organisation derives from Aristotle (*Constitution of Athens*) who was writing of fourth-century procedures.
95 R. Flaceliere, *Daily Life in Greece*, 1973, p. 249.
96 Aristophanes (*The Wasps*, line 578) reflecting the homosexual over-tones of the military life, makes a heliast to remark, 'when the young men come up for inspection, we get a good chance to see their genitals.'
97 Four obols per day per head.
98 Aristotle, *Constitution of Athens*, 42. 4.
99 Flaceliere, op. cit., p. 252 quoting J. Pouilloux, *La Fortress de Rhamnonte* [Rhamnous], 1954, pp. 81–2.
100 Thucydides II. 13.
101 In the fourth century BC, Xenophon (*On Horsemanship*) advised the cavalry to wear gauntlets and some form of cuirass. He also suggested that the horses too should be protected – perhaps with padded quilting to their undersides – a hitherto neglected practice among the Athenians.
102 Aristophanes, *The Knights*.
103 At the Battle of Marathon in 490 BC when the Athenians had routed a strong Persian force, they had neither cavalry nor archers, and

decided to make up for these deficiencies in future. Herodotus VI. 112.

104 Andrewes, *Greek Society*, p. 161.

105 Compare the prolonged siege of Tyre by the armies of Alexander in the fourth century BC, A. R. Burn, *Alexander the Great and the Middle East*, 1973.

106 For a general survey, see F. E. Adcock, *The Greek and Macedonian Art of War*, 1957.

107 Aeschines, *On the Embassy* quoted by Flaceliere, op. cit., p. 262. The Amphictyonic league, of whom more is known in the fourth century BC, was a pan-hellenic institution with traditional religious associations. It counselled self-knowledge and moderation, but had a limited practical influence.

108 See H. D. Kitto, *The Greeks*, 1951, p. 154.

109 Greek professional soldiers were in great demand in the ancient world, mainly in the fourth and third centuries BC fighting particularly for either Persia or Egypt. Perhaps the best known are the campaigns of the Ten Thousand in Asia recounted in the *Anabasis* of Xenophon.

110 The effectiveness of light-armed troops was particularly displayed by the Athenian Iphicrates in the fourth century BC against the Spartans, a lesson learned by his predecessors in campaigns in Western Greece during the Peloponnesian War.

111 See particularly, J. Fuller, *The Decisive Battles of the Western World* (ed. John Terraine), Paladin, 1970, vol. 1, chs 7–10.

112 H. Bengtson (ed.), *The Greeks and the Persians*, 1969, pp. 184–6.

113 Thucydides II. 93.

114 The term trierarchos, commander, is not to be confused with nauarchos, admiral.

115 The state often provided the hull and possibly the rigging of the ship, but the trierarchos would provide the rest as a form of leitourgia or public service. This practice began to die out later in the war when personal wealth became scarce and the burden of equipping triremes was shared by two or more citizens.

116 Flaceliere, op. cit., p. 265.

117 The helots of Messenia and Laconia revolted in 464 BC when an earthquake destroyed part of Sparta. The Athenian Cimon took a force of hoplites to aid the Spartans in putting down this very serious rebellion which lasted for some years.

118 It is probably fair to state that Corcyra and Corinth had been in conflict before, and were perhaps looking for the excuse to reopen hostilities. See V. Ehrenberg, *From Solon to Socrates*, 1968, p. 254.

119 The term arete is sometimes translated as 'virtue', but the modern connotations of this word are hardly appropriate, Arete comes nearer to the Roman 'virtus' which can be closely associated with 'manliness'. Compare the term ponos (toil) which came to connote endurance, and which – by Classical times – was associated with the upper order citizens who farmed, hunted and went to war.

120 Note A. W. Adkins, *Merit and Responsibility: a Study in Greek Values*, 1960.

121 A. Gouldner, *Enter Plato*, 1967, p. 13.

122 Note the Homeric account of the sack of Troy in the *Iliad*. M. I. Finley comments on similar practices in early Greece in *The World of Odysseus*, 1962, p. 61.
123 This is probably reflected in Plato (*Republic* V. 468 A): 'if any fall alive into the enemies' hands we shall make a present of him, and they may do what they like with their prey. . . .'
124 Some authorities use the disputable term 'class war' to describe the Corcyran incident. For example, Arnold Toynbee, *Greek Civilization and Character*, 1953, pp. 44–53.
125 Thucydides III. 70–85; IV. 46–8.
126 See G. Thomson, *Studies in Ancient Greek Society*, 1955, pp. 196–205.
127 Bengtson, op. cit., p. 193.
128 Aristotle, *Politics*, 1255A, 6–7.
129 See Yvon Garlan, *War in the Ancient World*, 1975, pp. 70–1.
130 See Chapter 12.
131 Plutarch, himself a priest of Apollo, wrote, 'when you see the god surrounded on all sides with tithes and spoils got by murder and war and rape, and his temple full of Greek . . . booty, does it not strike you as intolerable?' Plutarch, *On the Pythian Oracle*.
132 Flaceliere, op. cit., p. 259.
133 For the famous funeral oration of Pericles in 431 BC, see Thucydides, II. 34.
134 There is, however, a tradition that the Spartans may have been engaged in the suppression of a revolt in their own territory (Plato, *Laws* 692; 698).
135 Ehrenberg following Herodotus (VII. 206), is inclined to accept the ritual justifications, but admits that this is 'generally disbelieved by modern scholars' (op. cit., p. 151).
136 Herodotus IX. 61–2.
137 Excavations have uncovered evidence of dedications to the gods – particularly of bronze helmets – after the battle. Ehrenberg, op. cit., p. 137.
138 Compare B. d'Agostino, *Monuments of Civilization: Greece*, 1974, p. 40.
139 See J. M. Yinger, *Religion, Society and the Individual*, 1957.
140 Nicias was a devout man who carried images of the gods on the expedition together with a portable altar on which there was a perpetual altar flame lit at the city's altar-hearth. His staff also included diviners who advised him on crucial decisions.
141 Thucydides VIII. 1.
142 Thucydides on the class war quoted in Toynbee, op. cit., p. 50.
143 Fustel de Coulanges, *The Ancient City*, 1960 edn, pp. 326ff.
144 It is worth noting that there may be some correlation between naval development in Greece and proletarian participation. Thessaly, a non-naval power, with strong cavalry traditions, was also a non-democratic state. On the other hand, Carthage which was a very strong naval power, was an oligarchy. Carthage employed large numbers of mercenaries, but – unlike Egypt – was not troubled by attempted revolution. Her economic situation was similar to that of

the sixth-century Greek commercial states, but she was not significantly troubled by popular movements. See Andreski, op. cit., pp. 45–6.
145 See Etzioni and Wenglinsky, op. cit., pp. 169–70.
146 Ehrenberg, op. cit., pp. 204ff.
147 Alexis de Tocqueville, 'On War, Society, and the Military' in Bramson and Goethals, op. cit., p. 331.

## Chapter 12 Systems of ideation

1 Max Weber, *Sociology of Religion*, 1965.
2 See Roland Robertson, *The Sociological Interpretation of Religion*, 1970.
3 C. Hemple, *Fundamentals of Concept Formation in Empirical Science*, Cambridge University Press, 1952.
4 Note the form of essentialism taken by C. Lévi-Strauss (*The Savage Mind*, 1966) who argues in a neo-Kantian way that human categories of thought are really forms of a universal conceptual algebra which simply find different expressions in different societies. See also the criticisms by E. R. Leach, *Lévi-Strauss*, 1970.
5 For a very thorough treatment of these and related issues, see J. Hospers, *Human Conduct*, 1961.
6 See the excellent article by Clifford Geertz, 'Religion as a Cultural System' in M. Banton (ed.), *Anthropological Approaches to the Study of Religion*, 1966. Geertz cites examples of studies which merely highlight well-established propositions that 'initiation rites are means for the establishment of sexual identity' and that 'myths provide charters for social institutions', etc. (p. 2).
7 This expression was used by Janowitz about certain rather limited studies in anthropology generally. M. Janowitz, 'Anthropology and the Social Sciences', *Current Anthropology* 4: pp. 139, 146–54.
8 See E. O. James, *The Beginnings of Religion*, 1948.
9 L. T. Hobhouse, *Morals in Evolution*, 1906.
10 For a very clear explication of what is essentially a functionalist approach, see A. R. Radcliffe-Brown, *Structure and Function in Primitive Society*, 1952 and for a fairly typical example of a functionalist analysis, see W. Goode, *Religion among the Primitives*, 1964.
11 One of the best known proponents of the instrumental school is E. R. Leach, *The Political Systems of Highland Burma*, 1964. In a qualified way, Professor Leach has popularised a form of analysis which was developed much earlier in the century by W. Robertson-Smith in his treatise on the religion of the Semites (1908).
12 For a very clear elaboration of the cause-function problem, see P. Cohen, *Modern Social Theory*, 1968.
13 Geertz, op. cit., p. 4.
14 Note particularly the work of J. Wach, *The Sociology of Religion*, 1945 and A. D. Nock, *Essays on Religion and the Ancient World* (ed. Zeph Stewart), Cambridge University Press, 1972.
15 For a development of this theme with particular relevance to the modern world, see Peter Berger, *A Rumour of Angels*, 1972.

16 For an elaboration of these ideas, see G. Henningsen, 'Fatalism in Systematic Aspect and Fatalism in its Functional Context' in H. Ringgren, *Fatalistic Beliefs in Religion, Folklore and Literature*, SCM, 1967.

17 A. Wells, *Social Institutions*, 1970, p. 244.

18 H. Frankfort *et al.*, *Before Philosophy*, 1954, p. 12.

19 Note, for example, Jean Danielou, 'Phenomenology of Religions and Philosophy of Religion' in Morcea Eliade and Joseph Kitagawa (eds), *The History of Religions*, 1959, pp. 68–9.

20 The concrescent emphasis can be seen particularly in the influential writings of the theologian Dietrich Bonhoeffer.

21 Talcott Parsons (*Societies: Evolutionary and Comparative Perspectives*, 1966) also uses the Congruent and Contingent categories, but with a somewhat different emphasis.

22 R. H. Pfeiffer, *Introduction to the Old Testament*, Black, 1952.

23 The Herms were often little more than pillars surmounted by the sculpted heads of some Athenian dignitaries or heroes. Their phallic characteristics may have been the legacy of an earlier fertility emphasis in the Greek earth cults.

24 See V. Ehrenberg, *From Solon to Socrates*, 1968, pp. 291–2.

25 See, for example, among Petrie's voluminous output on Egyptian archaeology and civilisation, *Religion and Conscience in Ancient Egypt*.

26 Note the work of G. Steindorff and K. Seele, *When Egypt Ruled the East*, 1957, pp. 132–55.

27 Breasted, who was one of the fathers of modern Egyptology, produced the monumental *Ancient Records of Egypt* in five volumes (1906–7) and among his other writings, *The Development of Religion and Thought in Ancient Egypt* (1912).

28 H. Frankfort, *Kingship and the Gods*, 1948 and *Ancient Egyptian Religion*, 1961.

29 J. A. Wilson, Chapters 2–4 in Frankfort *et al.*, *Before Philosophy*.

30 For example, J. Vandier, *Egyptian Religion* (Paris, 1944), and A. Erman, *The Religion of Egypt* (Berlin, 1934).

31 J. E. Manchip-White, *Ancient Egypt*, 1970, p. 21.

32 Frankfort, *Ancient Egyptian Religion*, Chapter 1.

33 Manchip-White (op. cit.) tends towards an artistocratic-popular deities dichotomy. Note the similar division of official and popular deities suggested by the Ramesside specialist Dr K. A. Kitchen.

34 M. Covensky, *The Ancient Near Eastern Tradition*, 1966, p. 72.

35 Margaret Murray, *The Splendour that was Egypt*, 1963, p. 119.

36 *The Larousse Encyclopaedia of Mythology*, Hamlyn, 1968, p. 11.

37 Compare, for example, the dual nature of some ancient female deities such as the Egyptian Hathor and the Mesopotamian Innana who were endowed with both warmly beneficent and coldly aggressive characteristics. This may not only reflect the ambivalent attitudes to female deities found in some ancient cultures, it may also be an attempt to grapple with the contradictory elements in the human psyche.

38 Steindorff and Seele, op. cit., p. 142.

39 The position of vizier is not incompatible with that of kinsman; a brother or son might well also be vizier according to Old Kingdom practice.

40 Wilson in *Before Philosophy*, p. 81.

41 Ibid., p. 82.

42 The term 'mythopoeic' is commonly used by J. A. Wilson and particularly by Henri Frankfort in a rather speculative 'read-back' way to denote the conceptual orientations of 'ancient man'.

43 See S. Brandon, *Religion in Ancient History*, 1969, Chapter 8.

44 For a detailed analysis of the text, see Frankfort, *Kingship and the Gods*, Chapter 2.

45 The Memphite Theology is reminiscent of the Logos Doctrine of the New Testament (John, 1) – a point that Breasted noted – and may have influenced the philosopher Philo of Alexandria who was teaching immediately prior to the New Testament period.

46 See J. M. Plumley, 'The Cosmology of Ancient Egypt' in Carmen Blacker and Michael Loewe, *Ancient Cosmologies*, 1975, pp. 38–9.

47 Towns had sacred trees, and Egyptian art particularly emphasises the role of the sycamore as a cult-symbol. See P. Montet, *Everyday Life in Egypt*, 1958, p. 277.

48 Frankfort (*Ancient Egyptian Religion*, p. 10) insists that Ptah was never actually depicted as a bull or believed to be incarnate in a bull. But presumably there was some believed relationship between the procreative powers of the bull and the procreative powers of the earth-god, Ptah.

49 Steindorff and Seele, op. cit., pp. 140–1.

50 Herodotus II. 67.

51 These rituals are known primarily from the relief of Seti I (Nineteenth Dynasty) in the temple of Abydos.

52 For the later period, see Herodotus II. 59–60.

53 See F. L. Griffith, *Tomb Endowment in Ancient Egypt* (1925) quoted by Montet.

54 A. Gardiner, *The Attitude of the Ancient Egyptians to Death and The Dead*, 1935.

55 *The Book of the Dead* indicates that in the Netherworld man will inhabit the windswept Field of Rushes where he carries on life as before. But this is just the teaching of one particular tradition. See Erman, *The Religion of Egypt*, p. 229.

56 Miriam Lichtheim, 'The Songs of the Harpers', *Journal of Near Eastern Studies* IV (1945).

57 Frankfort, *Ancient Egyptian Religion*, p. 126. This should be compared with the view of H. W. Fairman, *The Triumph of Horus*, Batsford, 1974.

58 *The Book of the Dead*, Chapter 175.

59 *Bibliotheca aegyptiaca* I. 4. The Contendings of Horus and Seth.

60 There is, of course, the partial exception of Tutankhamun, although even in this case the evidence suggests that an unsuccessful attempt

to rob the tomb had actually been made. See H. Carter, *The Tomb of Tutankhamun*, 1922–3 and Penelope Fox, *Tutankhamun's Treasure*, 1951.

61 For example, a very early text of the Fifth Dynasty, reads: 'As for any people who take possession of this tomb ... or do any thing to it, judgement shall be had ... by the great god.' See R. O. Faulkner, *The Ancient Egyptian Pyramid Texts*, 1969 and *The Ancient Egyptian Coffin Texts*, vol. 1, Aris & Phillips, Warminster, 1973. It should be noted that curses were often directed not against the violators of the tombs themselves, but against the violators of the endowments which maintained the tombs and the mortuary-cults connected with them. Spiritual penalties were therefore being invoked for the enemies of the priesthood rather than the deceased. Murray, op. cit., p. 139.

62 For a specialised treatment, see T. E. Peet, *The Great Tomb Robberies of the 20th Dynasty*, vols 1 and 2 (1930).

63 Montet, op. cit., p. 266.

64 J. A. Wilson, *The Culture of Ancient Egypt*, 1956, p. 233.

65 Note the stories of the Twenty-first Dynasty King, Menkheperre at a time when – according to A. Gardiner (*Egypt of the Pharaohs*, 1961, p. 318) – women were becoming more influential in court circles. See H. Griffith, *Stories of the High Priests of Memphis*, Oxford University Press, 1900.

66 This position is taken by Wilson particularly in relation to the Old Kingdom. See *The Culture of Ancient Egypt*, p. 92.

67 Particularly the teachings of Ptahhotep, an Old Kingdom vizier. See Breasted, *The Development of Religion and Thought in Ancient Egypt*.

68 Frankfort, *Ancient Egyptian Religion*, pp. 61ff.

69 This is the position taken by Wilson (*Before Philosophy*, p. 104) who maintains that the earlier periods were characterised by an emphasis on action and life, whilst the later periods were marked by an emphasis on death and repose – resignation being a feature of a civilisation in decline.

70 As an ethico-social phenomenon, its investigation was a central feature of the work of Max Weber. Most famously in his work on *The Protestant Ethic and the Spirit of Capitalism*, and the many studies of religion in ancient societies which derive from it.

71 This pylon was found by Henri Chevrier during the 1953–4 excavations. See Charles Nims, 'Thutmosis III's Benefactions to Amon' in G. E. Kadish (ed.), *Studies in Honour of John A. Wilson*, 1969.

72 Note how in modern Christian movements it is possible to make radical criticisms of theological verities, but not the ecclesiastical procedures which affect the actual organisation and raisons-d'etre of the systems. See Eric Carlton, 'The Unitarian Movement in England', 1972.

73 Barbara Sewell, *Egypt Under the Pharaohs*, 1968, p. 108.

74 Wilson, *The Culture of Ancient Egypt*, p. 229.

75 For a discussion of this problem, see E. R. Dodds, *The Greeks and the Irrational*, 1951.

76 See Jacquetta Hawkes, *Dawn of the Gods*, 1968.

77 L. Pareti *et al.*, *The Ancient World*, 1965, vol. 2, Part 1, p. 232.

78 A number of Greek cults almost certainly derive from the pre-Mycenaean Minoan culture of Crete; that may even extend to the worship of Athena, the patron goddess of Athens. It may also be significant that early Attica and Argos, who have the longest royal genealogies known in Greece, had female deities – again a feature of the fertility religion of the Minoan civilisation. See H. D. Kitto, *The Greeks*, 1951, p. 18.

79 M. I. Finley (*The Ancient Greeks*, 1963, p. 30) agrees, but C. Seltman (*The Twelve Olympians*, 1952, p. 48) insists that most Greeks were probably untroubled by such 'wildly absurd' tales.

80 Kitto, op. cit., p. 19.

81 This relates to the famous story of the 'judgment of Paris', prince of Troy when, as a consequence of his unfortunate choice of the most beautiful goddess, he compounded the mistake by 'seducing' the legally unavailable Helen, wife of Menelaus of Sparta.

82 The term prodemic (pro + demos) is being used here to denote that which is done specifically to inculcate community-mindedness and aid community activity.

83 See Aristophanes, *Thesmophoriazusae*.

84 Artisans celebrated mainly at the Chalkeia, in honour of Athene Ergane (Athens the worker) their patron goddess, and Hephaistos, the patron god of the smiths. Marie Delcourt, quoted by R. Flaceliere, *Daily Life in Greece*, 1965, p. 200.

85 The term psychecentric is used here to denote what might best be termed a soul-centred approach to religion which was more developed in aspects of Egyptian religion.

86 M. Nilsson, *Greek Popular Religion*, 1940.

87 See A. H. Armstrong, *An Introduction to Ancient Philosophy*, 1968.

88 See particularly the *Apology* of Socrates (via Plato) in G. Lowes Dickinson, *Plato and His Dialogues*, 1947.

89 The term 'mystery' (mysterion) connotes something secret – in this case, a religious truth – which is restricted to a privileged minority.

90 M. Nilsson, *A History of Greek Religion*, London, 1952, pp. 179ff.

91 Orphism had a number of doctrines in common with contemporary Indian Jainism which 'emerged' at approximately the same time, i.e. in the middle of the sixth century BC.

92 See *The Republic* II. 364–5. Compare with the views of Herodotus in III. 129–38.

93 Armstrong, op. cit., p. 12.

94 See G. C. Field, *Plato and His Contemporaries*, 1967.

95 A. Andrewes, *Greek Society*, 1967, p. 258.

96 This may have been particularly feared where the dead had once been powerful people. See Suetonius on *Caligula* (59), and Andrewes, op. cit., pp. 258–9 re Agamemnon.

97 Plutarch, *Aristides* 21. See also Fustel de Coulanges, *The Ancient City*, 1960 edn, pp. 17–21.
98 Andrewes, op. cit., p. 270.
99 See H. W. Parke and D. E. Wormell, *The Delphic Oracle*, 1956.
100 It may not be possible to sustain the argument that oracles were merely a palliative for common superstitious people, simply because they are hardly mentioned in Homer (see Pareti, Part 1, p. 234). The Delphic oracle in particular was better established after Homer's time, and was consulted by all classes; there is little evidence anyway that ordinary citizens had a monopoly of superstition in this respect.
101 For oracular ambiguities, see Herodotus (VII. 140ff.) and Ehrenberg, op. cit., p. 150.
102 Of the daemonic forces, Isocrates (*To Philip* 117) wrote, 'we honour [them] neither in our prayers nor in our sacrifice, but seek to drive them off.'
103 Herodotus III. 10. Note also his accounts of Croesus (I, 32–4) and Polycrates (III. 39–43; 122–5). See too A. Toynbee, *Greek Historical Thought*, 1952.
104 T. B. L. Webster, *Athenian Culture and Society*, 1973, p. 97.
105 See B. D'Agostino, *Monuments of Civilization: Greece*, 1974.
106 Finley, *The Ancient Greeks*, p. 47.
107 Note the story reported in Flaceliere (op. cit., p. 211) of the polis which tore down a section of its city walls so as to welcome the hero through a 'gate' which had never been used before.
108 The bard of the games was Pindar (d. 441 BC) who is generally regarded as one of the great lyric poets of Greece.
109 The term 'autotelic' simply denotes activities or games which are played for their own intrinsic pleasure. See Omar Moore and Alan Anderson, 'Puzzles, Games and Interaction' in D. Braybrooke, *Philosophical Problems of the Social Sciences*, 1965.
110 See G. Simmel, *The Sociology of Georg Simmel*, 1950.
111 The word hypocrites – the one who wears the mask – became the common term for 'actor' i.e. one who plays a part.
112 R. M. Haywood, *The Ancient World*, 1971, p. 211.
113 Note Plato's strictures on the influence of the arts in *The Republic*. He argued that children particularly should only be exposed to 'the beautiful, the good and the true'.
114 Plato, *Protagoras*.
115 Aristophanes, *The Clouds* (produced in 423 BC).
116 See P. Green, *Ancient Greece*, 1973, p. 135.
117 See W. K. C. Guthrie, 'Religion and Mythology of the Greeks', *Cambridge Ancient History*, vol. 2, who certainly regards mythology as an aspect of religion.
118 B. Malinowski, *Magic, Science and Religion*, 1954.
119 See C. Lévi-Strauss, *The Savage Mind*, 1966.
120 G. S. Kirk, *The Nature of Greek Myths*, 1974, p. 18.
121 For an excellent general discussion of these and related problems, see G. S. Kirk, *Myth*, 1973, Section I and, with special reference to the Greeks, *The Nature of Greek Myths*.

122 For this approach, see Sir James Frazier, *The New Golden Bough*, 1961, and those influenced by this school, particularly Jane Harrison (*Prolegomena to the Study of Greek Religion*, 1903) and A. B. Cook (*Zeus*).

123 Pareti (op. cit., vol. 2, part II, p. 525) argues that this situation could not be prevented because of the lack of any powerful priestly class.

124 In a rather outmoded plea for sexual emancipation, Charles Seltman sees Greek religion as characterised by:
   (i) a lack of any class or caste of priests;
   (ii) the fact that humility and obedience were never Greek virtues since they presuppose an authoritarian system which demands or exacts them;
   (iii) a lack of dogma;
   (iv) an absence of missions – implying toleration and non-proselytism;
   (v) no martyrs – this, it is argued follows from the absence of missions and dogma. The Athenian impiety trials, and the later Roman persecution of the Christians are regarded as essentially *political* in motive;
   (vi) no Sacred Book, as such, although Homer may be regarded as a kind of moral reference point;
      Little preoccupation with sin – or therefore with misleading ideas about guilt or eternal punishment;
   (vii) tolerant attitudes to sex 'far more significant for mankind than anything as yet mentioned in the difference between Greek and most subsequent religious thought and practice concerned with the attitude to sex . . .' (p. 24).

(Seltman, *The Twelve Olympians*, pp. 15–25.) This book is characteristically dedicated to 'Pan and the Nymphs' and is really a eulogy of Greek religious and sexual practices. It is a work of some scholarship which is spoiled by a reiterated anti-Puritan bias. In effect, it is a polemic against authoritarian religion, particularly Christianity, and is consequently laced with the appropriate liberated conceits which are really no longer capable of shocking anyone. Compare the similar emphasis of his *Women in Antiquity*, 1956.

As a summary, this has its perceptions if, as an analysis, it has its prejudices. Many of the points need qualifying in terms of the substantive histories and, as we have seen, these are not without their ambiguities.

125 For example Alvin Gouldner, *Enter Plato*, 1967.

126 F. Nietzsche, *The Birth of Tragedy and the Genealogy of Morals*, Doubleday, 1956. See also F. M. Cornford, *From Religion to Philosophy*, 1957.

127 Gouldner, op. cit., pp. 116–21.

128 See Andrewes, *Greek Society*, pp. 260–1.

129 The 'spiritual' view is taken by Coulanges (*The Ancient City*, p. 19).

**Chapter 13   Conclusions**

1 Note the article by Barbara Bell, 'The Dark Ages in Ancient History',

in which a case is made that famine, due to a 'failure' of the Nile inundations, was mainly responsible for the political and social upheavals which attended the First and Second Intermediate periods. J. A. Sabloff and C. Lamberg-Karlovsky (eds), *The Rise and Fall of Civilizations*, 1974.

2 Direct democracies such as Athens did not require extensive bureaucracies, but political-administrative participation does require strict limits of citizenship and/or population if control is to be maintained, as Plato insisted in *The Republic*.

3 See P. Vinogradoff, *The Jurisprudence of the Greek City*, Oxford University Press, 1920.

4 M. Laistner, *Greek Economics*, 1923.

5 Of a later period, Herodotus II says that the Egyptians were most religious, and the only people he knew without some form of human sacrifice.

6 Rulers such as the Egyptian Pharaohs and, say, Dionysius, the tyrant of Syracuse – a contemporary of the later Classical period, paraded their wealth and often extolled their own virtues. But they were able to mobilise the men and resources which gave their states a grandeur which participatory systems have found difficult to match.

7 This is using the word 'tyrannical' as in common English expression. In Greek usage, a tyrannos was someone who seized power unconstitutionally, but did not necessarily exercise it cruelly.

8 This is not to assume a functionalist stance, but merely to recognise the 'competencies' of ideology to effect certain resolutions in social situations as discussed in Chapter 2.

9 The terms ademic and prodemic are used to denote the contrast between participatory and non-participatory systems.

10 See, for example, the collected essays in V. Ehrenberg, *Man, State and Deity*, 1974.

11 For an elaboration of this useful distinction between personal charisma and charisma of office see M. Weber, *The Theory of Social and Economic Organisation*, 1964.

12 '. . . the belief in superhuman beings and . . . their power to assist or to harm man approaches universal distribution, and . . . is the core variable which ought to be designated by any definition of religion.' Melford Spiro, 'Religion: Problems of Definition and Explanation' in M. Banton (ed.), *Anthropological Approaches to the Study of Religion*, p. 94, 1966. This view is also generally supported by a number of other anthropologists, e.g. R. Horton, 'A Definition of Religion and its Uses', *Journal of the Royal Anthropological Institute*, 90 (1960) and J. Goody, 'Religion and Ritual: the Definitional Problem', *British Journal of Sociology*, 12 (1961).

13 An interesting and curious problem for functionalists: why do societies insist on constructing ideal value-systems which are not observed in practice? Why is an accommodating congruency not contrived?

14 This approach to religion which is related to the work of Emile Durkheim has been applied with notable effect in a study of religious

values in the USA in the 1950s. See W. Herberg, *Protestant-Catholic-Jew*, 1956.
15 Emile Durkheim, *The Elementary Forms of the Religious Life*, 1968.
16 Among the many critical reviews of Durkheim's work on religion, see E. E. Evans-Pritchard, *Nuer Religion*, 1956; M. Ginsberg, *Reason and Unreason in Society*, 1957; A. Wells, *Social Institutions*, 1970, pp. 245ff.
17 Note the work of R. Redfield, *The Primitive World and its Transformations*, 1953 and 'On the Nature of Civilization' in C. Gabel (ed.), *Man Before History*, 1964. See particularly C. D. Darlington, *The Evolution of Man and Society*, 1969, Parts II, III and V.
18 Compare the experience of the Mesopotamian civilisations which were dependent on the less predictable Euphrates and Tigris rivers which were given to flooding. Here the gods could sometimes be awesome in their arbitrariness.

# Chronological outline of Ancient Egypt

(All dates are BC and approximate)

| | | |
|---|---|---|
| before 3200 | Pre-historic period | |
| 3200–2700 | Thinite period | |
| | Dynasties I–II | Menes as first king of United Egypt |
| 2700–2200 | OLD KINGDOM | Consolidation of theocratic rule |
| | Dynasties III–VI | Pyramid Age. Great Pyramid (Khufu) 2600. Pyramid Texts 2300 |
| 2200–2050 | First Intermediate period | |
| | Dynasties VII–X | Coffin Texts |
| | Dynasty XI | |
| 2050–1800 | MIDDLE KINGDOM | Vast irrigation projects at Fayum |
| | Dynasty XII | |
| 1800–1550 | Second Intermediate period | Hyksos rule 1730–1570 |
| | Dynasties XIII–XVII | |
| 1550–1090 | NEW KINGDOM | Creation of Empire reaching zenith under Tuthmosis III (1480–1450) and his son Amenophis II |
| | Dynasties XVIII–XX | Reforms of Akhenaten – decline with rise of Hittite power in Anatolia. Tutankhamun |
| | | Revival with Dynasty XIX. Seti I and Ramesses II (1300–1230) |
| | | Battle of Kadesh, c. 1295 |
| | | Monuments of Abu Simbel |
| | | Temple complex at Karnak (Thebes) |
| | | Invasions of the 'Sea-peoples' |
| | | Decline in later Ramesside period (Dynasty XX) |

| 1090–525 | Post-Empire period<br>Dynasties XXI–XXVI | Almost unremitting decline with successive defeats by Assyrians and Babylonians. Temporary recovery in Saite period (Dynasty XXVI) |
| 525 | Persian conquest | |
| 525–332 | Dynasties XXVII–XXX | Fluctuating Persian domination |
| 332 | Greek conquest under Alexander | |
| 332–30 | Ptolemaic period<br>Dynasties XXXI–XXXIII | |
| 30 | Roman conquest under Octavian (Augustus) | Death of Cleopatra – the last of the Graeco-Egyptian line<br>Egypt becomes Roman province |

# Chronological outline of Ancient Greece

(All dates are BC)

| | | | |
|---|---|---|---|
| 594 | Archonship of Solon | | |
| 545–510 | Tyranny of Peisistratids in Athens | | |
| 510 | Cleisthenes reforms the Athenian constitution | | |
| 499–494 | Ionian Revolt | | |
| 490–479 | Persian Wars | | |
| 478–404 | Delian league and Athenian Empire | 456 | Aeschylus dies |
| | | c. 450 | Aristophanes born |
| 431–404 | Peloponnesian War | | |
| 430–426 | Plague at Athens | c. 438 | Pindar dies |
| 429 | Death of Pericles | 432 | Parthenon completed. |
| 422 | Peace of Nicias | | Herodotus dies between 430 and 424 |
| | | c. 429 | Plato born |
| 415–13 | Sicilian expedition | 406 | Sophocles and Euripides die |
| | | 404 | Erechtheion completed |
| 399 | Trial of Socrates | | Thucydides dies between 404 and 399 |
| | | c. 385 | Aristophanes dies |
| | | c. 385 | Plato founds the Academy |
| | | 384 | Demosthenes born |
| 371 | Thebes defeats Sparta at Leuctra | | |
| 359–336 | Philip II King of Macedon | 347 | Plato dies |
| 338 | Battle of Chaeronea | 338 | Isocrates dies |
| 336–323 | Alexander the Great | | |
| 322 | End of democracy in Athens | 322 | Aristotle dies |

# Bibliography

## General

ABCARIAN, G. and PALMER, M., *The Human Arena*, Holt, Rinehart & Winston, 1971.

ADORNO, T. *et al.*, *The Authoritarian Personality*, Harper, 1950.

ALMOND, G. and POWELL, O., *Comparative Politics: a Developmental Approach*, Little Brown, 1966.

ANDRESKI, S., *Social Sciences as Sorcery*, Deutsch, 1972.

ANDRESKI, S., *Military Organisation and Society*, Routledge & Kegan Paul, 1968.

APTER, D. (ed.), *Ideology and Discontent*, Free Press, 1964.

ARON, R., *On War*, Anchor, 1963.

BAKER, J., *Race*, Oxford University Press, 1974.

BANTON, M. (ed.), *Anthropological Approaches to the Study of Religion*, ASA Monographs, Tavistock, 1966.

BELSHAW, C., *Traditional Exchange and Modern Markets*, Prentice-Hall, 1965.

BENDIX, R., *Max Weber: an Intellectual Portrait*, Heinemann, 1960.

BENDIX, R. and LIPSET, S. M., *Class, Status and Power*, Free Press, 1966.

BERGER, P., *The Social Reality of Religion*, Faber, 1967.

BERGER, P., *A Rumour of Angels*, Penguin, 1972.

BETEILLE, A., *Social Inequality*, Penguin, 1969.

BIRNBAUM, N., *The Sociological Study of Ideology 1940–60*, Blackwell, 1962.

BOTTOMORE, T., *Sociology*, Allen & Unwin, 1962.

BOTTOMORE, T., *Classes in Modern Society*, Allen & Unwin, 1965.

BOULDING, K., *Economic Analysis*, Harper & Row, 1941.

BRAMSON, L., *The Political Context of Sociology*, Princeton University Press, 1961.

BRAMSON, L. and GOETHALS, G. (eds), *War*, Basic Books, 1968.

BRAYBROOKE, D. (ed.), *Philosophical Problems of the Social Sciences*, Macmillan, 1965.

BREDEMEIER, H. and STEPHENSON, R., *The Analysis of Social Systems*, Holt, Rinehart & Winston, 1970.

BROWN, J., *Techniques of Persuasion*, Penguin, 1964.

CALVERT, P., *Revolution*, Pall Mall, 1970.

CARLTON, E., *Patterns of Belief*, vols 1 and 2, Allen & Unwin, 1973.

CARLTON, E., 'The Unitarian Movement in England', M.Phil thesis, University of London, 1972.

COHEN, P., *Modern Social Theory*, Heinemann, 1968.

COTGROVE, S., *The Science of Society*, Allen & Unwin, 1967.

DAHRENDORF, R., *Class and Class Conflict in an Industrial Society*, Routledge & Kegan Paul, 1959.

DAVIS, K., *Human Society*, Macmillan, 1966.

DURKHEIM, E., *The Division of Labour in Society*, Macmillan, 1933.

DURKHEIM, E., *Education and Society* (1911), Free Press, 1956.

DURKHEIM, E., *The Rules of Sociological Method*, Free Press, 1964.

DURKHEIM, E., *The Elementary Forms of the Religious Life* (1915), Allen & Unwin, 1968.

EISENSTADT, S. N. (ed.), *Readings in Social Evolution and Development*, Pergamon, 1970.

ELIADE, M. and KITAGAWA, J. (eds), *The History of Religions*, University of Chicago Press, 1959.

ETZIONI, A., *Studies in Social Change*, Holt, Rinehart & Winston, 1966.

ETZIONI, A. and WENGLINSKY, M. (eds), *War and its Prevention*, Harper & Row, 1970.

EVANS-PRITCHARD, E. E., *Theories of Primitive Religion*, Oxford University Press, 1965.

FIRTH, R., *Elements of Social Organisation*, Watts, 1951.

FLETCHER, R., *The Making of Sociology*, vol. 1 Michael Joseph, 1971.

FREIRE, P., *Pedagogy of the Oppressed*, Penguin, 1973.

FRIEDRICH, C. (ed.), *Totalitarianism*, Harvard University Press, 1954.

FRIEDRICH, C. and BRZEZINSKI, Z., *Totalitarian Dictatorship and Autocracy*, Praeger, 1965.

GARDINER, P., *The Nature of Historical Explanation*, Oxford University Press, 1961.

GARDINER, P. (ed.), *Theories of History*, Free Press, 1959.

GELLNER, E., 'Is Belief Really Necessary?', *Hibbert Journal* (1957).

GELLNER, E., *Thought and Change*, Weidenfeld & Nicolson, 1963.

GERTH, H. and WRIGHT MILLS, C., *From Max Weber*, Routledge & Kegan Paul, 1948.

GINSBERG, M., *On the Diversity of Morals*, Heinemann, 1956.

GINSBERG, M., *Reason and Unreason in Society*, Heinemann, 1957.

GOODE, W., *The Family*, Prentice-Hall, 1965.

GOODY, J., 'Religion and Ritual: the Definitional Problem', *British Journal of Sociology* 12 (1961).

GOULD, J. and KOLB, W. (eds), *Dictionary of the Social Sciences*, Tavistock, 1964.

HARRIS, M., FRIED, M. and MURPHY, R. (eds), *War: the Anthropology of Armed Conflict and Aggression*, Natural History Press, 1968.

HARRIS, N., *Beliefs and Society*, Penguin, 1971.

HEILBRONNER, R., *The Making of Economic Society*, Prentice-Hall, 1962.

HERBERG, W., *Protestant-Catholic-Jew*, Doubleday, 1956.

BIBLIOGRAPHY

HENRIQUES, F., *Prostitution and Society*, MacGibbon & Kee, 1962–8.

HOBHOUSE, L. T., *Morals in Evolution*, London, 1906.

HORTON, R., 'A Definition of Religion and its Uses', *Journal of the Royal Anthropological Institute* 90 (1960).

HOSPERS, J., *Human Conduct*, Harcourt Brace, 1961.

HOULT, T., *The Sociology of Religion*, Dryden, 1958.

ILLICH, I., *Celebration of Awareness*, Penguin, 1971.

JAMES, E. O., *The Beginnings of Religion*, Hutchinson, 1948.

JOAD, C. E. M., *Philosophy*, English Universities Press, 1960.

JOHNSON, H., *Sociology: a Systematic Introduction*, Routledge & Kegan Paul, 1965.

JOUVENEL, B. de, *The Art of Conjecture*, Weidenfeld & Nicolson, 1967.

KARDINER, A. and LINTON, R., *The Individual and His Society*, Columbia University Press, 1939.

KRICH, H. and GREENWALD, A., *The Prostitute in Literature*, Ballantine, 1960.

LAPIERE, R., *A Theory of Social Control*, McGraw-Hill, 1954.

LEACH, E., *Lévi-Strauss*, Fontana, 1970.

LEIRIS, M., *Race and Culture*, Unesco, 1951.

LENSKI, G., *Power and Privilege*, McGraw-Hill, 1966.

LÉVI-STRAUSS, C., *The Savage Mind*, University of Chicago Press, 1966.

LIPSEY, R., *Introduction to Positive Economics*, Weidenfeld & Nicolson, 1965.

LITTLEJOHN, J., *Social Stratification*, Allen & Unwin, 1972.

LOUCH, A. R., *Explanation and Human Action*, Blackwell, 1966.

MACRAE, D. G., *Ideology and Society*, Heinemann, 1961.

MALINOWSKI, B., *Magic, Science and Religion*, Garden City Press, 1954.

MANNHEIM, K., *Ideology and Utopia*, Harcourt, Brace, 1955.

MARX, K. and ENGELS, F., *The German Ideology*, Foreign Languages Publishing House, 1965.

MARX, K. and ENGELS, F., *The Communist Manifesto*, Penguin, 1967.

MAYER, K., *Class and Society*, Random House, 1955.

MERTON, R., 'Priorities in Scientific Discovery', *American Sociological Review* XXII (1957).

MERTON, R., *Social Theory and Social Structure*, Free Press, 1957.

MITCHELL, G. D., *Sociology*, University Tutorial Press, 1959.

MONTAGUE, M. ASHLEY, *Man's Most Dangerous Myth*, Oxford University Press, 1970.

NOTTINGHAM, E., *Religion and Society*, Random House, 1964.

NOWELL-SMITH, P., *Ethics*, Penguin, 1954.

OAKESHOTT, M., *Rationalism and Other Essays*, Methuen, 1962.

PARETO, V., *The Mind and Society*, Harcourt, Brace, 1935.

PARETO, V., *Sociological Writings* (ed. S. Finer), Pall Mall, 1966.

PARSONS, T., *The Social System*, Free Press, 1951.

PARSONS, T., *Societies: Evolutionary and Comparative Perspectives*, Prentice-Hall, 1966.

PARSONS, T., *Essays in Sociological Theory, Pure and Applied*, Free Press, rev. edn, 1954.

PARSONS, T. and SMELSER, N., *Economy and Society*, Routledge & Kegan Paul, 1956.

PLAMENATZ, J., *Ideologies*, Macmillan, 1971.

POPPER, K., *The Poverty of Historicism*, Routledge & Kegan Paul, 1960.

POPPER, K., *The Open Society and its Enemies*, vols 1 and 2, Routledge & Kegan Paul, 1965.

REITLINGER, G., *The Final Solution*, Valentine Mitchell, 1953.

REX, J., *Key Problems of Sociological Theory*, Routledge & Kegan Paul, 1961.

RICHARDSON, A., *Christian Apologetics*, SCM, 1947.

ROBERTSON, R., *The Sociological Interpretation of Religion*, Blackwell, 1970.

ROBERTSON, R. (ed.), *Readings in the Sociology of Religion*, Penguin, 1969.

RUSSELL, B., *A History of Western Philosophy*, Allen & Unwin, 1948.

RYAN, A., *The Philosophy of the Social Sciences*, Macmillan, 1970.

RYECROFT, C. (ed.), *Psychoanalysis Observed*, Constable, 1966.

SARGENT, W., *Battle for the Mind*, Pan, 1959.

SHIRER, W., *The Rise and Fall of the Third Reich*, Pan, 1965.

SIMMEL, G., *The Sociology of Georg Simmel*, Free Press, 1950.

SMELSER, N. and LIPSET, S. (eds), *Social Structure and Mobility in Economic Development*, Routledge & Kegan Paul, 1966.

SOREL, G., *Reflections on Violence*, Free Press, 1950.

SOROKIN, P., *Fads and Foibles of Sociology*, Regnery, 1956.

SOROKIN, P., *Social and Cultural Dynamics*, Bedminster, 1962.

SUTTON, F. et al., *The American Business Creed*, Harvard University Press, 1956.

TOYNBEE, A., *War and Civilization*, Oxford University Press, 1950.

TREVOR-ROPER, H. R., *The Last Days of Hitler*, Macmillan, 1947.

VAGTS, A., *A History of Militarism*, Free Press, rev. ed. 1959.

WACH, J., *The Sociology of Religion*, Kegan Paul, 1945.

WALTZ, K., *Man, War and the State*, Columbia University Press, 1959.

WEBER, M., *The Protestant Ethic and the Spirit of Capitalism*, Scribner, 1930.

WEBER, M., *Essays in Sociology* (trans. H. Gerth and C. Wright Mills), Routledge & Kegan Paul, 1948.

WEBER, M., *The Theory of Social and Economic Organisation*, Free Press, 1964.

WEBER, M., *Sociology of Religion*, Methuen, 1965.

WELLS, A., *Social Institutions*, Heinemann, 1970.

WORSLEY, P. et al., *Introducing Sociology*, Penguin, 1970.

WRIGHT, Q., *A Study of War*, University of Chicago Press, 1942.

WRIGHT MILLS, C., *The Sociological Imagination*, Oxford University Press, 1967.

YINGER, J. M., *Religion, Society and the Individual*, Macmillan, 1957.

## Traditional Societies

*General*

BALSDON, J. P. V. D., *Roman Civilization*, Penguin, 1965.

BELLAH, R., *Tokugawa Religion: the Values of Pre-industrial Japan*, Free Press, 1957.

BLANCH, L., *Pavilions of the Heart*, Weidenfeld & Nicolson, 1974.

BODDE, D., *China's Cultural Tradition*, Rinehart, 1957.

BULLOCK, A. (ed.), *Asia: the Dawn of History*, Marshall Cavendish, 1968.
CARCOPINO, J., *Daily Life in Ancient Rome*, Routledge & Kegan Paul, 1970.
CERAM, C. W., *A Picture History of Archaeology*, Thames & Hudson, 1957.
CHAMBERS, M. (ed.), *The Fall of Rome*, Holt, Rinehart & Winston, 1970.
CHUNG-LI-CHANG, *The Chinese Gentry*, University of Washington Press, 1955.
CHILDE, V. G., *Man Makes Himself*, Watts, 1948.
CHILDE, V. G., *What Happened in History*, Penguin, 1960.
COHEN, P., 'Theories of Myth', *Man* (September 1969).
COLLIER, J., *Indians of the Americas*, Mentor, 1956.
CONTENAU, G., *Everyday Life in Babylon and Assyria*, Edward Arnold, 1969.
COON, C., *The History of Man*, Penguin, 1962.
DARLINGTON, C., *The Evolution of Man and Society*, Allen & Unwin, 1969.
DAWSON, R., *Imperial China*, Hutchinson, 1972.
DRIVER, H. E. (ed.), *The Americas on the Eve of Discovery*, Prentice-Hall, 1964.
EBERHARD, W., *A History of China*, Routledge & Kegan Paul, 1950.
EISENSTADT, S. N., 'Oriental Despotism', *Journal of Asian Studies*, 1957–8.
ELIADE, M., *Myth and Reality*, Allen & Unwin, 1963.
EVANS-PRITCHARD, E., *Nuer Religion*, Oxford University Press, 1956.
FIRTH, R. (ed.), *Man and Culture*, Routledge & Kegan Paul, 1963.
FORDE, D., *Habitat, Economy and Society*, Methuen, 1968.
FRERE, S., *Britannia*, Routledge & Kegan Paul, 1967.
GABEL, C. (ed.), *Man Before History*, Prentice-Hall, 1964.
GIBB, H. A. R. and BOWEN, H., *Islamic Society and the West*, Oxford University Press, 1950.
GOODE, W., *Religion among the Primitives*, Free Press, 1964.
GRANT, M., *The Gladiators*, Penguin, 1971.
GREEN, P., 'The First Sicilian Slave War', *Past & Present* 20 (November 1961).
GURNEY, O. R., *The Hittites*, Penguin, 1964.
HARDEN, D., *The Phoenicians*, Penguin, 1971.
INNES, H., *The Conquistadors*, Collins, 1969.
JAMES, E. O., *Sacrifice and Sacrament*, Thames & Hudson, 1962.
JAMES, E. O., *The Beginnings of Religion*, Hutchinson, 1948.
JARVIS WOOD, H., *Pharaoh to Farouk*, John Murray, 1955.
KELLETT, S., *A Short History of Religions*, Penguin, 1960.
KENYON, F., *The Bible and Archaeology*, Harrap, 1940.
KENYON, K., *Archaeology in the Holy Land*, Benn, 1960.
KIEFFER, O., *Sexual Life in Ancient Rome*, Abbey, 1971.
KIRK, G. S., *Myth*, Cambridge University Press, 1973.
KRAMER, S., *The Sumerians*, University of Chicago Press, 1973.
*The Larousse Dictionary of the Ancient World*, Hamlyn, 1963.
LEACH, E. R., *The Political Systems of Highland Burma*, Bell, 1964.
LERNER, D., *The Passing of Traditional Society*, Free Press, 1958.
LEWIS, B., *A History of the Arabs*, Hutchinson, 1956.
MACRAE, D., 'Critique of Wittfogel's Thesis', *Man* (June 1959).
MAINE, SIR H., *Ancient Law*, Dent, 1906.
MALLETT, M., *The Borgias*, Bodley Head, 1969.

306

MARWICK, M. (ed.), *Readings in Witchcraft and Sorcery*, Penguin, 1972.
MILLAR, F., *The Romans and their Neighbours*, Weidenfeld & Nicolson, 1970.
MOOREHEAD, A., *The White Nile*, Hamish Hamilton, 1962.
MORRIS, DALE W., *The Christian Origins of Social Revolt*, Allen & Unwin, 1949.
MORRIS, D., *The Washing of the Spears*, Sphere, 1968.
NORBU, T., *Tibet is My Country*, Hart-Davis, 1960.
OLMSTEAD, H. *A History of Persia*, University of Chicago Press, 1948.
OLMSTEAD, H., *History of Assyria*, University of Chicago Press, 1960.
OPPENHEIM, A. LEO, *Ancient Mesopotamia*, University of Chicago Press, 1964.
PAYNE, R., *The Roman Triumph*, Robert Hale, 1962.
PRESCOTT, W., *The History of the Conquest of Mexico* (abridged), University of Chicago Press, 1966.
RADCLIFFE-BROWN, A. R., *Structure and Function in Primitive Society*, Cohen & West, 1952.
REDFIELD, R., *The Primitive World and its Transformations*, Cornell University Press, 1953.
RITTER, E., *Shaka, Zulu*, Panther, 1967.
ROEHL, R., *Patterns and Structure of Demand 1000–1500* AD, Economic History of Europe series, Fontana, 1970.
ROSTOVTZEFF, M., *Social and Economic History of the Roman Empire*, Oxford University Press, 1957.
ROSTOVTZEFF, M., *Rome*, Oxford University Press, 1963.
ROUX, G., *Ancient Iraq*, Penguin, 1964.
SCULLARD, H., *From the Gracchi to Nero*, Methuen, 1965.
SJOBERG, G., *The Pre-Industrial City*, Free Press, 1965.
SOUTHERN, R., *The Making of the Middle Ages*, Hutchinson, 1967.
THRUPP, S., *Medieval Industry 1000–1500* AD, Economic History of Europe series, Fontana, 1970.
TOYNBEE, A., *A Study of History*, Oxford University Press, 1970.
VAUX, R. de, *Ancient Israel*, Longmans, 1961.
WEBER, M., *The Religion of India*, Free Press, 1958.
WEBER, M., *The Religion of China*, Free Press, 1964.
WITTFOGEL, K., *Oriental Despotism*, Yale University Press, 1957.
ZAEHNER, R., *Hinduism*, Oxford University Press, 1962.

*Egypt*

ALDRED, C., *The Egyptians*, University of Chicago Press, 1956.
ALDRED, C., *Akhenaten*, Abacus, 1968.
ALDRED, C., *Egypt to the End of the Old Kingdom*, Book Club Associates, 1974.
BLACKER, C. and LOEWE, M., *Ancient Cosmologies*, Allen & Unwin, 1975.
BRANDON, S., *Religion in Ancient History*, Allen & Unwin, 1969.
BREASTED, J. H., *Ancient Records of Egypt*, University of Chicago Press, 1906–7.
BREASTED, J. H., *A History of Egypt*, Hodder & Stoughton, 1946.

307

BREASTED, J. H., *The Development of Religion and Thought in Ancient Egypt* (1912), Harper & Row, 1959.

BREASTED, J. H., 'Akhenaton: the First Monotheist' in R. Christen and H. Hazelton (eds), *Monotheism and Moses*, D. C. Heath, 1969.

*The Cambridge Ancient History*, Cambridge University Press.

CARTER, H., *The Tomb of Tutankhamun*, Cassell, 1922–3.

COTTRELL, L., *Life Under the Pharaohs*, Evans, 1955.

COTTRELL, L., *The Lost Pharaohs*, Pan, 1956.

COTTRELL, L., *The Penguin Book of Lost Worlds*, vol. 1, Penguin, 1966.

COVENSKY, M., *The Ancient Near Eastern Tradition*, Harper, Row, 1966.

DAVIES, N. de G. and FAULKNER, R. D., 'A Syrian Trading Venture to Egypt', *Journal of Egyptian Archaeology* XXXIII (1947).

DESROCHES-NOBLECOURT, C., *Tutankhamun*, Book Club Associates, 1972.

DUNNE, J., *The City of the Gods*, Sheldon, 1965.

EDGERTON, W., 'The Government and the Governed in the Egyptian Empires', *Journal of Near Eastern Studies* VI (1947).

EDWARDS, I. S., *The Pyramids of Egypt*, Michael Joseph, 1972.

EISENSTADT, S. N., *The Political Systems of Empires*, Free Press, 1969.

EISENSTADT, S. N. (ed.), *The Decline of Empires*, Prentice-Hall, 1967.

EMERY, W., *Archaic Egypt*, Penguin, 1972.

ERMAN, A., *Life in Ancient Egypt*, Macmillan, 1894.

ERMAN, A., *The Literature of the Ancient Egyptians*, Routledge, 1927.

ERMAN, A., *The Ancient Egyptians*, Harper & Row, 1965.

FAIRSERVIS, W., *Ancient Kingdoms of the Nile*, Mentor, 1962.

FAKHRY, A., *The Pyramids*, University of Chicago Press, 1961.

FAULKNER, R., *The Ancient Egyptian Pyramid Texts*, Oxford University Press, 1969.

FAULKNER, R., 'Egyptian Military Organisation', *Journal of Egyptian Archaeology* XXXIX (1953).

FINEGAN, J., *Light from the Ancient Near East*, Princeton University Press, 1969.

FOX, P., *Tutankhamun's Treasure*, Oxford University Press, 1951.

FRANKFORT, H., *Kingship and the Gods*, University of Chicago Press, 1948.

FRANKFORT, H. et al., *Before Philosophy*, Penguin, 1954.

FRANKFORT, H., *The Birth of Civilization in the Near East*, Anchor, 1956.

FRANKFORT, H., *Ancient Egyptian Religion*, Harper & Row, 1961.

GARDINER, A., *The Attitude of the Ancient Egyptians to Death and The Dead*, Cambridge University Press, 1935.

GARDINER, A., *The Wilbour Papyrus*, Oxford University Press, 1941, 1948–52.

GARDINER, A., *Ancient Egyptian Onomastica*, Oxford University Press, 1952.

GARDINER, A., *Egypt of the Pharaohs*, Oxford University Press, 1961.

GRANT, M., *Ancient History*, Hutchinson, 1952.

HARRIS, J., *Egyptian Art*, Spring Books, 1966.

HAYES, W., *The Sceptre of Egypt*, Cambridge University Press, 1953.

HERRMANN, S., *A History of Israel in Old Testament Times*, SCM, 1973.

*Introductory Guide to the Egyptian Collections*, British Museum, 1964.

KADISH, G. (ed.), *Studies in Honour of John A. Wilson*, University of Chicago Press, 1969.

MANCHIP WHITE, J., *Ancient Egypt*, Allen & Unwin, 1970.

MENDELSSOHN, K., *The Riddle of the Pyramids*, Thames & Hudson, 1974.

MONTET, P., *Everyday Life in Ancient Egypt*, Edward Arnold, 1958.

MOSCATI, S., *The Face of the Ancient Orient*, Anchor, 1962.

MURRAY, M., *The Splendour that was Egypt*, Sidgwick & Jackson, 1963.

PARETI, L. *et al.*, *The Ancient World* Vol. 2, Allen & Unwin, 1965.

PETRIE, W., FLINDERS, *Social Life in Ancient Egypt*, Constable, 1930.

POLANYI, K. (ed.), *Trade and Market in the Early Empires*, Free Press, 1957.

RINGGREN, H., *Religions of the Ancient Near East*, SPCK, 1973.

SABLOFF, J. A. and LAMBERG-KARLOVSKY, C. (eds), *The Rise and Fall of Civilizations*, Cummings, 1974.

SEWELL, B., *Egypt Under the Pharaohs*, Evans, 1968.

STEINDORFF, G. and SEELE, K., *When Egypt Ruled the East*, University of Chicago Press, 1957.

TOMPKINS, P., *Secrets of the Great Pyramid*, Allen Lane, 1973.

WEECH, E., 'Civilizations of the Near East' in W. Weech (ed.), *History of the World*, Odhams, 1946.

WINLOCK, H., *The Rise and Fall of the Middle Kingdom in Thebes*, New York, 1947.

WILSON, J. A., *The Culture of Ancient Egypt*, University of Chicago Press, 1956.

WILSON, J. A., 'Authority and Law in Ancient Egypt' in S. N. Eisenstadt, *The Decline of Empires*, Prentice-Hall, 1967.

*Greece*

ADCOCK, F., *The Greek and Macedonian Art of War* University of California Press, 1957.

ADKINS, A., *Merit and Responsibility: a Study in Greek Values*, Clarendon Press, 1960.

ANDREWES, A., *The Greek Tyrants*, Hutchinson, 1956.

ANDREWES, A., *Greek Society*, Penguin, 1967.

ARISTOPHANES, *Lysistrata* in D. Alastos (ed.), *Aristophanes: Two Plays*, Zeno, 1953.

ARISTOTLE, *Politics* (trans. B. Jowett), Clarendon Press, 1923.

ARMSTRONG, A. H., *An Introduction to Ancient Philosophy*, Methuen, 1968.

BEAZLEY, J. D. and ASHMOLE, B., *Greek Sculpture and Painting*, Cambridge University Press, 1966.

BECK, F., *Greek Education*, Oxford University Press, 1964.

BENGTSON, H. (ed.), *The Greeks and the Persians*, Weidenfeld & Nicolson, 1969.

BOARDMAN, J., *The Greeks Overseas*, Penguin, 1964.

BOWRA, C. M., *The Greek Experience*, Weidenfeld & Nicolson, 1957.

BOWRA, C. M., *Periclean Athens*, Penguin, 1971.

BURN, A., *Alexander the Great and the Middle East*, Penguin, 1973.

BURY, J., *A History of Greece to the Death of Alexander the Great* (rev. by R. Meiggs), Oxford University Press, 1974.

CARPENTER, R., *Beyond the Pillars of Hercules*, Tandem, 1973.

CARY, M. and HAARHOF, T., *Life and Thought in the Greek and Roman World*, Methuen, 1957.

CASTLE, E. B., *Ancient Education and Today*, Penguin, 1961.

CLASTER, J. (ed.), *Athenian Democracy*, Holt, Rinehart & Winston, 1967.

CORNFORD, F. M., *From Religion to Philosophy*, Harper, 1957.

COTTRELL, L., *The Lion Gate*, Evans, 1963.

COULANGES, F. de, *The Ancient City* (1864), Doubleday, 1960.

D'AGOSTINO, B., *Monuments of Civilization: Greece*, Cassell, 1974.

DEVAMBEZ, P. *et al.*, *The Praeger Encyclopaedia of Ancient Greek Civilization*, Praeger, 1967.

DODDS, E. R., *The Greeks and the Irrational*, University of California Press, 1951.

EHRENBERG, V., *Man, State and Deity*, Methuen, 1974.

EHRENBERG, V., *The People of Aristophanes*, Oxford University Press, 1951.

EHRENBERG, V., *From Solon to Socrates*, Methuen, 1968.

FERGUSON, J., *Socrates*, Macmillan, 1970.

FERGUSON, W., *Greek Imperialism*, Houghton Mifflin, 1913.

FIELD, G. C., *Plato and His Contemporaries*, Methuen, 1967.

FINLEY, M. (ed.), *Slavery in Classical Antiquity*, Heffer, 1964.

FINLEY, M. I., *The World of Odysseus*, Penguin, 1962.

FINLEY, M. I., *The Ancient Greeks*, Penguin, 1963.

FINLEY, M. I., *Early Greece: the Bronze and Archaic Ages*, Chatto & Windus, 1970.

FINLEY, M. I., *Aspects of Antiquity*, Penguin, 1972.

FINLEY, M. I., *The Ancient Economy*, Chatto & Windus, 1973.

FLACELIERE, R., *Daily Life in Greece*, Weidenfeld & Nicolson, 1965.

FLACELIERE, R., *Love in Ancient Greece*, Westport, 1973.

FORREST, W., *A History of Sparta*, Hutchinson, 1968.

FRAZER, SIR, J., *The New Golden Bough*, Anchor, 1961.

FREEMAN, K., *Greek City States*, Norton, 1963.

FRENCH, A., 'The Economic Background to Solon's Reforms', *Classical Quarterly* 1 and 2 (1956).

FULLER, J., *The Decisive Battles of the Western World*, vol. 1, Paladin, 1970.

GARDINER, E., *Athletics of the Ancient World*, Clarendon Press, 1930.

GARLAN, YVON, *War in the Ancient World*, Chatto & Windus, 1975.

GLOTZ, G., *Ancient Greece at Work*, Knopf, 1926.

GLOTZ, G., *The Greek City and its Institutions* (1929), Routledge & Kegan Paul, 1968.

GOMME, A. W., *Essays in History and Literature*, Blackwell, 1937.

GOULDNER, A., *Enter Plato*, Routledge & Kegan Paul, 1967.

GRAVES, R., *The Greek Myths*, Penguin, 1966.

GREEN, P., *Ancient Greece*, Thames & Hudson, 1973.

GREEN, P., *Alexander the Great*, Weidenfeld & Nicolson, 1973.

GUTHRIE, W. K. C., *The Greek Philosophers*, Cambridge University Press, 1950.

GUTHRIE, W. K. C., *A History of Greek Philosophy*, vols 1–3, Cambridge University Press, 1962–9.

HAMMOND, N. G. L., *A History of Greece to 322 BC*, Clarendon Press, 1967.

HASEBROEK, J., *Trade and Politics in Ancient Greece*, Bell, 1933.

HAWKES, J., *Dawn of the Gods*, Chatto & Windus, 1968.

HAYWOOD, A. M., *The Ancient World*, Mackay, 1971.

HERODOTUS, *Histories*, Penguin, 1954.

HESIOD, *Works and Days* (trans. R. Lattimore), University of Michigan Press, 1959.

HIGNETT, C., *History of the Athenian Constitution*, Oxford University Press, 1953.

HOMER, *The Odyssey* (trans. E. V. Rieu), Penguin, 1945.

HOMER, *The Iliad* (trans. E. V. Rieu), Penguin, 1947.

JONES, A. H. M., *Athenian Democracy*, Blackwell, 1957.

JONES, A. H. M., *Sparta*, Blackwell, 1968.

JONES, J., *Law and Legal Theory of the Greeks*, Oxford University Press, 1956.

KIRK, G. S., *The Nature of Greek Myths*, Penguin, 1974.

KITTO, H. D. F., *The Greeks*, Penguin, 1951.

LACEY, W., *The Family in Classical Greece*, Thames & Hudson, 1968.

LAISTNER, M., *Greek Economics*, Dent, 1923.

LESKY, A., *History of Greek Literature*, Barnes & Noble, 1966.

LIVINGSTONE, R., *The Legacy of Greece*, Oxford University Press, 1969.

LICHT, H., *Sexual Life in Ancient Greece*, Routledge, 1935.

LLOYD-JONES, H. (ed.), *The Greek World*, Penguin, 1965.

LOWES DICKINSON, G., *Plato and His Dialogues*, Penguin, 1947.

LOWES DICKINSON, G., *The Greek View of Life*, Methuen, 1957.

MACDOWELL, D., *Athenian Homicide Law*, Manchester University Press, 1963.

MARROU, H., *A History of Education in Antiquity* (trans. G. Lamb), Sheed & Ward, 1956.

MICHELL, H., *The Economics of Ancient Greece*, Oxford University Press, 1940.

MICHELL, H., *Sparta*, Cambridge University Press, 1952.

NILSSON, M., *Greek Popular Religion*, Columbia University Press, 1940.

PARKE, H. W. and WORMELL, D. E., *The Delphic Oracle*, Oxford University Press, 1956.

PLATO, *The Dialogues of Plato* (trans. B. Jowett), Clarendon Press, 1953.

PLATO, *The Republic* (trans. H. D. P. Lee), Penguin, 1964.

PLUTARCH, *The Rise and Fall of Athens*, Penguin, 1960.

RHODES, P., *The Athenian Boule*, Oxford University Press, 1972.

ROCHE, P., *The Orestes Plays of Aeschylus*, Mentor, 1957.

ROCHE, P., *The Oedipus Plays of Sophocles*, Mentor, 1958.

ROMILLY, J. de, *Thucydides and Athenian Imperialism*, Oxford University Press, 1942.

SELTMAN, C., *The Twelve Olympians*, Pan, 1952.

SELTMAN, C., *Women in Antiquity*, Pan, 1956.

SIHLER, E., *Hellenic Civilization*, Columbia University Press, 1920.

SINCLAIR, T., *History of Greek Political Thought*, Routledge & Kegan Paul, 1961.

SNODGRASS, A., *Early Greek Armour and Weapons*, Edinburgh University Press, 1964.

STARR, C., *The Origins of Greek Civilization*, Knopf, 1961.

STAVELEY, E., *Greek and Roman Voting and Elections*, Thames & Hudson, 1975.

STOBART, J., *The Glory that was Greece*, Sidgwick & Jackson, 1964.

THOMSON, G., *Studies in Ancient Greek Society*, Lawrence & Wishart, 1955.

THUCYDIDES, *History of the Peloponnesian War* (trans. R. Warner), Penguin, 1954.

TOYNBEE, A., *Greek Civilization and Character*, Mentor, 1953.

TOYNBEE, A., *Greek Historical Thought*, Mentor, 1952.

TRYPANIS, C., *The Penguin Book of Greek Verse*, Penguin, 1971.

USHER, S., *The Historians of Greece and Rome*, Hamish Hamilton, 1969.

WALBANK, F. W., 'The Causes of Greek Decline', *Journal of Hellenic Studies* 64 (1944).

WEBSTER, T. B. L., *Everyday Life in Classical Athens*, Methuen, 1969.

WEBSTER, T. B. L., *Athenian Culture and Society*, Batsford, 1973.

WILLETTS, R., *Ancient Crete*, Batsford, 1969.

XENOPHON, *A History of My Times* (*Hellenica*) (trans. R. Warner), Penguin, 1969.

ZIMMERN, A., *The Greek Commonwealth*, Clarendon Press, 1911.

# Index

This is primarily a subject index which covers the main text only. Further references, especially to the authors cited, can be found in the Notes pp. 244–98.

313

131–51; festivals, drama and music, 94–5, 96, 97, 121, 123, 145, 147, 148, 222, 226–8, 239; legal organisation, 145, 171–5, 235; metics (resident aliens), 62, 72, 112, 113, 114, 115–16, 144, 145, 170, 174, 176, 193, 194, 197, 222, 236; military organisation and militarism, 170, 180, 191–203; ostracism, 18, 169, 174–5; Peloponnesian War, 51, 70, 87, 117, 119, 120, 143, 147, 168, 169, 175, 194, 195, 196, 197, 198, 199, 201, 202, 225, 227; political processes, 32, 63, 111, 156, 157, 165–76, 202, 235; population and development, 10, 72ff, 111, 113–14, 143; punishments, 167, 172, 173–4; reforms, 34, 73–4, 111, 141, 166, 167–8; religion, 37, 38, 73, 89–90, 96–7, 115, 116, 149–50, 151, 161–2, 163, 169, 170, 175, 176, 200–3, 206, 207, 208, 209, 220–31, 235, 239; respect for aged, 89, 142; slavery, 10, 62, 88, 110, 112, 113, 114, 115–20, 144, 145, 147–8, 169, 173, 174, 194, 197, 198, 199, 223, 235, 236; taxes, taxation, 146–7, 149; tribute, 147, 148, 149; tyrants (tyranny), 73, 157, 199, 225; women, 18, 86–7, 96, 112, 121–3, 173; see also Socialisation and Social differentiation
Atlantis, 56
Attica, see Athens
Atum, 140, 210, 211, 216
Augustus, 50
Avaris, 185
Ay, 185
Aztecs, 6, 30, 43

Babylonia, see Mesopotamia
Bacchiadae, 73
Bakenkhonson, 162
Bast, Bastit (cat-goddess), 109, 214
Bellah, Robert, 126
Bengtson, H., 114
Berger, Peter, 30

Bocchoris, 163
Bogotia, 141
Bottomore, T. B., 2
Boule (Council), see Athenis, political processes
Bowra, C. M., 150
Braidwood, R., 44, 55
Breasted, J. H., 209
Buddhism, 101, 207
Buganda, 16
Buto, 65
Byblos, 215
Byzantium, 71, 127

Caligula, 50
Cambodia, 47
Cambyses, 82
Canaan, see Israel
Carthage, Carthaginians, 144, 145, 196
Ceylon (Sri Lanka), 47
Chalcedon, 71
Chalcis, 71
Childe, Gordon, 44, 52, 54, 55
China: Hwang-ho Valley culture, 42; traditional, 16, 29, 48, 49, 59, 91, 92, 101–2, 127, 130, 207
Chios, 196
Christianity, 36, 37, 130, 207
Class, see Social differentiation
Cleisthenes, 74, 167, 169, 171, 174
Cleon, 171
Coinage, see Economic systems
Comte, A., 5, 8, 153, 205
Concubinage, 83, 86, 87, 106, 121
Confucianism, 101
Corcyra, 118, 120, 197, 198, 199
Corinth, 71, 73, 118, 122, 198
Cortes, H., 30–1
Cosmic birth, 15–16
Coulborn, Rushton, 56
Covensky, Milton, 42, 43
Crete, 67, 70, 117, 118, 136, 145
Critias, 225
Cultures: Chalcolithic, 41, 44; Metal Age, 41ff; New Stone Age (Neolithic), 41, 44, 64; Old Stone Age (Palaeolithic), 40–1, 44
Cyprus, 69

Webster, T. B., 150
Wheeler, Sir Mortimer, 52
Whitehead, A. N., 33
Wilson, John A., 81–2, 108–9, 136, 159, 164, 210
Witchcraft, 17
Wittfogel, Karl, 47, 48, 49, 50
Women, position of, *see* Concubinage, Divorce, Education, Family, Prostitution, Social differentiation

Xenophanes, 223
Xenophon, 142, 143, 165, 181, 224

Zaleucus, 73
Zeus, 221, 222, 225, 226

# Routledge Social Science Series

Routledge & Kegan Paul    London and Boston

68–74 Carter Lane   London EC4V 5EL
9 Park Street   Boston   Mass 02108

# Contents

*Authors wishing to submit manuscripts for any series in*
*this catalogue should send them to the Social Science Editor,*
*Routledge & Kegan Paul Ltd, 68–74 Carter Lane,*
*London EC4V 5EL*

● *Books so marked are available in paperback*
*All books are in Metric Demy 8vo format (216 × 138mm approx.)*

# International Library of Sociology

*General Editor* John Rex

## GENERAL SOCIOLOGY

**Barnsley, J. H.** The Social Reality of Ethics. *464 pp.*
**Belshaw, Cyril.** The Conditions of Social Performance. *An Exploratory Theory. 144 pp.*
**Brown, Robert.** Explanation in Social Science. *208 pp.*
● Rules and Laws in Sociology. *192 pp.*
**Bruford, W. H.** Chekhov and His Russia. *A Sociological Study. 244 pp.*
**Cain, Maureen E.** Society and the Policeman's Role. *326 pp.*
●**Fletcher, Colin.** Beneath the Surface. *An Account of Three Styles of Sociological Research. 221 pp.*
**Gibson, Quentin.** The Logic of Social Enquiry. *240 pp.*
**Glucksmann, M.** Structuralist Analysis in Contemporary Social Thought. *212 pp.*
**Gurvitch, Georges.** Sociology of Law. *Preface by Roscoe Pound. 264 pp.*
**Hodge, H. A.** Wilhelm Dilthey. *An Introduction. 184 pp.*
**Homans, George C.** Sentiments and Activities. *336 pp.*
**Johnson, Harry M.** Sociology: *a Systematic Introduction. Foreword by Robert K. Merton. 710 pp.*
●**Keat, Russell,** and **Urry, John.** Social Theory as Science. *278 pp.*
**Mannheim, Karl.** Essays on Sociology and Social Psychology. *Edited by Paul Keckskemeti. With Editorial Note by Adolph Lowe. 344 pp.*
  Systematic Sociology: *An Introduction to the Study of Society. Edited by J. S. Erös and Professor W. A. C. Stewart. 220 pp.*
**Martindale, Don.** The Nature and Types of Sociological Theory. *292 pp.*
●**Maus, Heinz.** A Short History of Sociology. *234 pp.*
**Mey, Harald.** Field-Theory. *A Study of its Application in the Social Sciences. 352 pp.*
**Myrdal, Gunnar.** Value in Social Theory: *A Collection of Essays on Methodology. Edited by Paul Streeten. 332 pp.*
**Ogburn, William F.,** and **Nimkoff, Meyer F.** A Handbook of Sociology. *Preface by Karl Mannheim. 656 pp. 46 figures. 35 tables.*
**Parsons, Talcott,** and **Smelser, Neil J.** Economy and Society: *A Study in the Integration of Economic and Social Theory. 362 pp.*
**Podgórecki, Adam.** Practical Social Sciences. *About 200 pp.*
●**Rex, John.** Key Problems of Sociological Theory. *220 pp.*
  Discovering Sociology. *278 pp.*
  Sociology and the Demystification of the Modern World. *282 pp.*
●**Rex, John** (Ed.) Approaches to Sociology. *Contributions by Peter Abell, Frank Bechhofer, Basil Bernstein, Ronald Fletcher, David Frisby, Miriam Glucksmann, Peter Lassman, Herminio Martins, John Rex, Roland Robertson, John Westergaard and Jock Young. 302 pp.*
**Rigby, A.** Alternative Realities. *352 pp.*

**Roche, M.** Phenomenology, Language and the Social Sciences. *374 pp.*
**Sahay, A.** Sociological Analysis. *220 pp.*
**Strasser, Hermann.** The Normative Structure of Sociology. *Conservative and Emancipatory Themes in Social Thought. About 340 pp.*
**Urry, John.** Reference Groups and the Theory of Revolution. *244 pp.*
**Weinberg, E.** Development of Sociology in the Soviet Union. *173 pp.*

## FOREIGN CLASSICS OF SOCIOLOGY

●**Durkheim, Emile.** Suicide. *A Study in Sociology. Edited and with an Introduction by George Simpson. 404 pp.*
Professional Ethics and Civic Morals. *Translated by Cornelia Brookfield. 288 pp.*
●**Gerth, H. H.,** and **Mills, C. Wright.** From Max Weber: *Essays in Sociology. 502 pp.*
●**Tönnies, Ferdinand.** Community and Association. *(Gemeinschaft und Gesellschaft.) Translated and Supplemented by Charles P. Loomis. Foreword by Pitirim A. Sorokin. 334 pp.*

## SOCIAL STRUCTURE

**Andreski, Stanislav.** Military Organization and Society. *Foreword by Professor A. R. Radcliffe-Brown. 226 pp. 1 folder.*
**Coontz, Sydney H.** Population Theories and the Economic Interpretation. *202 pp.*
**Coser, Lewis.** The Functions of Social Conflict. *204 pp.*
**Dickie-Clark, H. F.** Marginal Situation: *A Sociological Study of a Coloured Group. 240 pp. 11 tables.*
**Glaser, Barney,** and **Strauss, Anselm L.** Status Passage. *A Formal Theory. 208 pp.*
**Glass, D. V.** (Ed.) Social Mobility in Britain. *Contributions by J. Berent, T. Bottomore, R. C. Chambers, J. Floud, D. V. Glass, J. R. Hall, H. T. Himmelweit, R. K. Kelsall, F. M. Martin, C. A. Moser, R. Mukherjee, and W. Ziegel. 420 pp.*
**Jones, Garth N.** Planned Organizational Change: *An Exploratory Study Using an Empirical Approach. 268 pp.*
**Kelsall, R. K.** Higher Civil Servants in Britain: *From 1870 to the Present Day. 268 pp. 31 tables.*
**König, René.** The Community. *232 pp. Illustrated.*
●**Lawton, Denis.** Social Class, Language and Education. *192 pp.*
**McLeish, John.** The Theory of Social Change: *Four Views Considered. 128 pp.*
**Marsh, David C.** The Changing Social Structure of England and Wales, 1871-1961. *288 pp.*
●**Mouzelis, Nicos.** Organization and Bureaucracy. *An Analysis of Modern Theories. 240 pp.*
**Mulkay, M. J.** Functionalism, Exchange and Theoretical Strategy. *272 pp.*
**Ossowski, Stanislaw.** Class Structure in the Social Consciousness. *210 pp.*
●**Podgórecki, Adam.** Law and Society. *302 pp.*

## SOCIOLOGY AND POLITICS

**Acton, T. A.** Gypsy Politics and Social Change. *316 pp.*

**Clegg, Stuart.** Power, Rule and Domination. *A Critical and Empirical Understanding of Power in Sociological Theory and Organisational Life. About 300 pp.*

**Hechter, Michael.** Internal Colonialism. *The Celtic Fringe in British National Development, 1536–1966. 361 pp.*

**Hertz, Frederick.** Nationality in History and Politics: *A Psychology and Sociology of National Sentiment and Nationalism. 432 pp.*

**Kornhauser, William.** The Politics of Mass Society. *272 pp. 20 tables.*

●**Kroes, R.** Soldiers and Students. *A Study of Right- and Left-wing Students. 174 pp.*

**Laidler, Harry W.** History of Socialism. *Social-Economic Movements: An Historical and Comparative Survey of Socialism, Communism, Co-operation, Utopianism; and other Systems of Reform and Reconstruction. 992 pp.*

**Lasswell, H. D.** Analysis of Political Behaviour. *324 pp.*

**Mannheim, Karl.** Freedom, Power and Democratic Planning. *Edited by Hans Gerth and Ernest K. Bramstedt. 424 pp.*

**Mansur, Fatma.** Process of Independence. *Foreword by A. H. Hanson. 208 pp.*

**Martin, David A.** Pacifism: *an Historical and Sociological Study. 262 pp.*

**Myrdal, Gunnar.** The Political Element in the Development of Economic Theory. *Translated from the German by Paul Streeten. 282 pp.*

**Wootton, Graham.** Workers, Unions and the State. *188 pp.*

## FOREIGN AFFAIRS: THEIR SOCIAL, POLITICAL AND ECONOMIC FOUNDATIONS

**Mayer, J. P.** Political Thought in France from the Revolution to the Fifth Republic. *164 pp.*

## CRIMINOLOGY

**Ancel, Marc.** Social Defence: *A Modern Approach to Criminal Problems. Foreword by Leon Radzinowicz. 240 pp.*

**Cain, Maureen E.** Society and the Policeman's Role. *326 pp.*

**Cloward, Richard A.,** and **Ohlin, Lloyd E.** Delinquency and Opportunity: *A Theory of Delinquent Gangs. 248 pp.*

**Downes, David M.** The Delinquent Solution. *A Study in Subcultural Theory. 296 pp.*

**Dunlop, A. B.,** and **McCabe, S.** Young Men in Detention Centres. *192 pp.*

**Friedlander, Kate.** The Psycho-Analytical Approach to Juvenile Delinquency: *Theory, Case Studies, Treatment. 320 pp.*

**Glueck, Sheldon,** and **Eleanor.** Family Environment and Delinquency. *With the statistical assistance of Rose W. Kneznek. 340 pp.*

**Lopez-Rey, Manuel.** Crime. *An Analytical Appraisal. 288 pp.*

**Mannheim, Hermann.** Comparative Criminology: *a Text Book. Two volumes. 442 pp. and 380 pp.*

**Morris, Terence.** The Criminal Area: *A Study in Social Ecology. Foreword by Hermann Mannheim. 232 pp. 25 tables. 4 maps.*
**Rock, Paul.** Making People Pay. *338 pp.*
●**Taylor, Ian, Walton, Paul,** and **Young, Jock.** The New Criminology. *For a Social Theory of Deviance. 325 pp.*
●**Taylor, Ian, Walton, Paul,** and **Young, Jock** (Eds). Critical Criminology. *268 pp.*

## SOCIAL PSYCHOLOGY

**Bagley, Christopher.** The Social Psychology of the Epileptic Child. *320 pp.*
**Barbu, Zevedei.** Problems of Historical Psychology. *248 pp.*
**Blackburn, Julian.** Psychology and the Social Pattern. *184 pp.*
●**Brittan, Arthur.** Meanings and Situations. *224 pp.*
**Carroll, J.** Break-Out from the Crystal Palace. *200 pp.*
●**Fleming, C. M.** Adolescence: Its Social Psychology. *With an Introduction to recent findings from the fields of Anthropology, Physiology, Medicine, Psychometrics and Sociometry. 288 pp.*
● The Social Psychology of Education: *An Introduction and Guide to Its Study. 136 pp.*
●**Homans, George C.** The Human Group. *Foreword by Bernard DeVoto. Introduction by Robert K. Merton. 526 pp.*
● Social Behaviour: *its Elementary Forms. 416 pp.*
●**Klein, Josephine.** The Study of Groups. *226 pp. 31 figures. 5 tables.*
**Linton, Ralph.** The Cultural Background of Personality. *132 pp.*
●**Mayo, Elton.** The Social Problems of an Industrial Civilization. *With an appendix on the Political Problem. 180 pp.*
**Ottaway, A. K. C.** Learning Through Group Experience. *176 pp.*
**Plummer, Ken.** Sexual Stigma. *An Interactionist Account. 254 pp.*
**Ridder, J. C. de.** The Personality of the Urban African in South Africa. *A Thermatic Apperception Test Study. 196 pp. 12 plates.*
●**Rose, Arnold M.** (Ed.) Human Behaviour and Social Processes: *an Interactionist Approach. Contributions by Arnold M. Rose, Ralph H. Turner, Anselm Strauss, Everett C. Hughes, E. Franklin Frazier, Howard S. Becker, et al. 696 pp.*
**Smelser, Neil J.** Theory of Collective Behaviour. *448 pp.*
**Stephenson, Geoffrey M.** The Development of Conscience. *128 pp.*
**Young, Kimball.** Handbook of Social Psychology. *658 pp. 16 figures. 10 tables.*

## SOCIOLOGY OF THE FAMILY

**Banks, J. A.** Prosperity and Parenthood: *A Study of Family Planning among The Victorian Middle Classes. 262 pp.*
**Bell, Colin R.** Middle Class Families: *Social and Geographical Mobility. 224 pp.*
**Burton, Lindy.** Vulnerable Children. *272 pp.*
**Gavron, Hannah.** The Captive Wife: *Conflicts of Household Mothers. 190 pp.*

George, Victor, and Wilding, Paul. Motherless Families. 248 pp.
Klein, Josephine. Samples from English Cultures.
   1. Three Preliminary Studies and Aspects of Adult Life in England.
   447 pp.
   2. Child-Rearing Practices and Index. 247 pp.
Klein, Viola. Britain's Married Women Workers. 180 pp.
   The Feminine Character. History of an Ideology. 244 pp.
McWhinnie, Alexina M. Adopted Children. How They Grow Up. 304 pp.
● Morgan, D. H. J. Social Theory and the Family. About 320 pp.
● Myrdal, Alva, and Klein, Viola. Women's Two Roles: Home and Work.
   238 pp. 27 tables.
Parsons, Talcott, and Bales, Robert F. Family: Socialization and Inter-
   action Process. In collaboration with James Olds, Morris Zelditch and
   Philip E. Slater. 456 pp. 50 figures and tables.


SOCIAL SERVICES

Bastide, Roger. The Sociology of Mental Disorder. Translated from the
   French by Jean McNeil. 260 pp.
Carlebach, Julius. Caring For Children in Trouble. 266 pp.
George, Victor. Foster Care. Theory and Practice. 234 pp.
   Social Security: Beveridge and After. 258 pp.
George, V., and Wilding, P. Motherless Families. 248 pp.
● Goetschius, George W. Working with Community Groups. 256 pp.
Goetschius, George W., and Tash, Joan. Working with Unattached Youth.
   416 pp.
Hall, M. P., and Howes, I. V. The Church in Social Work. A Study of
   Moral Welfare Work undertaken by the Church of England. 320 pp.
Heywood, Jean S. Children in Care: the Development of the Service for the
   Deprived Child. 264 pp.
Hoenig, J., and Hamilton, Marian W. The De-Segregation of the Mentally
   Ill. 284 pp.
Jones, Kathleen. Mental Health and Social Policy, 1845-1959. 264 pp.
King, Roy D., Raynes, Norma V., and Tizard, Jack. Patterns of Residential
   Care. 356 pp.
Leigh, John. Young People and Leisure. 256 pp.
● Mays, John. (Ed.) Penelope Hall's Social Services of England and Wales.
   About 324 pp.
Morris, Mary. Voluntary Work and the Welfare State. 300 pp.
Morris, Pauline. Put Away: A Sociological Study of Institutions for the
   Mentally Retarded. 364 pp.
Nokes, P. L. The Professional Task in Welfare Practice. 152 pp.
Timms, Noel. Psychiatric Social Work in Great Britain (1939-1962).
   280 pp.
●    Social Casework: Principles and Practice. 256 pp.
Young, A. F. Social Services in British Industry. 272 pp.
Young, A. F., and Ashton, E. T. British Social Work in the Nineteenth
   Century. 288 pp.

## SOCIOLOGY OF EDUCATION

**Banks, Olive.** Parity and Prestige in English Secondary Education: a Study in Educational Sociology. *272 pp.*

**Bentwich, Joseph.** Education in Israel. *224 pp. 8 pp. plates.*

●**Blyth, W. A. L.** English Primary Education. *A Sociological Description.*
   1. Schools. *232 pp.*
   2. Background. *168 pp.*

**Collier, K. G.** The Social Purposes of Education: *Personal and Social Values in Education. 268 pp.*

**Dale, R. R.,** and **Griffith, S.** Down Stream: *Failure in the Grammar School. 108 pp.*

**Dore, R. P.** Education in Tokugawa Japan. *356 pp. 9 pp. plates.*

**Evans, K. M.** Sociometry and Education. *158 pp.*

●**Ford, Julienne.** Social Class and the Comprehensive School. *192 pp.*

**Foster, P. J.** Education and Social Change in Ghana. *336 pp. 3 maps.*

**Fraser, W. R.** Education and Society in Modern France. *150 pp.*

**Grace, Gerald R.** Role Conflict and the Teacher. *150 pp.*

**Hans, Nicholas.** New Trends in Education in the Eighteenth Century. *278 pp. 19 tables.*

●   Comparative Education: *A Study of Educational Factors and Traditions. 360 pp.*

●**Hargreaves, David.** Interpersonal Relations and Education. *432 pp.*

●   Social Relations in a Secondary School. *240 pp.*

**Holmes, Brian.** Problems in Education. *A Comparative Approach. 336 pp.*

**King, Ronald.** Values and Involvement in a Grammar School. *164 pp.*
   School Organization and Pupil Involvement. *A Study of Secondary Schools.*

●**Mannheim, Karl,** and **Stewart, W. A. C.** An Introduction to the Sociology of Education. *206 pp.*

**Morris, Raymond N.** The Sixth Form and College Entrance. *231 pp.*

●**Musgrove, F.** Youth and the Social Order. *176 pp.*

●**Ottaway, A. K. C.** Education and Society: An Introduction to the Sociology of Education. *With an Introduction by W. O. Lester Smith. 212 pp.*

**Peers, Robert.** Adult Education: *A Comparative Study. 398 pp.*

**Pritchard, D. G.** Education and the Handicapped: *1760 to 1960. 258 pp.*

**Richardson, Helen.** Adolescent Girls in Approved Schools. *308 pp.*

**Stratta, Erica.** The Education of Borstal Boys. *A Study of their Educational Experiences prior to, and during, Borstal Training. 256 pp.*

**Taylor, P. H., Reid, W. A.,** and **Holley, B. J.** The English Sixth Form. *A Case Study in Curriculum Research. 200 pp.*


## SOCIOLOGY OF CULTURE

**Eppel, E. M.,** and **M.** Adolescents and Morality: *A Study of some Moral Values and Dilemmas of Working Adolescents in the Context of a changing Climate of Opinion. Foreword by W. J. H. Sprott. 268 pp. 39 tables.*

●**Fromm, Erich.** The Fear of Freedom. *286 pp.*
● The Sane Society. *400 pp.*
**Mannheim, Karl.** Essays on the Sociology of Culture. *Edited by Ernst Mannheim in co-operation with Paul Kecskemeti. Editorial Note by Adolph Lowe. 280 pp.*
**Weber, Alfred.** Farewell to European History: *or The Conquest of Nihilism. Translated from the German by R. F. C. Hull. 224 pp.*

## SOCIOLOGY OF RELIGION

**Argyle, Michael** and **Beit-Hallahmi, Benjamin.** The Social Psychology of Religion. *About 256 pp.*
**Nelson, G. K.** Spiritualism and Society. *313 pp.*
**Stark, Werner.** The Sociology of Religion. *A Study of Christendom.*
    Volume I. *Established Religion. 248 pp.*
    Volume II. *Sectarian Religion. 368 pp.*
    Volume III. *The Universal Church. 464 pp.*
    Volume IV. *Types of Religious Man. 352 pp.*
    Volume V. *Types of Religious Culture. 464 pp.*
**Turner, B. S.** Weber and Islam. *216 pp.*
**Watt, W. Montgomery.** Islam and the Integration of Society. *320 pp.*

## SOCIOLOGY OF ART AND LITERATURE

**Jarvie, Ian C.** Towards a Sociology of the Cinema. *A Comparative Essay on the Structure and Functioning of a Major Entertainment Industry. 405 pp.*
**Rust, Frances S.** Dance in Society. *An Analysis of the Relationships between the Social Dance and Society in England from the Middle Ages to the Present Day. 256 pp. 8 pp. of plates.*
**Schücking, L. L.** The Sociology of Literary Taste. *112 pp.*
**Wolff, Janet.** Hermeneutic Philosophy and the Sociology of Art. *150 pp.*

## SOCIOLOGY OF KNOWLEDGE

**Diesing, P.** Patterns of Discovery in the Social Sciences. *262 pp.*
●**Douglas, J. D.** (Ed.) Understanding Everyday Life. *370 pp.*
●**Hamilton, P.** Knowledge and Social Structure. *174 pp.*
**Jarvie, I. C.** Concepts and Society. *232 pp.*
**Mannheim, Karl.** Essays on the Sociology of Knowledge. *Edited by Paul Kecskemeti. Editorial Note by Adolph Lowe. 353 pp.*
**Remmling, Gunter W.** The Sociology of Karl Mannheim. *With a Bibliographical Guide to the Sociology of Knowledge, Ideological Analysis, and Social Planning. 255 pp.*

**Remmling, Gunter W.** (Ed.) Towards the Sociology of Knowledge. *Origin and Development of a Sociological Thought Style. 463 pp.*
**Stark, Werner.** The Sociology of Knowledge: *An Essay in Aid of a Deeper Understanding of the History of Ideas. 384 pp.*

## URBAN SOCIOLOGY

**Ashworth, William.** The Genesis of Modern British Town Planning: *A Study in Economic and Social History of the Nineteenth and Twentieth Centuries. 288 pp.*
**Cullingworth, J. B.** Housing Needs and Planning Policy: *A Restatement of the Problems of Housing Need and 'Overspill' in England and Wales. 232 pp. 44 tables. 8 maps.*
**Dickinson, Robert E.** City and Region: *A Geographical Interpretation 608 pp. 125 figures.*
    The West European City: *A Geographical Interpretation. 600 pp. 129 maps. 29 plates.*
● The City Region in Western Europe. *320 pp. Maps.*
**Humphreys, Alexander J.** New Dubliners: *Urbanization and the Irish Family. Foreword by George C. Homans. 304 pp.*
**Jackson, Brian.** Working Class Community: *Some General Notions raised by a Series of Studies in Northern England. 192 pp.*
**Jennings, Hilda.** Societies in the Making: *a Study of Development and Redevelopment within a County Borough. Foreword by D. A. Clark. 286 pp.*
●**Mann, P. H.** An Approach to Urban Sociology. *240 pp.*
**Morris, R. N.,** and **Mogey, J.** The Sociology of Housing. *Studies at Berinsfield. 232 pp. 4 pp. plates.*
**Rosser, C.,** and **Harris, C.** The Family and Social Change. *A Study of Family and Kinship in a South Wales Town. 352 pp. 8 maps.*
●**Stacey, Margaret, Batsone, Eric, Bell, Colin,** and **Thurcott, Anne.** Power, Persistence and Change. *A Second Study of Banbury. 196 pp.*

## RURAL SOCIOLOGY

**Chambers, R. J. H.** Settlement Schemes in Tropical Africa: *A Selective Study. 268 pp.*
**Haswell, M. R.** The Economics of Development in Village India. *120 pp.*
**Littlejohn, James.** Westrigg: *the Sociology of a Cheviot Parish. 172 pp. 5 figures.*
**Mayer, Adrian C.** Peasants in the Pacific. *A Study of Fiji Indian Rural Society. 248 pp. 20 plates.*
**Williams, W. M.** The Sociology of an English Village: *Gosforth. 272 pp. 12 figures. 13 tables.*

## SOCIOLOGY OF INDUSTRY AND DISTRIBUTION

**Anderson, Nels.** Work and Leisure. *280 pp.*

● **Blau, Peter M.,** and **Scott, W. Richard.** Formal Organizations: *a Comparative approach. Introduction and Additional Bibliography by J. H. Smith. 326 pp.*

**Dunkerley, David.** The Foreman. *Aspects of Task and Structure. 192 pp.*

**Eldridge, J. E. T.** Industrial Disputes. *Essays in the Sociology of Industrial Relations. 288 pp.*

**Hetzler, Stanley.** Applied Measures for Promoting Technological Growth. *352 pp.*

Technological Growth and Social Change. *Achieving Modernization. 269 pp.*

**Hollowell, Peter G.** The Lorry Driver. *272 pp.*

**Jefferys, Margot,** *with the assistance of Winifred Moss.* Mobility in the Labour Market: *Employment Changes in Battersea and Dagenham. Preface by Barbara Wootton. 186 pp. 51 tables.*

**Millerson, Geoffrey.** The Qualifying Associations: *a Study in Professionalization. 320 pp.*

● **Oxaal, I., Barnett, T.,** and **Booth, D.** (Eds). Beyond the Sociology of Development. *Economy and Society in Latin America and Africa. 295 pp.*

**Smelser, Neil J.** Social Change in the Industrial Revolution: *An Application of Theory to the Lancashire Cotton Industry, 1770–1840. 468 pp. 12 figures. 14 tables.*

**Williams, Gertrude.** Recruitment to Skilled Trades. *240 pp.*

**Young, A. F.** Industrial Injuries Insurance: *an Examination of British Policy. 192 pp.*

### DOCUMENTARY

**Schlesinger, Rudolf** (Ed.) Changing Attitudes in Soviet Russia.
2. The Nationalities Problem and Soviet Administration. *Selected Readings on the Development of Soviet Nationalities Policies. Introduced by the editor. Translated by W. W. Gottlieb. 324 pp.*

### ANTHROPOLOGY

**Ammar, Hamed.** Growing up in an Egyptian Village: *Silwa, Province of Aswan. 336 pp.*

**Brandel-Syrier, Mia.** Reeftown Elite. *A Study of Social Mobility in a Modern African Community on the Reef. 376 pp.*

**Crook, David,** and **Isabel.** Revolution in a Chinese Village: *Ten Mile Inn. 230 pp. 8 plates. 1 map.*

**Dickie-Clark, H. F.** The Marginal Situation. *A Sociological Study of a Coloured Group. 236 pp.*

**Dube, S. C.** Indian Village. *Foreword by Morris Edward Opler. 276 pp. 4 plates.*

India's Changing Villages: *Human Factors in Community Development.* *260 pp. 8 plates. 1 map.*

**Firth, Raymond.** Malay Fishermen. *Their Peasant Economy. 420 pp. 17 pp. plates.*

**Firth, R., Hubert, J.,** and **Forge, A.** Families and their Relatives. *Kinship in a Middle-Class Sector of London: An Anthropological Study. 456 pp.*

**Gulliver, P. H.** Social Control in an African Society: a Study of the Arusha, Agricultural Masai of Northern Tanganyika. *320 pp. 8 plates. 10 figures.*

Family Herds. *288 pp.*

**Ishwaran, K.** Shivapur. *A South Indian Village. 216 pp.*

Tradition and Economy in Village India: *An Interactionist Approach. Foreword by Conrad Arensburg. 176 pp.*

**Jarvie, Ian C.** The Revolution in Anthropology. *268 pp.*

**Little, Kenneth L.** Mende of Sierra Leone. *308 pp. and folder.*

Negroes in Britain. *With a New Introduction and Contemporary Study by Leonard Bloom. 320 pp.*

**Lowie, Robert H.** Social Organization. *494 pp.*

Peasants in the Pacific. *A Study of Fiji Indian Rural Society. 248 pp.*

**Smith, Raymond T.** The Negro Family in British Guiana: *Family Structure and Social Status in the Villages. With a Foreword by Meyer Fortes. 314 pp. 8 plates. 1 figure. 4 maps.*

### SOCIOLOGY AND PHILOSOPHY

**Barnsley, John H.** The Social Reality of Ethics. *A Comparative Analysis of Moral Codes. 448 pp.*

**Diesing, Paul.** Patterns of Discovery in the Social Sciences. *362 pp.*

●**Douglas, Jack D.** (Ed.) Understanding Everyday Life. *Toward the Reconstruction of Sociological Knowledge. Contributions by Alan F. Blum. Aaron W. Cicourel, Norman K. Denzin, Jack D. Douglas, John Heeren, Peter McHugh, Peter K. Manning, Melvin Power, Matthew Speier, Roy Turner, D. Lawrence Wieder, Thomas P. Wilson and Don H. Zimmerman. 370 pp.*

**Jarvie, Ian C.** Concepts and Society. *216 pp.*

●**Pelz, Werner.** The Scope of Understanding in Sociology. *Towards a more radical reorientation in the social humanistic sciences. 283 pp.*

**Roche, Maurice.** Phenomenology, Language and the Social Sciences. *371 pp.*

**Sahay, Arun.** Sociological Analysis. *212 pp.*

**Sklair, Leslie.** The Sociology of Progress. *320 pp.*

# International Library of Anthropology

*General Editor* Adam Kuper

**Brown, Paula.** The Chimbu. *A Study of Change in the New Guinea Highlands. 151 pp.*

**Hamnett, Ian.** Chieftainship and Legitimacy. *An Anthropological Study of Executive Law in Lesotho. 163 pp.*
**Hanson, F. Allan.** Meaning in Culture. *127 pp.*
**Lloyd, P. C.** Power and Independence. *Urban Africans' Perception of Social Inequality. 264 pp.*
**Pettigrew, Joyce.** Robber Noblemen. *A Study of the Political System of the Sikh Jats. 284 pp.*
**Street, Brian V.** The Savage in Literature. *Representations of 'Primitive' Society in English Fiction, 1858–1920. 207 pp.*
**Van Den Berghe, Pierre L.** Power and Privilege at an African University. *278 pp.*

# International Library of Social Policy

*General Editor*   Kathleen Jones

**Bayley, M.** Mental Handicap and Community Care. *426 pp.*
**Butler, J. R.** Family Doctors and Public Policy. *208 pp.*
**Davies, Martin.** Prisoners of Society. *Attitudes and Aftercare. 204 pp.*
**Holman, Robert.** Trading in Children. *A Study of Private Fostering. 355 pp.*
**Jones, Kathleen.** History of the Mental Health Service. *428 pp.*
   Opening the Door. *A Study of New Policies for the Mentally Handicapped. 260 pp.*
**Thomas, J. E.** The English Prison Officer since 1850: *A Study in Conflict. 258 pp.*
**Walton, R. G.** Women in Social Work. *303 pp.*
**Woodward, J.** To Do the Sick No Harm. *A Study of the British Voluntary Hospital System to 1875. 221 pp.*

# International Library of Welfare and Philosophy

*General Editors*   Noel Timms and David Watson

● **Plant, Raymond.** Community and Ideology. *104 pp.*

# Primary Socialization, Language and Education

*General Editor*   Basil Bernstein

**Bernstein, Basil.** Class, Codes and Control. *3 volumes.*
   1. *Theoretical Studies Towards a Sociology of Language. 254 pp.*
   2. *Applied Studies Towards a Sociology of Language. 377 pp.*
   3. *Towards a Theory of Educational Transmission. 167 pp.*
**Brandis, W.,** and **Bernstein, B.** Selection and Control. *176 pp.*
**Brandis, Walter,** and **Henderson, Dorothy.** Social Class, Language and Communication. *288 pp.*

**Cook-Gumperz, Jenny.** Social Control and Socialization. *A Study of Class Differences in the Language of Maternal Control. 290 pp.*
●**Gahagan, D. M.,** and **G. A.** Talk Reform. *Exploration in Language for Infant School Children. 160 pp.*
**Robinson, W. P.,** and **Rackstraw, Susan D. A.** A Question of Answers. *2 volumes. 192 pp. and 180 pp.*
**Turner, Geoffrey J.,** and **Mohan, Bernard A.** A Linguistic Description and Computer Programme for Children's Speech. *208 pp.*

# Reports of the Institute of Community Studies

**Cartwright, Ann.** Human Relations and Hospital Care. *272 pp.*
● Parents and Family Planning Services. *306 pp.*
Patients and their Doctors. *A Study of General Practice. 304 pp.*
**Dench, Geoff.** Maltese in London. *A Case-study in the Erosion of Ethnic Consciousness. 302 pp.*
●**Jackson, Brian.** Streaming: *an Education System in Miniature. 168 pp.*
**Jackson, Brian,** and **Marsden, Dennis.** Education and the Working Class: *Some General Themes raised by a Study of 88 Working-class Children in a Northern Industrial City. 268 pp. 2 folders.*
**Marris, Peter.** The Experience of Higher Education. *232 pp. 27 tables.*
Loss and Change. *192 pp.*
**Marris, Peter,** and **Rein, Martin.** Dilemmas of Social Reform. *Poverty and Community Action in the United States. 256 pp.*
**Marris, Peter,** and **Somerset, Anthony.** African Businessmen. *A Study of Entrepreneurship and Development in Kenya. 256 pp.*
**Mills, Richard.** Young Outsiders: *a Study in Alternative Communities. 216 pp.*
**Runciman, W. G.** Relative Deprivation and Social Justice. *A Study of Attitudes to Social Inequality in Twentieth-Century England. 352 pp.*
**Willmott, Peter.** Adolescent Boys in East London. *230 pp.*
**Willmott, Peter,** and **Young, Michael.** Family and Class in a London Suburb. *202 pp. 47 tables.*
**Young, Michael.** Innovation and Research in Education. *192 pp.*
●**Young, Michael,** and **McGeeney, Patrick.** Learning Begins at Home. *A Study of a Junior School and its Parents. 128 pp.*
**Young, Michael,** and **Willmott, Peter.** Family and Kinship in East London. *Foreword by Richard M. Titmuss. 252 pp. 39 tables.*
The Symmetrical Family. *410 pp.*

# Reports of the Institute for Social Studies in Medical Care

**Cartwright, Ann, Hockey, Lisbeth,** and **Anderson, John L.** Life Before Death. *310 pp.*
**Dunnell, Karen,** and **Cartwright, Ann.** Medicine Takers, Prescribers and Hoarders. *190 pp.*

# Medicine, Illness and Society

*General Editor* W. M. Williams

**Robinson, David.** The Process of Becoming Ill. *142 pp.*
**Stacey, Margaret,** *et al.* Hospitals, Children and Their Families. *The Report of a Pilot Study. 202 pp.*
**Stimson, G. V.,** and **Webb, B.** Going to See the Doctor. *The Consultation Process in General Practice. 155 pp.*

# Monographs in Social Theory

*General Editor* Arthur Brittan

●**Barnes, B.** Scientific Knowledge and Sociological Theory. *192 pp.*
**Bauman, Zygmunt.** Culture as Praxis. *204 pp.*
●**Dixon, Keith.** Sociological Theory. *Pretence and Possibility. 142 pp.*
**Meltzer, B. N., Petras, J. W.,** and **Reynolds, L. T.** Symbolic Interactionism. *Genesis, Varieties and Criticisms. 144 pp.*
●**Smith, Anthony D.** The Concept of Social Change. *A Critique of the Functionalist Theory of Social Change. 208 pp.*

# Routledge Social Science Journals

**The British Journal of Sociology.** *Managing Editor – Angus Stewart; Associate Editor – Michael Hill. Vol. 1, No. 1 – March 1950 and Quarterly. Roy. 8vo. All back issues available. An international journal publishing original papers in the field of sociology and related areas.*
**Community Work.** *Edited by David Jones and Marjorie Mayo. 1973. Published annually.*
**Economy and Society.** *Vol. 1, No. 1. February 1972 and Quarterly. Metric Roy. 8vo. A journal for all social scientists covering sociology, philosophy, anthropology, economics and history. Back numbers available.*
**Religion. Journal of Religion and Religions.** *Chairman of Editorial Board, Ninian Smart. Vol. 1, No. 1, Spring 1971. A journal with an interdisciplinary approach to the study of the phenomena of religion.*
**Year Book of Social Policy in Britain, The.** *Edited by Kathleen Jones. 1971. Published annually.*

Printed in Great Britain by Unwin Brothers Limited
The Gresham Press Old Woking Surrey
A member of the Staples Printing Group          June 1975